Dante, Chaucer, and the Currency of the Word

Dante, Chaucer, and the Currency of the Word

MONEY, IMAGES, and REFERENCE

in LATE MEDIEVAL POETRY

By

R. A. Shoaf

PILGRIM BOOKS, INC.
NORMAN, OKLAHOMA

This book was published with the kind assistance of the Frederick W. Hilles Publication Fund of Yale University.

Pilgrim Books, P.O. Box 2399, Norman, Oklahoma 73070

Library of Congress Cataloging in Publication Data

Shoaf, R.A. (Richard Allen), 1948–
    Dante, Chaucer, and the currency of the word.

    Bibliography: p.
    Includes index.
    1. Poetry, Medieval–History and criticism.
2. Money in literature. 3. Dante Alighieri, 1265–1321. Divina commedia. 4. Chaucer, Geoffrey, d. 1400. Troilus and Criseyde. 5. Chaucer, Geoffrey, d. 1400. Canterbury tales. I. Title.
PN688.S56 1983   809.1'9355   82-12108
ISBN 0-937664-62-6

To the memory of

My Father
Henry Lee Shoaf, 1919–1968

and

My Brother
William Starling Shoaf, 1950–1975

They sin who make discord between wisdom and eloquence, but what is all eloquence without wisdom except, as Cato says, glossaries of the dead? We are able to live without language, although not comfortably, but without wisdom we are not able to live at all. He is perhaps not humane who is unfamiliar with polite letters, but he who is deprived of philosophy is no longer even a man.

(Pico della Mirandola)

Contents

Acknowledgments

I would like to recognize and thank the following:

Yale University, for a Morse Fellowship in the academic year 1980–81, which provided full leave to finish this book; an A. Whitney Griswold Research Grant, which defrayed the costs of microfilming and typing; and a subvention from the Frederick W. Hilles Publications Fund, which helped pay the costs of producing the book.

Judson B. Allen, Stephen A. Barney, Thomas G. Bergin, Anthony K. Cassell, Roger Ferlo, Margaret Ferguson, John Hollander, Robert Hollander, Thomas Leitch, Dorothee Metlitzki, Winthrop Wetherbee, and James Winn for meticulous and learned criticism of all or parts of the book.

J. Hillis Miller, for support, encouragement, and, above all, belief in my work.

Mary Christoforo, for typing the manuscript and Daniel Kiefer, for proofreading it.

Mildred Ann Raper, for introducing me to Dante and Chaucer in 1966.

Mary Ann Stallings Calloway, for talking me out of quitting school in 1964.

Ralph Stewart Smith, for showing me what a passion for literature really is.

My students in Yale College, 1977–82, for listening to me.

Judy and Brian, for putting up with me—for loving me so much.

Abbreviations Used in This Book

Aen.	Aeneid
AHDLMA	Archives d'histoire doctrinale et littéraire du moyen âge
AM	Annales du Midi
Anglia	Anglia: Zeitschrift für Englische Philologie
Aug	Augustiniana
BGDSL	Beiträge zur Geschichte der Deutscher Sprache und Literatur
CAIEF	Cahiers de l'Association internationale des études françaises
CCSL	Corpus Christianorum series latina
ChauR	Chaucer Review
CkT, CkP	The Cook's Tale, The Cook's Prologue
CL	Comparative Literature
ClT, ClP	The Clerk's Tale, The Clerk's Prologue
Conf.	Confessions
Conv.	Convivio
CR	Centennial Review
CSEL	Corpus scriptorum ecclesiasticorum latinorum
CT	The Canterbury Tales
DA	Dissertation Abstracts
Dante Studies	
De cons.	De consolatione philosophiae
DSpir.	Dictionnaire de spiritualité
ED	Enciclopedia Dantesca
ELH	English Literary History
ELN	English Language Notes
FrT, FrP	The Friar's Tale, The Friar's Prologue
GD	Giornale Dantesca
GDI	Grande dizionario italiana
Genre	

Godefroy	*Dictionnaire de l'ancienne langue française*
GP	*The General Prologue*
GR	*Georgia Review*
HthR	*Harvard Theological Review*
Inf.	*Inferno*
JEGP	*Journal of English and Germanic Philology*
JEH	*Journal of Economic History*
JMRS	*Journal of Medieval and Renaissance Studies*
JS	*Journal des savants*
KnT, KnP	*The Knight's Tale, The Knight's Prologue*
LGW, LGWP	*The Legend of Good Women, The Legend of Good Women Prologue*
MÆ	*Medium Ævum*
M&H	*Medievalia et humanistica*, New Series
MED	*Middle English Dictionary*
Mediaevalia	*Mediaevalia: A Journal of Mediaeval Studies*
MerT, MerP	*The Merchant's Tale, The Merchant's Prologue*
Met	*Metamorphoses*
MilT, MilP	*The Miller's Tale, The Miller's Prologue*
MkT	*The Monk's Tale*
MLN	*Modern Language Notes*
MLQ	*Modern Language Quarterly*
MLT	*The Man of Law's Tale*
MP	*Modern Philology*
MQR	*Michigan Quarterly Review*
MS	*Mediaeval Studies*
N&Q	*Notes and Queries*
NLH	*New Literary History*
NM	*Neuphilologische Mitteilungen*
NPT, NPP	*The Nun's Priest's Tale, The Nun's Priest's Prologue*
OED	*Oxford English Dictionary*
OL	*Orbis litterarum*
Par.	*Paradiso*
PardT, PardP	*The Pardoner's Tale, The Pardoner's Prologue*
PG	*Patrologia graeca*
Phy–PardL	*Physician–Pardoner Link*
PL	*Patrologia latina*
PMASAL	*Publications of the Michigan Academy of Sciences, Arts, and Letters*
Politiques	*Le Livre de politiques d'Aristote* (Oresme)

PQ	Philological Quarterly
Purg.	Purgatorio
REA	Revue des études augustiniennes
REI	Revue des études italiennes
REL	Review of English Literature
RH	Revue historique
RHPR	Revue d'histoire et de philosophie religieuses
RIN	Rivista italiana di numismatica
RvT, RvP	The Reeve's Tale, The Reeve's Prologue
SAC	Studies in the Age of Chaucer
Scholastik	
ShT	The Shipman's Tale
SMC	Studies in Medieval Culture
SP	Studies in Philology
Speculum	Speculum: A Journal of Medieval Studies
SqT	The Squire's Tale
ST	Summa theologiae
Symposium	
TAPS	Transactions of the American Philosophical Society
TC	Troylus and Criseyde
Traditio	Traditio: Studies in Ancient and Medieval History, Thought, and Religion
TSLL	Texas Studies in Language and Literature
UR	University Review
UTQ	University of Toronto Quarterly
Vivarium	Vivarium: An International Journal for the Philosophy and Intellectual Life of the Middle Ages and Renaissance
WBT, WBP	The Wife of Bath's Tale, The Wife of Bath's Prologue
YIS	Yearbook of Italian Studies
ZPF	Zeitschrift für philosophische Forschung

Note: Conventional abbreviations for books of the Bible are employed.

Dante, Chaucer, and the Currency of the Word

Introduction

The Discourse of Man
"by Nature a Political Animal"

All goods to be exchanged, then, should be measurable by some standard coin or measure. . . . In reality, this measure is the need which holds all things together; for if man had no needs at all or no needs of a similar nature, there would be no exchange or not this kind of exchange. So a coin is a sort of substitute (or representative) for need and came into being by convention; and it is because of this that its name is "coin" ($= \nu\acute{o}\mu\iota\varsigma\mu\alpha$), for it exists by regulation($= \nu\acute{o}\mu\psi$) and not by nature, and it is up to us to change a given coin or make it useless. . . . Now this money, too, is subject to the same fluctuation in need, for its worth does not always remain the same, but it has a greater tendency to remain the same. In view of this, all things should have a price on them; for in this way an exchange is always possible, and if so, also an association of men.

(Aristotle)

And if there were no buying and selling, there would be no communication.

(Nicole Oresme)

Coinage can always bring back into the hands of its owner that which has just been exchanged for it, just as, in representation, a sign must be able to recall to thought that which it represents. Money is a material memory, a self-duplicating representation, a deferred exchange.

(Michel Foucault)

Love is more serious than Philosophy
Who sees no humor in her observation
That Truth is knowing that we know we lie.

(W. H. Auden)

Introduction
The Discourse of Man
"by Nature a Political Animal"[1]

N 1252, thirteen years before Dante was born, Florence stamped her lily on one face of a gold coin, the figure of John the Baptist on the other; the coin was the florin (It. *fiorino*: "little flower"). It would be hard to exaggerate the importance of this event: it marked both a culmination and a beginning. The florin was the culmination of Florence's extraordinary commercial growth and vitality of the preceding two centuries.[2] It was the beginning of another century or so of commercial preeminence in Italy, Europe, and the Mediterranean generally.[3] Of 3.5 to 4.5 grams of fine gold, the florin at its height was the "dollar" of Europe.[4] To be sure, the Venetian ducat soon participated in this honor, too; but when Dante came of age, he entered the political life of a commune whose coin was of incontestable value, power, and prestige. Consequently, he also necessarily encountered the features and the behavior of money which had already compelled Aristotle to call it "nonsense" (lễros).[5]

Dante was not alone in this encounter; many of his contemporaries were as disturbed as he by the irrationality and the mystery of money. Lauro Martines, in a recent study (1980:85), has described the situation well: "As attested by the performance of its poets, communal society was still struggling to absorb the moral consequences of money and credit mechanisms into its religious view of the world." Perhaps no better evidence of this struggle or of its vehemence comes down to us than the story of "il poverello," Francis of Assisi (Fleming 1977:73–109). His life is unimaginable outside the context of money and the triumph of a money economy. From his repudiation of his father's mercantile values to the anonymous treatise *Sacrum commercium Sancti Francisci cum domina paupertate*, the events and the consequences of his words and deeds are inextricably involved with money.[6] Dante's own celebration of Francis (*Par.* 11.43–117) emphasizes this involvement also. In addition to the story of Francis, we have many lyrics of the Trecento which lash out against money or try to discover some sort of rationality in it.[7] Moreover, the triumph of money led to a revision of the hierarchy of the seven deadly sins so that avarice came to share with pride the position of root or beginning of evil.[8] Finally, the writings of Italian merchants themselves, which proliferated in the thirteenth and fourteenth centuries (Bec 1967:49–247), attest to the dominance which money had assumed over the lives and thoughts of men.

In all ages, poets, like other men, need money, and they get it when and how they can. But Dante and Chaucer obviously thought about money even when they did not need it to put bread on the table. Because of the age in which they lived, they encountered all around them the independent life as image and image maker which the coin also leads. They could see, even as clearly as we, how the coin once produced produces more of itself. They could see that to create debt is to create currency (though not necessarily wealth). They could see the coin generate credit: the image beget belief. Seeing all this, considering it, they were also necessarily considering issues poetic in structure and content. Money and poetry are both fictions, as we who live with paper money know only too well, and they are both strangely alike – so much so that the problem of the meaning of money is analogous to the problem of the meaning of language, especially poetic language. Because the one problem was for Dante, Chaucer, and their age both starkly visible and in the process of changing its structure and scope, the other was necessarily rendered visible in intense and variable lights. This relation, this analogy, and the concomitant problems, make up the subject of this book. To study them is to focus our attention on the power of language to mean, both because the analogy itself between language and money insists on the question of reference and because this is the power the fourteenth century's concern with the analogy found most problematic.

This book begins to deal with the analogy by mapping Dante's reaction to money in the *Commedia*. My method is cross-disciplinary and from time to time uses history, economics, sociology, philology, and literary criticism. Dante's reaction to money, the map makes clear, leads to the structure from which his poem comprehends imagery and the operation of poetic discourse. This map I next follow to Chaucer. Chaucer, I argue, is no mere quoter of virtuoso passages. Rather, he is a great interpreter of Dante. He is so, in part, because of his own efforts to come to grips through poetry with the power and the meaning of money. Oftentimes Chaucer's texts show a feel for the problem of the meaning of money similar to that encountered in the *Com-*

media; this is especially the case in *Troylus and Criseyde* (see chap. 5 n. 1 below), and if it is only indirectly the case in *The Canterbury Tales*, where Chaucer is most his own if not on his own, still the context of money in the *Commedia* and the *Troylus* contributes greatly to understanding that extraordinary "fragment." Indeed, my book argues that the structure of *The Canterbury Tales* is economics and that Chaucer derived this structure in part from his understanding of the *Commedia* – understanding won from the process of "translating" *Troylus and Criseyde*.

This argument is neither as cold nor as abstract as it might at first appear to be. Both Dante and Chaucer are love poets. It is peculiarly the gift of such a poet that he understands that there is no taking in love without giving, no giving without taking. Love is (at least) an exchange. Hence the love poet's fascination with economics. Hence also the profound similarity between Dante and Chaucer.

At the same time, however, it would not do to lose sight of the differences between Dante and Chaucer (and I try throughout this book to keep them in sight). Whereas the former begins in a blurred and fragmented vision of his own condition but ends in a whole vision of primal unity, the latter, in *Troylus and Criseyde*, begins in a pseudo-unity of vision but ends in a whole vision of human fragmentariness. Dante goes from the fallen world to the Other World of Paradise; Chaucer goes from an illusory paradise of *fin'amors* to the real world of ordinary mortals making do. Then, from and within that world, he goes on to explore, in *The Canterbury Tales*, that typical confusion of self-understanding and self-deception which makes ordinary mortals uncommonly interesting and lovable.

The analogy between language and money is of some modern interest, especially since Saussure and Derrida. Indeed, many might even call it "trendy." But it is also, I am arguing, seriously medieval, and it was present to Dante and Chaucer not only through "experience" but also through impeccable "authority" – that of Boethius, in his comment on Aristotle's *De interpretatione*. Boethius translated *Peri Hermenias* in A.D. 510 and wrote two commentaries on it subsequently, one in 511, and another two years later. In the second of these commentaries he argues that a word is formed in a manner similar to that by which a coin becomes current money. For this argument he assumes a structural relationship between language and money which, I believe, Dante and Chaucer also assume. Different as the two poets are (and I hope never to lose sight of those differences, I repeat), it is possible that they shared a knowledge of Boethius's argument – it was easily available to them if they wanted it (Isaac 1953:96–7) – and hence also a common understanding of the resemblance between language and money, a resemblance often the cause of dangerous confusion. The phrase Boethius is discussing when he presents his argument is "those things which are in sound" (I print the Latin first and then follow with a translation which makes no pretense to elegance, since my desire is the optimum construction of Boethius's sense):

> vox enim universale quiddam est, nomina vero et verba partes. pars autem omnis in toto est. verba ergo et nomina quoniam sunt intra vocem, recte dic- tum est ea quae sunt in voce, velut si diceret: quae intra vocem continentur intellectuum designativa sunt. sed hoc simile est ac si ita dixisset: vox certo modo sese habens significat intellectus. non enim (ut dictum est) nomen et verbum voces tantum sunt. sicut nummus quoque non solum aes inpressum quadam figura est, ut nummus vocetur, sed etiam ut alicuius rei sit pretium: eodem quoque modo verba et nomina non solum voces sunt, sed positae ad quandam intellectuum significationem. vox enim quae nihil designat, ut est garalus, licet eam grammatici figuram vocis intuentes nomen esse conten- dant, tamen eam nomen philosophia non putabit, nisi sit posita ut designare animi aliquam conceptionem eoque modo rerum aliquid possit. etenim nomen alicuius nomen esse necesse erit; sed si vox aliqua nihil designat, nullius nomen est; quare si nullius est, ne nomen quidem esse dicetur. atque ideo huiusmodi vox id est significativa non vox tantum, sed verbum vocatur aut nomen, quemadmodum nummus non aes, sed proprio nomine nummus, quo ab alio aere discrepet, nuncupatur. ergo haec Aristotelis sententia qua ait ea quae sunt in voce nihil aliud designat nisi eam vocem, quae non solum vox sit, sed quae cum vox sit habeat tamen aliquam proprietatem et aliquam quodammodo figuram positae significationis inpressam.[9]

(For sound is a kind of universal; names and words, on the other hand, are parts. Every part, however, is in the whole. Words, therefore, and names, since they are within sound, rightly is it said, "those things which are in sound," as if he [Aristotle] had said, "things which are contained within sound are designative of thoughts"; but this likening is as if he had spoken thus: "a sound having itself in a certain way signifies a thought." For, as it has been said, names and words are not sound merely. Thus just as a coin is copper impressed with a certain figure not only in order that it might be called a coin but also in order that it might be the price of some specific thing, so, in the same way, words and names, are not only sounds, but are imposed to a certain signification of thoughts. For a sound which designates nothing, such as "garalus," although grammarians looking at the shape ["figuram"] of the sound, might contend that it is a name, nevertheless philosophy does not consider it to be a name, unless it may be imposed to designate some conception of the soul, and in that way is able to signify something real, since a name shall necessarily be the name of some thing.

But if some sound designates nothing, it is the name of nothing; wherefore, if it is the name of nothing, neither is it said to be a name. And thus, in this way, a sound – that is, a significant sound – is not sound only, but is called a verb or a name, just as a coin is not called copper, but is called, by its proper name, a coin, by means of what distinguishes it from other copper. Therefore, this sentence of Aristotle by which he says "those things which are in sound" designates nothing other than a sound which is not sound only, but which, while it may be sound, has nevertheless a certain property and a certain, as it were, impressed figure of the imposed significance.)

For Boethius, a "vox," comparable because of similarity to any and all other sound, becomes a "verbum" by being "imposed" to or for a significance, just as copper impressed with a figure is so impressed that it might as currency become the price of some specific and obviously different thing. Note that, in constructing the analogy, Boethius is very careful to make a subtle but important distinction. "Aes figura inpressum" is not necessarily a coin; it could be a medallion, for example, or a "symbolon," in the original sense of that word (Shell 1978:32–35). "Aes figura inpressum" is not a coin until it is legal tender, until it is further differentiated by being the price of something else – current for something else. Hence Boethius is very exact: ". . . not only in order that it might be called a coin but also in order that it might be the price of some specific thing." To illustrate again with his concluding remarks, a sound, "vox," is a word, "verbum," when, like a coin stamped with the appropriate effigy and current for another thing, it bears the impressed figure of an imposed significance. For Boethius, then, the stream of sound must be differentiated by the exchange of a sound and a significance just as a coin must be differentiated not only by its stamped effigy but also by its exchange for some specific and different thing. Thus Boethius recognizes that value, linguistic and economic, depends on relativity and differentiation which are elements of exchange (cf. Saussure 1966:115; Derrida 1974:6–14).

If Boethius is Dante's and Chaucer's authority for an analogy between language and money at the level of formation, there are other authorities for the analogy at the level of work or function. Aristotle, for example, insists that "all goods to be exchanged. . .should be measurable by some standard coin or measure."[10] From this need, universally recognized, for a common measure, arises what in this book I will call the *reductive power* of money – the power of money to reduce anything and everything to itself. Although the Middle Ages did not know Averroes's *On Plato's Republic*, they would have understood his very typical (Aristotelian) teaching that money "is potentially all things valuable" (Lerner 1974:110). In fact, money means nothing because it is worth everything.[11] Everything has its price, and when it is reduced to that price – that node of value in a skein of relativity – it sacrifices all its dense, tangible difference to the common denominator. Money is the more or less temporary disappearance of difference; it is the reduction of the random to quantifiable system.[12] Money is not precisely mute (we all know that money talks) but it appears silent – the supreme ventriloquist. Money can talk only through the mouths of dummies because its own character, giving the lie to the "sharp point" of that word (charaktḗr) is flat; etched into the surface of the coin, the "character" is dead – the institutionalized physiognomy of the dominant power instantly interchangeable with the "character" of the next regime. Moreover, a field of corn, a porcelain vase, a pint of blood, and a pro-stitute's tricks can be rendered equal in value at $500 or $1,000 or 10¢. Little wonder Aristotle called money "nonsense."

As money reduces everything to arbitrary exchange values, so language reduces experience to meaning. The universalizing or generalizing power of language is necessarily if also paradoxically reductive – we accord that poetry the highest respect which successfully counters this reductiveness (Wimsatt 1954:69–83) – and as in the former system the coin displaces the distinctive otherness of the object, so in the latter system the word can supplant reality by substituting itself for the thing to which it supposedly refers. We see this best in ethnic slurs and slogans – the words "nigger" and "Jew" and "national security" are good examples. Reality disappears into such words even as it disappears into coins. Both because they are so full are empty signifiers: both fill with the selfishness of those who would possess and manipulate the world rather than share it (cf. Serres 1982:149, 168). If I choose words which are ex-tremely prejudicial, I do so only to emphasize that all words can be prejudi-cially reductive even though and sometimes perhaps precisely because we are not always aware of as much. Only in the past thirty years has the word "nig-ger" been felt as prejudicially reductive by most people. And even now, women are trying to counter the reductive power of "feminine" and "female." To use a word is *always* to commit an act of reduction – and so much the analogy with money helps us clearly see; it need not always be, however, to commit an act of *prejudicial* reduction. The use of a word can be free of the selfishness structural in coin. With coin I buy or spend my own; with language I share or translate my own. There is a difference, though it is often obscured. And the difference is the motive which Dante and Chaucer share; they seek to raise it from its obscurity. In the process they both from time to time emphasize the similarity between language and money, finding in it much that is positive and even creative. Dante, more frequent and consistent with this gesture, likens faith, for example, to "moneta" (*Par.* 24.84; and see p. 93

below). Chaucer, typically more indirect and less insistent, discovers character, for example, from the ways in which people spend words (see *CT, WBP* D 425: "'I ne owe hem nat a word that it nys quit'"; and Chap. 10 below). But both poets will more often focus on the difference between language and money since it is so frequently lost to sight and thought in the baneful *confusion* of language *as* money. Language *would* generate meaning, but, confounded with the coin it so nearly resembles, it only reifies desire. To break language from a thing and to restore it to things is the goal and the achievement of Dante's and Chaucer's poetry, different as the two of them are.

In making such a claim, the reader will have already observed, I necessarily skirt some of the more formidable positions of postmodernist criticism; and I suppose I should say, at the outset, that the nostalgia for an idealist and idealizing signification which certain schools will detect in this book is real and intended. If difference is the ever unstable ground of presence and plenitude, still presence and plenitude are viable experiences of the human intellect, hardly delusions even if perhaps illusions (cf. Derrida 1976:44–73). If, as this book supposes, Dante and Chaucer alike feared the initial inhuman rigor of idealist and idealizing signification, they also sought a poetry which would for that very reason relate the human and the ideal harmoniously.[13] The modernist anxiety that predication is a kind of original violence throwing up an illusory presence and plenitude and plenitude of presence is the extreme of the fear which Dante and Chaucer, emerging from Platonism into an intellectual environment increasingly Aristotelian, also experienced. But they understood their fear in very different terms, and thus their reactions were very different from those of their modern counterparts: similarly suspicious of metaphor, they discovered in metaphor nevertheless liberation from the fear of definition and category and nomination.[14] To say that they relaxed into faith will perhaps strike some as an "easy out," but that, I will argue, is exactly what they did (and it was no easier for them to do than it is for me to argue that they did it). And their faith was predicated not on ecclesiastical pronouncement but on the common realization that, without faith, exchange – whether of love or of money – is simply not possible. We must believe to love (and we must love to believe).

This faith, first and foremost, was faith in the ontological relation between word and thing. To illustrate just briefly here, with Chaucer: As often in his poetry, we find the ideal or the positive first appearing as its opposite. Hence in *The Shipman's Tale*, where money and language obviously relate to each other as a thematic concern,[15] the words "cosyn" and "cosynage" repeatedly appear in each character's discourse, only to assert the contrary, however, without fail, that neither of the three is really the other's "cosyn" in any meaningful sense.[16] Word and thing (*vox et res*) are obviously disjunct. This ontological problem receives, with typical Chaucerian wit, sexual and marital inflections in the poetry. When the Merchant's wife exclaims, in one of the more famous of Chaucer's lines, "'I am youre wyf; score it upon my taille'" (*ShT* B² 416), the word "taille" exquisitely points the problem. Its equivoca- tion—"tally" or "pudendum"? (Davis 1979:150)—insists on the disjunction be- tween word and thing, on the difficulty inhering in any assumption of an a priori conjunction between word and thing *innocent of intervening interpreta- tion: we* have to *interpret* or to *decide* to what thing the word refers or whether, indeed, it refers to both things at once? *The* referent is absent.

But the word's equivocation in context is hardly all; the word's original meaning also points the problem. For the "taille" is a notched stick recording debt, or some other obligation, which is split lengthwise on the understanding that the two parts, because originally one, when rejoined, will *unambiguously* indicate the obligation (*OED* T:60). No more brilliant choice than this, for the situation or for the philosophical dilemma, could have been made. Both marital and verbal infidelity are implicated in "taille." Where is the other half of the Wife's "taille"? In whose keeping is the other part of her "taille"? Who puts notches in it and when? The answers to these questions, of course, are far less important than the questions themselves. For the questions insist on the disjunction, the split, the severance, the absence, which is a "taille" itself. The word refers to a thing, a thing like human being itself, not whole but broken and only with difficulty brought back into wholeness again. The word refers to a thing which is a symbol of the very crux of the tale, or the failure of the two pieces word and thing ("cosyn," for example) to conjoin. And yet. The word "taille" does *refer* to a thing and the thing *is* a successful *symbol* —for us, Chaucer's readers. For us, Chaucer's readers, as he intended them to do, word and thing tally.

The faith which assumes that word and thing do—and, moreover, shall—tally is the subject of this book. It seeks a late medieval poetics of reference. I have no illusions about "completing" this task; for that many more years will be required and many more laborers. But I do hope to begin clearing the path with my concentration on the currency of the word.

Part One of the book explores the imagery of the coin in Dante's *Commedia* and particularly in the *Paradiso*. I am hardly the first to have studied this im- agery, but I do think a great deal remains to be said about it. Dante positions it in a rich context of allusions to Narcissus, and his story in Ovid, and hence also to the thematics of metamorphosis; moreover, he links it directly to the

14

theology of the Image of God and the reformation of that Image; all this he further complicates with the dialectics of reading and the question of literary paternity, itself directly tied to the question of God's paternity of the individual soul. He reaches full complexity when he joins all these issues to the problem of vision and its limits. I will argue that his theory of vision is ultimately a poetics of reference and that he articulates both in terms of the coin.

Part Two proceeds to *Troylus and Criseyde*, where imagery of coinage and exchange, occurring principally in books 4 and 5, shows a direct relationship to similar imagery in the *Commedia*. Many other sources doubtless intervene (I note some of them), and the climate of philosophical opinion in which Chaucer received the *Commedia* differed greatly, we know, from that in which it was written; still, only the *Commedia* was rich enough to give Chaucer not only the imagery he needed but also the full poetic, philosophical, and theological context which would enable that imagery to communicate the complex and poignant fate of Troylus and Criseyde. The imagery attaches chiefly to Criseyde, and after an analysis of its relevance to her character and her role, I go on to argue that Chaucer uses the imagery as a strategy for the problem of authority—the problem of his poetic career. The strategy applies to Troylus and Pandarus both, but most importantly to the Narrator himself, whose role as translator, I suggest, is one of the principal concerns of the poem. Translation became for Chaucer, I think, the very crisis of authority which compelled him to seek, with Dante's help, a poetics of reference. And although he and Dante differ profoundly, I will argue that they resemble each other profoundly too. They each seek a way to tell the truth without prejudicial reduction of the complexity of experience. They each seek a personal position which is not in opposition to reality or an imposition on others.

The poetics of reference which Chaucer discovered in the *Troylus* he uses, Part Three argues, in *The Canterbury Tales*. After a brief analysis of fragment A and particularly of the issue of "falsification" in that fragment, this part proceeds to chapters on the Wife of Bath, the Merchant, and the Pardoner. Many other pilgrims and their tales could have been included, and I hope eventually to write on them too. For the purposes of this book, however, these three are most significant because the relationship between language and money in them is as obvious as it is in *The Shipman's Tale* and at least as problematical if not more so. Each of these three illustrates the narcissism involved in the instrumentality of language, and thus each provides a crucial example of Chaucer's complex play of positions for humanizing and containing narcissism. Each of them is a type of the poet Chaucer will *not* be.

The conclusion is not only a summary but also a prediction of the kinds of studies which will recover an accurate sense of poetic discourse and its ontology in the late Middle Ages. These will be studies of politics in the widest and most fundamentally Aristotelian sense of the word—studies of how men relate to one another in the daily commerce of communication within a world public and private alike.

PART ONE

Dante's *Commedia*
and the
Promise of Reference

For patience is necessary for you: that, doing the will of God, you may receive the promise.

(Hebrews 10.36)

For all the promises of God are in him.... Who also hath sealed us and given the pledge of the Spirit in our hearts.

(2 Corinthians 1.20–22)

You were signed with the Holy Spirit of promise, Who is the pledge of our inheritance, to the redemption of acquisition, unto the praise of his glory.

(Ephesians 1.12–14)

Where there is an image, there is similitude but not equality.... as in a mirror, there is the image of a man because it is expressed from him; and it is also necessarily a similitude; nevertheless, there is no equality because many things are lacking in the image which nevertheless are in the thing from which it is expressed. And where there is equality, there is similitude but no image.

(Saint Augustine)

For what God is not is clearer to us than what He is. Therefore similitudes drawn from things farthest away from God form within us a truer estimate that God is above whatsoever we may say or think of Him.

(Saint Thomas Aquinas)

Comedy is an imitation of life, a mirror of custom, an image of truth.

(Cicero)

Chapter 1
Introduction: Narcissus and the Poet

N THE FINAL lines of *Paradiso*, Dante enjoys the vision of God. As he gazes into the Trinity he sees "nostra effige" (*Par.* 33.131): he sees our image. Dante's gesture is identical with that of Narcissus as he bends over the pool and gazes at his image.[1] But if the gestures in each case are the same, their intentions and results define the difference between beatitude and damnation. Dante sees *our* image, which includes his but which is not his *own*. And this sight, which at once identifies him with and distinguishes him from Narcissus, is the culmination of his entire pilgrimage. At the end, Dante is Narcissus "transhumanized" (*Par.* 1.70).

The story of Narcissus was so popular and widely known in the Middle Ages that Dante probably counted on his readers' recognition of the similarity between the two of them in *Paradiso* 33.[2] Moreover, it is possible that he had to do so since contemplation, or the ascent to mystic vision of God, under one of its names in the Middle Ages, is *speculatio*;[3] and "speculation" if a way of seeing God is also Narcissus's error. Further, the turning inward, which mystic theologians agree is necessary to the vision of God, is also the movement of consciousness, though belated, characteristic of Narcissus.[4] In their structures, then, mystic vision and narcissism are perilously similar. And Dante, profound theologian as well as poet, acknowledges that this peril is a crucial element in the pilgrimage. The poet remembers the pilgrim's slow and painful emergence from narcissism to a just self-love; and, scribe that he is (*Par.* 10.27), he transcribes that memory in canto 30 of each canticle and in cantos 3 and 33 of *Paradiso*.[5]

The numerology at work in *Paradiso* is important to grasping Dante's meaning. The three cantos of that canticle in which Narcissus and narcissism figure most prominently are 3+30=33. Obviously the text is releasing Trinitarian energies; and while the Trinity is not the main focus of this book, it is a crucial part of the relevant context. That context, seen most inclusively, is

Dante's concern with the Image of God in man and the reformation of that image. Speculation and reflection obviously involve images and image making, while Narcissus, of course, errs in regard to an image and the proper construction of an image. Dante can hardly deploy the Narcissus narrative without involving his text in the theology of the Image. That theology is a subject vast in scope, and I cannot pursue its relevance to the *Commedia* as a whole.[6] Nor is that my aim. On the contrary, I am concerned with the narrower but related issue of Dante's vision, both his sight and what he sees. While the purification of Dante's vision is a necessary part of the reformation of his image to the likeness of God, I think it can and should be studied separately for two reasons.

First, Dante obviously lays more emphasis on vision than on any other sense of the human body. So much is this the case that near the end of his vision (the pilgrimage, of course, is a *vision*) he figures the whole of his experience in an image of the eyebrow. In the Celestial Rose, Saint Bernard points out to the pilgrim, "'Lucia, che mosse la tua donna, / Quando chinavi, a rovinar, le ciglia'" ("'Lucy, who moved your Lady when you were bending your brows downward to your ruin'"; *Par.* 32.137–38). The implication is that Dante "ruined"—the same verb is used of the pilgrim's fall at *Inferno* 1.61—because he lowered or, perhaps better, closed his eyes. In keeping with this implication, the whole of *Paradiso* is an opening and a clearing of Dante's eyes.[7] To return to God, a man must open his eyes, open them to and into a just self-love.

Open eyes and purified vision chasten the Narcissus in every man since in such a condition he can begin to see the narcissism in all human instrumentality. Hence my second motive for isolating Dante's vision and studying it separately. His poetics of reference originates in the perception that human instrumentality is narcissistic. To articulate that poetics, therefore, we must follow the intermediate step of the purification of Dante's vision. Then we may turn to Chaucer, who derives his own poetics of reference, in part, from Dante's. For the aim of this book is to read Chaucer, with Dante's help.

To begin the study of Dante's vision, we must read the three cantos 30, for they are a systematic meditation on narcissism and, in particular, on narcissism in art. Just as we must read the three cantos 26 vertically to map Dante's exploration of the historicity and temporality of language, so we must read the three cantos 30 vertically to map his strategy for the recovery of speculation and reflection in art and in life.

Common to each canto 30 in all three canticles is the problematics of imagery. Each canto tests the reality of imagery. Thus, in Hell there is no reality except imagery ("ombra"). There is matter, materiality, but no substantiality, where "substance" is understood to be the real (*Par.* 29.15). In Paradise there is no imagery, only light, and the images we see are cast by the poet's eyes. Though transhumanized (*Par.* 1.70) the poet still sees with bodily eyes (see especially *Par.* 33.31–37), and we, who are hardly transhumanized, to whom he must communicate his vision, see it and read it through bodily eyes. The poet, then, darkens the light of Paradise with shadows or "ombra" (see *Par.* 1.22–27). In Purgatory there is reality which is a complex of imagery and light. Most like this world which we inhabit, Purgatory is the space of confusion and subsequent correction where "ingegno" and "arte" (*Purg.* 27.130) divide and distinguish the fictional and the real (*Purg.* 26.12).

In Hell—to describe the pattern now metaphysically—images refer without a referent; they "mean" only themselves. It rains, for example, only to assert that it is not raining (*Inf.* 30.95); or, trees grow only so that they may never ripen (*Inf.* 13.97–100). In Paradise, on the other hand, is perfect reference; light is always the In-Light-of-Whom or the Universal Mediation through whom creation means. Dante never sees this unmediated Light; rather, at the end, his "mente" is "percossa / da un fulgore in che sua voglia venne" ("smitten by a flash wherein its wish came to it;" *Par.* 33.140–41); rather than see, Dante is enlightened ("fulgore"). In Purgatory imagery and light mix so that reality is experienced as a confusion of signs and referents. For example, in *Purgatorio* 10 at first the pilgrim is unable to make out the proud (lines 112–14). Virgil, similarly confused (line 117), subsequently tells Dante to look again, more intently (lines 118–19). Whereupon, having discerned the proud, Dante proceeds to describe them in a crucial simile (*Purg.* 10.130–35):

> Come per sostentar solaio o tetto,
> per mensola talvolta una figura
> si vede giugner le ginocchia al petto,
> la qual fa del non ver vera rancura
> nascere 'n chi la vede; così fatti
> vid'io color, quando puosi ben cura.

(As for corbel to support a ceiling or a roof, sometimes a figure is seen to join the knees to the breast—which, unreal, begets real distress in one who sees it—so fashioned did I see these when I gave good heed.)

The reality ("ver") of the proud beneath their stones appears like the unreality ("non ver") of "una figura" which nevertheless begets reality ("vera rancura"): here sign or figure and reality have no stable margins or demarcated boundaries, and the eye is always in danger of error and misconstruction.

Finally to describe the pattern with regard to the pilgrim-poet. In *Inferno*, canto 30, Dante lapses into a Narcissus and almost realizes or substantiates mere shades or "ombre"; Dante proves himself a son of (Master) Adam. In *Paradiso*, canto 30, Dante darkens the pure, unmediated Light with the "umbriferi prefazi" (line 78) in his mortal eyes; he still carries Adam with him. In *Purgatorio* 30, Dante begins to understand the confusion of reality in the light and dark of signs and referents by learning, or beginning to learn, the nature of imagery; Dante begins to know who Adam is when he sees what Adam lost.

The act which grounds Dante's discourse about imagery is falsification. *Inferno*, canto 30, is the canto of Master Adam, who falsified the florin with "'tre carati di mondiglia'" ("'three carats of alloy or dross'"; line 90); it is also the canto of Myrrha "'falsificando sé in altrui forma'" ("'falsifying herself in another's form'"; line 41) so as to be "'al padre fuor del dritto amore amica'" ("'loving of her father beyond rightful love'"; line 39) and of Sinon who spoke "falso" (line 115) regarding the Horse. *Purgatorio* 30 is the canto in which Beatrice rebukes Dante for following "'imagini di ben. . .false / che nulla promession rendono intera'" ("'false images of good, which pay no promise in full'"; lines 131–32), where the phrase "nulla promession rendono intera" is economic and refers to redeeming or covering the value of a coin (read "image"). *Paradiso*, canto 30, ends with Beatrice's last words in the poem; these are words in condemnation of "'cieca cupidigia'" ("'blind cupidity'"; line 139) and in particular of simony, or the buying and selling of office – which is a kind of falsification;[8] in this canto Dante's eyes "coin" the light of Paradise into topazes, rivers, sparks, flowers, and so on, before they finally adjust to the brilliance of the Empyrean. Finally, falsification and coinage figure in many other cantos which bear directly or indirectly on the three cantos 30: an obvious case in point is the likening of faith to a coin in *Paradiso* 24.84.

Next in importance to the act of falsification is the imagery of water. Indeed, words for water abound in all three cantos. The most important "water" is the Mirror of Narcissus. "'Lo specchio di Narcisso'" is actually named at *Inferno* 30.128, and Dragonetti (1965:121–22) explains the importance of its being named there. If not named, the Mirror of Narcissus also figures in *Purgatorio* 30, where, following Beatrice's rebuke, Dante looks down and sees himself in the "chiaro fonte" (line 76) only to withdraw his eyes instantly and thus interrupt the narcissistic vision. Finally, the Mirror of Narcissus is evoked only to be rejected in *Paradiso* 30, where Dante's eyes become mirrors (lines 84–85) in which reality, or the light of Paradise, now no longer subject to mirroring, is itself mirrored. Supplementing the Mirror of Narcissus, this image of imagery in *Inferno* 30, is the water which Master

Adam imagines, "'li ruscelletti'" ("'the little brooks'"), and which, as image, parches him (lines 64, 68); the water of the rain he imagines himself to have been when he rained down into Hell (line 95); the water which is poisonously dammed up in his dropsical body; and, finally, the water of the shame which washes Dante's face (line 142). In *Purgatorio* 30 there is the water of the rain of "'grazie divine'" ("'divine graces,'" line 112) which fertilized Dante's soul; the water of the ice which melts from around his heart, issuing in his tears (lines 97–99); the water of the "chiaro fonte"; and the water of the river Lethe. In *Paradiso* 30 there is the water of the light which Dante sees in the form of a river (lines 61–62) and the water of the same light which Beatrice tells Dante he must drink (lines 73–74). Connected with the imagery of water is the physical sensation of thirst, which is explicit in *Inferno* 30 and *Paradiso* 30 and implicit in *Purgatorio* 30, where, I assume, Dante means us to realize that he thirsts for the water of Lethe. As always in Dante, thirst ("sete") carries with it the connotation of the desire to know, a connotation which he owes to his reading of Aristotle (*Conv.* 1.1.9–10; *Metaphysics* 980a22; Boyde 1981:51). Furthermore, accompanying the imagery of rain is the closely related phenomenon of growth – "maturo"/"acerbe" ("ripe"/"unripe") – which is explicit in *Purgatorio* 30 and *Paradiso* 30 at a number of points and implicit in *Inferno* 30, where all the damned are by definition immature and unripe.

Answering to the imagery of water is the imagery of its natural opposite of fire. This imagery, more so than the water imagery, is indebted to its source in Ovid, where both fire and water are crucial to the peculiar Ovidian pathos (*Met.* 3.426, 464, 487–88, 490). But Dante is primarily interested in fire as an agent, successful and unsuccessful, of transformation, or "transhumanization" (*Par.* 1.70). *Inferno* 30 begins with an allusion to Zeus and Semele (lines 1–3); the latter was burned to death by Zeus in his glory when she foolishly demanded that he reveal himself to her as he appeared to Juno in lovemaking. And since in Ovid the story of Narcissus follows that of Zeus and Semele with that of Teiresias intervening, it is possible to recover a pattern there of revelations destroying by reveiling which Dante may have read, too, since he pursues the problematics of "velo," especially in *Paradiso* 30.[9] This pattern, however, is probably subsidiary, in both Ovid and Dante, to the theme of madness which they each explore through the image of Narcissus. Equal in importance to the Zeus-Semele allusion as an insistence on fire is the burning of Master Adam's body (Singleton 1970:1, 2, 556–57). If the false coiner is to be understood as a figure of Narcissus, then he is a disfigured figure, since the fire which burned the beautiful boy has been grossly literalized in the actual burning of Master Adam's flesh.[10] Then, too, Master Adam burns with thirst as does Sinon, his opponent in debate, and Dante recurs to their parched suffering, by dropsy and by fever, respectively, several times (e.g., lines 63, 68, 99, 127–28). In *Purgatorio* 30, Dante turns "sinisterly" to Virgil to confess, "'conosco i segni de l'antica fiamma'" ("'I know the tokens of the ancient flame'"; line 48), only to learn quickly that, one, these signs, like those of another "fiamma antica," or Ulysses (*Inf.* 26.85), are fraught with ambiguity and error, and, two, that the flame he feels through these signs is perilously similar to that which burns Narcissus and Master Adam. Indeed, insofar as Dante is (a son of) "Adam," they are identical flames – the reason's version of and to a truth which it only projects from within itself (Dragonetti 1965:91–92). Also in *Purgatorio* 30 the ice melts from around Dante's heart just as if it were snow melting under the sun's heat (lines 85–99). And, finally, when, having rebuked Dante, Beatrice asserts that he must pay some "scotto" of penitence (line 144), the word "scotto" imports into the text not only another economic image but also a connotation of fire since Italian knows a verb "scottare" meaning to burn (Vernon 1907:2, 533). Presumably it is Dante's tears which burn him or are about to burn him, and this burning too may be some punishment of the "Adam" in Dante. Finally, in *Paradiso* 30, Beatrice tells Dante that every soul who enters the Empyrean is a candle which God prepares so that it may burn with His light (line 54); and indeed Dante is said to be kindled by the light (line 58). Moreover, Beatrice remarks that desire burns Dante (line 70), and eventually she herself is said to be the sun in Dante's eyes (line 75), where the suggestion is that those eyes envision because they contain the cosmos.

The last notion common to each canto in the three canticles is that of reflection, which is expressed in *Inferno* and *Paradiso* by the word "specchio" or some form thereof.[11] In *Inferno* 30, "specchio" is of course the Mirror of Narcissus (line 128). In *Purgatorio* 30, the word "specchio" is not mentioned, but Dante obviously "reflects" in the "chiaro fonte"; and the absence of the word for mirror is significant. In *Paradiso* 30, "specchio" occurs twice in a crucial simile describing the "reflection" of the Celestial Rose (lines 109–14), and a related word, "spegli," is used of Dante's eyes when they drink of the light (line 85).

This already long list could be extended by many items which are common to two of the three cantos 30, but these are probably better left until they arise in the context of discussion, since there is no apparent rank to them. On the other hand, preliminaries must be extended by a careful consideration of Ovid's story of Narcissus and of that story as the Middle Ages received and revised it. Included among the stories of Zeus and Semele and of Teiresias and of Bacchus's arrival in Thebes, the story of Narcissus forms part of a very

dense text of unreason and madness; this Dante acknowledges and emphasizes as *Inferno* 30 opens; for example, "tanto il dolor le [Hecuba] fé la
mente torta" ("so did grief twist her mind"; line 21). Madness is the dominant
note of this canto's exordium because it is the canto of the fraudulent. As
Dragonetti has shown (1965:94–106), fraud vitiates the reason, inducing
madness, because it is a covert and self-masking perversion of the reason. Furthermore, as such, fraud is a falsification of the Image of God in man, for the
reason is just that. Moreover, sin of any sort is always a turning to the self to
the exclusion of the Other – a gesture identical with that of Narcissus. And
so, sin, especially fraud, falsification and narcissism provide Dante with a
system of discourse about imagery. And since the poet is obviously a worker
in images, this system also doubles as Dante's discourse about his own craft
and his practice of it.

The connection from unreason or madness to the poet's craft of working in
images is formed by vision itself. The sane or healthy, the mature, mind sees
the truth, and, seeing the truth, it makes and uses images without falsification. Such a mind Dante wants to become and eventually does become. We
can see the process clearly at a crucial moment in its unfolding in *Paradiso* 21,
where we also see Ovid's text return to underwrite Dante's intricate design.
In this canto Beatrice explains that Dante cannot, because of his mortality,
look on her smile: "'tu ti faresti quale / Fu Semelè, quando di cener fessi'"
("'You would become such as was Semele when she turned to ashes'"; *Par.*
21.5–6). She then goes on to issue this extraordinary command (*Par.*
21.16–18):

> "Ficca di retro a li occhi tuoi la mente,
> E fa di quelli specchi a la figura
> Che 'n questo specchio ti sarà parvente."

("Fix your mind after your eyes, and make of them mirrors to the figure
which in this mirror shall be shown to you.")

Note that here, for the first time in *Paradiso*, Dante's eyes become, or begin to
become, mirrors, and Dante's seeing thus becomes reflecting. The whole
movement of vision in *Paradiso* is from sight to reflection, and here in canto 21
that movement takes a crucial turn. The purification of Dante's vision involves the reversal of Narcissus's: whereas Narcissus saw and did not reflect
(until it was too late), Dante must reflect and cease seeing altogether;
whereas the world or the Other was a mirror to Narcissus, Dante's eyes must
become mirrors to the Other. He must fix behind his eyes his mind – as lead or
silver lines the back of a glass – thus to make of his eyes a mirror for reflecting
the figure which will appear to him in the mirror of Saturn. Where everything

is a mirror reflecting Supreme Reality, no image or figure can usurp reality; where everyone reflects and no one sees, no one can mistake an image or figure because everyone reflects that image or figure. In the world we know, this condition is impossible; it is the condition of Paradise to reflect God eternally. But Dante is approaching this condition through—the multiple senses resonate—his vision. And here, in canto 21, when he reverses Narcissus's vision, himself reflecting and no longer merely seeing, Ovid's text underwrites his design through the allusion to Semele. If Dante were *merely to see* Beatrice's smile, he would be another Semele, burned to ashes, and another Master Adam, we might add, who was also burned to ashes. He would go mad, lose his reason; he would suffer the fate of the characters in Ovid's text. The allusion to Semele at the moment when Dante begins to master the Narcissus in himself affirms that he is moving away from madness and toward sanity—"di Fiorenza in popol giusto e sano" ("from Florence to a people just and sane"; *Par.* 31.39). Ovid's text and *Inferno* 30 supply this affirmation. With "la mente retro a li occhi," Dante's seeing becomes reflecting; when the mind is applied to sight, vision in the sense of reflective understanding follows—when a man thinks about what he sees he reflects on it, and is not blind like Teiresias, or mad like Pentheus, or drunk like Bacchus, or burned like Semele.

If Dante exacts so much from *Metamorphoses* 3 in this oblique allusion, that text provokes him even more in his direct confrontation with it in *Inferno* 30. For example, it inscribes the concept of reflexivity itself: "Dumque *petit petitur* pariterque accendit et ardet" ("At once he seeks and is sought, himself kindling the flame with which he burns"; line 426, emphasis added; see also line 440; Innes 1955:92). Next in importance to this concept is the question on which the text insists of self-knowledge. Teiresias's prophecy regarding Narcissus, when asked "an esset/Tempora maturae visurus longa senectae" ("Whether this boy would live to a ripe old age"; lines 346–47)—namely, "si se non noverit" ("yes, if he does not come to know himself"; line 348; Innes 1955:90)—locates the pathos of narcissism, or self-knowledge that so far from liberating rather only binds. Incidentally, it is worth noting here, though it anticipates later parts of the argument, that to Ovid's "maturae...senectae" answers Dante's concern with maturity and ripeness in the three cantos 30; Master Adam is precisely an unripe Narcissus, immature and imperfectly grown. After reflexivity and self-knowledge, the issue of desire probably attracted Dante most to Ovid's text. Narcissus laments "uror amore mei" ("I am on fire with love for my own self"; line 464), and again "Quod cupio mecum est; inopem me copia fecit" ("What I desire, I have. My very plenty makes me poor"; line 466; Innes 1955:93); obviously he laments a desire which can never be fulfilled, and such is also, of course, the condition of Master Adam and Sinon. Moreover, and of equal importance, the cry "inopem me copia fecit" answers, with searing irony, to Narcissus's earlier refusal of coition with Echo: "'ante,' ait, 'emoriar, quam sit tibi *copia* nostri'" ("'I shall die,' he says, 'before you enjoy the *plenty* of my beauty'" *Met.* 3.391; emphasis added)–he who would not part with and share his "copia" now festers in poverty because of that very "copia." Selfishness destroys the self. Desire which refuses the Other is only a simulacrum of itself; it is not itself if it is not Other. Just so, Master Adam is not himself but only an image ("ombra") of himself. Finally, Ovid touches on the problem of imagery. He writes, for ex-ample: "Ista repercussae, quam cernis, imaginis umbra est. / Nil habet ista sui; tecum venitque manetque; / Tecum discedet, si tu discedere possis" ("What you see is but the shadow cast by your reflection; in itself it is nothing. It comes with you, and lasts while you are there; it will go when you go, if go you can"; lines 434–36; see, further, lines 416–17; Innes 1955:92). Such lines, we will see, were crucial to Dante's strategy. In addition to these concepts and problems, Ovid's text is also provocative in its emphasis on water, thirst, fire, light, and eyes (see lines 417, 430, 431, 439, 470, 490).

Such a preliminary sketch hardly does justice to Ovid's poetry, but it does serve to suggest the spur Dante might have found there. Also provocative were later, medieval versions of Narcissus's story. The most important of these, for present purposes, is that of the *Roman de la Rose.*[12] This is the ver-sion of the story, in both Guillaume de Lorris's and Jean de Meun's parts, that after Ovid probably spurred Dante on the most. He would have found, in Guillaume, that, because of his perverse love for himself, Narcissus "perdi d'ire tot le sen / et fu morz en poi de termine" ("lost his reason and died in a short time"; lines 1500–1501).[13] In Jean's part, certainly the more provocative part, he would have also read that "quant [Amans] s'i mira, / maintes foiz puis an soupira, / tant s'i trouva grief *et pesant*" ("when Amans looked at himself in it [the Fountain of Narcissus], he found himself *so heavy* and full of grief that many times thereafter he sighed over it" lines 20387–89; Dahlberg 1971:334; emphasis added). Master Adam of course is precisely "pesant" and thus corporealizes or materializes Amans's narcissistic condition.[14]

Dante would also have read in Jean the crucial observation that "'n'est nule chose qu' ele tiegne / qui tretout d'ailleurs ne li viegne'" ("'there is nothing about it that does not come to it from elsewhere'"; lines 20399–400; Dahlberg 1971:335). Precisely the curse on the mirror of Narcissus is its total incapac-ity for origination: everything comes to it "tretout d'ailleurs." It is perhaps as extreme a parody of the creative fullness of God, whence comes everything, as the poet could have found. And he found it already in large measure worked out in the *Roman*.

Jean himself opposes the Fountain of Narcissus to the Fountain of Life: "'cele les vis de mort anivre, / mes ceste fet les morz revivre'" ("'the other makes the living drunk with death, while this fountain makes the dead live again'"; lines 20596–97; Dahlberg 1971:337). For him, the Fountain of Life is clearly analogous to the Trinity (see lines 20349–448), and because of the Trinitarian structures of the *Commedia*, and especially of the *Paradiso*, Dante, I suspect, was much attracted to this opposition between the two fountains, as much as he was to the opposition between the Rose of the *Roman* and the Celestial Rose of Paradise, and this especially because Jean establishes the opposition principally in terms of vision. In Guillaume's part, the Fountain of Narcissus is clearly to be assimilated to the Lover's eyes, and like any other pair of human eyes, their field of vision is restricted to 180 degrees: "car torjors, quel que part qu'il soit, / l'une moitie dou vergier voit; / et c'il se torne, maintenant / porra veoir le remenant" ("for always, wherever they are, they see one half of the garden, and if they turn, then they may see the rest"; lines 1561–64; Dahlberg 1971:51). Now to Jean this is partial and all-too-human vision. Indeed, he complains of the "cristauz" which Guillaume praises that "'certes ainz sunt trouble et nueus'" ("'on the contrary, these stones are murky and cloudy'"; line 20418; Dahlberg 1971:335). He then goes on to celebrate the very different kind of vision to be enjoyed in the Fountain of Life. The Trinitarian carbuncle (see line 20500) which is the sun of this fountain is such that when people look into it and see themselves in it (lines 20541–47; Dahlberg 1971:336–37),

> tourjorz, de quelque part qu'il soient,
> toutes les choses du parc voient
> et les connoissent proprement,
> et eus meismes ansement;
> et puis que la se sunt veu,
> ja mes ne seront deceu
> de nule chose que puisse estre.

(They always, no matter where they may be, see all things in the park and understand them rightly, themselves as well. After they have seen themselves there, they become such wise masters that they will never be deceived by anything that can exist.)

In these lines we can see, as Dante must have seen, how vision in the Trinitarian Fountain is whole, where vision in the Fountain of Narcissus is partial, and how self-knowledge in the Trinitarian Fountain is true and complete, where self-knowledge in the Fountain of Narcissus is distorted and vain (see, further, lines 20407–408 and 20537–60).[15] In a way, the entire project of *Paradiso* resides in Jean's opposition between the two fountains: Dante in that canticle goes from the partial sight of merely human eyes to the whole vision of divine reflection—from the Fountain of Narcisssus to the Fountain of Life.

Although Dante certainly turned to the Ovidian and to the medieval versions of Narcissus's story, in his text all these versions cohere in a new structure. They all serve his fundamental premise that the ultimate falsification of images is sin which falsifies the Image of God in man or the reason. Falsification, as the figuration of money in Dante's text suggests (*Inf.* 30.90), consists in adding alloy or dross ("mondiglia") to a coin after subtracting from it pure substance, or three carats of gold in this case. Hence, in keeping with the figure, sin should also be an addition after subtraction if it does falsify the Image of God in man. But sin, all evil, is a negativity: in the classic Augustinian formulation it is a corruption of the good.[16] Hence while sin certainly subtracts from the soul it corrupts, what can it be said to add if it is itself nothingness? The question appears more formidable than it is. Sin adds that very nothingness; sin "adds" what it "leaves behind," a residue of corruption. And this Dante expresses in the word "mondiglia." The word is formed off Latin *mundus*, "clean," and expresses the leavings or the waste or the chaff which remains after cleaning.[17] "Mondiglia" consists of matter, not substance—of a something that is nothing. As matter, existing merely, it is important and it is necessary, but it is not to be confused with substance, living and inspirited.

Sin, however, precisely confuses matter and substance, thus corrupting substance. So much is explicit, we now can see, in the sin of Master Adam: he so confuses matter and substance that matter *passes for* substance—"mondiglia" for gold. He generates "as": three carats of dross are seen *as* gold. Thus his sin derives from and in one sense repeats the sin of the original Adam (and thus also original sin, we might pause here to note, is for Dante basically a sin of falsification). Adam our father generated "as" when he committed "il trapassar del segno" ("the transgression of the sign"; my translation; *Par.* 26.117). When Adam transgressed the sign of the apple, he suddenly knew evil—signs of evil were suddenly everywhere. The whole of creation, however, was good—God had created it so—and hence the only way he could know evil was to know the good *as* evil; just so, his first experience after the transgression was shame, or knowledge of his good body *as* evil, *as* something to be ashamed of. When Adam transgressed the sign, he incurred the punishment of naming one thing by another thing—one leaf after another leaf, to adapt Dante's (and Horace's) image (*Par.* 26.137–38). The sin of Adam issued in the mutability of the sign (as did that of Lucifer—after Lucifer, "serpent" can no longer unambiguously name the creature snake). Gone now the singleness and purity of prelapsarian naming (Gen. 2.19–20); in its place, men, simply by reasoning, name A *as* B. They never know A; they only know A as . . . something else. And B is always a mutation of A because unlike A as well as like A.

For men, in their fallen state, there are necessarily both, likeness and unlikeness: this is the lot of men—"as" always threatens them with illusion through the confusion of like and unlike which it generates. To prevent such illusion, likeness and unlikeness must cooperate in a diacritical or differential relationship: the sign must be different from the thing it signifies (Weiskel 1976:140–41). Some sons of Adam, however, actually exploit the mutability of the sign, to erase the unlikeness, thus concealing the confusion "as" generates in the illusion "as" generates. They make signs so like the original that it is impossible to tell the difference between sign and original. Thus they corrupt reference itself, for reference respects difference—and there, of course, is the ground of the analogy between language and money. Master Adam is the type of these. A counterfeiter, he further damages the already mutable sign by rendering it "irreferent"; his florin refers to *the* florin—it is like it—but it has no reverence for the florin because it erases, by concealing, its unlikeness to the florin. A counterfeit or "irreferent" sign is a false image because it is identical with its exemplar and thus disdainful of "as." But it is not granted the sons of Adam to nullify their Father's sin by evading, however intricately, *as*; they must take the route through "as" if they would arrive at "is."

With the mutability of the sign we enter the arena of the poet's agon. He, the maker of images, always struggles with the indeterminacy of signs. Moreover, as maker of images, he is identical with Master Adam in one respect, namely, that he makes images of images just as the counterfeiter made false images of the image of Florence's credibility. Saint Paul teaches the Middle Ages that "the invisible things of him from the creation of the world are clearly seen, being understood by the things that are made" (Rom. 1.20). The things that are made, the "ea quae facta sunt," are themselves images, and the poet produces images of them. Hence the great risk of falsification that he constantly runs. To avoid this risk, the poet must take great care in his response to the mutability of the sign. He must not be tempted by the illusion of permanent identity between the sign and his meaning. And yet this is a great temptation. Everyone would like, without misunderstanding, to mean what *he* says, even if hardly anyone ever says what he means.

The sign *is* mutable; its meanings *are* indeterminate. As a consequence, the sign is inseparable from dissension in human communities.[20] In such dissension men practice fraud on each other: one faction attempts to wrest control of the sign to itself—to determine its indeterminacy (to fix it and "fix" it) in its favor. Analogously, the counts of Fonte Branda hire Master Adam to falsify the florin, so that they may control part of its gold—masking their self-determination by the illusion of truth in the false florin. Thus the sin of Master Adam is a further perversion of the issue of Adam's sin: from mutability to the corruption of reference.

Men can take this step, so fraught with perilous consequence, because signs and coins are subject to their will. Aristotle made the point that "it is up to us to change a given coin or make it useless" (*Ethics* E1133a–b). And his medieval commentators followed suit; for example, Saint Thomas declared that "if the disposition of men who use riches should change, then coins will not buy a thing, nor will they bring anything of necessity to living, if, say, it pleases the king or community that they be of no value."[21] At the same time, medieval-language theory, early and late, recognizes that signs are instituted by an arbitrary *impositio ad placitum*.[22] Indeed, theorists acknowledge that it is in the community's power to change a sign's significance if they so choose.[23] Such power does not constitute ownership of the sign, since the same sign in a different community at the same time might have a different significance. But it does demonstrate that by concord men agree—as one theorist puts it, "mutualiter"—on the "property" a given sign possesses; moreover, it also demonstrates that the community is the steward of this "property." According to Emile Benveniste (1971:277), "*Communis* signifies literally 'one who shares in the *munia* or *munera*.'... Charges and privileges are the two faces of the same thing, and this alternation constitutes the community." When we *communicate*, we are sharing the *wealth* and the *gifts* of lanruage; in the word itself, we confront how language is a kind of wealth. But this wealth is more than and other than coin: with coin I *possess* wealth; with language I *share* wealth. Signs, in short, are never private property.[24]

Except when a malicious will wrests the sign to itself, ap-propr-iating the sign to itself as if it were a coin. Gradually I have been letting the words "proper" and "property" and "appropriate," "appropriating" and "appropriation" rise to the surface of my text. In the notion of the proper lies the crux of this book. In the Middle Ages "proper" denoted what we mean by the word "literal"—the first, the primary sense of a word.[25] This sense is the "property" of the word. Extraliteral or metaphoric senses of a word were indicated, most suggestively, by terms like "usurpata translatio."[26] These senses are "improper": they are not the property of the word; they are brought to the word, added to it, imposed upon it. Metaphor, then, is the ex-propr-iation of words in favor of an alien sense ("the meadow laughs"), while, in keeping with this reasoning, the natural opposite of metaphor (which for that very reason closely resembles it), or mendacity, is the ap-propr-iation of words to covert realities. Metaphor and mendacity are both "improper" uses of words; so it is, for example, that poetry, always dense with metaphors, in antiquity and the Middle Ages was called a lie.[27] But metaphor and mendacity are "improper" uses in different ways. A metaphor is improper because it is a usurpation of sense; a lie is improper because it is a divagation of sense and reality. However, although they differ thus, and differ crucially, both are violations of the *proper* sense of words. And as such, both are demonstrations that words possess property (cf. de Man 1974:39).

Words possess property; coins *are* property. The distinction is crucial: coins can be owned, words cannot. Even to say that words are "community prop-erty," which is close to the truth, is to violate (by metaphor) the property of words. No one, no group either, owns words; owned, words cease to be words, become counters or ciphers of the arrogating will. The just use of words respects the property of words – which is to say, it respects the others who live in the community of the language and thus share the property of words. My coins are mine though issued by the state; my words are ours though issued by me.

The notion of the proper thus leads to the relationship of justice to money and language. This subject is crucial to the present argument, since justice is always inevitably the first victim of fraud, which is as much as to say that community or social relations are also fraud's first victim; for justice in the Middle Ages was preeminently the social virtue, and especially so in the later, Aristotelian Middle Ages. And Dante so passionately loathes fraud, damns it so deeply and so precisely, because it undermines justice – for him the supreme virtue – hence also society. Saint Thomas makes the connections abundantly clear: "It is proper to justice, as compared with the other virtues, to direct man in his relations with others: because it denotes a kind of equal-ity, as its very name implies; indeed, we are wont to say that things are ad-justed when they are made equal, *for equality refers to some other*. On the other hand the other virtues perfect man in those matters only which befit him in relation to himself" (*ST* 2a. 2ae. 57, 1 reply; emphasis added). Justice always looks outward, to the other. Thomas goes on to define justice as "a habit whereby a man renders to each one his due by a constant and perpetual will" (*ST* 2a. 2ae. 58, 1 reply). Moreover, he insists – and this is important to the present argument – that "justice is first of all and more commonly exercised in voluntary interchanges of things, such as buying and selling, where the expressions 'loss' and 'gain' are properly employed; and yet they are transferred to all other matters of justice. The same applies to the rendering to each one of what is his own" (ST 2a. 2ae. 58, 11, 3). In buying and selling, or the use of money, we find the primary and the most frequent exercise of justice— Thomas, it is clear, lived and wrote in a commercial society dominated by money. So did one of his contemporaries, Brunetto Latini, who offers an even more startling pronouncement on the relationship between justice and money: "And money is also like justice without a soul, because it is one means by which things unequal and different are reduced to equality."[28] If Brunetto cites what I have called the reductive power of money, he does so in order to liken it to "justice *without a soul*." Justice *with* a soul, it would seem to follow, generates equality by rendering each his due in such a way as not to eliminate the distinctions and the differences, the natural inequalities, of various sub-jects. The soul of justice is to render *each* man *his* due.[29] Money, however, reduces each man's due to itself, and his due disappears in this universal sol-vent (cf. Serres 1982:150, 163, 172). Similarly, if signs are perverted into coins, they too resemble justice *without* a soul: they respect no differences and distinctions, dissolving them rather, and are exactly meaningless. The word "nigger," for example, *the* verbal coin of white racism in America, has no *meaning*, although from time to time it co-opts force. Words *with* meaning, however, words which respect differences and distinctions, are not coins; rather they resemble justice *with* a soul. Meaningful words are words of justice. And the just use of meaningful words respects their property pre-cisely because, to repeat, it respects the others who live in the community of the language and thus share that property. *I* can only share *our* words.

When the just work of language is interrupted and words are perverted into coins, thus to resemble justice *without* a soul, they become counterfeit. Wrested to the appropriating self, they are no longer just or true but, soulless, like counterfeit coins, are "irreferent." The counterfeiter, the falsifier, it is who exploits the arbitrariness of the mutable sign to privatize it and thus corrupt its reference. And the poet is constantly in danger of becom-ing a falsifier because *he* has a *meaning* which he desires to communicate. Mutable and arbitrary signs the poet is under compulsion to make refer.[30] He is tempted to fix and "fix" the sign in his meaning—to appropriate it to himself, thus becoming a liar, demanding that it *reflect* his meaning and *only* his mean-ing. But that meaning, to be a *meaning*, must become Other and the meaning of others'.[31] Failing that, it is no meaning but an echo, and Narcissus is gazing at himself in the mirror of language. If the poet would shun the identity of Narcissus, he must first accept the mutability and arbitrariness of signs in the hope of their eventual reference to and reverence for reality. Such hope must have faith as its substance—faith which, for good reason, Dante calls "moneta" (*Par.* 24.84).

Accepting the mutability and arbitrariness of signs, the poet realizes that if he were to fix and "fix" the sign in his meaning, he would nullify the seminality of history, the ongoing interpretative labor which inscribes human beings in time and the world—which marks them as human. Rather than succumb to this temptation and thus demean the sign, the poet must *contribute* his meaning to the sign. Nothing could be further from falsification. Since a sign is formed as a coin is formed, it can be deformed as a coin is deformed. A coin is deformed or falsified by the subtraction of gold and the subsequent addition of dross; a sign is deformed by the subtraction of reference and the subsequent addition of personal desire. Reference is the "gold" of signs, the property because of which they are "valuable," though it is a property immaterial and intangible. If the poet wrests the property to himself—makes it his coin—if he materializes it *as his own*, if it becomes synonymous with his reality, then the sign becomes false, fixed in and by a private will. If, for example, my pun "irreference" fails to communicate a valid insight, exhibiting instead only my wit, then it is a counterfeit coinage. If, on the other hand, the poet contributes his meaning to the temporal and communal inheritance of the sign, he *adds without subtracting* even as he inserts the sign into the seminality of history. As long as he *owns up* to his meaning, without presuming to own *the* meaning, of the sign, the poet does not falsify or "fix" the sign; rather, he historicizes and personalizes the sign (cf. the narrators of *Troylus and Criseyde*, Chap. 9 below, and of *The Canterbury Tales*, Chap. 10 below). He publishes his personal meaning. Put another way, as long as the reference of the sign is intact, the poet may figure it as he will. As long as the Celestial Rose refers to a rose—and to the *Roman de la Rose* and to every other rose in medieval literature—Dante may make of it the awesome and intimidating figure he does. And so much, in fact, is the case: Dante's Rose is part of the common fund, the common store or treasury, of literary tradition.

Dante the poet, we can begin to summarize, confronts the question of imagery in the canto of the falsifiers, and in the vertically related cantos, because he must differentiate his coinage as poet from the false coinage of Master Adam. We his readers must be able to spend his coin—read his language—for the vision which he experienced. So it is that, from his position of the allegory of the theologians (Hollander 1969:15–24), he must convince us that his coin or language is not fraudulent, not false, but a true and a valuable representation of what he saw when grace dispensed with the ordinary limits on human sight. He has no alternative but to use images or coins; they are all that a son of Adam has with which to communicate. He must therefore accept the mutability and the arbitrariness of the sign without impatiently fixing it in a meaning. Rather than fix and "fix" the sign in a meaning, he must liberate in the sign its energies of meaning and meaningful energies. Hence, even as he strikes the image ("batter li fiorini"), he must strike it from reality—lest it falsify reality in the illusory fixity of identity. Rather than in the spurious security of self-aggrandizing meanings, the poet must reside in the tension of reference. Such is the residence of the viator who has no true home here. And its name is faith. The lot of Adam and his sons and daughters is this, that if they would pass from mutability and arbitrariness to reverence, they need the sub-stance of faith (Heb. 11.1); and faith Dante names "moneta" (Par. 24.84) to insist that the sub-stance is only one more if the most fundamental means. It is not an end, not a fixity. It is an "as"—not yet an "is."

Here emerges a serious question for Dante's text, and, indeed, for all of medieval literature. The coin is valuable. It has so much gold. The flower too is valuable. It has beauty. Why then strike the medium from reality? Why discard the sign? The question, of course, is venerable. Its more familiar medieval form is, what has Ingeld to do with Christ? What has literature and all its mediations—images and figures and "beautiful lies"—to do with divinity and the purity of Christ's truth? We recognize the trenchant problem for the whole of the Middle Ages of the justification for poetry.[32] Necessary to any answer to this question is a distinction between the flower (or gold) and the "leavings" ("mondiglia"). The "fiore" is good in the measure to which it is current and exchangeable for the good. Saint Paul's phrase "ea quae facta sunt" (Rom. 1.20) is helpful here. The "ea quae facta sunt" are good for the "invisibilia Dei." But the "ea quae facta sunt" are flowers—evanescent, temporary, mutable, historical (and if gold seems permanent, that is precisely the curse on gold because of which it so often leads to idolatry). All media because they are historical disappear and are consumed in mediation (even the coin is abraded).[33] This is the most immediate consequence of the seminality of history. And in their historicity, all media must be struck from reality because they are less real than reality—not unreal, less real.

From this vantage point—namely, his Platonistic trust and distrust simultaneously of figures and figurativity—Dante's strategy in the three cantos 30 is completely visible. It originates in coinage because in the word "fiore" is the very value (coin) but also evanescence (flower) of all media of exchange. Thus when Dante's eyes in Paradise "coin" the spirits in the Empyrean into "fiori" (Par. 30.65, 95), we are suddenly aware that all "fiori"—coins, images, flowers, even (historical) persons—must be struck from reality or the light of

Paradise because all "fiori" are finally, however beautiful, also evanescent. Whatever coin the poet contributes, it is still coin—a promise and not the reality.

Furthermore, some "fiori" are like the Narcissus narcissistic: to them have been added the leavings of the self's desire for itself. To adapt John of Salisbury's reading of Narcissus's story, such flowers are "sine fructu" ("without fruit") because they mediate no reality—rather interrupt it to replace it with themselves.[34] The florin with three parts dross does not mediate, does not represent, the credit or creditability of Florence because in such a flower the fruit of Florence is blasted: such a flower cannot yield the fruit of Florence. Rather, it contains dead, useless matter which shadows and blights the fruit of Florence: such a flower is false, a false image, which "pays no promise in full" (*Purg.* 30.132). All flowers ("fiori") then are false in the sense that they fade and pass away—their "as" is only an afterglow of the being Adam man's father lost—but even so (and here is the Aristotelianism of Dante's Platonism) they can be trusted—one can have faith in their coinage—to mediate while they last the "invisibilia Dei."[35] The Celestial Rose is a "fiore" even as it also is not a "fiore." The faith which accepts, endures, and rejoices in this paradox is the faith of the *via affirmativa*.[36] And it is the faith which substantiates Dante's naming faith "moneta"—supreme tautology since money is itself based on faith (credit). Faith is "moneta" because faith and the creation are simultaneous and reciprocal: the goodness and the value of the creation depend on faith, while faith depends on the goodness and the value of the creation. And so it is that, for the poet of the *via affirmativa*, if all flowers or images are false, only those flowers or images *must be* repudiated which have been *intentionally falsified* by the addition of narcissistic "mondiglia." All images must be struck from reality, yes, but only some images belong in Hell.

Chapter 2
Narcissus Damned, or the Failure of Reference
(*Inferno* 30)

LTHOUGH a vertical reading of the three cantos 30 is necessary to understanding the synoptic vision of imagery in the *Commedia*, Dante is also of course a narrative and an autobiographical poet; equally necessary, therefore, is a reading of each canto 30 in its narrative situation. The reading of the cantos, in fact, must be cumulative: the synoptic vision depends on our accumulation of detail about the error of imagery.[1] Only as we see more and more lucidly that our seeing is dark and darkening can we come to grasp the necessity for the vision of Paradise of simultaneous affirmation and negation of imagery. Narrative accumulation and vertical synopsis lead us to the one goal: the purgation of vision and the achievement of reflection.

Although he is not directly named in *Inferno* 30, Narcissus is a brooding presence in that canto; in fact, Dante disfigures the figure of Narcissus in the two shades of Master Adam and Sinon. That Master Adam is such a disfigured figure is quickly established. One of the "mal nati" ("ill-born"; line 48), he is also an "idropico" ("one who suffers from dropsy"; line 112) whose body is distended "con l'omor che mal converte" ("with ill-digested humor"; line 53); consequently, he forever thirsts even though he is filled with water (lines 56, 63, 121–22).[2] Moreover, as punishment for falsifying the florin, Master Adam was condemned to the stake, burned to death (lines 75, 109–10). Finally, the *contrapasso* which he suffers is to be parched by images of water (lines 64–69). Now these three distinctions—dropsy with perpetual thirst, flesh consumed by fire, and a throat parched by images—confirm that Master Adam is a gross and literalized version of Ovid's Narcissus.[3] Yet even as Dante corporealizes or materializes him, he also plays with the loss of body which Narcissus suffers. If Narcissus wastes away until "nec *corpus* remanet quondam quod amavɛrat Echo" ("nothing remains of that *body* which Echo once had loved"; line 493; emphasis added; Innes 1955:94), Master Adam also laments "'io nel volto mi *discarno*'" ("'I in the face *unflesh* or *discarnate* myself'"; line 69; emphasis added). Master Adam "discarnates" in the face even as Narcissus loses his flesh, and this disfigurement, as its location suggests, attacks that very beauty which, initially anyway, hides his despair and loss from Narcissus.

Dante's word "discarno" provides convenient access to his strategy in *Inferno* 30. He disfigures the figure of Narcissus, or discarnates it, in Master Adam because disfigurement or discarnation is the opposite of falsification. Falsification leaves the figure intact—that of the Baptist, for example (line 74)—so as to conceal the falsity: the intact figure suggests a true coin.[4] Disfigurement or discarnation, on the other hand, mars the surface or appearance and compels testing and questioning—who or what is this figure? and to what extent should I trust him or it? A disfigured or discarnate figure can never be a false figure of an original. Correspondingly, a dis-figuring or dis-carnating figure always proclaims that it is a copy and no more than a copy of an original. A figure that dis-figures or dis-carnates is an image struck from reality, in the crucially double sense of that phrase. Such are the figures in Paradise and especially, as we shall see, in *Paradiso* 30. They figure the Light or incarnate it only to dis-figure or dis-carnate it at the same time, in order to proclaim how much greater than they the Light "really" is. We will return to this point again and again, but for now we should emphasize how systematic the synoptic relationships among the cantos 30 are.

If Dante disfigures or discarnates Narcissus in Master Adam so as to oppose falsification, he opposes falsification because he, too, is a maker of images. He feels compelled to distinguish himself from Master Adam and Narcissus alike. If, finally, he as poet proves not to be a falsifier, it is because of Beatrice. She it is who makes his images true. And so much is reasonable: she is "loda di Dio vera" ("true praise of God"; *Inf.* 2.103); moreover, her eyes are "i vivi suggelli / D'ogne bellezza" ("the living seals of every beauty"; *Par.* 14.133). As long as Dante is "stamped" with these "seals," he and the images he makes will be true copies. Through Beatrice, Dante is "signed or sealed with the holy Spirit of promise" (Eph. 1.13); he and his images "rendono promession intera" (*Purg.* 30.132). With Beatrice's help Dante is neither Narcissus nor Master Adam.

And yet briefly Dante *was* a falsifier. There was a time when he had abandoned Beatrice. Not long after her death Dante, seeking consolation, abandoned Beatrice for a "pargoletta"—Lady Philosophy, we eventually learn.[5] And, as we know, only slowly and painfully did he return from the "selva oscura" of philosophical rationalization and abstraction to the "loda di Dio vera." Had he remained enamored of Lady Philosophy, he and the images he made would have continued false because—and here Dragonetti's arguments are crucial (1965:193–40)—the reason, which is Philosophy's instrument in man, would have interrupted and interfered with his vision—the reason and not Beatrice's eyes would have been the "suggelli" stamping his images. And the reason, without Beatrice, is the fallen and unreformed Image of God. Only the reason stamped by Beatrice can see by reflecting God.

We will have occasion in the reading of *Purgatorio* 30 to return to the issue of Beatrice versus Lady Philosophy. Here we need to pursue further Dante's disfigurement of Narcissus in Master Adam. The principal means of disfigurement are the "ruscelletti" and their "imagine." The falsifier of coins, maker of false images, is now parched by an image: "'Li ruscelletti...sempre mi stanno innanzi, e non indarno, / ché l'imagine lor vie più m'asciuga'" ("'The little brooks...are always before me, and not in vain, for the image of them parches me'"; lines 64, 67–68).[6] If images of water parch Master Adam, a severe disjunction has opened between image and referent. The figure of water, like Master Adam himself, is disfigured. Obviously water cannot parch. It is contrary to the nature or the reality of water to parch. And in fact it is the *image* and not the water that parches. Hence, here in Hell, so Dante implies, the image is real—or, say, palpable and effective—but its referent is denatured—impalpable and uneffective. Indeed, Dante adds "e non indarno" ("and not in vain"; line 67) to emphasize that the image *without a referent* is effective, real, and palpable. Here in Hell the image is the only reality, the only matter, the only efficacy. It is precisely reference that has been repudiated: none of these souls would, for example, grow to maturity, that is, become one with his referent, or God. Each one is an "ombra"—"shade" but also "image"—without a referent. This is his fraudulence; he is a false image of God because, having corrupted reference itself, he can no longer refer to any Other, least of all God.[7] Fraud, then, *is* the vice which corrupts reference. In Master Adam's particular case, by adding "mondiglia" to the florin, he corrupted the reference of the florin to the credit and the creditability of Florence. And so it is that, by the law of the *contrapasso*, he who corrupted reference himself suffers and suffers from a corrupt reference: images of water parch him; disfigured figures of water discarnate him—fraudulent images of water defraud him.

A similar *contrapasso* works on Sinon, in whom also Dante disfigures Narcissus. Sinon, to be precise, suffers and suffers from disfigured fame. Sinon's introduction points the way. Dante the pilgrim asks Master Adam: "'Chi son li due tapini / che fumman come man bagnate 'l verno, / giacendo stretti a' tuoi destri confini?'" ("'Who are the two wretches that are smoking like wet hands in winter, lying close to your confines on the right?'"; lines 91–93). The latter replies: "'L'una è la falsa ch'accusò Giuseppo; / l'altr'è 'l falso Sinon greco di Troia: / per febbre aguta gittan tanto leppo'" ("'The one is the false woman who accused Joseph; the other is the false Sinon, Greek from Troy. Burning fever makes them reek so strongly'"; lines 97–99). And immediately, "l'un [Sinon] di lor, che si recò a noia / forse d'esser nomato sì oscuro, / col pugno li percosse l'epa croia" ("one of them [Sinon], who took offense perhaps at being named so darkly, with his fist struck him on his stiff paunch"; lines 100–102). Sinon is enraged at "being named so darkly or obscurely." Several commentaries on Ovid's story of Narcissus agree in reading it as an allegory of the pursuit of glory and consequent rejection of good fame; this reading was widespread (Vinge 1967:75, 86). And Dante may have relied on it for his description of Sinon's violent reaction to being "nomato sì oscuro." Sinon, like Narcissus, sacrificed "good fame," or recognition and visibility, by the pursuit of "inania gloria," in his case, through perpetrating the downfall of Troy. And his present obscurity is his *contrapasso*. The phrase "greco di Troia," suggesting as it does an unclassifiable hybrid—a Greek? from Troy?—is a disfigured fame—it is fame, but it is disfigured. As with Master Adam, so with Sinon, disfigurement is Dante's strategy.

And of most importance, Master Adam and Sinon form *together* Dante's disfigured figure of Narcissus. By halving Narcissus into these two figures, Dante can, in the "tenzone" between them,[8] demonstrate more profoundly than he otherwise could how narcissism corrupts reference. As frauds, Master Adam and Sinon are identical; as "ombre" they have shadowy differences. In their debate they think to insist on their differences; in fact, they only prove their identity. So much is clear from the form of their debate where each refers to the other with the referent also proper to himself. For example, "'S' io dissi *falso*, e tu *falsasti* il conio'" ("If I spoke *falsely*, you *falsified* the coin'"; line 115; emphasis added); or, "'e *sieti reo* che tutto il mondo sallo!' / 'E te *sia rea* la sete onde ti criepa . . . la lingua'" ("'and *may it torture* you that all the world knows of it!'" "'And *to you be torture* the thirst that cracks your tongue'"; lines 120–21; emphasis added); or "'S' i' ho *sete* e omor mi rinfarcia, / tu hai l'*arsura* e 'l capo che ti duole'" ("'If I have *thirst* and if humor stuffs me, you have the *burning* and an aching head'"; lines 126–27; emphasis added). So far from establishing difference, this exchange insists on identity. The pronouns "I" and "you" are mere shifters positioning identical formulas on two (non) sides of a (non) divide. Master Adam and Sinon are mirrors each to the other; each reflects the other. Each is a Narcissus; together they are Narcissus talking to himself. And it is hardly fanciful to hear in their exchange Echo, especially in the pair "sieti reo" and "sia rea." The Other is the Same, and in this illusory difference there is reference, but it is the corrupt reference of the sign signifying only itself signifying, referring only to its own referring—Echo.

When such a sign forms an image, it completes the corruption of reference by falsifying the image to refer without a referent. The image, its reference now completely corrupt, only repeats its referral (Echo). Dante exemplifies this final corruption at the end of the "tenzone" between Master Adam and Sinon in the strategic and crucial image of "lo specchio di Narcisso." Master Adam is speaking (*Inf.* 30.127–29):

> "tu hai l'arsura e 'l capo che ti duole
> e per leccar lo specchio di Narcisso,
> non vorresti a 'nvitar molte parole."

("you have the burning and an aching head, and to lick the mirror of Narcissus you would not want many words of invitation.")

If not many words would bring Sinon to lick Narcissus's mirror, then Sinon would seem to be more nearly Narcissus. But we must remember that Master Adam, when he addresses Sinon, is also actually speaking to and of himself; he is also licking Narcissus's mirror. He is referring to his own referral. He appears to be referring to *water*—that is, Sinon is so thirsty that he would lick any water—but he actually refers to an image which itself refers to images. Never, in fact, is there a referent; there is only an endless series of referrals. Dragonetti is of help here:

> The poet who speaks of a mirror apropos of water, then, does not speak only of water, but of a reflecting, even hardened, surface which sends back the image of a Narcissus in love with his reflection. Thus the cool, clear water of verse 128 is in fact this water, but transmuted into a mirror, a water changed into an image of water (Dragonetti 1965:87–88).

Instead of water and instead of simple reference, Master Adam names "lo specchio di Narcisso": on the one hand, as a mirror, this is an image and an inexhaustible source of images—"a water changed into an image of water"; on the other hand, this is not a mirror at all but water "transmuted into a mirror." Not only does Master Adam not refer to water; he does not refer to a mirror either. "Lo specchio di Narcisso" as an image with putative reference fails completely; in context it refers to nothing. It is not a mirror but water, and yet it is not water but an image of water. The image and the signs of which it is made never attach—in the necessarily nontactile sense of that tactile metaphor—to a thing. The image refers, well enough; indeed, it is an energetic succession of referrals. But it refers without a referent. When Narcissus or the falsifier makes an image, he contaminates it with his own mode of signifying – he never refers except to himself, he only signifies his own signifying (cf. Deleuze 1968:104); hence whatever image he makes, insofar as it is an image, it *will* refer – it will obey the process – but it will never refer to a real referent; it will only repeat its referrals.

Another example of such falsification, less dramatic, perhaps, but no less compelling, is Master Adam the "raindrop": "'piovvi in questo greppo'" ("'I rained down into this trough'"; *Inf.* 30.95). Rain figures in all three cantos 30; here in *Inferno* 30, Master Adam "rains" only to insist that he is false rain. The poisonous water backed up inside him will never break forth – unlike that frozen around Dante's heart when we see him as "Adam" in Purgatory (canto 30, lines 85–99) – and he will never moisten anything, least of all the ground of Hell. The irony in "piovvi in questo greppo" is too great – distended to the very boundary of meaninglessness. The rain is *only* the image of rain – the reality impalpable and ineffective because excluded and repudiated. Again Master Adam makes an image which refers without a referent. He cannot rain, and when he makes an image that says he did, he falsifies the word "piovvi" – it is *only* a word and therefore fraudulent.

If Master Adam makes images which refer without a referent, he is himself just such an image. He is Adam, the Image of God. But he has repudiated God – that is why he is in Hell – by corrupting reference, falsifying images. He refers endlessly. But he refers (in Hell) to no Other.

With one near exception, namely, Dante the pilgrim. Dante the pilgrim, in Hell, almost adds a referent, himself, to the fraudulent process of signifying which Master Adam and Sinon conduct in their "tenzone." Their empty signs, only signing and otherwise without a referent, Dante the pilgrim almost fills with himself. We know the gravity of Dante's situation and imminent error from the description of his posture when Virgil interrupts him: he is "tutto fisso ad ascoltarli" ("all intent to listen to them"; line 130). The phrase "tutto fisso" is as ominous here as it is in *Purgatorio* 2 (line 118), where the souls are "tutti fissi" in Casella's song when, as Cato quickly reminds them, they should be proceeding to their purgation.[9] Here in *Inferno* 30 it is a signal that Dante, and in particular the Adam in him, is bound to and by the evil before him.

To be precise, at the moment when Virgil vents his anger at Dante, the latter is providing reality for, or, say, lending substance to, the empty *signa* of Master Adam and Sinon. Dante is becoming that which is *behind* or *beyond* or *referred to* in the signs which Master Adam and Sinon hurl back and forth. The condition of images and/or shades in Hell is lack, insubstantiality, and yet Dante, by taking Master Adam and Sinon as seriously as he does, lends them his being, materializes their lack, and thus becomes the substance behind them. In effect, Dante the narcissist sees himself in the two halves of the disfigured Narcissus—hence Virgil's "'Or pur *mira*'" ("'Now just you keep on *looking*'"; *Inf.* 30.131; emphasis added): Virgil obviously understands precisely the error Dante is committing. To recur to Dragonetti's argument (1965:94–106), Dante sees the reason perverted—he is seeing an image of fraud—and he materializes the perversion by the fixity of his gaze as he tries to reason through, to understand (cf. line 145), an exchange radically unreasonable, reasonless, damned. He, Dante, almost becomes the significance or the referent—perverted human reason—of the otherwise empty signs of Narcissus in Hell. Dante almost gives the damned what they lack and what they have lost all right to, namely, reality or substance. Even perverted human reason would be more substantial than the reasonless echos of Master Adam and Sinon.

If Dante had continued to lend his substance to the empty signs, eventually they would have consumed him, and he would have become identical with Master Adam and Sinon, his reason as perverted as theirs. Happily, the process is not allowed to complete itself. Virgil calls Dante back from marmoreal fascination with the signs of Narcissus. Dante's response to this recall is crucial. He does, in fact, repent, though his repentance, too, is troubled by narcissism (lines 133–41):

> Quand'io 'l senti' a me parlar con ira,
>   volsimi verso lui con tal vergogna,
>   ch'ancor per la memoria mi si gira.
> Qual è colui che suo dannaggio sogna,
>   che sognando desidera sognare,
>   sì che quel ch'è, come non fosse, agogna,
> tal me fec'io, non possendo parlare,
>   che disïava scusarmi, e scusava
>   me tuttavia, e nol mi credea fare.

(When I heard him speak to me in anger, I turned to him with such shame that it circles through my memory even yet. And as is he who dreams of something hurtful to him and, dreaming, wishes that it were a dream, so that he longs for that which is, as if it were not, such I became that, unable to speak, I wanted to excuse myself, and did excuse myself all the while, not thinking I was doing it.)

Of most importance initially in reading this passage is the fact that shame is, in the influential Augustinian terms Dante would have known, an instance of "signa naturalia":

Those signs are natural which, without any desire or intention of signifying, make us aware of something beyond themselves, like smoke which signifies fire. . . . and the face of one who is wrathful or sad signifies his emotion even when he does not wish to show that he is wrathful or sad, just as other emotions are signified by the expression even when we do not deliberately set out to show them.[10]

Distinctive of the "natural sign" is the absence of intention in the presence of signification: Where there's smoke, there's fire, with no intention; where there's a twisted face, there's wrath, with no intention; where there's a blush, there's shame, with no intention – Dante himself insists on as much later in the poem (*Purg.* 21.105–108). A blush and shame, then, form an in-stance of pure reference where no will or intention interrupts or interferes with the process of reference; a blush and shame form an instance of pure readability. But Dante, through a tortuous and almost serpentine simile, does interrupt the process of reference; and he does so by introducing desire ("desidera") or lack and belief ("credea") or faith. He perverts the natural sign by his intention, an intention thoroughly narcissistic and falsifying because it subtracts the "gold" of reference from the sign only to replace it with the "mondiglia" of personal desire.

The force of the simile is to suggest that the shame : sign which is real and in real relation to a real referent is disfigured "come non fosse" – figured "as if it were not" to be thus disfigured. Dante *is* ashamed and the shame : sign *does* communicate; Virgil makes this abundantly clear (lines 142–44). But desire – the intention to excuse himself – forces Dante to believe or to have faith otherwise, so that the shame : sign, in his belief or faith, is emptied and becomes a *signum Narcissi* – such a sign as Master Adam and Sinon make, a false sign. Through his desire and in his belief, what is, is "as if it were not": the excuse or shame which *is* on his face is *not* in his belief or faith. Sign and referent are radically sundered, their exchange interrupted, even though this sign and its referent are in an ontically pure relationship. Dante disfigures the sign by his denial of its referent, and it is his desire which motivates the disfigurement. Dante's desire to excuse himself, to feel shame, precludes his feeling shame, and thus he believes that he is not excusing himself. He desires to feel shame, but he believes that the shame is not accommodated to any ex-ternal sign; he believes that he cannot communicate – "non possendo parlare" – and yet he *is* communicating and communicating shame to Virgil. Desire separates the red blush and the shame, and belief keeps them separated. Still desiring to feel shame, Dante does not believe in his shame. The sign thus without a referent precisely *is*, only as if it were not, "come non fosse." It refers, but it refers without a referent. It is thus a sign of Narcissus and of narcissistic, or selfish and unreflective, desire – "bassa voglia" (line 148).

Dante's frame of mind, his *faith* ("credea"), when Virgil reprimands him, indicates the extent to which, "tutto fisso" in the "tenzone," he *has* become Narcissus. To restore Dante's faith, and especially his faith in signs, Virgil must, having stopped the process by which Dante was becoming Narcissus, now go on to reverse it by affirming and confirming Dante's penance: "'Maggior difetto men vergogna lava,' / disse'l maestro, 'che 'l tuo non è stato; / però d'ogne trestizia ti disgrava'" ("'Less shame washes away a greater fault than yours has been,' said the master, 'therefore disburden yourself of all sadness,'"; lines 142–44). Note that if shame washes ("lava") shame is somehow liquid—has something to do with water. Now obviously, even ostentatiously, Virgil is speaking in metaphor. And through this metaphor, water enters this *bolgia* of Hell. Thus the only "real"—that is, palpable and effective—water in Hell is this metaphoric "water" which washes Dante's "difetto." The implication seems to be that reality obtains—in this case, the reality of water—when the exchange between sign and referent is true and complete; Dante's shame, even so excessive and self-conscious a shame as his is, is the only case of such exchange here in the *bolgia* of the falsifiers. Thus the poet seems to say that when the sign—in this case, shame—is referential it can be the foundation of a metaphor—or, washing—because both partners in the meaning are real. The sign truly referential attaches to the Other, and the Other validates the sign. And a valid sign, not fraudulent, is the ground of every metaphor.

The narcissist, however, having lost faith in signs, does not believe this, and thus, in the present example, does not feel the laving effects of his penance, his shame. So it is that Virgil must go on to say, "'pero d'ogne trestizia *ti disgrava*.'" Master Adam is laden with "membra che son *gravi*" (line 107), and as long as Dante "si grava" with "trestizia" or any other infernal emotion or desire, he must remain the narcissist, unredeemed by reference, the Adam in him masterful still. So it is that Virgil tells Dante to "disAdam" himself ("ti disgrava"); which is also as much as to tell him to "disNarcissus" himself.

Having reasoned thus with Dante, Virgil—himself the figure of human Reason—concludes by insisting on the Reason and its involvement in the scene which has just transpired (lines 145–48; emphasis added):

> "e fa *ragion* ch' io ti sia sempre allato,
> se più avvien che fortuna t'accoglia
> dove sien genti in simigliante piato;
> ché voler ciò udire è bassa *voglia*."

("and do not forget [lit.: "do you *reason* that"] that I am always at your side, should it again fall out that fortune find you where people are in a similar dispute, for the wish to hear that is a base *wish*.")

"Ragion" and "voglia" – "reason" and "desire" or "will" – are elemental structures of the human being, according to the theology with which Dante is working.[11] The reason, or "ragion,"[12] is generally understood to reflect the Second Person of the Trinity, or the Son, the Word or *Intellectus*. By trying to reason through the reasonlessness of Master Adam's and Sinon's "tenzone," Dante has been not only reducing himself to a Narcissus but also deforming the Image of God in himself. Virgil, the figure of Reason, has just arrested this deformation. And now, reasoning further with Dante, he orders him "to reason" ("fa ragion") that he, Virgil, will be with him *always* in similar circumstances. The extraordinary precision of Dante's language insists on the proces of *re*formation of the Image which Virgil is initiating here. Note also that Virgil cites "fortuna" as the agent of Dante's predicament; and precisely, throughout medieval philosophy and theology, reason is the opponent of "fortuna," its mandate being *to see through* the illusory "order" which "fortuna" establishes.[13] Finally, Virgil condemns the desire or will to hear such "piato." In Dante's theological optic it is the duty of the will to obey the reason (see *Par.* 28.109–11); if it does, it is then rightly ordered. This right ordering of the will under the guidance of reason is the process and the result of Dante's ascent of Purgatory in Virgil's company: when Virgil crowns and mitres Dante, it is because "libero, dritto e sano" is his "arbitrio" (*Purg.* 27.140). Hence, when Virgil condemns the pilgrim's "voler" as a "bassa voglia," Dante once again calls attention to the deformation and reformation of the Image of God. For the "bassa voglia" to hear reasonlessness itself can only follow upon a perverted reason; only a perverted reason could lead the "voler" thus astray; only a deformed Image could further vitiate itself by bending the will so low ("bassa").[14]

    With this analysis of its concluding lines, the rigor of the structure of *Inferno* 30 is evident. It begins with allusions to madness, or the loss of reason, and ends with Virgil just managing to prevent Dante from going mad, losing his reason. Because the Reason is the Image of God, throughout the canto Dante articulates a theology and a poetics of imagery. Falsification is the act which grounds Dante's discourse. And Narcissus is the figure (disfigured) that represents – which is to say, successfully refers to – the failure of reference which falsification of imagery perpetrates. And it is the success of this reference of Narcissus that suggests that Narcissus need not be damned, that, on the contrary, he can be purged, and, indeed, even redeemed.

Chapter 3
Narcissus Purged, or the Renewal of Reference
(*Purgatorio* 30)

URGATORIO, canto 30: Dante sees and meets Beatrice again, loses Virgil. In the next canto he confesses—to infidelity (*Purg.* 31.34–36). In this canto Beatrice delivers a brief biography of him which chronicles the circumstances of that infidelity. All this and more unfold in the presence of the twi-form griffon, figure of Christ. The very density of the symbolic environment suggests that if this is the Garden of Eden it still resembles the "selva oscura" where Dante "came to himself." The verb "mi ritrovai" stems from the same root that generates North French (*langue d'oïl*) "trouvère" and South French (*langue d'oc*) "trobador"—both words meaning "poet."[1] When Dante "finds" himself, in a sense he "poets" himself; underwriting this sense is the Latin equivalent of "trov-" or "inventio," the rhetorical term for that process by which a poet "finds" or "invents" or "discovers" his matter.[2] Dante's "self-discovery" is very much of, by, and in poetry. On the one hand, explicitly, is Beatrice's mandate to Virgil to aid Dante with his "parola ornata" ("fair or ornate speech"; *Inf.* 2.67). On the other hand, implicitly, is the suggestion that the "selva oscura" itself is language. Three times in the *De vulgari eloquentia*, Dante likens the Italian language to a "silva" ("wood" or "forest").[3] In keeping with this metaphor, the "selva" of poetic language would be precisely "oscura"—dark with allegory, multivalence, and hidden intention—and only the poet could find his way through it. Much more "oscura," however, if not exactly a "selva," is the Garden of Eden, which mortal man has not seen since the Fall of his first parents. Here, because of deeper, more primal obscurity more than "invention," more than "poet-ing," more than facility with the "ornata parola" of poetry are required for finding oneself. Here being a poet is not enough. Here interpretation demands that the nature of imagery itself be questioned even as the sonship of the poet be tested. Here discovery is often an ambiguous re-covery. Here, if Beatrice chastens Narcissus, falsifier of images, only forgetfulness (the river Lethe) purges him; and even then he does not die. Here it is still possible for Dante to be "troppo fiso" in Beatrice's smile (*Purg.* 32.9). Moreover, "sotto l'ombra / ...di Parnasso" ("under the shade [also, image]...of Parnassus"; *Purg.* 31.140–41), the poet still sees shades—"ombra"/images. Here, the light is still dark.

If Dante in *Inferno* 30 barely escapes the fate of Narcissus ("tutto fisso"), in *Purgatorio* 30, he only barely endures the self-consciousness of his narcissism. That he becomes self-conscious of his narcissism before he drinks of Lethe is evident from his physical reaction to Beatrice's outraged rebuke (lines 76–78):

> Li occhi mi cadder giù nel chiaro fonte;
> ma, veggendomi in esso, i trassi a l'erba,
> tanta vergogna mi gravò la fronte.

(My eyes fell down to the clear fount, but, seeing myself in it, I drew them back to the grass, so great shame weighed on my brow.)

We will be involved with these lines and those that follow for some time to come, but for the present most important is the interruption of the narcissistic gesture (lines 77–78); if interrupted, it must have begun. Dante, then, *does* see himself, and in that measure he *does* repeat Narcissus's error. But he nonetheless recoils from the image. And note that the image is not reflected in a "specchio" or even in "acqua" but in a "chiaro fonte." It is as if the absence of "lo specchio di Narciso" confirmed the possibility of Dante's interrupting the fascination—as if the "chiaro fonte" could not be the space of such deceit. At any rate, Dante's behavior suggests that he is both guilty of narcissism—as is, in some measure, every son of Adam—and at the same time reluctant to submit to it. This doubleness and mixture of good and bad are proper to Purgatory and to the pilgrim's askesis there.

Now Dante's shame, "vergogna," further proves his self-consciousness of narcissism and consequent repudiation of it, or refusal to continue speculating. Note that the shame "*gravò* la fronte." The word "gravò" asks to be read in conjunction with Virgil's "disgrava" in *Inferno* 30.144. There Virgil told Dante to disburden himself of all sorrow; in effect, this was to tell him to "disAdam" himself. Virgil's argument for this advice was that Dante's "vergogna" was already sufficient to excuse him. To the burden of shame Dante should not add the burden of "trestizia": the shame is valid and valuable—it is true—and Dante ought to feel it; not so with the infernal "trestizia," however. Moreover, Virgil also told Dante to remember that he, Virgil, would be with Dante in other like cases and that, therefore, Dante should not give in to such emotions again (*Inf.* 30.145–47). Consequently, when in *Purgatorio* 30 "vergogna gravò la fronte," the word "gravò" not only suggests a burden which Dante ought to bear but also suggests that, although Virgil has just moments earlier disappeared (lines 49–54), he is still, just as he promised in Inferno, with Dante. His legacy to Dante, it will be remembered, is a will "libero, dritto e sano" ("free, upright and whole"; *Purg.* 27.140), a will set in order under reason's guidance. To be sure, Virgil was only human reason, inspired (by Beatrice) but not yet reformed, not yet illumined. Hence Dante, the Image of God, though much healed, remains in the region of dissimilitude[4] – his mind is still essentially dark – but his will or intention is strong enough now at least to interrupt the narcissistic gesture. Hence, if he does speculate in the "chiaro fonte," he sees with Virgil's aid his shame-burdened brow. In Inferno, he did not, at first, see his shame and consequently desired it so as to will it "come non fosse"; in Purgatory, on the other hand, with his will healed, Dante does see his shame, and the vision finally triumphs over narcissism, since neither desire nor belief impedes correct construction of his behavior and subsequent right action.

Dante continues to comment on his behavior under Beatrice's rebuke with an important simile of maternity and sonship: "Così la madre al figlio par superba, / com' ella parve a me; perché d'amaro / sente il sapor de la pietade acerba" ("So does the mother seem harsh to her child as she seemed to me, for bitter tastes the savor of stern [lit.: unripe] pity"; lines 79–81). We will have occasion, in the reading of *Paradiso* 30, to return to this extraordinary and in many ways pivotal simile, but for present purposes the crucial point is the implication of Dante's immaturity. He is like a boy overwhelmed by his mother. Although Dante's will is now "libero, dritto e sano," his reason, image in him of God, is still immature; this, of course, is why Virgil has left him – Another must reform the reason. And to the immature, naturally, the taste of pity will be bitter; moreover, the immature will predictably assign his subjective state to the pity, sensing it as unripe. "Pietade," however, is "pietade" and not "acerbe." A mother's "pity" is her love for her son, and she corrects her son because she loves him; that it should seem otherwise to him is his emotion and his projection, not her behavior. Because of his projection, the "sapor" of "pietade" *does* taste "d'amaro" to the boy – taste is taste, completely subjective – but the "pietade" itself is "acerba" *only* because it seems so to the boy. The boy, in short, has confused the "sapor" with the "pietade" – he has *added* his taste to the "pietade," subtracting from it its reference to the mother's love – with the result that it seems "acerba," its reference corrupt, just as Master Adam added "mondiglia" to the "fiorino," thus corrupting its reference to the credit and the creditability of Florence. Dante in his reason is as yet far from mature because he is still, as Master Adam will be forever, a narcissist, corrupting reference.

Not only does Dante's speculation in the "chiaro fonte" prove that he is still a narcissist, even though his will has been healed; there is also his extra-ordinary resemblance, even here in Purgatory, to Master Adam himself. Three particulars insist on the resemblance; and we will take up each in order. First, he contains within him a flame, a burning; second, he bears water pent up inside him; third, he thirsts with a thirst no ordinary water can satisfy (the thirst for Lethe). Dante feels the "antica fiamma" of Didonian ar-dor (line 48); he releases a torrent of tears when the ice melts from around his heart (lines 97–99); and he burns with stinging tears, paying thus his "scot," before passing through and drinking of Lethe (lines 142–45).

Dante's recognition of Beatrice, the event which first exposes Narcissus still within him, is a moment of profound emotional disturbance (lines 43–54):

> volsimi a la sinistra col respitto
>   col quale il fantolin corre a la mamma
>   quando ha paura o quando elli è afflitto,
> per dicere a Virgilio: "Men che dramma
>   di sangue m'è rimaso che non tremi:
>   conosco i segni de l' antica fiamma";
> ma Virgilio n'avea lasciati scemi
>   di sé, Virgilio dolcissimo patre,
>   Virgilio a cui per mia salute die' mi;
> né quantunque perdeo l'antica matre
>   valse a le guance nette di rugiada,
>   che, lagrimando, non tornasser atre.

(I turned to the left with the confidence of a little child that runs to his mother when he is frightened or in distress, to say to Virgil, "Not a drop of blood is left in me that does not tremble: I know the tokens of the ancient flame."

But Virgil had left us bereft of himself, Virgil sweetest father, Virgil to whom I gave myself for my salvation; nor did all that our ancient mother lost keep my dew-washed cheeks from turning dark [lit.: black] again with tears.)

Bracketing the famous quotation of *Aeneid* 4.23, "Adgnosco vestigia veteris flammae," are several allusions to maternity and paternity. Noteworthy in the first such allusion (lines 43–46) is a crucial error: Dante, after his first sight of Beatrice, is so disturbed that he turns to Virgil as would an infant to its mother. Virgil, however, is hardly a mother; rendering the image further suspect is the fact that Dante turns to the left "sinisterly."[5] The corrupt image and the movement leftward emphasize a regression, a reversion, by Dante to a narcissism from which in a moment Beatrice will brusquely recall him.

Before she does, however, the mirror in which Dante the narcissist is at this moment gazing becomes visible. It is the *Aeneid*, and in particular the figure of Dido: "conosco i segni de l'antica fiamma." In effect, upon his first sight of Beatrice, Dante turns back to look into poetry and into *the* epic poem, where he sees *not* Beatrice but his Didonian version of the fire which consumed Narcissus. The *Aeneid* is here a distorting mirror which mediates only to interrupt the first vision of Beatrice. Dante the pilgrim sees himself, not Beatrice, and sees himself in the famous lines of epic ardor. Such a reaction after so long a separation was perhaps predictable, but it is hardly pardonable, as Beatrice will make clear. Dante sees an *old* love when he should see a *new* love; he reverts to an *old* life when he should turn at last to a *new* life ("vita nova"). If Dante's will is healed, his reason is still corrupt, not yet reformed, and it corrupts the text of Virgil to substitute the Virgilian name of desire, or Dido, for the new reality which confronts him. Here it is important also to recall that the poet had already named Ulysses, whose "ardore" (*Inf.* 26.97) for experience is the very type of self-fascination, a "fiamma antica" (*Inf.* 26.85). Ulysses the rhetor is swathed in the flame of rhetoric; and this flame is "old."[6] Dante, then, in *Purgatorio* 30 quotes himself as well as Virgil, so as to insist that the fire which consumed Narcissus and consumes him is not only Didonian but also Ulyssean. Love and rhetoric, desire and language, vicious with a nostalgia for "esperïenza" (*Inf.* 26.116) and "il disïato riso" ("the longed-for smile"; *Inf.* 5.133), both bend Dante equally to the poetic text where his own "ardore" is mirrored—represented to replace reality.

Dante the pilgrim is not only Narcissus but also Dido and Ulysses; he reduces the *Aeneid* to a mirror, corrupting Virgil's text, and founds his recovery of Beatrice on error. A terrible emblem. But there is more. There is another poet in Purgatory who reads and who read Virgil. He is Statius. And Dante the pilgrim's reading is itself a distorted reflection of the true maternity of the *Aeneid* for this other poet (*Purg.* 21.94–99):

> "Al mio ardor fuor seme le faville,
>   onde sono allumati più di mille;
> de l' Eneïda dico, la qual mamma
>   fummi e fummi nutrice poetando:
>   sanz' essa non fermai peso di dramma."

("The sparks which warmed me from the divine flame whereby more than a thousand have been kindled were the seeds of my poetic fire: I mean the

Aeneid, which in poetry was both mother and nurse to me – without it I had achieved little of worth" [lit.: I had not weighed a dram].)

Here too is a "fiamma," only it is "divina," not "antica." Here too is the Aeneid, but a wholly different Aeneid from the one into which Dante gazes later. Note further that here too is a "dramma," or coin (Gr. "drachma"),[7] of which Dante's "dramma" – "Men che dramma / di sangue m'è rimaso che non tremi: / conosco i segni de l'antica fiamma" (Purg. 30.46–48; emphasis added) – is only a falsification. Perhaps most important, here too is an "ardor" wholly different from Ulysses' and Dido's.

Statius was converted to Christianity by his reading of Aeneid 3.56–57. This reading, according to Dante, was a deliberate "spoiling" of Virgil's letter so as to take from it the meaning which conduced to salvation (Shoaf 1978:195–99). Statius's relationship to the Aeneid then is not a passive one; he did not merely gaze into a mirror. Quite the contrary, he violated the poem just as every infant violates its mother, in birth, and its nurse, in suckling. But before such violation there must be conception; and in Statius's case, "seeds" of fire begot his "ardor." In other words, the "divina fiamma" was the father – who, in Dante's physiology, is the source of the seed or the image (Purg. 25. 37–51) – and Statius is saying, in effect, that Virgil was his father while the Aeneid was his mother. I admit that the locution "de l'Eneïda dico" appears to contradict this position. Yet I would argue that this locution is not in apposition to the preceding tercet. Given Dante's physiology (and how seriously he took it),[8] Statius would hardly go from speaking of "seme" to speaking of "mamma" with the intent of equating the two; for Dante, the mother provided no seed. Hence, rather than an apposition between "la divina fiamma" and "de l'Eneïda dico," I would suggest that the latter locution serves for emphasis and specification – something like, "in all this I am referr-ing to the Aeneid, which was. . . ."

Certainly the suggested reading serves the logic of Statius's discourse. Virgil, the father, begot Statius's "ardor" upon the Aeneid, the mother. If, in fact, this is the correct reading, immediately apparent in its light is the seriousness of Dante's error when he turns "sinisterly" to Virgil as to a mother: if, at that moment, Virgil is "mother," then the Aeneid is "father" – and just so, as from the seed or source of the image, Dante takes from the Aeneid Dido's image as his own. Dante approaches the Aeneid as if it were a father when, as Statius rather proves, it can only be a mother. Statius's description of the birth of his "ardor" is physiologically correct: the poet pro-vides the seed; the text, the matter. And the flame of the father always ex-ceeds the matter of the mother; the mother, then, as Statius implies, can always be violated to recover more of the father—as he himself does, when he spoils Virgil's text for the meaning which tends to his own salvation. The birth, on the other hand, of Dante's "ardor" when he first sees Beatrice again is unnatural: the father, Virgil, is the mother; the mother, *Aeneid* 4.23, is the father. In a sense, we see now, it is Beatrice's task to reverse this unnatural birth as she, in some measure to be adequated to Scripture and revelation, becomes the text-mother (*Purg.* 30.79–81, especially) of Dante.

At this point the coin image is intelligible. The child receives matter, precisely weight, from the mother (*Purg.* 25.51); just so, Statius notes, "'sanz' essa non fermai *peso* di dramma'" (*Purg.* 21.99). To have even so much weight as a "dramma," Statius had to have the *Aeneid*'s matter; without "her" matter he would have weighed nothing—he would not have been alive. Dante, on the other hand, as a result of seeing Beatrice again, turns to the false "mother" Virgil and measures his blood in "dramma"—the blood which, in his physiology, is the source of seed or the image (*Purg.* 25.37–45)—and then takes his image, of Dido, from the text. Dante, in short, is so confused that he measures paternal blood with maternal weight, applying "dramma" to the source of the image rather than, as did Statius, to the source of weight. Dante confuses substance and matter, which is also the sin of Master Adam. The image (not the infernal but the generative and creative image) is substantive, not material (the infernal image is material only), and that substance may join matter but must never be seen *as* matter. Dante, however, precisely sees his "sangue" as "dramma"—substance *as* matter and therefore necessarily matter *as* substance—and thus, in effect, falsely *coins* substance into "dramma" of matter. As Narcissus would body his image in water ("corpus putat esse quod unda est"—"he thinks that a body which is water only"; *Met.* 3.417; cf. Innes 1955:92), so Dante would body his image in a text.[9] He has the wrong text, however. He must have a text, yes; but his text is Scripture (Beatrice : revelation), not the *Aeneid*.[10] He is Dante, not Statius.

A brief summary here, before the next step in the argument, will be of great help. Dante the pilgrim's vision of his Didonian ardor and flame is a distorted reflection of the birth of Statius's "ardor"; as a poet, in comparison with Statius, Dante has not yet found, or—perhaps better—returned, to his "inspiration." He is about to rejoin Beatrice, whose eyes are the "suggelli" of his craft. But to fold himself within her inspiration once again, Dante must transcend his narcissism, and to do that, he must acquiesce in the passing of poetry's authority. This he is reluctant to do because the fascination of Narcissus is still so strong in him, and he does see himself in the epic text. He is still a son of (Master) Adam, and he falsely coins substance by confusing it with matter. The flame with which he burns does not yet illumine; he cannot yet see his text. Dante the pilgrim, on the way to being the poet, does not yet know who his father and mother are.

Dante, of course, does not quite complete the narcissistic reversion to Virgil; it remains, fittingly, in his imagination. This because, when he has turned, before he speaks, he finds Virgil gone; and now he *must* accept the passing of poetry's authority. And now, also, he is suddenly and painfully aware that Virgil is a *father*, in fact *the* "dolcissimo patre," to whom he gave himself "per salute." Only the loss of his image establishes Virgil as the source of images, or the father. The father lost, Dante thinks of the "ancient mother" responsible for loss itself. He thinks of Eve and behaves very much like a son of Eve, undoing the work of the father Virgil: "And all that the ancient mother lost {=Eden} could not avail that the cheeks washed with dew did not turn black with weeping." This extraordinary periphrasis, besides introducing yet another (and not the last) mother, also recalls Virgil's cleansing of Dante's image just before they begin the ascent of Purgatory. When he and Dante first arrive on the shores of the mountain, Cato instructs him to wash Dante's face "'sì ch'ogne sucidume quindi stinghe'" (*Purg.* 1.96). Shortly thereafter Virgil puts both his hands in the grass wet with *dew* ("rugiada"; *Purg.* 1.121). Dante says: "ond'io, che fui accorto di *sua arte*, / porsi ver' lui *le guance* lagrimose: / ivi me fece tutto discoverto / quel color che l'inferno mi nascose" ("I therefore, aware of *his purpose*, reached toward him my tear-stained *cheeks*, and on them he wholly disclosed that color of mine which Hell had hidden"; *Purg.* 1.126–29; emphasis added).

Dante is "aware of Virgil's purpose," but Virgil's "purpose" is also, fittingly, an "art," and by that "art" he washes Dante's tear-stained cheeks with dew so that he "dis-covers" the color which Hell had hidden there.[11] When, however, Virgil suddenly disappears, and with him "sua arte," Dante's cheeks, though washed with dew, turn black with more weeping. Obviously Virgil's efforts were limited and their effects temporary: "art" can only wash away the stain of Hell, and the "dis-covery" of normal color is far from that "reformatio imaginis Dei" which it is the purpose of Dante's askesis to achieve. Virgil is Dante's father in poetry—not the only one, to be sure (see *Purg.* 26.97–99), but the most important, without doubt—and yet the image which he provides is fleeting as well as secondary. It is, of course, only a poetic image ("sua arte") and therefore, inevitably, transitory. Dante's true Image—true Image of both the pilgrim and the poet, his personal and primary Image—has its source elsewhere, in a Father whom he has yet to see. He has yet to see that Father because the Image of Him which he bears, the Fall, and especially the sin of pride, has seriously deformed. And Virgil's "arte" cannot reform this Image. So temporary is Virgil's "arte" that, when he disappears, its effects disappear too, and the black stain of Hell reappears on the as yet unreformed Image of God, or Dante's face.

Now, for the same reason that Dante's Image exceeds Virgil's "arte" (and, ultimately, his paternity too), it also defeats restoration by Eden, or "quantunque perdeo l'antica matre" ("all that our ancient mother lost"). The key is "antica" and hence the periphrasis. The *old* mother, Eve, wrought the deformation of the Image, and only the *new* mother, Mary, Mother of God, can reform the Image through the agency of her Son. Because Eve is the *old* mother and because her "antiquity" taints Eden, neither she nor what she lost can prevent the tears which blacken the Image of God in Dante. As Virgil finally is not the true Father, neither is Eve the true mother. Dante's Father is God; his mother, Beatrice: the Trinity reforms him to similitude with Itself through the mediation of Scripture.

This reformation, of course, is very far off. Here and now, surrounded by what the ancient mother lost, Dante *falsifies* the Image of God in him by blackening his face with tears. He is still a son of (Master) Adam and of the "antica matre," Adam's wife. And so it is that Beatrice must rebuke Dante (*Purg.* 30.55–57, 73–75).

The effect in him of this rebuke Dante describes in an elaborate simile, far-reaching in its many implications, of ice melting from around his heart.[12] Initially, for present purposes, the most important element of this simile is the word "liquefatta" (line 88), since it answers directly to Ovid's description of Narcissus's "dissolution": "sic attenuatus amore / Liquitur et tecto paulatim carpitur igni" ("thus worn away by love, he *dissolved* and was slowly consumed by its secret fire"; *Met.* 3.488–90; emphasis added). Obviously the processes of "liquefaction" in the two cases are similar: although Dante introduces subtle changes of Ovid in his version of the simile (Brownlee 1978:202–203), he retains the basic notion of the sun melting snow or frost (lines 85–90), and he does repeat the crucial term "liquefatta." The emphasis on liquid is necessary to continue the thematization of Adamic parallels. But if the processes of "liquefaction" are similar, the end results of these processes, we know, are widely different. Unlike Narcissus, who as a result of "liquefaction" dies, Dante, dying rather in the sense of "conversion," begins to return to the "new life" (*Purg.* 30.115) and to return under the guidance of the one who first revealed it to him (cf. Eph. 4:22–24).

So that he may finally enjoy the fruit of his "new life," Beatrice must bring Dante to confess his sins. The Adam in him must confess his betrayal of Beatrice, and this betrayal took precisely the form of falsification, the sin of

(Master) Adam. So it is that Beatrice proceeds to report Dante's biography (*Purg.* 30.109–41) in such a way as to emphasize his Adamic error.

Two moments of the biography are crucial for the special emphasis she seeks. First is the metaphor of the rain (*Purg.* 30.112–20):

> "per larghezza di grazie divine,
> che sì alti vapori hanno a lor piova
> che nostre viste là non van vicine,
> questi fu tal ne la sua vita nova
> virtüalmente, ch'ogne abito destro
> fatto averebbe in lui mirabil prova.
> Ma tanto più maligno e più silvestro
> si fa 'l terren col mal seme e non cólto,
> quant' elli ha più di buon vigor terrestro."

("through largess of divine graces, which have for their rain vapors so lofty that our sight goes not near thereto, this man was such in his new life, virtually, that every right disposition would have made marvelous proof in him. But so much the more rank and wild becomes the land, ill-sown and untilled, as it has more of good strength of soil.")

This is extremely dense figuration, requiring extensive analysis. Of most importance initially is to recognize that it responds to Master Adam's "piovvi in questo greppo" (*Inf.* 30.95). At the same time, it depends for this response on Genesis 2.4–5 and Saint Augustine's magisterial commentary on these verses. The verses themselves read:

> These are the generations of the heaven and the earth, when they were created, in the day that the Lord God made the heaven and the earth: And every plant of the field before it sprung up in the earth, and every herb of the ground before it grew: for the Lord God had not rained upon the earth; and there was not a man to till the earth.

The emphasis in these verses on rain and earth relates directly to Dante's "piova" and "terren." Moreover, in Augustine's commentary, he would have found a meditation on the Fall and the pride which brought it about. As part of this meditation Augustine recognizes that the Fall necessitated mediation for the human creature:

> Now [after the Fall] God makes the fields green, but by raining upon the earth [as opposed to before the Fall when he "had not rained upon the earth"]—that is, he makes souls to flower again through his word; but He waters them from clouds—that is, from the Scriptures of the Prophets and the Apostles. And rightly are they called clouds, since these are words which sound and pass away, having struck the air. Moreover, they have

the added obscurity of allegories, as if they were darkened with a sort of mist, just as happens with clouds. But when by explication they are glossed, it is as if the rain of truth is poured out on those who understand them.[13]

From this position Augustine can go on to celebrate the Incarnation as an acceptance of, and triumph through, the curse, also blessing, of mediation:[14]

Our Lord deigned to assume the cloud of our flesh and pours out the most generous rain of the holy Gospels, promising also this, that if someone drinks of his water, he may return to that fountain within, so that he will not seek the rain without (PL 34:199).

Then, as part of his conclusion, he turns, within his theology of the Image and its Pauline vocabulary, to our ultimate transcendence of mediation:

. . . for man laboring in the earth–that is, settled in the dryness of sin–divine doctrine, from human words, is necessary, just like rain from clouds. Such knowledge, however, will be destroyed. For we see now in aenigmas, as if seeking food in a cloud: then, however, we will see face to face (1 Cor. 13.8, 12), when the whole face of our earth shall be watered by the inner fount of leaping water (PL 34:199).

I have quoted at such length so as not to impoverish the context of Dante's own reading. He modifies Augustine's searching interpretation to articulate his own moving figure of the "piova" and the "terren." Dante, like every other man, is earth, and earth needs rain–to be fertile, to be strong, to be good and not sterile and waste. But once the land is moist, it can grow rank with weeds. Early in his "vita nova," in the pristine moment of his conversion by and to Beatrice's beauty, Dante enjoyed the "larghezza" of divine graces, which include the Scriptures, raining down upon him from "alti vapori"; here the poet draws on Augustine's "imbrem largissimum" which pours from the "nubilum carnis" of the Lord. Enjoying this largess–the term's economic resonances are crucial–Dante participated in the promise the Lord made– "promittens etiam quod si quis biberit de aqua ejus, rediet ad illum intimum fontem." But Dante abandoned this promise when he abandoned Beatrice, "'imagini di ben seguendo false / che nulla promession rendono intera'" ("'following false images of good, which pay no promise in full'"; lines 131–32). Following these images, Dante made himself "terren maligno e silvestro col mal seme e non cólto": he squandered the rain on weeds. In doing so, he falsified the Image of God in himself, since, as Augustine suggests, the Image is the "facies terrae nostrae"; this extraordinary phrase authorizes

Dante's figuring his deformation of the Image as "terren" he has made "maligno e silvestro."

Although these various elements of Augustine's text provoked Dante, he must have found most compelling the image of "nubes" itself, to which his own word "vapori" answers. It is here that Augustine's discourse and his own thematization of Narcissus meld. And the interface is mediation. Augustine's figure of the "nubes" must be seen in the context of his anxiety of figuration itself.[15] Throughout his career Augustine lamented the temporality and spatiality of language because of which it is limited to figuration when it would describe God and his acts. A word is "quod videtur et transit" ("what is seen and passes away"), as he expresses it elsewhere.[16] Clouds, then, figure the fault in language which necessitates figures: they thunder, then blow over; and sometimes they are black, obscuring. And, as in a thunderstorm the rain must break through the clouds, so in an allegory the truth must descend through the obscurity of the letter.

Dante, who shares Augustine's anxiety, adapts his figure to his own. He understands that mediation is the error in which narcissism originates. Because men must use media to communicate, they always risk contaminating the media with their own selfish desires. Indeed, if men could reach the clouds, they would try to control even them for their own selfish interests. Hence, Beatrice's insistence that the divine graces have "clouds so high for their rain / that our sight does not come near them." Dante is anxious to stress that this rain, unlike the rain which Master Adam rains, could never be contaminated with any "mondiglia" of desire. Indeed, so distant is the source of this rain that not even Beatrice's sight—she insists on "*nostre viste*"—can reach it. So invisible and impenetrable by sight are these "vapori" that no Narcissus can ever look into them and see himself. These "vapori" originate in God, and no man hath seen the Father except the Son (Matt. 11.27).

If safe from Narcissus, these "vapori" are also proof against Master Adam's false coining. Since God is the origin of the "vapori," the rain of divine graces is obviously and even ostentiously a metaphor, insisting on its figurativity. It never rains in Heaven, and there are no clouds in Heaven (however many there may be in the heavens), just as it never rains and there are no clouds in Hell. But this similarity masks a crucial difference. In Heaven, although it never rains, the referent of the figure of rain is real, namely God. In Hell, on the other hand, it may "rain," but it is the *sign* "rain" and *only* the sign "rain" which is real (though it is not true), as in the "rain" which punishes the glut-tons (*Inf.* 6.7–9)—hardly true "rain" in the sense we know it ("regola e qualità mai non l' è nova"—"its measure and its quality are never new") even if very real (*Inf.* 6.34–35). In both Heaven and Hell, which resemble each other as original and disfigured copy, the sign "rain" is *qua* sign false in that it cannot function *qua* sign in either region. In Hell the sign is false because reference is corrupt: the sign "rain" *does* communicate (it is real), but it communicates only itself disjunct from any referent (it is not true). When Master Adam claims "piovvi in questo greppo," the sign infinitely defers the referent; it is a false coin not to be exchanged for any reality other than itself. In Heaven, on the other hand, the sign is false because the referent exceeds it: both it and its reality, or water, are inadequate to circumscribe or circumrealize the referent, God. Not only absent and invisible, this referent is also incomprehensible. God, however, is never not real and efficacious. Hence "rain" can be predicated of Him and of His actions: He will "condescend" to this predication (see *Par.* 4.43–48). Moreover, such condescension is always available if only there is never any admixture of personal desire in the sign so as to substitute it for the referent. In that event the sign is so many parts dross and a falsification of the pure light of Heaven. To forestall such an event, Beatrice insists "che nostre viste la non van vicine." She excludes the possibility of narcissistic pollution of the image. Hence she speaks in a figure of *pure* figurativity—which is the only way to speak to Narcissus about his narcissism.

Beatrice's biography of Dante continues with a description of the help she gave him in this life; she then recounts her "mutation" of life (lines 121–26). Shortly thereafter Dante "volse i passi suoi per via non vera, / imagini di ben seguendo false, / che nulla promession rendono intera" ("turned his steps along a way not true, following false images of good, which pay no promise in full"; lines 130–32). Many words here are crucial as Dante prepares the way for the final purgation in him of Narcissus. Of most importance initially are the "imagini false."

Necessarily, these images evoke the false images which Master Adam made, or the coins three-parts dross. And in the systematics of the three cantos 30, Beatrice, we can see, is accusing Dante of having been a Master Adam. The accusation is the more obvious for the word "promession": in Italy by the fourteenth century one spoke of "promession" in the sense of indebtedness, or obligation to pay, and so Dante could presume that the economic connotation of the word would not be lost on his readers.[17] And that connotation contributes to the sense of the "imagini" as coins. Dante, then, so Beatrice implies, by following false images, as much as falsely "coined" them: he added to them the "mondiglia" of his concupiscence and rendered them thus good for nothing.

It will be helpful to recall at this point Dante's Christian Platonism. This Platonism posits that all creation is but an image of a Good which is absent and invisible though always operant. That the creation is an image hardly means that it is not good; quite the contrary: "viditque Deus cuncta quae fecerat, et erant valde bona" ("and God saw all the things He had made, and they were very good"; Gen. 1.31). Indeed, one could go further: the good of creation is that it is an image, an Image of God. Hence the dilemma confront-ing man fallen, his reason benighted. He often, in fact usually, mistakes the image for the Good of which it is an image. He appropriates the creation or some part of it as an absolute or end in itself, whereupon it becomes, *as image*, a *false* image of the Good in which it participates as a creature of the Good. In such a case, from this image or creature has been subtracted the good of its Good, and in its place has been added the dross ("mondiglia") of personal desire—the desire to find the person satisfied or quiescent in an image now belonging to and therefore of the person. From the optic of Christian Platonism, desire falsifies the only substantiality which the image or creature has—namely, its creatureliness, its middled if also muddled being—and thus the image becomes a false coin "che nulla promession rendono intera."

A coin is a promise—no matter how pure its gold—of faith and exchange-ability: a coin is not the thing itself (gold is not God, though some men make it a god) but a medium of exchange for other things. A coin, however, three-parts dross is no longer a valid promise—it no longer "covers" the promise—because the whole promise cannot reside in the less than whole or false coin: a false coin cannot render the promise whole. Just so with the false image of the Good. Through created goods, "ea quae facta sunt" (Rom. 1:20), God *promises* to man forgiveness, salvation, eternal life. If to the created good is added the "mondiglia" of narcissistic desire, then the image, thus falsified, cannot render God's promise whole. The image, of course, can never re-present God—it can never "purchase" God—it is *only* the promise, where the promise is of something else which, until death, is absent and invisible. But if the image can never re-present God, it can, as long as it is *not* falsified, render the promise whole: the "ea quae facta sunt" rightly read and rightly loved show forth the glory of God—the goods of creation are "good for" the Good because they are the promise of the Good.

But Dante, Beatrice is saying, was a false coiner just like Master Adam, whose son in a sense he is. When Dante followed false images of the good, they were ontically true images which *he* was falsifying with personal desire. The question pressing on us now is, With exactly what desire did Dante falsify the images?

The answer to this question emerges from the revision of the *Vita nuova* which Dante is prosecuting in the three cantos 30. We have already briefly considered this revision in the discussion of *Inferno* 30. There we learned that, following Beatrice's death, Dante met and became enamored of a *donna pietosa* who is almost certainly the "pargoletta" whom Beatrice mentions in *Purgatorio* 31.59 and who is to be identified with Lady Philosophy. Here, in the continuation of the revision, we learn in greater detail the exact nature of Dante's betrayal of Beatrice for this *donna pietosa*.

First recall that, when Beatrice accuses Dante of following false images, she claims that he "volse i passi suoi per *via non vera*, / imagini *di ben* seguendo false." The claim and especially the emphasized phrases suggest that Beatrice is also describing Dante lost in the "selva oscura" since there the "diritta *via* era smarrita" ("the direct *way* was lost"; *Inf.* 1.3; emphasis added), and *there* ("vi") all along was the *good* though Dante was so late in finding it—"ma per trattar *del ben* ch' i' *vi* trovai" ("but to treat of *the good* which I found *there*"; *Inf.* 1.8; emphasis added). Now if the direct way was lost and if Dante lost the good, so as to have to find it again, behind these events lay, doubtless among other causes, his attempt at a too narrowly philosophical conversion.[18] Dante had attempted to reason his way through "del bel monte il corto andar" (*Inf.* 2.120). Much like Boethius in his time of loss, Dante, when he had lost Beatrice, desired to console himself with philosophy; the fragmentary *Convivio* is probably best understood as Dante's "Consolation of Philosophy." But the consolations of philosophy are severely limited; they are wholly inadequate to supernatural happiness (Freccero 1973:77). And they certainly do not constitute the short way to the Garden of Eden. Indeed, theirs is the long and winding and often tortuous way of rationalization, abstraction, and hypothesis—the way, in short, of the reason still in the darkness of the Fall, the way "non vera." Philosophy is not the true way; it cannot finally lead to the good, because the philosopher's desire is for rationality when the reason, unillumined by grace and unreformed to similitude with God, can only see its own rationality, its own order (often specious) wherever it looks.[19] Images, however, which do lead to the good, always exceed rationalization or escape it, and if reduced to counters of philosophy, they are in that measure falsified. Hence, we can infer from Beatrice's words that the desire with which Dante falsified the images was the philosopher's desire for rationality in the world.

Confirmation of this inference is available from *Purgatorio* 31, where Dante actually confesses to his betrayal of Beatrice. First, she asks him (*Purg.* 31.22–30):

> "Per entro i mie' disiri,
> che ti menavano ad amar lo bene
> di là dal qual non è a che s'aspiri,

> quai fossi attraversati o quai catene
>   trovasti, per che del passare innanzi
>   dovessiti così spogliar la spene?
> E quali agevolezze o quali avanzi
>   nella fronte de li altri si mostraro,
>   per che dovessi lor passeggiare anzi?"

("Within your desires of me that were leading you to love that Good beyond which there is nothing to which man may aspire, what pits did you find athwart your path, or what chains, that you had thus to strip you of the hope of passing onward? And what attractions or what advantages were displayed on the brow of others, that you were obliged to dally before them?")

These questions bring into focus the major points of Beatrice's case. Note, first of all, that she explicitly cites "disiri" for her as Dante's motive: desire for her must obviously have differed from the philosopher's desire for rationality in the world; and the measure of the difference was her *image*. Unlike the disembodied abstraction, the personification, Lady Philosophy, Beatrice was a person and hence a living image of the living God, "lo bene / di là dal qual non è a che s'aspiri." She led Dante to love the good ("lo bene") because he could love her, his whole person engaged by the love of and in her whole person. Not just his reason but also his body found salvation in the love of Beatrice. Dante's desire for Beatrice was not the desire of reason for order, more or less specious, but the desire of the whole man for the good of wholeness itself, "di là dal qual non è a che s'aspiri." This desire and only this desire does not falsify the image because this desire desires that the image be; it desires above all the being of the image.[20] This desire would never reduce the image to its version of the image – Narcissus is always and forever alone.

But when Beatrice's image disappeared, Dante's desire for her was diverted. Seeking the consolations of philosophy, Dante was reduced to reason's version of beatitude, its version of happiness in a fallen world. The twisted, tortuous, painful, and binding experience of reason in its search for happiness is communicated in Beatrice's words "attraversati" and "catene": the latter word speaks for itself, but "attraversati" should be analyzed so as to hear its insistence on turning, on version, which leads astray. Dante himself, in his confession a few lines hence, will admit to the *turning* of his steps in a wrong direction. But before that Beatrice actually hints at the mode of this "attraversion": she says that he *found* ("trovasti") the cross ditches and the chains, which is as much as to say that he "poeted" them in the allegorical and philosophical *canzone* of the *Convivio* and elsewhere – songs which, however beautiful, are also fraught with the "attraversions" and "concatenations" of reason in its search for happiness. Such songs, in fact, are reason's efforts *to mirror* itself in the unpredictable creativity of history; and Beatrice precisely goes on to suggest that Dante's *version* from her was an act of Narcissus. She says that the "agevolezze" and "avanzi"—exactly what they were is not immediately relevant—"nella fronte delli altri si mostraro." Now if Dante was looking "nella *fronte* delli altri," it is likely that he was seeing *his* image in those images and *his* face in those faces—in short, seeing himself instead of the Other and his reason's version of the real instead of the real. Beatrice, then, does not hesitate finally to suggest that Dante was a Narcissus, diverted if not perverted when he should have been converted.[21]

Dante himself confirms the suggestion—and does so, little wonder, weeping (*Purg.* 31.34-36):

> Piangendo dissi: "Le presenti cose
> col falso lor piacer volser miei passi,
> tosto che'l vostro viso si nascose."

(Weeping I said, "The present things, with their false pleasure, turned my steps aside, as soon as your countenance was hidden.")

Dante's words continue the emphasis on steps and direction—on error physical and mental—and on turning, "volser," which as "version" is a strategic figure of his discourse. Most important, though, is his use of the word "falso." Necessarily, it reverberates loudly from its other occurrences in the cantos 30: in acknowledging the falsity of the pleasures of the images, Dante is also acknowledging the falsity of the images themselves; neither they nor their pleasures rendered any promise whole. Moreover, if he was like Master Adam in these pleasures, falsifying them with his desire when they turned his steps toward them, he was also like Master Adam, seeing himself in them, for they attracted his gaze only when Beatrice's "viso si nascose." The implication is clear: her face was the true mirror, the mirror in which, as long as Dante looked into it, he saw not himself but the good which he *would* be, "lo ben" for which he longed. When, however, her "viso si nascose," Dante *turned* to other "fronti" (other mirrors and other faces), where he began to see only himself and his reason's version of the real. The Adam in him began to falsify "le presenti cose" by desiring them since they seemed (the reason found them) so pleasurable. And instantly no promise could be rendered whole, for the promise is of things *not* present—of things which "le presenti cose / col falso lor piacer" can only obscure. Narcissus can see no promises; he can see only a thing—"*iste* ego sum" (*Met.* 3.463; emphasis added).

Responding to Dante's confession, Beatrice asserts that he must now bear the "'vergogna / del suo errore'" ("'shame for his error'"; *Purg.* 31.43–44). Shame, we have seen, is a motion of the will rightly ordered by the reason and a motion which, as such, interrupts the narcissistic gesture; where there is shame, there is consciousness of the Other and no (or at least less) narcissistic emphasis on the self. Hence it is most fitting that Dante now should bear the "vergogna / del [suo] errore" since earlier it was precisely his "shameless" reason which erred or wandered in pursuit of the "pargoletta," Lady Philosophy, thus leading the will and its desires astray. The darkened reason and disordered will of that time could feel no shame, and now Dante must compensate for that omission.

In addition to his shame, Dante must also pay some "'scotto / di pentimento che lagrime spanda'" ("'scot of penitence that may pour forth tears'"; *Purg.* 30.144–45). He must pay this "scot" before he may drink of Lethe: this is the draught of cool water, even a single drop of which Master Adam cannot have because he is a falsifier; and the implication is clear that Dante can drink of this water only when the falsifier is purged from within him. Hence the tears—"che lagrime spanda." These tears are true coin because they are natural signs of Dante's contrition; he cannot falsify them, as the whole of canto 31 makes abundantly clear: he hurts too much. Moreover, these tears *burn* Dante, as the verb *scottare* = "to scald" suggests, and thus they inflict him for a moment with the same pain Master Adam suffers. Thus, too—and this is crucial—they are a water that *burns* but that burns naturally: this in rebuttal of that denaturing of water in imagery—that image of water that parches—in the vicious materiality of Hell. Hence, in summary, Dante "is" Master Adam (and a son of Adam) suffering the pain of Master Adam just as he "is" Narcissus enduring the sorrow of Narcissus, but only as preparation for "transhumanizing" Narcissus and (Master) Adam on the way to his ultimate reflection of the New Adam—the "vista nova" (*Par.* 33.136) of his now revised "vita nova."

Chapter 4
Narcissus Redeemed,
or Transference Crowns Reference
(*Paradiso* 30)

ITH THAT passion for accuracy true of the whole *Commedia* but
most characteristic of the last canticle, *Paradiso*, canto 30, transcribes Dante's "transhumanization" from narcissism to a just self-
love. Here Dante's eyes become mirrors (line 85) so that, instead
of seeing, he now reflects, and, reflecting, he is no longer physically capable of
the error of Narcissus. To be sure, he cannot adequately "reflect" God; as
Adam informs him, God is the "'verace speglio / che fa di sé pareglio a l' altre
cose, / e nulla face lui di sé pareglio'" ("'the truthful Mirror which makes of
itself a reflection of all else, while of It nothing makes itself the reflection'";
Par. 26.106–108). But if unable to "reflect" God because an inadequate mirror, Dante is also unable to mistake God through sight for some "thing" He is
not. On the contrary, now, when he "looks into" the "verace speglio," he
reflects the reflection of the light which was *in principio*. Now, in Paradise, it
is only God who "sees" since nothing exists except in the sight of God. Now,
in Paradise, no creature "sees"; it only reflects–for only in reflecting the glory
of God is the creature glorious (cf. *Par.* 31.70–72).

Paradiso is a poem of vision, in every sense which that word will bear. No
study such as this one can begin to do justice to the vision; hence I think it
wise to detail right away what I hope to do in this chapter so as to distinguish
it from what I have no intention of even attempting. Only so can I prevent
misunderstanding.[1]

Narcissus, coinage, falsification: these are my primary concerns. Canto 30 is
my principal focus. The "transhumanization" of Dante into a redeemed Narcissus is the term of my argument. That "transhumanization" involves first
and foremost a reformation of sight; hence I will isolate moments of the
Paradiso which record major alterations in the nature and quality of Dante's
sight. Crucial to this project is to remember that Dante and his sight con-

stitute *our* reference point – and our transference point also, I will eventually argue – in Paradise: he is *the only human being* in Paradise to whom we can turn for bearings. Consequently, he must figure and figure in our sight but dis-figure and dis-figure in our sight, too. Against the cry of "jargon," let me insist that *we* never "see" Paradise: we see only the figures which Dante's eyes brought to Paradise and with which those eyes remember the vision of Paradise; he and his eyes are our reference and transference point. But these figures are by definition (the definition of the human body) inadequate to Paradise; they are a darkening of the Light in our behalf, because pure and un-differentiated the Light would be invisible to us – we see only by contrast (cf. Serres 1982:70). Hence these figures *do* disfigure the pure Light of Paradise, in the Adamic sense of their fallenness: all human similitudes originate in the region of dissimilitude; they are all dark with exile. Consequently, they would also falsify the Light of Paradise if they did not dis-figure even as they figure: so as not to be a falsifier, Dante charges every figure with so much figurativity that the very ostentation of the figure initiates its dis-figurement – the figure figures only to dis-figure, or to cease figuring so as to transfer us beyond figurativity itself. Only thus can we see even as we know we do not see; only thus can Dante represent Paradise even as he knows he does not re-present Paradise; only thus can the Light, invisible without con-trast, be purged of the shadow ("ombra") which makes it, not visible – it is never visible – but present by its absence.

The one occurrence in *Paradiso* of the verb *figurare* in its active form con-firms this argument and, indeed, furthers it. In *Paradiso* 23.46–48, Beatrice commands Dante:

> "Apri li occhi e riguarda qual son io;
>   tu hai vedute cose, che possente
>   se' fatto a sostener lo riso mio."

("Open your eyes and look on what I am; you have seen things such that you are become able to sustain my smile.")

Dante's reaction to this "proffer," as he terms it (line 52) is complex, and his report of it is fraught with ambiguities and hesitancies and perhaps even a tinge of awe (*Par.* 23.52–69):

> io udi' questa proferta, degna
>   di tanto grato, che mai non si stingue
>   del libro che 'l preterito rassegna.
> Se mo sonasser tutte quelle lingue
>   che Polimnïa con le suore fero

> del latte lor dolcissimo più pingue,
> per aiutarmi, al millesmo del vero
>   non si verria, cantando il santo riso
>   e quanto il santo aspetto facea mero;
> e così, figurando il paradiso,
>   convien saltar lo sacrato poema,
>   come chi trova suo cammin riciso.
> Ma chi pensasse il ponderoso tema
>   e l'omero mortal che se ne carca,
>   nol biasmerebbe se sott' esso trema:
> non è pareggio da picciola barca
>   quel che fendendo va l'ardita prora,
>   né da nocchier ch'a sé medesmo parca.

(I heard this proffer, worthy of such gratitude that it can never be effaced from the book which records the past. Though all those tongues which Polyhymnia and her sisters made most rich with their sweetest milk should sound now to aid me, it would not come to a thousandth part of the truth, in singing the holy smile, and how it lit up the holy aspect; and so, depicting Paradise, the sacred poem must needs make a leap, even as one who finds his way cut off. But whoso thinks of the ponderous theme and of the mortal shoulder which is laden therewith, will not blame it if it tremble beneath the load. It is no voyage for a little bark, this which my daring prow cleaves as it goes, nor for a pilot who would spare himself.)

These extraordinary verses deserve much more commentary than I can afford here, but certain points need emphasis. First, note that Dante cannot "rassegnare" Beatrice's smile; he can only record, in the sense of "sign," the *proffer*. Not the reality, only the preface to the reality, or, say, the invitation, is transcribable. Indeed, all the efforts of poetry, as suggested by Polyhymnia and her sisters, would be inadequate to this Paradisal reality, or Beatrice's smile. Hence, and this is the crucial observation, "figuring paradise, / it is necessary for the sacred poem to leap, / as with one who finds his way cut off." The one and only time Dante uses the verb *figurare* of his transcription of Paradise is to tell us that the poem *cannot* figure paradise.[2] On the contrary, figuring, it must leap, its way cut off. Dante uses the verb at the very moment when its signification is wholly inapposite. The way of figuring is cut off; the poem must leap. In contrast, in the Aristotelian natural theory which Dante inherits, it is a crucial axiom that "natura non facit saltum" (Boyde 1981:129); on the contrary, nature establishes all the levels of being without a "leap" between any two of them. Dante's poem, on the other hand, is precisely *not* "natural" because it is concerned with *supra*nature. Hence it must *leap* – that is, do the opposite of nature. In the terms I am proposing from the vertical reading of the three cantos 30, the poem must dis-figure. The space defined by the hyphen in *dis-figure* is the gap the poem must leap every time it would "figure" Paradise. Since the way from figure to reality is cut off, the poem must leap across the absence of figuration into dis-figuration where the sudden cessation of figuration, the gap or absence or blank space (marked by a hyphen [-] in my reading) dis-figures Paradise, in this case Beatrice's smile, simultaneously figuring and not figuring it. Dante figures the smile by saying that it cannot be figured; the poem, instead, can only leap. The leap, marking the absence, is the (dis-)figuration. Note, finally, Dante's insistent and poignant emphasis on the body. The mortal shoulder—also the mortal Homer ("omero" / "Omero"—*Inf.* 4.88), mortal because blind. Dante, with this pun, is at once bold and humble: bold to say he is Homer; humble to assume the mortality implied by Homer's blindness. To be sure, the boldness is every bit as important as the humility: Dante *is* arrogating to himself something of Homer's *fama*, which is a kind of *im*mortality. But it is the humility, the mortality, which receives the accent here. Dante is confessing that the sacred poem must leap because a human being, a human body, is bearing it. And it cannot go where the body cannot go. At the same time, of course, the body has the strength to leap the gap: this pilot will not spare himself, and the very confession of weakness becomes the occasion, as the weakness itself is the origin, of triumph.

At this point two corollaries of the argument should be emphasized. First, by the very fact that he is a son of Adam in Paradise, Dante risks being a Master Adam or false coiner of the Light of Paradise. Dante has no alternative but to coin the Light. Hence, time and again Beatrice warns him to be quiet and to look again, so that she may rid his eyes of images false in the sense of inadequate to reality. For example, she upbraids him at the beginning of the ascent (*Par.* 1.88–91; emphasis added):

> "Tu stesso ti fai *grosso*
> col *falso imaginar*, sì che non vedi
> ciò che vedresti *se l'avessi scosso.*
> Tu non se' in terra, sì come tu credi;"

("You make yourself *dull* with *false imagining*, so that you do not see what you would see *had you cast it off*. You are not on earth, as you believe.")

The allusion in "grosso" to the ponderous Master Adam is hardly mistakable. If Dante does not "throw off" the "false imagining"—if he clings to it and to the earth—then he will be a Master Adam, a gross falsifier of the Light of Paradise. So it is that the whole of Dante's experience of Paradise is a "scossare," a "throwing off" or purging of images from his eyes.[3]

But when Dante returns to earth and to transcribe the experience for us, he is in a quandary, for—and this is the second corollary—his only recourse is once again the discourse of imagery. Upon his return, in point of fact, Dante is himself, in his person, the coin which "purchases," or, more exactly, "repre-sents," Paradise for us: "l'ombra del beato regno" is "segnata" in his head (*Par.* 1.23–24). Dante is the coin of God, *stamped* with the *image* of Paradise.[4] Hence the precision of his earlier promise (*Par.* 1.10–12; emphasis added):

> Veramente quant'io del regno santo
> ne la mia mente potei far *tesoro*,
> sarà ora materia del mio canto.

(Nevertheless, so much of the holy kingdom as I could *treasure up* in my mind shall now be the matter of my song.)

Dante makes a "tesoro" of the "regno santo" in his mind because his mind is the coin of the "beato regno."[5] Dante is obviously adapting and extending the theology of the Image here; if man is the Image of God, then the figure of man as God's coin follows compellingly. Moreover, there is considerable patristic authority behind the figure: Saint Augustine, for example, refers to man as "nummus Dei" ("the coin of God").[6] If Dante, returned from Paradise, is the coin of the realm, it follows that his poem is to be understood as the figure ("ombra") on the coin. While he was a pilgrim in Paradise, Dante coined the Light of reality with images which he brought with him; after his return from Paradise, Dante is its coin, stamped with its figure; but his substance—his body as well as his soul and mind—affects that figure, that "ombra segnata," when it accommodates it to itself. His substance, being human, humanizes the figure and thus reduces it to figurativity. And so, this figure, *Paradiso*, strictly speaking, the coining of a coining, made up of so many figures, must also dis-figure. This coin must be struck from reality, in the crucially double sense of the phrase, lest, disdainful of "as," it attempt identity with its exemplar. In fact, no poem ever more revered "as"; in fact, this poem is struck from reality (*Par.* 1.70–72; emphasis added):

> Trasumanar significar *per verba*
> non si poria; però l'essemplo basti
> a cui esperïenza grazia serba.

(The passing beyond humanity may not be set forth in words: therefore, let the example suffice any for whom grace reserves that experience.)

The "essemplo" is *not* the "esperïenza": it is struck from the "esperïenza."[7] And Dante escapes his quandary by assuming it. *Paradiso* is only an example of Paradise. It is *only* a coin and a true coin because it is *only* a promise. It is not falsified with any presumption of appropriation. Quite the contrary, it is a piece of the "moneta" of faith (*Par.* 24.84).

This argument and its corollaries enable us to see that the process of dis-figurement is itself a figure of the reformation of Dante's sight *during the vi-sion.* The reformation of Dante's sight is a constant and incremental "scossare," or casting off, of images and figures, which is a dis-figuring, where the images and figures are the more similar to God the nearer Dante ap-proaches to Him, until the figure of the circle (*Par.* 33.116ff.), which, since it is as close to God's primal unity as a human figure can come, constitutes the purest figurativity in the poem. Moreover, since Dante is the Image of God, the reformation of his sight is simultaneous with (though not the same thing as) the reformation of his Image to similitude with God; and at the term of this reformation, when and because Dante has achieved similitude, figurativity ceases—his mind "percossa" with the vision of God, Dante has no need of figures. We, of course, never reach this term. We have no vision: we have not had the experience; we have only Dante's "essemplo" (*Par.* 1.70–72). Hence, for example, Dante transcribes the last moment as: "la mia mente fu percossa / da un *fulgore* in che sua *voglia* venne" ("my mind was smitten by a flash wherein its wish came to it"; *Par.* 33.140–41). "Fire" and "desire" or "will," the figures (and the figure) of Narcissus, still remain; and they must, otherwise we could not see. Dante's sight is now beyond even reflection; he is with God. We, however, are still looking into a mirror, struggling to reflect; and because we see a Narcissus, we know that we are not looking into the mirror of Narcissus.

From this vantage point we can articulate the last distinction of the analysis which I am attempting here. If dis-figuration is the figure of the reformation of Dante's sight, which is part of his total "transhumanization," we never reach the term of that figure or the absence of all figures. We remain, on the con-trary, with figures, in the space of reference, the space of the poem, which is language. However, when figures dis-figure in Dante's sight, we *do* see the dis-figuration; we do see beyond, though we do not see *what* is beyond. I can see that angels are not "faville" (*Par.* 30.64) but something beyond "faville." The dis-figuration of "faville" transfers me beyond "faville": transference ex-tends and crowns the reference of "faville." I do not because I cannot see God with Dante; but in his poem I am at least beyond this world—almost, for a moment, transhuman.

Canto 30 transcribes the most drastic changes in Dante's sight during the pilgrimage through Paradise before his actual vision of God at the end.

However, his sight undergoes other important changes at earlier stages of the journey, and some of these deserve separate emphasis as preparation for analysis of those transcribed in canto 30. In particular cantos 21, 22, and 26 should be singled out.

I undertook an analysis of the opening of canto 21 in my discussion of the allusion to Semele in *Inferno* 30. Here I want to emphasize again that this is the canto in which for the first time Dante's eyes become mirrors (lines 16–18), and I want to add, for special emphasis, that this is the canto in which Dante enters the heaven of Saturn. Dante's eyes, then, become mirrors when he enters the heaven of the contemplatives, or those who *speculate*. As usual, Dante is precise. And the precision continues into the next canto, where, having begun to reflect, Dante, desiring to exercise his new vision, asks Benedict to assure him "'s'io posso prender tanta grazia, ch'io / ti veggia con imagine scoverta'" ("'if I am capable of receiving so great a grace, that I may behold you in your uncovered shape'"; *Par.* 22.59–60). This request is momentous for the reformation or redemption of Narcissus.

To understand its importance, we must remember that Benedict answers Dante in terms of desire – desire which is the "mondiglia" with which the narcissist falsifies signs (*Par.* 22.61–69; emphasis added):

> "Frate, il tuo *alto disio*
> s'adempierà in su l'ultima spera
> ove s'adempion tutti li altri e 'l mio.
> *Ivi è perfetta, matura e intera*
> ciascuna disïanza; in quella sola
> è ogne parte là ove sempr' era,
> perché non è in loco e non s'impola;
> e nostra scala infino ad essa varca,
> onde così dal viso ti s'invola."

("Brother, your *high desire* shall be fulfilled up in the last sphere, where are fulfilled all others and my own. *There every desire is perfect, mature, and whole.* In that alone is every part there where it always was, for it is not in space, nor has it poles; and our ladder reaches up to it, wherefore it steals itself from your sight.")

Dante's sight does not yet reach there where desire is quiet – "perfetta, matura e intera," and does not because Dante is still in the body, origin of desires, very locus of that "inquietum cor" (*Conf.* 1.1) which can rest only in God. And because he is still in the body, his "alto disio" turbulent and strained, Dante cannot see Benedict "con imagine scoverta," because the eyes of that body, though beginning to reflect, still see with images ("coverings").

In particular, they see Benedict with the image or covering of the "margherite" (*Par.* 22.29). Here is a moment of extraordinary, Dantesque precision. The moon, we have already learned, is also a "margarita" (*Par.* 2.34), and it is in the Moon that Dante fell "dentro a l'error contrario... / a quel ch'accese amor tra l'omo e 'l fonte" ("into the contrary error to that which kindled love between the man and the fountain"; *Par.* 3.17–18). Dante here mistook "reality" for an image whereas Narcissus mistook (the contrary error) an image for reality. He explains that he made this mistake because the spirits before him appeared only very faintly (*Par.* 3.10–16; emphasis added):

> quali per vetri trasparenti e tersi,
>   o ver per acque nitide e tranquille,
>   non sì profonde che i fondi sien persi,
> tornan d'i nostri visi le postille
>   debili sì, che *perla* in bianca fronte
>   non vien men forte a le nostre pupille;
> tali vid'io più facce a parlar pronte.

(As through smooth and transparent glass, or through clear and tranquil waters, yet not so deep that the bottom be lost, the outlines of our faces return so faint that a *pearl* on a white brow comes not less boldly to our eyes, so did I behold many a countenance eager to speak.)

When Dante sees Benedict and the others as "margherite," he is seeing – the echo in that word of "perla" suggests it unmistakably – with the sight of Narcissus. Although he has begun to reflect (in canto 21), he still sees with images or coverings; and until his "alto disio" is satisfied with the "fulgore" of the end, he will continue to see with images.

And so it is that where speculation begins, in the heaven of Saturn among the contemplatives, the sight of Narcissus if not also his error is recalled. Speculation if a way of seeing God is also the way Narcissus died. So it is also that in this same heaven Dante undergoes a radical change of sight – through seeing "this little threshing floor" of the earth (*Par.* 22.151). In a sense this sight of the "aiuola" is Dante's last "sight" in the poem; hereafter he only reflects, progressing in degrees of reflection. Fittingly, his last sight concludes with seeing the earth, ground of ordinary mortal seeing. Moreover, he sees this last time in order "'aver le luci...chiare e acute'" ("'to have his eyes clear and keen'"; *Par.* 22.126), where the word for eyes, or "luci," suggests that they are continuous with though hardly the same thing as the Light which they are being prepared to reflect (see also *Par.* 1.66). This last sight, with these "luci chiare e acute," so far reforms or redeems the Narcissus in Dante, as he enters the Heaven of the Fixed Stars, that hereafter he can bear because he reflects more and more of the "lux quae erat in principio."

And yet, of course, he is still far from capable of the final vision. Hence, for example, not long after he has entered Saturn, he can, in fact, see and sustain Beatrice's smile (*Par.* 23.46–48). But if he can "see" Beatrice's smile, that sight only prepares him for a more exalted sight which he cannot "see." Beatrice directs his sight to Christ and Mary above them (*Par.* 23.76–87):

> e io, che a' suoi consigli
> tutto era pronto, ancora mi rendei
> a la battaglia de' debili cigli.
> Come a raggio di sol, che puro mei
> per fratta nube, già prato di fiori
> vider, coverti d'ombra, li occhi miei;
> vid' io così più turbe di splendori,
> folgorate di sù da raggi ardenti,
> sanza veder principio di folgóri.
> O benigna vertù che sì li 'mprenti,
> sù t'essaltasti per largirmi loco
> a li occhi lì che non t'eran possenti.

(and I who to her counsels was all eager, again gave myself up to the battle of the feeble brows.
As under the sun's ray, which streams pure through a broken cloud, ere now my eyes, sheltered by shade, have seen a meadow of flowers, so saw I many hosts of splendors glowed on from above by ardent rays, though I saw not whence came the glowings. O benign Power, which doth so imprint them, Thou didst ascend so as to yield place [lit: to bestow the largesse of a place to me] there for the eyes that were powerless before Thee!)

There is a sense in which the whole of Dante's experience is a "battaglia de' debili cigli." The eyebrows are weak because in the body, and the battle is the battle of the body with that which transcends the body. Moreover, as Dante engages the battle, he is, the simile suggests, under a shadow, also, therefore, under an image: he still "sees" with images/shadows and does not yet reflect reality. Indeed, Christ must depart upward so as to bestow upon Dante the largesse of a place for his eyes. "Largirmi loco" is literally an accommodation (a certain economy) for Dante's eyes as well as metaphorically an accommodation to Dante's mortality. Dante's eyes still need room to grow.

Before they reach full maturity, however, they will err again a number of times, and notably when he strives to gaze on the Apostle John (*Par.* 25.118–29). This attempt for a moment blinds Dante; his vision is, crucial description, "smarrita" (*Par.* 26.9) according to John, who goes on, however, to assure Dante that Beatrice can heal his eyes. Thereupon, the latter replies (*Par.* 26.13–15):

"Al suo piacere e tosto e tardo
vegna remedio a li occhi, che fuor porte
quand' ella entrò col foco ond' io sempr' ardo."

("At her good pleasure, soon or late, let succor come to the eyes which were the doors when she did enter with the fire wherewith I ever burn.")

The phrase "foco ond' io sempr' ardo" reminds us that Dante is still, indeed, always, Narcissus, burning because of and through his sight, his eyes. But if Everyman is Narcissus, his pilgrimage to the Light can transhumanize the fire with which Narcissus burns even as it transhumanizes the eyes through which that fire enters Narcissus. And Dante's present error, just so, initiates another momentous turn of such transhumanization; for when Beatrice does heal his sight, he sees "mei che dinanzi" (*Par.* 26.79) and sees Adam, in an image of imagery itself (*Par.* 26.97–102):

Talvolta un animal coverto broglia,
sì che l'affetto convien che si paia
per lo seguir che face a lui la 'nvoglia;
e similimente l'anima primaia
mi facea trasparer per la coverta
quant' ella a compiacermi venìa gaia.

(Sometimes an animal that is covered so stirs that its impulse must needs be apparent, since what envelops it follows its movements: in like manner that first soul showed me, through its covering, how joyously it came to do me pleasure.)

This simile and the scene which it sets deserve far more attention than I can pay them here.[8] I do, nonetheless, want to emphasize how the terms of the simile provoke the dilemma of Narcissus in Paradise, who can only see with images. "Coverto," "coverta," and above all "invoglia" insist on imagery, and especially "invoglia" since it is equivalent to Latin "involucrum" or "integumentum," technical terms for image or for allegory.[9] Adam, father of Everyman, is also author of imagery since only with the Fall did mediation become necessary (recall Saint Augustine's "nubes"). The author of imagery appears to Dante as the image of an image – of a covering following, or perhaps tracing, the movement ("affetto") internal to its referent. Against a poetics and a metaphysics of absence, which would posit that the internal/external distinction is merely a nostalgia for an idealist signification, Dante opposes and affirms a Christian Platonist reference. Adam *is* within and beyond the "invoglia" which covers him (and should be compared, therefore, with Ulysses, similarly swathed, but not *both* beyond *and* within his covering – he is only [and eternally] within his covering). And so, looking on him, Dante "sees" (i.e., reflects) imagery, which Narcissus (the Narcissus in Everyman) must do before he can cease seeing *with* imagery. Dante cannot see imagery until it is an image because human beings cannot see without images. He must see imagery *with* an image, but once he has seen with that image, he knows thereafter when he is seeing with images, and he can allow for such seeing. No longer bound to images, he can come to full self-consciousness. Once Dante has "seen" imagery imaging, he knows imagery (in the sense of Fr. *connaître*) and can allow for it. He can, dis-figuring because of the error of imagery, reflect that imagery is inadequate to ultimate vision. His eyes ("luci") are one grade closer to the Light. And they "see"/reflect imagery, so as to allow for seeing *with* imagery when – profound accuracy of the poet – they "see"/reflect Adam, author of imagery through "il trapassar del segno" (*Par.* 26.117).

The transhumanization of Dante's sight reaches in canto 30 the next grade, where the reformation or redemption of Narcissus is clearly evident and also eminently available for analysis. We begin with yet another moment of blindness (*Par.* 30.46–54):

> Come sùbito lampo che discetti
>   li spiriti visivi sì che priva
>   de l'atto l'occhio di più forti obietti,
> così mi circunfulse luce viva;
>   e lasciommi fasciato di tal velo
>   del suo fulgor, che nulla m'appariva.
> "Sempre l'amor che queta questo cielo
>   accoglie in sé con sì fatta salute,
>   per far disposto a sua fiamma il candelo."

(As a sudden flash of lightning which scatters the visual spirits so that it robs the eye of the sight of the clearest objects, so round about me there shone a vivid light and left me so swathed in the veil of its effulgence that nothing was visible to me.

"Ever does the love which quiets this heaven receive into itself with such like salutation, in order to prepare the candle for its flame.")

The dis-figuration of this figure consists in the obvious fact that there are no candles in Heaven.[10] But because of the dis-figuration, we look beyond the figure, transferred, and not into it. Moreover, the candle dis-figures also because of the contrasting figure in *Purgatorio* 30: "pur che la terra che perde ombra spiri, / sì che par foco fonder la candela" ("if only the land that loses

shadow breathes, so that it seems a fire that melts the candle"; *Purg.*
30.89–90). Here, in Purgatory, the figure supplements the experience of snow
melting so as to suggest that the fire in Dante is becoming capable of illumination. The figure is necessary, then, not only for its visual properties but also
for its spiritual connotations: without the figure we would see less. The excess of the figure is necessary. If we express the matter in terms of *our*
mystical ascent, here in Purgatory the self still needs a palpable image which
provides a help, so to speak, up to the referent. Mystic vision here is imperfect, far from reflection. In Paradise, however, reflection is possible; while
our eyes are not transhumanized, our sight definitely improves through
transference. Hence, in Paradise, without the figure, we see more, though
what we see cannot be seen: we reflect, and, reflecting, we are conscious that
we must go beyond this image of the candle. Like Dante himself, initially we
are blinded by the figure, its excess, but then it dis-figures upon reflection,
and our eyes adjust, as do Dante's (lines 55–60).

But our eyes adjust only to more figuration, for we have not had the experience; Dante's eyes, on the other hand, adjust to reality, for he did have
the experience which is our "essemplo." Dante experienced the initial blindness as a "velo del fulgor" in which he was "fasciato." The "velo" assimilates
Dante to other characters in the poem. Ulysses "si fascia" with flame (*Inf.*
26.48); Adam "si fascia" with "letizia" (*Par.* 26.135); Beatrice appears "velata"
in Purgatory (30.65, 67). Moreover, the figure calls up only to deflect the
burned bodies of Master Adam, Narcissus, and Semele: if Dante is consumed
by "fulgor," it is light and not flame that consumes him and which renders him
new. In fact, it is the difference between Dante, on the one hand, and all
these various characters, on the other, that the figure succeeds in
establishing. Not only is Dante not burned to death, he is not veiled for the
sake of concealment. He is veiled, rather, that reality might be re-vealed to
him. This veil in a moment will fall away, and Dante will see more and purer
light. More and yet more will be revealed to him. Each re-vel-ation will be
another veil – another image, another "ombra," another "accommodation" –
but these veils also will fall away. To Dante "veiled," he tells us, "nulla ap-
pariva." He was blind. But after blindness, greater vision. And as the veil falls
away from Dante, so it will fall away from every re-vel-ation. Dante experiences, subjectively, the process of re-vel-ation, and he learns from the experience that the veil shall be taken away (2 Cor. 3.16).

As much is figured in Beatrice's words, "per far disposto a sua fiamma il
candelo" (line 54). If Dante is a candle, he is an in-light-of-which, a source of
illumination, and no longer a passive viewer. He no longer merely receives the
veil of each re-vel-ation; he is the in-light-of-which it is reveiled; he does not

merely see, as by a *virtus exemplaris*, rather, he makes visible. He is, if you will, one candlepower of the Light of the Empyrean: this is his "salute" (line 53)—"welcome" but also "salvation." Part of the Light (and God is Light though the light is not God), Dante makes visible what he sees because he is part of God in the sight of whom all things exist. Any veil of re-vel-ation, therefore, which Dante sees *he* makes visible, and if he makes it visible, then when he ceases to look on it, it disappears. He is by no means the source of the re-vel-ation, but he is the in-light-of-which it is re-veiled; and when his light is one with God (mystical union) there will be no more veils because God and he will look on each other, light in light, and not need veils. When Dante looks on God, the veil *shall* be taken away. And "we all, beholding the glory of the Lord with open face, [will be] transformed into the same image from glory to glory, as by the Spirit of the Lord" (2 Cor. 3.18).

But the vision of God is as yet far off, and Dante still sees veils. His eyes however *are* adjusting to the light of the Empyrean as he "transhumanizes" into a "candle" of God (lines 58–60):

> di novella vista mi raccesi
> tale, che nulla luce è tanto mera,
> che li occhi miei non si fosser difesi.

(such new vision was kindled in me that there is no light so bright that my eyes could not have withstood it.)

Of most importance initially is the verb *raccesi*: it indicates that the candle is now lit, and it is alight with vision. But Dante qualifies this "transhumanized" condition by saying that "no light is so bright, / that my eyes could not make defenses for themselves." Now *mera* can be translated "bright," but, as Dante would certainly have known, it is Latin for "pure" also. And if we translate it as "pure," the self-defense of Dante's eyes is more readily intelligible. The light of the Empyrean is pure, unmixed, and therefore immeasurably bright, so that eyes in a merely human condition would be obliterated by it. Dante's eyes, however, because he is becoming a "candle" of God, have light of their own, and so, if "attacked" by light, from their perspective unnaturally bright, they can "defend" themselves and remain Dante's eyes. Dante, unlike Nar- cissus or a certain kind of mystic, is not melting away.[11] Dante must be Dante when he sees/reflects God because the Father does not consume the child. Dante must have his eyes, and that is why he must also, for the time being, have veils, figures, and shades.

Hence the very next vision he has (lines 61–63):

> E vidi lume in forma di rivera

> fulvido di fulgore, intra due rive
> dipinte di mirabil primavera.

(And I saw a light in form of a river glowing tawny between two banks painted with marvelous spring.)

The remainder of this vision is less important for our purposes than the phrase "in forma di" and the word "primavera." Dante sees/makes visible, but only "in forma di": form still mediates and therefore interrupts reality; the figure must still dis-figure. This river, of course, and the river Lethe and the "ruscelletti" whose images parch Master Adam are all related; we have moved from carnalized images of water, to water that heals, to a river which is a form of light; the progression is one of increasing figuration whose term is dis-figuration, or radical appearance. But the word "primavera" chastens impatience. As we know from *Vita nuova* 24, where Giovanna precedes Beatrice, "primavera," to which Dante assimilates Giovanna, is only the forerunner, the precursor (Singleton 1949:21–24). It is the "first truth," not the "last truth"; it is a shadow and not the light. Dante still sees-makes visible images: he still bears Narcissus within him, and he still remotely resembles Master Adam.

So Beatrice (lines 70–74):

> "L'alto disio che mo t 'infiamma e urge,
> d'aver notizia di ciò che tu vei,
> tanto mi piace più quanto più turge;
> ma di quest' acqua convien che tu bei
> prima che tanta sete in te si sazi."

("The high desire which now inflames and urges you to have knowledge concerning that which you see pleases me the more the more it swells; but first you must needs drink of this water before so great a thirst in you be slaked.")

Desire burns Dante, and this flame both is and is not the fire which consumes Narcissus, just as the thirst with which he thirsts and the swelling with which he swells both are and are not the thirst which parches Master Adam and the swelling which distends him. On the one hand, no matter how "alto" his "disio," it is still "disio" and therefore heavy with mortality. As long as "inquietum est cor nostrum," Narcissus still lives. On the other hand, this flame and this thirst ("sete") are of and for "notizia di ciò che tu vei." Not just what he sees but knowledge of what he sees is Dante's desire and thirst, and for this desire and thirst there *is* satisfaction. Hence Dante dis-figures Narcissus and Master Adam as he drinks of "acqua" that is only figure, that in the reality of the Empyrean is light. The "acqua" as figure or "ombra" is false, but it is precisely the "acqua" which Dante must drink before the light will cease to be falsified. When he has drunk of this "acqua," it will no longer be "acqua" (and false) because Dante will no longer see "acqua"—rather, light. Insofar as Dante burns and thirsts, he is not yet pure, and thus he needs the "acqua," itself impure because a figure shadowing the light; but when he has drunk the shadow, it will dis-figure, and he will see light, "have knowledge of that which he sees."

Before this happens, however, he must have further understanding of the Narcissus within him. Hence Beatrice continues (lines 76–81):

> "Il fiume e li topazi
> ch'entrano ed escono e'l rider de l'erbe
> son di lor vero umbriferi prefazi.
> Non che da sé sian queste cose acerbe;
> ma è difetto da le parte tua,
> che non hai viste ancor tanto superbe."

("The stream and the topazes which enter and issue, and the smiling of the grasses, are the shadowy prefaces of their truth; not that these things are defective in themselves, but on your side is the defect, in that you do not yet have vision so exalted.")

Note first of all that verses 79 and 81 of *Purgatorio* 30 reverse verses 79 and 81 of *Paradiso* canto 30 in the rhyme words *superba* and *acerba* (*Purg.* 30.79, 81: *superba-acerba*; *Par.* 30.79, 81: *acerbe-superbe*). Thus, these terzine suggest, Paradise is the reality or the truth of which Purgatory is only the reflection. In Paradise we see the "reality" (itself, of course, only figure about to dis-figure) which is reflected in the imperfect mirror of mortality, light and shade mixed, in Purgatory. What we see, in Purgatory, when we merely see is only reflection as in a glass darkly, only shadow; and we always run the risk of taking the shadow *as* reality. What we see, in Paradise, on the other hand, when seeing is reflecting—when *we* reflect—is reality; and narcissism is impossible since reality is no longer a mirror.

Beatrice's phrase "umbriferi prefazi" facilitates understanding this position. When Dante merely sees, he sees "pre-speakings bearing shadow" of the reality of light. These "pre-speakings bearing shadow"—topazes, a river, laughter, flowers, spring, and so on—are all mortal, this-worldly objects which Dante's eyes, still his own eyes though transhumanizing, bring with them. These "umbriferi prefazi" are a coinage of the Light of Paradise, but not a false coinage, because mortal desire does not substitute them for the light of Paradise. They are rather the necessary coinage which (a son of) Adam brings to Paradise and continues to practice, not out of fraud but out of his very fallenness. They are "prefazi"–"already spoken"–because mortal words have named them; and they are "umbriferi"–"shadow-bearing"–because everything mortals see, when they merely see, is shadow, since they cannot see without the contrast of light and dark. When, however, seeing is reflecting, "umbriferi prefazi" disappear, because then reality is wholly itself and thus wholly other, distinct from the "reflector."

Now from the vantage point afforded by Beatrice's phrase we can proceed to the "mirror" verses. Their content is a continuation of Beatrice's explanation of the things which Dante sees:

> Not that of themselves are these things unripe   *acerbe*
>   but is the defect on your part
>   that not have you sight yet with such exaltation   *superbe*

Now the verses in *Purgatorio* 30 read

> Thus the mother to the son appears proud   *superba*
>   as she appeared to me since bitter
>   tastes the taste of pity unripe.   *acerba*

The "reality" in the Empyrean is the correct *version* of "superba"/"acerba" because in it the two words are "imparadised." "Imparadised," "superba" means "exalted," and "acerba" is negated ("unripeness" is impossible in Paradise). In the shadowy version of Purgatory, the "amaro" is taste which the immature or unripe child adds to the "pietade," corrupting thus its reference to his mother's love. The "pietade" can only *seem* "acerba" and seem so *only* to the immature youth. This subjectivity Dante emphasizes when he says that the mother *appears* "superba." In fact, she is true and loving, but the appearance of her love *as* "superba" is an "umbriferous preface" which the child cannot pierce. It is in his eyes. And it is in his eyes because he is "unripe" or immature. Dante's syntax ("perché") rightly indicates that the cause of the appearance is the son's subjective state ("sente"); "il sapor" of pity is separate from the youth; "il sapor" is the objective taste of the pity, while "amaro" is the subjective taste. In fact, "il sapor" is unknowable since it will be different for each tongue. Hence the only proper locution in such a situation is "d'amaro sente il sapor de la pietade": one *can* say that the taste of pity is bitter, for one may feel it so; but if one says that the taste of *unripe* pity is bitter, one has redundantly added one's feeling to the pity, making one's subjective taste part of its objective taste. And the "unripeness"/immaturity which commits this error is the same "unripeness"/immaturity through which, in the son's eyes, the mother "par superba."

Now answering to the "unripe" son in Purgatory is Dante in Paradise in-creasing in ripeness. Increasing in ripeness, he learns that, one, reality, or the original light which is the body of each of the blessed, is ripe, "non...da sé...acerbe," and that, two, he does not see/reflect this ripeness because his eyes are not yet "superbe"; the implication, of course, is that he will when they are. And that will be when the "umbriferi prefazi" of the mother in Purgatory, or "superba" (behind which her "pietade" *is* ripe), becomes the true condition of Dante's eyes. When Dante's eyes have transcended by in-corporating that "umbriferous preface," they will have been prepared to penetrate all other "umbriferous prefaces," and that because with an "exalted" eye Dante will be mature enough to know that all such appearances are in his eyes. If he "looks away" (the action, of course, is not physical) from the ap-pearance of pride, it will disappear—such is the power of "superbic" eyes—and visible instead will be reality, whether of pity or of the elect. The "umbriferous preface" of "superba" will become in Paradise what it substan-tially is, or a condition of the eye. Thus Dante "imparadises" the word "superba"—it no longer means "proud"—and "realizes" its substantial meaning or the opposite of its shaded meaning. And the "imparadised" word indicates that Dante's eyes now comprehend this, "superba," and all other "um-briferous prefaces." Finally, if "superba" corrects so as to "realize" or "im-paradise" its reflection, so does "acerba"; and "realized," or "imparadised," it is negated, since perfect or paradisal creatures cannot be unripe; and this nega-tion, in turn, asserts that "pietade," perfect because it is love, is not unripe. The ripening Dante will see the ripeness of perfected creation, which includes the ripeness of mother love.

But Dante is far from ripe yet. He is in fact an infant again (lines 82–90):

> Non è fantin che sì sùbito rua
>   col volto verso il latte, se si svegli
>   molto tardato da l'usanza sua,
> come fec'io, per far migliori spegli
>   ancor de li occhi, chinandomi all'onda
>   che si deriva perché vi s'immegli;
> e sì come di lei bevve la gronda
>   de le palpebre mie, così mi parve
>   di sua lunghezza divenuta tonda.

(No infant, on waking far after its hour, so suddenly rushes with face toward the milk, as then did I, to make yet better mirrors of my eyes, stoop-ing to the wave which flows there that we may be bettered in it. And even

as the eaves of my eyelids drank of it, so it seemed to me out of its length to
have become round.)

Dante is still immature in vision, and he must grow. So it is that he must turn
toward the milk, toward precisely the food which is meant for the
immature.[12] Because he is immature, Dante needs both the image of milk and
the milk of images. When Dante turns to the "milk," he is actually turning to
light; but because he is an "infant," he sees and drinks "milk" where the "milk"
is only and necessarily an image. The ostentation of the image, its excess or
surplus, is its significance: it must obviously disfigure the light of Heaven
even as it figures it, and thus it also dis-figures when Dante has drunk of the
light for then he will no longer need the "milk." The simile figures Dante's subjective condition—and "molto tardato" finely if obliquely suggests his
apostasy—even as its very excess predicts its imminent dis-figuration.

Now Dante turns to the light, momentarily "milk," so as "to make better
mirrors still of his eyes." This, I take it, is the still center of the canto. If and
when Dante's eyes become mirrors, they will reflect rather than see; and in
this condition Dante will be incapable of narcissism. That version of self-
consciousness peculiar to Narcissus and mystic vision alike will, in this condition, be completely purged of confusion; and the redeemed soul will never
again see itself in or projected on its environment. In fact, it will never again
"see" itself at all. Rather it will reflect itself reflected in the "'verace speglio'"
("'truthful Mirror'") of God and "'tanti / speculi...in che si spezza, /
[though] uno manendo in sé'" ("'so many mirrors...wherein it is reflected,
[though] remaining in itself One as before'"; *Par.* 29.143–45). It will know
(and know itself) even as it is known (1 Cor. 13.12). Become the Image of
God now reformed to similitude with God, the soul will know as God knows:
it will reflect every creature, what the creature is (without intervening image), the image of its Creator.

To attain this "transhuman" condition, Dante bends to the water "che si
deriva perché vi s' immegli" (line 87). The verb *s'immegli* is Dante's *coinage*
(Vernon 1972: 2.403). And it is coinage here and now to insist that all expression in this light and of this light is accidental, subjective, "ab-out." Here
Adam can only coin; and we can only spend his coin.

Because it is our lot to deal in coin, we see Dante bend to the water, which
is not water but light, where the eaves of his eyelids drink of it. Again the
ostentation and excess of the figure are important. The image is almost too
much and thus signals its disfigurement of Paradise. If Dante's lashes drink of
the light in the manner of eaves, then his eyelids are roofs or coverings intended to protect and to defend his eyes, while the lashes or eaves are projec-

tions or overhangs intended to collect runoff rain and so on, so as to discard it. The figure continues the emphasis on defense introduced earlier (line 60) and suggests that Dante's eyes, in becoming better mirrors, are opened wide but, as it were, under a roof there to receive the light as an excess dripping over the eaves. The figure is so excessive because Dante is still in the body as he experiences the vision. If Dante took in the light as do Beatrice and the other "speculi" of Heaven, it would, I think we are to assume, destroy him. Hence his body protects itself. And even as the eyes of his body drink the light in the only way the eyes of a *body* could drink the light—namely, through the interference of a medium—so we, who deal in images and coins, see them drink it through similar interference: we see a figure, an image, a coin because we are seeing a *body*, primary cause of media.

Dante, the pilgrim, on the other hand, as soon as the eyes of his body have drunk the light, is prepared to "reflect" a radical disappearance of figuration (lines 91–99):

> Poi come gente stata sotto larve
>   che pare altro che prima, se si sveste
>   la sembianza non süa in che disparve,
> così mi si cambiaro in maggior feste
>   li fiori e le faville, sì ch'io vidi
>   ambo le corti del ciel manifeste.
> O isplendor di Dio, per cu'io vidi
>   l'alto triunfo del regno verace,
>   dammi virtù a dir com'io il vidi.

(Then, as folk who have been under masks seem other than before, if they do off the semblances not their own wherein they were hid, so into greater festival the flowers and the sparks did change before me that I saw both the courts of Heaven made manifest. O splendor of God whereby I saw the high triumph of the true kingdom, give to me power to tell how I beheld it!)

First, we should note, in concert with all other commentary on the poem, the repetition of "vidi" in the rhyme scheme at verses 95, 97, and 99. The only other occasions in *Paradiso* when Dante rhymes three times on the same word are those on which he names "Cristo."[13] With this rhyme scheme he is obviously calling up Trinitarian energies, and he is doing language's best to communicate a "transhumanizing" in process. Dante has here passed to a seeing much nearer "reflection" than any he has enjoyed so far. His eyes have endured the light of the Empyrean, remaining his and physical if also "transhumanized," and they have now sufficient "candlepower" to illumine, to be the in-light-of-which for, the creatures of the Empyrean. And so it is that he sees them "manifest" by their change, their differentiation, into a greater festival. This change is like a removal of masks, a dis-figuring, where the word for "masks," or "larve" connotes the "unripeness" which was in the "non-superbic" eyes. The creatures, not "da sé acerbe," were not under masks; they only seemed so to the immature eyes of Dante (hence the reflexive emphasis: "mi si cambiaro"). Now they appear otherwise because they have, as it were (and only in the simile), divested themselves of the "sembianza" not theirs—not theirs, precisely Dante's—in which they had disappeared. Dante had clothed the creatures in the "larve" of his own vision ("fiori," "faville," etc.), and the creatures had then disappeared ("disparve") into these semblances. The crux here is the meaning of disappearance, and we need to proceed carefully. To disappear is *not* not to appear; it is rather to appear not to appear: that which has disappeared has appeared and then appeared not to appear. The creatures of the Empyrean appear not to appear, i.e., disappear, when in the various "sembianza," but when these are, as it were, divested, the creatures appear. Hence Dante communicates the dis-figuration, the sudden removal of figures, which occurs when eyes are "superbic" and reflective—purged of "larve"—able to see what is otherwise "visible" only in the "coinage" of faith.

We are here at the optimum vantage point for falling back to retrieve Dante's understanding of faith as "moneta" so as to proceed with it to the conclusion of our analysis. The relevant text is *Paradiso* 24, during Saint Peter's examination of Dante on faith. Dante responds to the first question as follows (*Par.* 24.64–66):

> "fede è sustanza di cose sperate,
> e argomento de le non parventi;
> e questa pare a me sua quiditate."

("Faith is the substance of things hoped for and the evidence of things not seen; and this I take to be its quiddity.")

Obviously, Dante quotes Hebrews 11.1; the subsequent two verses are also important:

> Now, faith is the substance of things to be hoped for, the evidence of things that appear not. For by this the ancients obtained a testimony. By faith we understand that the world was framed by the word of God: that from invisible things visible things might be made.

First, the issue of invisibility. Dante himself elaborates on this issue a few lines later (*Par.* 24:70–78): faith, very much of the mind, is, he argues, a position on, an attitude toward, the invisible, which presumes original blindness in man, and which, consequently, "stands under" ("sub-stance") the absent good for which men hope, as if by looking on faith and with faith they might see that to which they are otherwise blind; from this foundation men reason ("silogizzar") or argue to the nonapparent, the invisible. Faith is not itself blind; it is man who is blind. Faith is first and foremost the acceptance of this blindness – of reality's invisibility – as the beginning of any and all understanding: "intellectus enim merces est fidei" ("Understanding is the recompense of faith").[14] As such, faith is substantive and argumentative. At the same time Dante's images and the language of his images constitute the substance and the arguments of his poem. Hence the language of Dante's poem is his faith. *And just as language is a kind of coin, or medium of exchange, so is faith.*

As Hebrews 11.3 suggests, the Word of God brings visibles from invisibles. Just so, Dante's words, though vastly inferior, bring visibles from invisibles; faith, seeing these visibles – language showing them – reasons or argues back to the Word of God. Faith, in short, exchanges the visibles for the invisibles. *And so it is that Peter likens faith, at the end of the first part of Dante's examination, to money*: "'Assai bene è trascorsa / d'esta moneta già la lega e 'l peso'" ("'Now the alloy and the weight of this coin have been well enough examined'"; lines 83–84). To set this bold and brilliant maneuver in perspective, we need to see it in its total theological context. At one extreme, St. Ambrose, for example, writes: "For Christ is not bought with money, but rather with grace: the price you pay is faith (pretium tuum fides est), with this divine mysteries are bought (hac emuntur divina mysteria)"; at the other, Hugh of St. Victor argues that "your heart is a mirror if only it is clean and polished and clear. And an image in the mirror is faith in your heart. For faith itself is an image and a sign."[15] If faith is image, nothing is more natural or compellingly logical than Dante's likening faith to money, itself an image too. Like money, faith is a promise (see Heb. 11.17; Heb. 6.13–18). Like money, faith purchases what it is not; like money, it is a medium of exchange for an Otherness. Like money, faith has a value of its own, and yet that value is subject to supply and demand – if indulgences are easy to buy, faith will be cheap. Like money, faith is not the thing itself, it only refers. Like money, faith can be falsified, and, false or "bad," it is incapable of rendering the promise whole. So it is that, to insist that his faith is true, Dante replies, when Peter asks him whether he has this money in his purse, "'si ho, sì lucida e sì tonda, / che nel suo conio nulla mi s'inforsa'" ("'Yes, I have it so shining and so round that in its stamp nothing is doubtful to me'"; lines 86–87). Dante's faith is true because of its stamp or "conio," so true, in fact, that he has no doubt of it. And he proves his faith as well as its truth by relying on its "conio" to *coin* or

stamp the word "s'inforsa": Dante boldly coins a word in this line to demonstrate, as by a kind of intellectual onomatopoeia, that the "conio" of his faith
coins faithfully or truthfully (Singleton 1975:3.2, 392). Dante can be this sure
of the "conio" of his faith because that "conio" is Christ, the Image of God.
Since, moreover, he, Dante, is made in the Image of God, he already bears
within him this "conio," or at least the potential for receiving it. Hence, for example, his later description of his faith in the Trinity: he says that evangelic
doctrine *stamps* ("sigilla") his mind with it (*Par.* 24.143). If Scripture "sigilla"
Dante's "mente" with the "conio" of faith in the Trinity, it is because his
"mente" is the Image of God primed, as it were, to receive it.

Now Dante's strategy begins to emerge in complete clarity. A poet, he can
work only with images – say, with visibles – and yet everything he would
communicate to us is invisible because archaic, original, divine. Hence in a
radical sense Dante must purchase invisibles with visibles. The only coin he
has for such a purchase, once the vision has passed, is faith. Faith and imagery or language are ultimately one; ultimately either each is sealed with
Christ, or it is false.

The most important consequence of this metaphysical identity is that
money becomes a common metaphor adequate to both faith and imagery or
language. An important corollary of this consequence for *Paradiso* 24 is the
wealth imagery. When Dante first sees the blessed, they "de la sua *ricchezza*
[si] facieno stimar" ("of their *riches* made [him] judge"; lines 17–18) and when
he acknowledges the invisibility of the heavenly mysteries, he says, "'le pro-
fonde cose / che mi *largiscon* qui la lor parvenza'" ("'the deep things which
grant to me here the sight of themselves'"; lines 70–71). The money of faith
and the money of imagery or language are exchanged, just as money normally
is, for other wealth. But implicit in Dante's words is the sense that faith and
imagery are by no means adequate to the riches and the largess of the "invisibilia Dei." The bounty of Heaven far exceeds the purchasing power of
both.[16]

In addition to this corollary, the metaphor of money also imports manifest
Narcissus imagery into *Paradiso* 24, particularly fire and water. When Peter
tells Dante, "'Dì, buon cristiano, fatti manifesto: / fede che è?'" ("'Speak,
good Christian, and declare yourself: Faith, what is it?'"), Dante turns to
Beatrice, and she "sembianze femmi perch' io spandessi / l' acqua di fuor del
mio interno fonte" ("signaled to me that I should pour the water forth from my
inward fountain"; lines 52–53, 56–57). The ice melting from around Dante's
heart so that he wept before Beatrice (*Purg.* 30.97–99) not only purged the
dropsical and fetid waters of (Master) Adam and Narcissus but also, it seems,
left room for new water to rush into their place. Instead of those waters

Dante now has an internal fountain. This new "water," however, does in one way resemble the "water" in *Inferno* 30: it is only an image. This resemblance is purposeful. Dante insists on it so as to expose the overwhelming difference between the two images. Here in Heaven the referent, or, better, the transferent—the faith in which Dante shares—is real, if transcendent, and because the transferent is real, the image has value; say, it is stamped as cur-rent for its transferent. At the same time, though, its palpability or thingness is a disfigurement of the Light of Paradise, and so it must also necessarily dis-figure; and as and because it does, all threat of infernal imagery vanishes. The difference between Paradise and Hell is this, that, in Paradise the referent-transferent being real, the image or figure is *both* true *and* real without, however, being materialized and thus burdened with the death imminent in matter.

The other Narcissus image follows directly on the "stamping" of Dante's mind. Dante says (*Par.* 24.145–47):

> "Quest'è 'l principio, quest' è la favilla
> che si dilata in fiamma poi vivace,
> e come stella in cielo in me scintilla."

("This is the beginning, this is the spark which then dilates to a living flame and like a star in heaven shines within me.")

This "favilla" replaces the fire which burns Master Adam and Narcissus; this "fiamma" replaces the "antica fiamma" of Dido and Ulysses. Dante has found a new fire on the way to becoming essentially fire (light). Finally, this "favilla" is not unlike that which ignited Statius. The difference though is important: the authority or source of the "favilla" in this case is not the *Aeneid* but precisely Scripture (line 144). Dante reads the way Statius read, but he reads a different book—the Book of faith.

Faith is a money which exchanges visibles for invisibles. So is language. Dante demonstrates this truth in a stunning maneuver in *Paradiso* 30 at the moment when his "mirror eyes" are finally able to see the blessed as they really are, without "sembianza" emanating from his eyes to clothe them. He com-municates his "sight"/reflection of the blessed in a simile whose principal verb openly challenges faith. The simile insists on the gesture of Narcissus, but the gesture is completely free, to the eyes of faith, of the content of narcissism (lines 109–14; emphasis added):

> E come clivo in acqua di suo imo
> si *specchia*, quasi per vedersi addorno,

> quando è nel verde e ne' fioretti opimo,
> sì, soprastando al lume intorno intorno,
> vidi *specchiarsi* in più di mille soglie
> quanto di noi là sù fatto ha ritorno.

(and as a hillside *mirrors itself* in water at its base, as if to look upon its own adornment when it is rich in grasses and in flowers, so above the light round and round about in more than a thousand tiers I saw *reflected* all of us that have won return up there.)

The challenge is obvious: if we stop with the verb *specchiar*, we see only Narcissus; and in that case, we are certainly blind. Rather than stop with the verb and merely see, we must reflect, and, reflecting, exchange it for the invisible to which it would transfer us. We must pass through faith beyond the sign to its referent-transferent; and Dante insists on this necessity with the very word which inscribes the potential for disdain of this necessity. Dante transcribes a moment of innocent reflection with the verb certain, were it not for faith, to question and disturb that innocence. Dante demands of the word of Narcissus that it name a vision (invisible to us) the opposite of that of Narcissus. Paradoxically, Dante thus "imparadises" the word by (the phrase is necessarily inelegant) re-literalizing it, by renewing its proper sense apart from the context of the myth of Narcissus.

A careful analysis of the simile itself will aid our vision. The verb *specchiar* is present here in the Empyrean as the "reality" of which "lo specchio di Narcisso" in Hell is only the perverted and insubstantial "ombra." Next in importance to the verb itself are the two subjects of which it is predicated: an imagined cliff, slightly personified, and as many of the saved as have returned to the Rose. Neither of these subjects is logically capable of the error of Narcissus. The cliff, "quasi"-personified, looks not to see itself but to see itself *adorned*, in the handiwork of Another. The blessed, seated in the Rose, "reflect themselves"/"are reflected" simply because Dante is looking at "sommo del mobile primo" ("the summit of the Primum Mobile"), where the extent of the Rose is "fassi di raggio. . . reflesso" ("made of a ray. . . reflected"; lines 106–107). Dante's first "sight" of the Rose is a reflection in his mirror eyes of its reflection "al sommo del mobile primo"; and this first "sight" serves to demonstrate that the gesture of Narcissus in Paradise is innocent of narcissism. Where all "sight" is reflection, the only Being "visibile" is the One on Whom reflection depends, or "lo creatore" ("the Creator"), in seeing Whom every creature "ha la sua pace" ("has his peace"; lines 100–102). And so it is that "specchiar" can have its proper sense renewed; here it is impossible that Narcissus should ap-propr-iate the word to his own perverse "meaning."

Among its many other distinctions, *Paradiso* 30 concludes with Beatrice's last words in the poem (lines 128–48). She lashes out against "la cieca cupidigia" ("blind cupidity"; line 139) and its manifestation in simony. Such a peroration would mystify and perplex us were we not prepared by the vertical reading of the three cantos 30 for this violent emphasis on buying and selling. With this preparation, however, we can grasp Dante's strategy whole. First, we must go back to canto 29 to get, as it were, a running start with Beatrice's condemnation of false preachers because of whom false pardons flood the world (*Par.* 29.121–26):

> "per cui tanta stoltezza in terra crebbe,
>   che, sanza prova d'alcun testimonio,
>   ad ogne *promession* si correbbe [sc. the people].
> Di questo ingrassa il porco sant'Antonio,
>   e altri assai che sono ancor più porci,
>   *pagando di moneta sanza conio*."

("from which such folly has grown on earth that without proof of any testimony they would flock to every *promise*. On this the pig of St. Anthony fattens, and others also, who are far more pigs, *paying with money that has no stamp of coinage*.")

The repetition from *Purgatorio* 30 of "promession," though in a new context, and the appearance of "false money" ("sanza conio") from *Inferno* 30 are crucial to Dante's strategy at this point. Simony, indulgences, and frivolous preaching (lines 115–16), along with innumerable other perversions of the Word, are all instances of falsification because they involve the referral of an image—most generally, some medium or other—to an end obviously narcissistic, i.e., personal, selfish, and cupidinous. Now I did *not* say "to an end not intended for the image or medium"—as if divine intentionality were in any sense recoverable by human insight; rather I said (because Dante suggests that this is all a mortal can say) that the medium—ecclesiastical office, ecclesiastical seal on a written indulgence, the words of Scripture in a preacher's mouth, what have you—is obviously referred to the self instrumentalizing it such that this self finds itself in the medium. Not every "promession" is "intera," just as not every "moneta" possesses "conio" because the residue of self, "mondiglia," contaminates the instrument unless the self knows the truth which Dante learns in the Empyrean, namely, that *instrumentality itself is narcissistic in fallen man*. Whatever we do, we do as fallen men—through and with desires whose selfishness we cannot finally control. Even the best of us, sometimes, gives in to desiring blindly; even the best of us, when his eyes are opened, may feel remorse, or, if Providence has smiled on him, relief that his desires "turned out for the best" after all. Even the best of us, sometimes, wants more than he needs, and because of this primal failure of control, any means may at any moment become an end; any end may at any moment become a means. Furthermore, no means which man employs to any end can fail to influence that end and possibly contaminate it.[17] Narcissus sees himself everywhere.

We arrive here, by the logic of the relationship between cantos 29 and 30, at the term of Dante's argument on the error of Narcissus, though we are far as yet from the term of his, Dante's, vision. Beatrice's last speech in the poem, the conclusion of canto 30 — the canto of the redeemed Narcissus — is an attack on "blind cupidity" because cupidity is the Christian name for the error which Dante has followed throughout the canticle — the error of Narcissus. Cupidity is the narcissism of instrumentality understood as a corruption of images:

> But in that apostatizing pride, which is called "the beginning of sin," [the soul] sought for something more than the whole; and while it struggled to govern by its own laws, it was thrust into caring for a part, since there is nothing more than the whole; and so by desiring something more, it becomes less, and for this reason covetousness is called "the root of all evils." The efforts by which it urges its own interests against the whole, and against the laws by which the whole is governed, are made through its own body which it possesses as part of the whole; and so, having found its delights in those corporeal forms and movements, since it cannot have them with it within itself, *it becomes entangled with their images which it has fixed in its memory, and is foully defiled by the fornication of the phantasy*; and it refers all its functions towards those ends for which it curiously seeks corporeal and temporal things through the senses of the body. . . . When the soul, therefore, consults either itself or others with a good will for the purpose of perceiving interior and superior things which are possessed in a chaste embrace, *not privately but commonly*, without any narrowness or envy by all who love such things, even though it may err in something through its ignorance of temporal things because it also directs these things in a temporal way, and may not observe the manner of acting that it should, this is a human temptation. . . . But when it does anything in order to obtain those things which are perceived through the body, because of its lust for experiencing them, excelling in them, or handling them, *so that it places the end of its own good in those things*, then whatever it does, it does shamefully; it commits fornication, sinning against its own body, while it *snatches the deceptive images of corporeal things from within and combines them together by empty thought*, so that nothing seems to it to be divine unless it be such a kind as this; covetous of its own selfish possessions it becomes prolific in errors, and prodigal of its own selfish goods it is emptied of strength.[18]

Augustine gives here pure expression to his mature theory of reference, which is also Dante's and, I will argue, Chaucer's. Indeed, Augustine frequently uses the verb *referre* itself to describe the instrumentality of the creation.[19] I am not interested in, nor do I wish to be accused of, the excesses of Robertsonian "exegetical criticism"; I trust that it is evident by now that my commitment lies elsewhere. I am, rather, interested in the brilliant way in which Augustine realizes the problem of imagination in the cupidity or narcissism of instrumenting the creation.[20] The "fornication of the phantasy" is precisely what Dante condemns as the falsification of images by the "mondiglia" of desire; when the phantasy fornicates with images, it corrupts them. Moreover, the cupidity or narcissism of instrumentality is a lust for private possession, a lust of private interest (*commoda privata*), and as such it is the bane of the poet tempted as he is always to fix and "fix" signs in a private meaning (see Chap. 1 above).[21] Augustine's words constitute the profoundest moral theology the West has known; they also suggest, more narrowly, why Dante has Beatrice attack "blind cupidity" in the canto of the redeemed Narcissus: redeemed, Dante-Narcissus can appreciate the full heinousness of the love which seeketh its own, "pagando di moneta sanza conio."

If instrumentality is narcissistic or cupidinous, then the poet, because of his unique temptation, either confronts this problem or remains forever a fornicator with images, a falsifier of the instruments of creation. The very language with which Dante represents the Other World threatens to falsify it in the measure to which it appears to re-present it, where repetition, distance, and the human hand in figuration open the possibility of error and forgetfulness, absence and lapse. But Dante does confront the problem, and consequently he thwarts such an appearance. He radicalizes every mediation in his own body and resigns himself to temporality and to the secondariness of writing. Every image Dante writes would be a "moneta sanza conio" did it not betray the body, both in the sense that the image is bodily and in the sense that the body is inadequate to the space of the Other World. All that separates Dante from Narcissus and (Master) Adam is the New Adam, Christ, the Word or Idea or Image of God. The Image of God, Christ, is the "conio" of Dante's imagery because He, the Son, is the resurrected and transfigured *body*. He is the "testimonio" (cf. Heb. 11.2) and the promise that flesh and mortality, however alien to the Joy of Light, can (at least) "transhumanize." He is the only Means also His own End. Without Him, Dante is only looking at himself, Narcissus.

With him, however, Dante coins true words. With Him and the faith which He makes real, Dante figures language in *Paradiso* at its purest: language not mimetic—how could any human instrument mime Paradise? – not indicative – how could any human instrument point to Paradise? – but creative, productive of provocations of the invisible and the transhuman. Dante's text is no transparency, rather a darkening ("ombra") by which the light becomes more bearable for fallen eyes. Dante's figures are his *faith* (which is "moneta") because they substantiate and argue for the transhuman and the invisible. They are his *hope* with which "'nfiora / la mente sua" ("his mind blossoms"; *Par.* 25.46–47) because they are "fiore" making visible the invisible. They are his *charity* because they *imprint* his mind as does "amor" itself (*Par.* 26.27).[22] None of this is to say that Dante's language embeds itself in a residual *archē*, nostalgic for a covert security of origination. The substance is not bedrock, the argument not a dogma; the hope is as fragile as a flower; and love's print is subject to effacement (*Par. 33.*64–66). Dante's language is open, anxious, patient, nervous, dynamic, and historical. Its futurity and incompleteness are the authority of the figures it generates. Dante himself, at the end, wheels with the love that moves the sun and the other stars. But his language knows no end. What is more, it has fallen into writing.

In writing, the creativity of language suffers secondariness, belatedness, and illusory stasis. In *Paradiso*, Dante finds this fall felicitous. The futurity and incompleteness of his figures constantly strain against the graphic and hence fixed reference of writing; differentiating themselves from it, they break it down (cf. Deleuze 1968: 28, 36–37, 375). Writing is the mask his figures are always removing so as to become other. Other than writing, breaking out of writing in writing, his figures re*call* their *vocal*ity and say, for example, "I saw the two courts of Paradise change into a greater festival." Other than writing, breaking out of writing in writing, their vocality recalled, Dante's figures refer to what he saw by transferring us beyond what he says: we hear "festival" and know that "festival" is not enough. Transference revokes reference. But both remain: that is the privilege of the "essemplo." The "essemplo" is a simultaneous reference and transference. It is written and spoken, universal and particular, present and absent. It is a relation and a translation. Finally, the "essemplo" is not a work of "cieca cupidigia" because it is not a false coin, nor is it the mirror of Narcissus.

By the end of canto 30, Dante-Narcissus is almost ready to "see"-reflect God. He is almost ready for the final "outrage" ("oltraggio"; *Par.* 33.57). And it is an "outrage," in part, because Dante never does "see" or, in fact, even reflect; he wishes to do so, but cannot (*Par.* 33. 137–38). Rather, when his own feathers, "penne" (*Par.* 33.139), and therefore also his pen, prove inadequate to the vision, his "mente fu percossa / da un fulgore in che sua voglia venne" ("mind was smitten by a flash wherein its wish came to it"; *Par.* 33.140–41). Hence the vision violates even "transhumanized" sight – arrives as a piercing flash. All the preparation of bodily eyes, even preparation as extraordinary as Dante's, is insufficient ultimately to strengthen them for the vision of God, the joining with Him. It follows that every sight up to the sudden penetration of Dante's mind, however "transhumanized," is still bodily sight. Everything Dante sees is measured by and is a measure of the bodily eye, and the communication to us of what he sees must follow that measure. His vision exceeds his eye (*Par.* 33.76–78):

> Io credo, per l'acume ch'io soffersi
>   del vivo raggio, ch'i' sarei smarrito,
>   se li occhi miei da lui fossero aversi.

(I believe that, because of the keenness of the living ray which I endured, I should have been lost if my eyes had been turned from it.)

But the eye must be present so as *to be exceeded*, else we who have no vision can see nothing. And if Dante is not now "smarrito," it is precisely because the eye does not *turn* from the Light: there is no *version* ("aversi") – rational, poetic, or otherwise – of or from the Light (recall Beatrice's "attraversati" and "catene" of *Purg.* 31.25); there is only the Light and the eye in the Light being exceeded. And even as the eye, there and not "aversi," is exceeded, Dante's "aspetto" increases in strength (lines 79–81):

> E mi ricorda ch'io fui più ardito
>   per questo a sostener, tanto ch'i' giunsi
>   l'aspetto mio col valore infinito.

(I remember that on this account I was the bolder to sustain it, until I united my gaze with the Infinite Goodness.)

But it is strengthened only that it might be overcome. When Dante-Narcissus finally gazes into the "verace speglio," he must be strong enough *not* to see himself. He must be strong enough not to project himself on reality but to take-receive reality as himself.

Dante insists on as much in a crucial description of the metamorphosis or transhumanization of his sight (*Par.* 33.109–14; emphasis added):

> Non perché più ch'un semplice sembiante
>   fosse nel vivo lume ch'io mirava,
>   che tal è sempre qual s'era davante;
> ma per la vista che s'avvalorava
>   in me guardando, *una sola parvenza,*
>   *mutandom'io, a me si travagliava.*

Following is a translation of these extraordinary terzine (emphasis added):

> Not because more than a simple semblance
>   was in the living light [God, the Trinity] which I gazed at,
>   for such it is always as it was before;
> but through my sight which increased in strength
>   in me looking, *one sole appearance*,
>   *I myself changing, to me travailed itself.*

My painfully (and necessarily) literal English suggests with what vehemence Dante tests the limits of syntax. Indeed, the syntax also travails. And it produces, at first sight, an absurdity, namely, an impassable, eternal, and infinite God travailing or suffering—"si travagliava." "Parvenza" provides no way out of the absurdity, since, if it is an appearance which Dante sees, it is an appearance necessarily of God. To abandon the text to such an absurdity would be intolerable. Hence it is necessary to look again. And when we do, we see Dante "seeing" and see a very different appearance.

Again Saint Augustine will help us sharpen our focus. In book 5 of *De Trinitate*, Augustine confronts a problem very similar to Dante's own: How can he talk about God coming to be the friend and father of a man, a man who has converted, without suggesting that God suffers change ("coming to be" : "esse incipit")? Obviously, Augustine hastens to affirm, God does not suffer change, in this or any other event. It is the man who changes. He goes on to extend this point in a crucial way: "So, too, when we speak of [God] as being angry with the wicked and gentle towards the good; it is they who are changed not He: *just as light is painful to weak eyes and pleasing to strong eyes, namely by their change, not its own.*"[23] Augustine's analogy takes us back to Dante's text with new vision. Light is always light, Augustine suggests: if it hurts one pair of eyes and not another, it remains the same light, identical with itself. Now, of course, for Dante and in the Christian tradition, God is light—"vivo lume," to quote Dante's words—and with Augustine's analogy in mind, we can see why Dante constructs the crucial terzina the way he does. Repeatedly he emphasizes that it is *he* who is changing as he approaches the unchanging "vivo lume." *His* sight increases in strength—the appearance remains "sola," identical with itself, self-contained; *he* is mutating—and the action is reflexive, as the verb indicates, "mutando mi io"; and finally, it is "to" or "in" *him*—"a me"—that the "parvenza si travagliava." Everything in the construction of the second terzina insists on Dante and his body and his body's sight. Everything insists that, just as Augustine would have it, it is Dante who is changing. God, the Trinity, does not travail except *to* Dante; "si travagliava" is the way it seems to *Dante*.

And because that is the way it seems to Dante, we see the limits of Dante's vision. As Dante was changing, the Trinity seemed to travail. In reality – the only reality we can know – it was Dante who travailed. The travail was in him – "a me" – and in that travail Dante saw the Trinity. Dante saw the Trinity in *his* travail and yet was strong enough, his language suggests, not to see the Trinity *as* his travail. Dante saw himself but did not project himself; he was self-conscious, but he was not beside himself ("para" + "noia" = "beside the mind" or "out of the mind").[24] He was Narcissus redeemed.

So it is that if the son of (Master) Adam still generates "as" even now when "is" looms imminent, he does not – crucial difference – confuse "as" and "is." On the contrary, "as" remains the servant of "is." With "as" he goes on toward "is," and the measure remains the bodily eye (lines 127–32):

> Quella circulazion che sì concetta
>   pareva in te come lume reflesso,
>   da li occhi miei alquanto circunspetta,
> dentro da sé, del suo colore stesso,
>   mi parve pinta de la nostra effige;
>   per che 'l mio viso in lei tutto era messo.

(That circling which, thus begotten, appeared in Thee as reflected light, when my eyes had dwelt on it for a time, seemed to me depicted with our image within itself and in its own color, wherefore my sight was entirely set upon it.)

Several details here insist on Dante, his body, and his body's "sight." Any creaturely reflection of God will necessarily be partial and incomplete. Hence, for example, the phrase "da li occhi miei alquanto circunspetta." "Alquanto" can be translated with temporal denotation – "for a while." But the obvious spatial denotation of "circun" as well as the principle of the body as measure suggests that the more accurate translation is "somewhat."[25] Dante's eyes "somewhat looked around" the Circulation; and, Dante thus insists, they limited and restricted, or gave a circumference to, what is Itself the Circumference of all being. Hence, necessarily, his eyes eliminated ultimate vision, which can only come to a "mente percossa," or a mind, by the definition of "percossa" (something like "exploded"), incapable of "looking around" anything. Note, further, in concert with the emphasis on the limits of creaturely "sight," that, although with its own color, "nostra effige" appears *painted* to Dante's eyes. The word "painted" can not fail to call attention not only to mortal art but also to *the* mortal art of the eye.[26] The mortal eye, our eyes, remains the measure.

Even of what is painted there: "nostra effige." On the one hand, "nostra effige" is the Trinity; on the other hand, it is the body of man. The gesture of the vision is that of Narcissus. So much so that Dante's "viso"—sight and face—was *sent* ("messo") all the way into it. Even more (lines 97–105):

> Così la mente mia, tutta sospesa,
>   mirava fissa, immobile e attenta,
>   e sempre di mirar faceasi accesa.
> A quella luce cotal si diventa,
>   che volgersi da lei per altro aspetto
>   è impossibil che mai si consenta;
> però che 'l ben, ch' è del volere obietto,
>   tutto s'accoglie in lei, e fuor di quella
>   è defettivo ciò ch'è lì perfetto.

(Thus my mind, all rapt, was gazing, fixed, motionless and intent, ever enkindled by its gazing. In that Light one becomes such that it is impossible he should ever consent to turn himself from it for other sight; for the good, which is the object of the will, is all gathered in it, and outside of it that is defective which is perfect there.)

Here is Narcissus: "fissa"; "accesa"; "volgersi impossibil." But he is a Narcissus fixed, aflame and unable to turn, all in regard to "lo ben." [27] His image is the good; the good is his image. Narcissus remains. But he remains transformed, "transhumanized," on the edge of "is."

And Narcissus must remain because, as Dante rightly says, it is an "effige" which he sees. Dante-Narcissus sees "a thing from which it is made" (="e+fingere"). [28] Now the "fictio" (="fictus," ppl. "fingere") is the very scandal of Dante's profound faith as well as the testimony that he is *made* in the Image of God. Dante does not see his *own* image, nor does he see just the good. He sees the source from which he is made and sees, moreover, that it is *ours*, where this plural, like the plural of "nostra vita" (*Inf.* 1.1), claims the community of men because of which Narcissus need never again die. It must be Narcissus who looks into "nostra effige"; but it is not Narcissus who sees himself.

This paradox is more readily intelligible if we turn to the one other occurrence of the word "effige" in the poem. After Beatrice has left Dante and just before Bernard assumes the role of guide, Dante sees his lady in her seat in the Rose: "süa *effige* / non discendëa a me per mezzo mista" ("her image came down to me unblurred by aught between"; *Par.* 31.77–78). Of Beatrice and the Trinity, and of them only, Dante uses the word "effige": Beatrice is the "effictio" or source from which Dante's "vita nova" was made, just as the Trinity is the "effictio" or source from which his "vista nova" (*Par.* 33.136) is made. But there is rather too much of the critic's virtuosity in this reading. Such a reading, in fact, elides Dante's boldness. He believes Beatrice made his new life, just as he believes the Trinity makes his and all human life. And when he reflects her in the Rose, the im-mediacy he insists upon—"non per mezzo mista"—is itself only and necessarily a mediation of the incomprehensible but real fact that he and Beatrice are identical in effigy—it *is* Narcissus who looks into the effigy—but radically different and separate in being—it is *not* Narcissus who sees himself.

Both Beatrice and Dante are mirrors reflecting the same effigy, the Trinity, the source from which they are made. And if they reflect that effigy, it follows that the Trinity is gazing into them even as the Trinity itself is gazing each member of itself into the other (*Par.* 33.124–26). And here, I would like to suggest in conclusion, is the full measure of Dante's vision—namely, his celebration of the self-reflexivity of the Trinity. Whereas Narcissus, without "nostra effige" and beside himself, sees an image of a body which is only water, the Father reflects, and the Son is born, Image made flesh (not water); and the love with which they love each other, unlike the sterile ardor of Narcissus, breathes into Being, the Holy Spirit, and moves the sun and the other stars.

To conclude what is obviously little more than a fragment is an insult to intelligence, I know. But I must be on to Chaucer. Hence let me make only one final point. When Dante-Narcissus looks into the Trinity, he does not see himself as God, but he does see God as himself. Bear with me. A fine distinction, yes, but of absolute importance. Say it this way, though this way diffuses Dante's vision: he does not see his person as God, but he sees God personally. At the supreme moment Dante resembles God, though God does not resemble Dante at all. At the supreme moment Dante is God, but God is not Dante. This is the mystery of the Judaeo-Christian God: He is a personal God. This is the genius of Dante: in assimilating himself to Narcissus, he is able to insist that he sees himself in God but does not see himself as God.[29]

Dante's vision, then, is personal. When Chaucer saw this, he saw that the personal vision of the truth must also necessarily be a personal version of the truth. No one else could see God the way Dante saw God, "Dantesquely." And yet everyone can see and participate in if he likes the "Dantesque" way of seeing God. Dante's version, then, is not such a version as reason's "at-traversion" nor Master Adam's perversion. No. Version though it be, Dante's version of the truth is a true version arising in and from the whole man. Indeed, the purpose of the vision was to make Dante whole so that his version would be true. From all of this Chaucer reasoned, I will now go on to argue, that one's personal version of the truth is true in the measure to which it is not a subversion of oneself or a perversion of the truth of others.

PART TWO

Troylus and Criseyde
and the
"Falsing" of the Referent

pose: poser, expose, propose, suppose, presuppose, compose, depose, decompose, impose, oppose, repose, purpose, posture, imposter

A strong egoism is a protection against disease, but in the last resort we must begin to love in order that we may not fall ill, and we must fall ill if, in consequence of frustration, we cannot love.

(Sigmund Freud)

Critical motherliness has been at too great pains to keep Chaucer genial and cheerful. . . . we still hesitate to look at his somberer side.

(E. Talbot Donaldson)

For al that evere is iknowe, it is rather comprehendid and knowen, nat aftir his strengthe and his nature, but aftir the faculte (*that is to seyn, the power and the nature*) of hem that knowen.

(*Boece* 5, pr. 4)

In fact, what does the coincidence between the representation and the object mean, since the object itself is only a representation?

(Lucien Goldmann)

And when we wish to signify something true or false, necessarily first we impose and transume a sound for the purpose of so signifying ("prius imponimus et transsumimus vocem ad significandum").

(Roger Bacon)

Chapter 5
A Brief Visit to *The House of Fame*

N The House of Fame, the first of his texts to know and to cast a searching eye on Dante, Chaucer poses often as somewhat doltish, certainly diffident, and frequently wide-eyed. But at one point in book 3 he strikes a much somberer pose (lines 1878–82):

> "I wot myself best how y stonde;
> For what I drye, or what I thynke,
> I wil myselven al hyt drynke,
> Certeyn, for the more part,
> As fer forth as I kan myn art."

The tonal change is unarguably abrupt and startling: this is the voice of a collected intelligence, of a mature citizen of an obviously untrustworthy world, the voice of a man with a position, as well as poses, and the courage to hold it. This is no bumbling narrator. And if the man of "gret auctorite" (3.2158) is never named, there may be good reason, not far to seek.

So far as we know, it is 1378. About seven years later Chaucer will be finishing *Troylus and Criseyde*.[1] In the intervening years, much doubtless changed, including Chaucer himself, but the courage to take a position, even in the midst of poses, did not change. To be sure, the understanding of what it means to take a position grew and deepened, but this was a change of what remained the same. And it, the understanding along with all the implications that flow from it, became part of the substance and the texture of the greatest of his poems. The hero of this poem is the Narrator because he survives the cruelest disillusionment English poetry knows to take his stand at the end, his position, with a serenity more convincing than the highest seriousness imaginable.

Chapter 6
Criseyde

OVE FOR Chaucer, as for Dante, is the only viable response to our middled and muddled condition. For all the pain it brings, its absence is unbearable. We must love, then, but how do we love with a minimum of selfishness and hence also with a minimum of deception, self-deception and deception of others? This, I take it, is the fundamental question for Chaucer. To begin to answer it, he structures the *Troylus* with imagery of narcissism and coinage, which, as his allusions and quotations prove, he assumes from Dante's *Commedia*; and he uses this structure of imagery to probe the imagination's invention of ideals in love. The result is nothing less than a theory of mediation—a theory which, while transformed in them, nonetheless informs *The Canterbury Tales*.

This theory is henceforward my subject. As I explicate it and follow it to its often surprising conclusions, I will from time to time recommend positions and suggest interpretations which will at first seem disturbing. But it is only like pouring water into a half-full pitcher: when the new hits the old, at first there is a splash, disturbance, but then, very soon, calm and continuity return; the pitcher is a little bit fuller. In particular, I will be found to insist, both with his characters and with his plots, more on the somber than on the merry in Chaucer. This is not because I do not think Chaucer merry; I do. It is rather because I believe his capacity for merriment is directly dependent on his often too carefully qualified sympathy with the misery of the human condition. My hope for the rest of this book is that it can see and show the merry Chaucer and the somber Chaucer as the one, inimitable, loving and lovable Chaucer.

The theory of mediation is most visible in the poem's coinage imagery. This imagery asserts itself in Book 4 at a number of points but most forcefully near the end of the book. Here, through an oblique allusion to *Inferno* 30, Chaucer suggests that Criseyde is like a coin (4.1534–40; emphasis added):

"For thilke day that I for cherisynge
Or drede of fader, or of other wight,
Or for estat, delit, or for weddynge,
Be *fals* to yow, my Troylus, my knyght,
Saturnes doughter, Juno, thorugh hire myght,
As wood as Athamante do me dwelle
Eternalich in Stix, the put of helle!"

In the context of the allusion to Dante through Athamante, the word "fals" announces the problem of corrupt or fraudulent reference. Although she claims otherwise, Criseyde will in fact betray Troylus and be "fals" to him even as a false coin betrays the authority of the prince or the community which issued its original.[1] Chaucer reinforces this reading with the allusion to Juno: under one of her aspects she is Juno Moneta, goddess of the temple of the moneyers in ancient Rome.[2] Moreover, he has already repeated ten times in Book 4 the words "chaunge" and "exchaunge"[3]—Criseyde, of course, is to be exchanged for Antenor—and, although Hector claims early in the book, "We usen here no wommen for to selle" (line 182), his heroic sentiment serves serves to pass economic sentence on Criseyde's future. She will, in fact, be sold, more goods for Troy than good for Troylus.

Now Chaucer supplements the image of Criseyde as coin with many suggestions that she is also like a sign or text: for example, her face is "lik of Paradys the ymage" (4.864); and Troylus himself declares, "'Though ther be mercy writen in youre cheere, / God woot, the text ful hard is, soth, to fynde'" (3.1356–57). If Criseyde is a text or a sign or even perhaps the parchment, she is already written before Pandarus, in Troylus's behalf, begins his effort to rewrite her. In the language of medieval grammar, she has already been "imposed" to signify a meaning. The *impositio ad placitum* by which signs receive a meaning, in her case, has occurred "at the pleasure" of an Authority far greater and more original than either Pandarus or Troylus. If Pandarus attempts Criseyde's "herte for to grave" (2.1241; 3.1499), he not only wounds flesh with his stylus or chisel but also violently effaces an original character, imprinted by that greater Authority (it matters little whether we call it Nature or God) and substitutes for it a character of his own making (*poesis*) which, to Troylus's sorrow, must necessarily prove false.

Chaucer's strategy with Criseyde and the coinage imagery is, briefly, this: Troylus, by means of Pandarus, intentionally falsifies Criseyde; Troylus, by means of Pandarus, renders Criseyde "irreferent." Criseyde is both word and coin on which Troylus imposes and stamps the meaning of his idealism: she is the gold which his love would mint; she is the voice with which his love would speak. But, as the analogy makes only too clear, he is doomed to failure. Criseyde is *already* gold and minted; she is *already* a sign.[4] Troylus is belated (and in this, perhaps, is most the poet since the poet must always work tradition's vein).

To open out the analogy: Criseyde is, as it were, an alloy of all those characteristics which make her who she is. She is already a person, an individual, as Chaucer (and E. Talbot Donaldson) make abundantly clear.[5] Criseyde is a woman, a human being, with a will of her own, and she is therefore changeable and capable of changing others. Because she is a self and hence changeable, she can receive Troylus's relentless *fin'amors* idealism only as a "mondiglia," or a dross which falsifies: Troylus reduces Criseyde to identity with his ideal. Necessarily, therefore, she is "fals"; necessarily, "irreferent." Indeed, exchanged for Antenor and circulated to the Greek camp, her own alloy dominant again, her own character visible again, especially her "slydynge corage" (5.825), Criseyde becomes Diomede's coin, and he wastes no time in spending her.

But he spends *her* character. She *has* a character, and it cannot be, ought not be, effaced. It *must* out. Hence Criseyde is not to blame alone. Nor, at the same time, is Troylus to blame alone. They are to blame together. Chaucer is as humane as he is profound. If a man imposes such idealism on a woman, *even if* his motive is helpless love, falsification is bound to result. By its very intensity, the idealism imposed upon others becomes "mondiglia," a dross of personal desire. Humankind cannot bear very much idealism. The "irreference" of the sign, we have seen, derives from the tendency of the sign to replace that which it mediates. Criseyde appears for a brief, blissful moment to be the ideal woman whom Troylus imagines in the privacy of his heart; she appears to be the ideal incarnate, so absolute is Troylus's desire, so irrevocable his narcissism, so helpless his love. But she, the woman, as medium, is changeable, with a will of her own, and she cannot be the private hoard or the blank parchment which Troylus imagines and desires. All signs, words or coins, have always already been "imposed," and the "pleasure" of the authority is absent if not inscrutable. Away from Troylus's desire, Criseyde's alloy asserts itself; and she is "fals" – by her own curse condemned, along with all the other false signs, "'as wod as Athamante'" to "'dwelle / Eternalich in Stix, the put of helle.'" Criseyde *is* to blame for being "slydynge of corage"; but Troylus and Pandarus are also to blame for inhumanely, if in the one case very humanly and even desperately, refusing to see who and what she, the woman, really was.

Chapter 7
Troylus

ROYLUS and Pandarus are false coiners, in a sense, though they are hardly as guilty as Master Adam, because they take a creature, the coin of another Authority, and try the one to remint it and the other to efface it in order to make it current for Troylus, his idealism, and his passion. The image of that other Authority, however, who, Chaucer says, "nyl falsen no wight" (5.1845), is ineradicable. Criseyde is a person and will not, cannot, be Troylus's ideal. This Pandarus, in fact, knew all along and is thus, if charmingly industrious, also more reprehensible, finally, than Troylus, who is so thorough a narcissist that he cannot see, seeing himself, that he sees only himself in Criseyde (cf. 3.1499).

Although his own image blinds him, and although he never becomes Narcissus transhumanized, Troylus, we must insist, is more than just Ovid's self-indulgent boy or Dante's disfigured figure. He is also, to put it most simply, a philosopher, the most consistent Platonist in Chaucer's poetry. His Boethian idiom, however distorted from its original, identifies him unmistakably.[1] And just because he is a Platonist, his immersion in images and the flesh is catastrophic. The discrepancy between the "forms" which his spirit perceives and the reality of the world is finally so vast that he cannot bear it, and he rides out on the Trojan Plain to kill or be killed. Any reading of Troylus's character which omits or slights the purity of his idealism and the breathlessness of his love, even though every reading must insist on his narcissistic falsifications, misses the poignancy of his condition. Had he been able to emerge from the cave, Troylus would have seen the sun. As it turned out, Mercury "sorted hym to dwelle" (5.1827) we know not where.

At the same time, though, he is a narcissist. Chaucer is at pains to plot many allusions to Troylus's narcissism in Book 1. Manifestly, for example, when we first see him, Troylus disdains the love of women (1.190–203); and although his motives are not those of Ovid's Narcissus, he is also vain, or, at the least, presumptuous, assuming an invulnerability (1.204–05) which does indeed suggest that "se non noverit" ("he does not know himself"; *Met.* 3.348). Moreover, when he does come at last to know himself–that, although he has loved another, he loved more his image of her than her–his self-knowledge that he has loved not wisely but too well will cost him, as it did Narcissus, his life.

The beginning of Troylus's self-knowledge is the God of Love's vengeance upon his presumption (1.206–10). Immediately Troylus, like Dante in *Inferno* 30, is "fixed" in narcissistic fascination: "in his hertes botme gan to stiken / Of hir his *fixe* and depe impressioun" (1.297–98; emphasis added). Furthermore, even now Troylus begins to fabricate false images: he repeatedly dissimulates his real condition (1.320–22, 488–90). And, most telling of all, he is like Narcissus trapped now in a mirror (1.365–67, 372; emphasis added):

> Thus gan *he make a mirour of his mynde*,
> In which he saugh al holly hire figure,
> And that he wel koude in his herte fynde.
> . . . .
> *Imaginynge* that travaille nor grame. . .

Note well that Chaucer, as did Dante before him, takes pains to emphasize the connection between mirroring and image making. Troylus is already succumbing to the temptations of (Master) Adam.

Supplementing these direct allusions are suggestions of Troylus's narcissism through images of fire and water. Besides simple references to fire and fever (1.490–91), there are almost certain evocations of Ovid's and Dante's texts. For example, Troylus laments (1.523–25; emphasis added):

> "But also cold in love towardes the
> Thi lady is, as frost in wynter moone,
> And thow fordon, *as snow in fire is soone.*"

In the same way Narcissus "melted" for "unrequited love" (*Met.* 3.487–90). Again, Troylus complains that "desir so brennyngly me assailleth" (1.607); and in the complaint he sounds like both Ovid's Narcissus (*Met.* 3.464) and Dante's Master Adam (*Inf.* 30.64–69).

As for the suggestion of Troylus's narcissism through the imagery of water, Chaucer is shrewd indeed (1.871–74; emphasis added):

> But tho gan sely Troylus for to quake
> As though men *sholde han led hym into helle,*
> And seyde, "Allas! of al my wo *the welle,*
> Thanne is my swete fo called Criseyde!"

This is the moment when at last Troylus confesses to Pandarus who it is that he loves, and, however oblique the allusion through "the welle" to "lo specchio di Narcisso," the rhyme with "helle" and the suggestion that his confession leads Troylus to Hell combine with the allusion to evoke not only Narcissus but also the very scene in which Dante confronts Narcissus. In this "welle" Troylus will see not only himself but also, after Criseyde has betrayed him, the prospect of Hell itself. In light of Chaucer's dependence on and transformations of Dante, this moment carries chilling force, and we can only admire the care the poet has taken to set the stage.

At least one more detail of that setting needs special emphasis. At the end of Book 1 (lines 1083–85) we learn of Troylus that

> Dede were his japes and his cruelte,
> His heighe port and his manere estraunge,
> And ecch of tho gan for a vertu chaunge.

Troylus, in short, has converted (cf. 1.999); but this conversion, unlike Dante's, does not transhumanize. In fact, that is Troylus's tragedy: he does turn to love, but his version of love does not turn *him* to the sun and the other stars.

Chapter 8
Pandarus

ROYLUS reaches the stars only after death and complete disillusionment with human love (disillusionment, we should note, is
compatible with maintaining "trouthe"). Pandarus is interested in
the stars, if at all, only as a means to forecast the weather
(2.74–75); he never had any illusions, and that may be why he never cared
much for "trouthe." Pandarus is an instrument—"'swich a meene / As maken
wommen unto men to comen'" (3.254–55)—and he constantly practices instrumentality or expediency. His narcissism is relentless and finally more
vulgar than Troylus's—as opportunism is always more vulgar than idealistic if
naïve striving.

But Pandarus is not to be dismissed in neat moral judgments. If he is an op-
portunist, he is also a consummate master of props. If he is illusionless, he is
also remarkably sensitive. If he is expedient always, he is also aware—it may
be only dimly—that there is more to life than expediency. No, Pandarus has
too much energy to be simply dismissed. Moreover, he is too compelling an
authority. Indeed, the narcissism and false coining of Pandarus are inseparable from his *auctoritas* in the story. To be sure, brief references, almost
like cues, point to his narcissism: for example, in his first attempt to rewrite
Criseyde for his and Troylus's script, at one point he looks into her face and
muses to himself, "'on swich a *mirour* goode grace!'" (2.266; emphasis added).
But it is chiefly as a poet or *auctor*, a worker in images, that Pandarus betrays
his narcissism and falsification.

Pandarus emerges as the poet who will write or invent the "romance" of
Troylus and Criseyde at the end of Book 1, where he goes musing like the
poet in Geoffrey of Vinsauf's famous description (lines 1065–71).[1] He is most
obviously at work as the poet in Book 2, where, as Criseyde rightly perceives,
he is about a "paynted proces" (lines 423–25):

> "Is this the verray mede of youre byheeste?
> Is al this paynted proces seyd, allas!
> Right for this fyn?"

The word "paynted" can hardly fail to call attention to the "colores rhetorici" or indeed to the Horatian "ut pictura poesis."[2] Criseyde recognizes Pandarus's dubious *auctoritas*. Moreover, she also discerns that, if Pandarus is poet and rhetorician, he is also lawyer, since "proces" means not only "story" but also "plea" or "case" (as explicitly at 2.1615); her sense, however dim, that Pandarus is prosecuting her is close to the truth.[3] Finally, she also rightly intuits that, in addition to poet, rhetorician, and lawyer, Pandarus is also a merchant, trying very much to sell her and to sell her on something. "Mede," as we know from *Piers Plowman*, is an extremely volatile economic and commercial word; its meaning cannot be restricted merely to "reward."[4] Furthermore, as the Man of Law makes clear, "biheste is dette" (*MLT* B¹ 41), and, as we already know, the "pandar" is a bargainer – little doubt can remain then that Pandarus is merchandizing with his "paynted proces." And, indeed, that is just what we would expect from a certain kind of poet and his rhetoric. In one of the most famous of the dictaminal treatises of the high Middle Ages, the *Flores rhetorici*, Alberic of Montecassino describes metaphor and its effect much as Pandarus would have probably done:

> Metaphor's way of speaking is, as it were, a twist away from the proper meaning; a twist, so to speak, for innovation; innovation as if for dressing in a nuptial gown; *and such dressing as if for selling at a dignified price* (lit.: price of dignity). For what else is it, shall I say, except for *selling*, when, a story base in its simplicity, you celebrate by a kind of snootiness of variety and variation, representing it as always new, always pleasing?[5]

The dictaminist commits metaphor with intent to sell. The dictaminist, of course, writes for a living; and in a sense, Pandarus does, too. His "paint job," with its elaborate *fin'amors* tropes and metaphors, is definitely meant to sell Criseyde – he wants her to buy a "historiam," which is "vilem" in more than one sense. And, as she knows only too well, he would not go into debt for nothing: in exchange for the "mede" he would sell her, he will have – she probably already suspects as much – the vicarious enjoyment of her and Troylus's affair. As Donaldson (1975:288) so finely puts it, "Those who can, love; those who cannot, write about it."

Chaucer has several other ways, too, of suggesting that, because Pandarus cannot, he writes about it. Again in Book 2, for example, he is careful to assimilate Pandarus to the archetypal artist of this sublunary sphere, or Goddess Natura. Chaucer presents the Goddess in this role in *The Physician's Tale*

(C 11–28), and there he is almost certainly indebted to the Chartrians, especially to Alain de Lille's *De planctu naturae* (PL 210:456–60 especially). So also in the *Troylus*, where, after Criseyde, in Pandarus's company, has seen Troylus pass by on the street below, she begins to meditate favorably upon him and his suit, and "Pandare, which that stood hire faste by, / Felte iren hoot, and he bygan to smyte" (2.1275–76). The image calls forth Natura at her forge, where she hammers out new creatures to replenish the fallen world (*Roman de la Rose* 15861–16083). Related to this figure and its iconography is Natura's role, in the *De planctu*, as the moneyer of creation: for example, early in her instruction of Alain, she affirms "'Me...He [God] appointed as a sort of deputy, a coiner for stamping the orders of things.'"[6] Hence the assimilation of Pandarus to Natura also suggests that he is "coining" Criseyde. Also in Book 2, Pandarus is most like Grammar personified. Near the end of Book 2 "this Pandarus gan newe his tong affile, / And al hire cas reherce, and that anon" (2.1681–82). Such *filing* is, with various tools, the business of Grammatica in Alain de Lille's *Anticlaudianus* and Martianus Capella's *De nuptiis*.[7] Pandarus is, then, Grammar as well as Nature, writing as well as forging and coining the story of Troylus and Criseyde. Finally, and, as it were, crowning these many suggestions of Pandarus's *auctoritas* is the famous scene in Book 3, where he "fond his contenaunce / As for to looke upon an old romaunce" (3.979–80)–this posture, almost emblematic, confirms and consummates the whole pattern of allusions.

Motivating this insistence on Pandarus's *auctoritas* is Chaucer's desire to separate and distinguish it from his own. Indeed, the whole of the *Troylus* can be seen as Chaucer's repudiation of the pandar's poetics–a poetics of imposition generating an *auctoritas* of "trecherye" (3.274–80; emphasis added):

> "And were it wist that I, thorugh myn *engyn*
> Hadde in my nece *yput* this *fantasie*,
> To doon thi lust and holly to ben thyn,
> Whi, al the world upon it wolde crie,
> And seyn that I the werste *trecherie*
> Dide in this cas, that evere was bigonne,
> And she forlost, and thow right nought ywonne."

The text folds in a new complexity at this moment. "Engyn" translates medieval Latin *ingenium*, a word and a concept of crucial importance to later medieval literature.[8] Among its many meanings, "ingenium" connotes that faculty of imagination by virtue of which poets invent their poems. Here, then, Pandarus is speaking explicitly as a poet, and his is definitely a poetics of imposition ("yput"). As if the theory of *impositio ad placitum* had been taken literally and to a physical and possibly violent extreme, Pandarus has *put* his "fantasye" into his niece; and the sexual connotation, we should note, is as audible as the grammatical. He has to some extent made her his creature; and although he probably hopes to exorcise or at least to deflect the charge by remorsefully and self-protectively acknowledging his "trecherye," he cannot suppress the truth in his confession—truth which exceeds or escapes his intention. He is guilty and he knows it. And his is the guilt of perverted *auctoritas*—a guilt which Chaucer would just as soon not have to bear.

Pandarus perverts *auctoritas* to the point of playing god with the lives of Troylus and Criseyde. He manipulates them as if they were his "characters" and not creatures in their own right. As a poet and worker in images, he desires to make Troylus and Criseyde in his own image—and in his own image of "romance." This desire is his narcissism and hence the motive for his falsification of images. In the actual practice of his craft, then, Pandarus will betray himself—how he "handles" his "characters." With the pandar as his *auctor*, Troylus will become a perfect "character" of Amor, true to the type—until, of course, he walks out of the story Pandarus is writing and into one Pandarus can hardly understand, much less complete. Troylus will eventually discover a meaning in love beyond the rhetoric of love, though at a staggering price. But until such time, he remains a "character" in Pandarus's story, to be "written" as Pandarus sees fit. Hence, for example, Pandarus falsifies Troylus into a falsifier, the very image of his *auctor*, when he persuades him to lie to Criseyde about Horaste (3.701–702, 1156–58).[9] Pandarus "writes" this image of Troylus, and many others, because he is finally more adept at talking love than loving. We know, of course, that he is involved in an affair of his own during the "writing" of Troylus and Criseyde's "romance"; but all that we ever hear of it is that it is not prospering.[10] The increment of hints that his affair is not working out forces us to suspect that for Pandarus words replace reality. He experiences in language what he cannot experience in fact, and that is why Troylus is so important to him: Troylus and so also Criseyde (though any woman would do—see 4.400–406) represent the opportunity for Pandarus's words to take on flesh—to assume more reality than they and he would otherwise enjoy. Pandarus, in short, desires his word made flesh—and for Chaucer and his world that is the ultimate perversion of *auctoritas*.

If Pandarus falsifies Troylus, still Criseyde is his principal victim. He falsifies her so as to please or to pandar to Troylus. Up till now my judgments may have seemed excessively harsh, since Pandarus is so very attractive, though I have tried to be fair. Now, however, we enter a depth of the text where harsh judgments are inevitable if also regrettable. Pandarus does violate the integrity of Criseyde's self or person to reduce her to his "character" and Troylus's ideal. The text adumbrates this violence with the allusion to Proigne which opens Book 2 (lines 64–70, 75–77):

> The swalowe Proigne, with a sorowful lay,
> Whan morwen com, gan make hire waymentynge,
> Whi she forshapen was; and ever lay
> Pandare abedde, half in a slomberynge,
> Til she so neigh hym made hire cheterynge
> How Tereus gan forth hire suster take,
> That with the noyse of hire he gan awake,
>
> . . . .
>
> and took his weye ful soone
> Unto his neces palays ther biside.
> Now Janus, god of entree, thow hym gyde!

It is hard not to imagine Pandarus as another Tereus about to "take" another Philomela in Criseyde. Indeed, the metaphors of violence which he freely uses of her strengthen our tendency to imagine just that. For example, as part of his effort to encourage Troylus's good hope and patience, he likens Criseyde in her Daunger to an oak tree hard to bring down (2.1380–86); or again, as he prepares Troylus for the first meeting with Criseyde, he exclaims, "'Lo, hold the at thi triste cloos, and I / Shal wel the deer unto thi bowe dryve'" (2.1534 35). Whether by ax or by bow, Criseyde is to suffer violence, and it is Pandarus who "engineers" that suffering. He, like another Tereus, will be the cause "whi she forshapen" is: not only will she be stamped with a new impress, that impress will also "metamorphose" her into a new creature (for a while, at least). Chaucer's verb "forshapen" is his way of acknowledging Ovid's *Metamorphoses* in the telling of one of its tales, as it is also his way of announcing the kind of change Criseyde is about to undergo at Pandarus's hands—violent, partly irrational, and in some sense moral.[11] If we add to the suggestion of Pandarus as Tereus his status as augurer or diviner (2.74–75), then his potential for violence, for calling up darkness or calling down thunder (3.519–22), as well as for releasing irrational forces, is, as Chaucer intended it to be, even more starkly visible. The concluding allusion to Janus (line 77) only confirms what by now is an unavoidable suspicion—that Pandarus is potentially a two-faced traitor, someone whose face may have only another face in back of it.

At the same time, of course, Criseyde is hardly an innocent. No widow could be. Moreover, her obscure but nonetheless certain intimate relationship with her uncle suggests in fact that she is in some ways a coconspirator with him.[12] All the same, she does not begin as guilty either. However guilty she eventually becomes, she begins as an ordinary, complicated, anxious, and partly self-deceived woman. Her fear, nearly a constant condition with her, is mentioned no fewer than seven times in Book 2;[13] and her anxiety about appearances, which expresses itself pointedly enough in terms of religion, argues a person who cannot afford an easy commerce between her inner and her outer self. She is, in short, a very human woman, and she is therefore also very vulnerable. Pandarus knows this.

And he knows that she is most vulnerable perhaps in the area of appearances. Her father a traitor and herself a widow, she lives, she must feel, under surveillance in Troy. She must at all costs be proper—even to the point perhaps of *falsifying herself* in order to be proper—and the propriety she imagines (almost, "counterfeits") is that of religion. When Pandarus suggests, at their first meeting, that they "'daunce / And...don to May som obser-vaunce'" (2.111–12), she exclaims, apparently in shocked dismay (2.113, 117–18; emphasis added):

> "I? God forbede!" quod she....
>
> . . . .
>
> "It sate me wel bet *ay in a cave*
> *To bidde and rede on holy seyntes lyves.*"

Now Chaucer uses the imagery of conversion of both Troylus (1.999) and Criseyde (2.903): each converts to *fin'amors*. And it seems obvious that each has a predisposition to convert. But in Criseyde the predisposition is more an anxiety than a habit of will as it is, I feel, in Troylus's case. She is anxious to appear proper, and she assumes that propriety for a woman in her position would be that of the recluse or the anchorite (the anachronism—there were no anchorites in ancient Troy—flavors the text with just enough strangeness to call just enough of the wrong kind of attention to Criseyde at this point). It would be premature as well as harsh to claim that she is interested *only* in appearances—such a claim would reduce her to a very banal schemer, a falsifier merely, like Myrrha or Master Adam—but it would be just as erroneous to take the anxiety altogether seriously. Rather, Criseyde is a woman with enough fineness of character to sense the propriety of opting for religion in a case like hers, but she is also shrewd enough to know that it is "a case like hers"—that is, that her motive would not be free of expediency and hence of some degree of falsification, too (cf. 5.1149). Hence the peculiar sense of release when she later exclaims, trying (successfully) to persuade herself to love, "'What, par dieux! I am naught religious!'" (2.759)—she is just as happy to be rid of the anxiety, though she is aware of what she is now rid of. And it is just this very ordinary if also very complex mixture of anxiety, fineness of character, and shrewdness which Pandarus presupposes for his opening ploy: when he adds to it Troylus's passion and his own rhetoric (itself a kind of passion), he will have his counterfeit coin.

Criseyde's curiosity, then, has intricate and deep origins; all Pandarus needs to do is play to it if he would falsify her. Consequently, in precisely a two-faced way, he sets up an obvious, even ostentatious discrepancy between his words and his intent so that the former compel Criseyde to guess at the latter, her curiosity whetted all the while. The more she hears, the more she does *not* know, and therefore the more and all the more she wants to know (2.309–12):

> "Now, my good em, for Goddes love, I preye,"
> Quod she, "come of, and telle me what it is!
> For both I am agast what ye wol seye,
> And ek me longeth it to wite, ywys'"

This discrepancy between words and intent is a crucial element in Chaucer's strategy to expose the pandar's poetics. The word "entente" occurs many times in Book 2 – more than fifty times in the whole poem. The word usually occurs with reference to some form of *auctoritas*;[14] and although the adjective often accompanies it, "entente" in the poem is rarely ever "playn." In fact, if Pandarus claims, as he does at one point in the first attempt to rewrite Criseyde, that "'this al and som, and pleynly oure entente. / God help me so, I nevere other mente'" (2.363–64), we can be fairly certain of just the opposite. Pandarus always "means other." And if Chaucer repeats the word "entente" so insistently, it is because he is problematizing authorial intentionality as an instance of the narcissism of instrumentality. His theory of mediation, unlike the pandar's poetics, will presuppose the direct interference of authorial intention in the text; and it will therefore also include a position on the necessary morality of the author – who must discount for his narcissism if he is to tell his story truly, if his version of the story is not to be a perversion of the story.

Pandarus never discounts for his narcissism, and because he always means himself he never says what he means: he always means more than and other than he says. He is forever undoing the prior text in order to construct his own. His "paynted process" is always a re-vel-ation, and for him the truth is only another veil – precisely a process of substitution (recall Adam's "trapassar del segno"). Pandarus is the origin of representation in Chaucer's poem. To Troylus's ideal love he brings the body of Criseyde, and along with that body all the metaphoricity of *fin'amors* – Daunger, for example. Criseyde was not "daungerous" until Pandarus said she was (2.384)—if you will, coined her so. Pandarus writes the story and consumes the present in re-presentation. Hence, when Troylus and Criseyde couple for the first time, he "fond his contenaunce, / As for to looke upon an old romaunce" (3.979–80). The origin of representation, Pandarus is also the "engineer" of "as" in the poem and hence the vector of the problem of reference. Twice, for example, he poses "as if's."[15] The most comprehensive "as" of this archposer and type of all of Chaucer's posers to come, however, is his version of "romance," the version with which Troylus and Criseyde begin. Even so, his is not the ver-sion with which they end. To his claim that "it is but casuel plesaunce" (4.419) and to his offer to substitute another woman for Criseyde (4.400–406), Troylus opposes a "newe qualite" (3.1654) which writing and representation cannot consume. Rather than fit Pandarus's genre, Troylus dies. He does not reduce to Pandarus's (per)version of the lover. Pandarus cannot write the end of Troylus's romance. His last words in the poem are "'I kan namore seye'" (5.1743). Deprived of words—of representation, writing, and metaphoricity—Pandarus ceases to exist. In his stead the Narrator must finish the text.

Chapter 9
The Narrator

NLY GRADUALLY do we register that the Narrator is as much a character in the poem as is Troylus, Criseyde, or Pandarus, and this because, at least in part, only gradually does he become conscious of his role and responsibility as translator of the Book of Lollius. He begins the poem claiming that he is "the sorwful instrument, / That helpeth loveres, as I kan, to pleyne" (1.10–11). Not until well into the third book, however, does he recognize the threat of narcissism in his *instrumentality* so as to confess that he might have "any word in eched" (3.1329). And only by the end of the poem does he realize that he, the fourteenth-century translator, must make the best of it he can and without the production of "irreferent" signs. By then he, much like Dante, has become a redeemed Narcissus. He turns (converts), and urges others to turn, to God—who made man "after his ymage" (5.1839)—because "he nyl falsen no wight" (5.1845). With this emphasis on "ymage" and "falsen" the poem resumes and completes the structure of coinage and narcissism imagery; and Chaucer has mapped his theory of mediation in the conversion of the Narrator from un-self-conscious "instrument" to master poser of the many versions of the truth.

In the beginning the Narrator is secure in a chrysalis of various formulas: the formula for tragedy—"Fro wo to wele, and after out of joie" (line 4); the formula for decorum—"For wel sit it, the sothe for to seyne, / A woful wight to han a drery feere, / And to a sorwful tale, a sory chere" (1.12–14); a formula for "clerkly" subservience— "I, that God of Loves servantz serve" (1.15); a formula for erotic bliss—"ye loveres, that bathen in gladnesse" (1.22); the formula for *losengiers*—"for hem that falsly ben apeired / Thorugh wikked tonges" (1.38–39).[1] Moreover, from this formulaic security the Narrator presumes to chastise and even to sermonize to Troylus and other such "foles" (1.211–17):

> O blynde world, O blynde entencioun!
> How often falleth al the effect contraire
> Of surquidrie and foul presumpcioun;
> For kaught is proud, and kaught is debonaire.
> This Troylus is clomben on the staire,
> And litel weneth that he moot descenden;
> But alday faileth thing that fooles wenden.

The Narrator might do well to heed his own homily. There is something of a presumption of "omniscience" in remarks like these and others which he makes in Book 1 (lines 253–59, for example; Rowe 1976:159). Add to this presumption and its formulaic security his self-quarantine from "the fyr of love—the wherfro God me blesse" (1.436), and the Narrator does seem some-one too concerned with security and with avoiding eros—someone, that is, potentially vulnerable. And when he is eventually wounded, it is in fact by a Love which he could not have imagined from the severely limited and hence spurious security of his initial formulas.

The Narrator's already shaky defenses have begun to crumble by the Proem to Book 2. Here he visibly differs from the Narrator in Book 1. The crux of the difference is Pandarus: by the Proem to Book 2 the Narrator has had ample opportunity, not just as a reader but as a translator, to observe Pandarus's authority, as he exercises it on Troylus, and thus equal opportunity to measure the difference between Troylus's love and idealism, on the one hand (however tainted with narcissism), and Pandarus's cynicism and smug wisdom, on the other (1.1030–40 especially). The Narrator has begun to fear that he might become a Pandarus and a pandar of words who imposes his meaning upon his matter with little or no respect for its original composition. How can he tell a tale already told without treating it the way Pandarus treats Troylus and Criseyde?

The measure of the Narrator's fear in the Proem to Book 2 is his *self-consciousness* of his retreat into the *pose* of translator. He is now searching for security—no longer secure (2.8–21; emphasis added):

> O lady myn, that called art Cleo,
> Thow be my speed from this forth, and my Muse,
> *To ryme wel* this book til I have do;
> *Me nedeth here noon other art to use.*
> Forwhi to every lovere I me excuse,
> That *of no sentement I this endite,*
> But out of Latyn in my tonge it write.

> Wherfore I nyl have neither thank ne blame
> Of al this werk, but prey yow mekely,
> Disblameth me, if any word be lame,
> *For as myn auctour seyde, so sey I,*
> Ek though I speeke of love unfelyngly,
> No wondre is, for it nothyng of newe is;
> A blynd man kan nat juggen wel in hewis.

Self-evidently, the Narrator protests too much. "Me nedeth here noon other art to use" suggests definite awareness of other art, while the disavowal of "sentement" intimates at least enough "sentement" to deplore its alleged absence (as much could also be argued of his claim that he speaks of love "unfelyngly"). The Narrator, having observed how Pandarus imposes his *auctoritas* upon Troylus—how he adds to the latter's amorous predisposition the metaphoricity of *fin'amors*—has begun to fear that he might impose his *auctoritas* upon his matter, perhaps in the form of "other art" or through the absence of "sentement." Hence the insistence on the *pose of translator*. If he is "only" a translator, then (he can reason) he need not and will not *add* anything to the original. If his version is rigorously faithful to the original, then he is completely in the clear. Note, in this regard, the emphasis "to ryme wel": "ryme" is the most mechanical, least ideological or "sentimental" feature of the poet's craft, even more so if the poet is only a translator. Mere "ryming" can hardly be guilty of adding to or imposing upon the original. And the Narrator is eager to be an innocent instrument—merely a historian (i.e., servant of Cleo)—at most only "sorwful" (line 10), for that, after all, is only decorum. And yet he is aware already that he cannot be innocent (2.22–37):

> Ye knowe ek that in forme of speche is chaunge
> Withinne a thousand yeer, and wordes tho
> That hadden pris, now wonder nyce and straunge
> Us thinketh hem, and yet thei spake hem so,
> And spedde as wel in love as men now do;
> Ek for to wynnen love in sondry ages,
> In sondry londes, sondry ben usages.

> And forthi if it happe in any wyse,
> That here be any lovere in this place
> That herkneth, as the storie wol devise,
> How Troylus com to his lady grace,
> And thenketh, 'so nold I nat love purchace,'
> Or wondreth on his speche or his doynge,
> I noot; but it is me no wonderynge.

For every wight which that to Rome went
Halt nat o path, or alwey o manere.

To measure the change in the Narrator which these extraordinary qualifica-
tions and hesitations register, the stanzas must be compared with his introduction of Troylus's first lyric in 1.393–98 (emphasis added):

And of his song *naught only the sentence*,
As writ myn auctour called Lollius,
But *pleinly, save oure tonges difference*,
I dar wel seyn, in al that Troylus
Seyde in his song, *loo! every word right thus*
As I shal seyn.

The vexed issue of Lollius to one side, these lines are remarkable for the
display of confidence the Narrator indulges in them. Here "oure tonges difference" is a mere trifle, mentioned only to be summarily ignored, so that the
Narrator can fairly exult in the transparency of his translation—"loo! every
word right thus...pleinly." Both tone and diction suggest a complete lack of
anxiety about the practice and the results of translation; the Narrator is an
"innocent instrument."

How different matters are in the Proem to Book 2. Here the Narrator cannot ignore time, "a thousand yeer," nor can he be innocent of it. The "prys" of
words changes and so also the "forme of speche." Consequently, if he
translates with absolute fidelity, the Narrator will be translating words
whose value or "prys" is, at least in part, lost; and thus time itself will impose
on his story. By the very act of translating, the Narrator, however
faithful—indeed, because faithful—names and marks the story as old and thus
adds strangeness to it: his presence is the story's absence. And inevitably,
because of the strangeness, someone, perhaps many, will remark, "'so nold I
nat love purchace'": he or they would not pay such a "prys" for love—he or
they would not "purchace" love with such old, strange words. Here emerges
the importance of the economic terms "prys" and "purchace." Economics is
preeminently the sphere of relativity (as in measurement), of subjectivity, and
of the will in its private desires.[2] Hence, used of language and love and the
language of love, such terms insist on the residue of arbitrariness and subjectivity—*affectio* and *complacibilitas*—in both language and love. The "prys" of
words changes because the market for them, namely, the human construction
of meaning, changes.[3] The "prys" of a word may come to seem no value at all,
only "nyce" and "straunge." Moreover, people "purchace" love because love is
exchange, and in love the will is always giving up one thing for another; love
is structurally a transaction in which people purchase according to *affectio* and

complacibilitas. The words "prys" and "purchace," then, suggest the Narrator's growing awareness of the necessary residue of self in language and love and the language of love. Even the translator desires to translate, and with that desire the self imposes on the text, whereupon the question of narcissism in reference inevitably arises, Why bother awakening the old text and its strange usages? What is the "prys" of a translation? Can the story be told by a native of fourteenth-century England without the imposition upon it of his values and perspectives and desires?

If time raises such questions and forces the Narrator thus to realize that he cannot be innocent, so does space (2.38–49):

> Ek in som lond were al the game shent,
> If that they ferde in love as men don here,
> As thus, in opyn doyng or in chere,
> In visityng, in forme, or seyde hire sawes;
> Forthi men seyn, ecch contree hath his lawes.
>
> Ek scarsly ben ther in this place thre
> That have in love seid lik, and don, in al;
> For to thi purpos this may liken the,
> And the right nought, yet al is seid or schal;
> Ek som men grave in tree, some in ston wal,
> As it bitit; but syn I have bigonne,
> Myn auctour shal I folwen, if I konne.

Mutability is as spatial as it is temporal: "ecch contree hath his *lawes*" but also "ecch contree hath *his* lawes." So it is that law and potentially irrational subjectivity sit side by side. "Ek som men grave in tree, some in ston wal," and some, as the Narrator is about to observe, in human hearts (2.1241). Faced with such bewildering variety and relativity, and the consequent doubt, and having already observed Pandarus's disturbingly easy presumption of omniscience and of deific control of his matter, the Narrator concludes his proem on a note of hesitancy and almost fear. Suggesting that the only reason to go on with the story is that he has begun it, the Narrator ends by clearly expressing doubt whether he *can* translate his original faithfully: "Myn auctour shal I folwen, *if I konne.*" The very assumption of the pose of translator has ended in grave doubt about the possibility of translation—not unpredictably, since to take translation seriously is to be forced to realize that the translator is necessarily a guilty instrument because of time and space. The Narrator knows now, or at least can guess, that the task of purging the Pandarus in him is going to be an arduous one, even as he also knows, and probably with certainty, that a pose is by definition insecure.

His awareness so much more sensitive, the Narrator next enters his story *on a level with its characters* and *not* as if from a superior, omniscient position. In fact, he has begun to fall a little in love with Criseyde (Donaldson 1972:65–83). But rather than conceal this fact, he exposes it by openly defending her (2.666–79):

> Now myghte som envious jangle thus:
> "This was a sodeyn love; how myght it be
> That she so lightly loved Troylus,
> Right for the firste syghte, ye, parde?"
> Now whoso seith so, mote he nevere ythe!
> For every thyng, a gynnyng hath it nede
> Er al be wrought, withowten any drede.
>
> For I sey nought that she so sodeynly
> Yaf hym hire love, but that she gan enclyne
> To like hym first, and I have told yow whi;
> And after that, his manhod and his pyne
> Made love withinne hire herte for to myne,
> For which, by proces and by good servyse,
> He gat hire love, and in no sodeyn wyse.

Given that Diomede is "sodeyn" (5.1024), the threefold repetition and negation of "sodeyn" in these two stanzas (lines 667, 673, 679) suggests that the Narrator is making a concerted effort to remember him and to differentiate Criseyde and Troylus from him. Moreover, and more important, the Narrator comments directly, without subterfuge, openly taking his position ("For I sey nought") while going out of his way to notice that of the opposition ("som envious"). In short, he does not pretend to a translator's or "rymer's" putative objectivity, nor does he shrink from open "sentement." At the same time, he has abandoned the pose of authorial omniscience, knowing it now for a pose and a very insecure one. Instead, recognizing the inner life of his text and its obscure though nonetheless certain demands on his affections, he has entered the text, as much character as Narrator. And this appearance of subjectivity, this extroversion of himself in the text, helps save him from a narcissistic version of the text.

Just how it helps save him we can learn from a consideration of Antigone's lyric (2.827–76) and the role it plays in Criseyde's decision to love. Scholars have recognized the importance of this lyric and the many others which punctuate the poem.[4] Here, therefore, I will be selective in my emphases. I am most interested in the valorization of "entente" in the lyric and in the remarks which follow it, for it is the problem of intentionality with which the Narrator is grappling. As we know, "entente" in *Troylus and Criseyde* is rarely ever "playn," but sometimes it is, and can be, good. And just such an occasion Antigone's lyric illustrates. The opening of the lyric insists on the importance of "entente" in love: "'O Love, to whom I have and shal / Ben humble subgit, trewe in myn entente'" (2.827–28); and the intellectual center of the lyric carries this insistence to its moral and philosophical conclusion (2.851–54):

> "This is the righte lif that I am inne,
> To flemen alle manere vice and synne;
> This dooth me so to vertu for t'entende,
> That day by day I in my wille amende."

This is *fin'amors* at its most "fine," and the rhyme "entende-amende" beautifully captures the ideal to which *fin'amors* aspired. Before it lapsed into sterile formalism, such as Dante devastatingly censures in Francesca's amorous rhetoric (*Inf.* 5.100–07; 121–38),[5] *fin'amors* inscribed the possibility of human behavior as decorous and as beautiful and as ordered as the form of a lyric. The virtuosity of lyric form and the "vertu" of human behavior approximated each other, interpenetrated each other. But eventually virtuosity consumed virtue. Hence Dante's palinodes to *fin'amors* lyricism; hence, as I have already argued here and elsewhere, Chaucer's repudiation of this mode too (Shoaf 1981a:179–85).

But if Chaucer repudiates the sterile formalism of *fin'amors*, he does not categorically reject the possibility of purified intent, the possibility of transcendence. He leaves open the possibility of a *fine amors* and an amended will. When Antigone finishes singing her lyric, Criseyde asks, obviously in wonder, "'Now nece... / Who made this song now with *so good entente?*'" (2.877–78; emphasis added). Criseyde *feels* the goodness of the "entente" of the author of this song, and apparently her feeling is wholly justified, for Antigone answers, in three momentous lines (2.880–82; emphasis added):

> "Madame, iwys, the *goodlieste* mayde
> Of gret estat in al the town of Troye,
> And *let hire lif in moste honour and joye.*"

The maker of this song *was* a good woman, who led her life in honor and joy: "'Forsothe, so it semeth by hire song,'" exclaims Criseyde. The song, in other words, is evidence of virtuous intent and trustworthy evidence at that—we have no reason to doubt Antigone. Chaucer goes out of his way, then, to insist, within the fiction, *that there is here no discrepancy between the intent of the maker and the formal expression of that intent in the made thing.* The lyric is not guilty, that is, of any form of falsification: it harbors no covert designs upon the life of another. To be sure, neither is the lyric innocent of narcissism: the woman who made it desired to make it and her desires everywhere influence it; but her desires *do* influence it—that is, they are visible—and therefore the lyric is not a falsification. She, the maker of this lyric, is not, in other words, a Pandarus or a Master Adam. And her lyric is not a lie, either in the rhetorical sense of a "bella menzogna" or in the moral sense of mendacity.

Chaucer has succeeded in representing a true representation. The lyric is a true representation of its maker's character and intent. Hence it cannot be accused of false transcendence or of propagandizing false transcendence. This lyric, in other words, cannot be guilty of falsifying another's life; on the contrary, only those who hear it can be guilty of such misapplication. The audience can fail to perceive the unrepeatability, the distinctive uniqueness, of the lyric's reference. And just such a failure is, Chaucer insists, Criseyde's. She asks Antigone (2.885–96; emphasis added):

> "Lord, is ther swych blisse among
> Thise loveres, as they konne faire endite?"
> "Ye, wis," quod fresshe Antigone the white,
> "For alle the folk that han or ben on lyve
> Ne konne wel the blisse of love discryve.
>
> "But wene ye that every wrecche woot
> The parfite blisse of love? Why, nay, iwys!
> They wenen all be love, if oon be hoot.
> Do wey, do wey, they woot no thyng of this!
> *Men mosten axe at seyntes if it is*
> *Aught fair in hevene (why? for they kan telle),*
> *And axen fendes is it foul in helle.*"

In other words, direct personal experience—"'why? for they kan telle'"—is necessary for a true representation, and even then, that representation is an individual, personal version of the truth *which may not apply in every case.* (cf. *LGWP* F1–9). But "Criseyde unto that purpos naught answerde" (2.897). Criseyde, because she is already under the mesmerizing, "ad placitum" influence of Pandarus's authority, pays no heed to the warning implicit in Antigone's opinion. Rather (2.899–903; emphasis added):

> every word which that she of hire herde,
> She gan *to prenten* in hire herte faste,
> And ay gan love hire lasse for t'agaste
> Than it dide erst, and synken in hire herte,
> *That she wex somwhat able to converte.*

Criseyde *prints* in her own heart another's personal version of the truth of love; she makes her own heart another's book. She misreads. Even as did Paolo and Francesca.[6] She has made another the author in and of her heart. But this is not the fault of the lyric or of its author; so much Chaucer has made clear. Language is not the culprit.[7] Poetry is not guilty (though the disillusioned envy the lucidity of its form). The culprit is, on the one hand, Pandarus, the falsifier, who conceals his narcissism as he designs on his niece's affections and fears. On the other hand, the culprit is Criseyde, partly complicit with her uncle and partly disposed by temperament to the quasi religious ambience of *fin'amors* lyricism. The culprits, in other words, are a deceitful author and an impressionable (and for the moment at least) unwary audience.

Chaucer the poet would stand up to and stand up against both. The Narrator is slowly recognizing that he is just such an audience of the poem he is translating as is Criseyde of Antigone's lyric; and as this recognition increases, he struggles against the tendency to "print" the poem in his own heart, finally achieving the distance of the last two books.[8] At the same time, if he is audience, he is also translator, and, as we have seen, he is already sharply cognizant of the threat of the pandar's poetics. He confronts, then, a twofold peril, of becoming a false author and an irresponsible (literally "ir-respons-ible") audience. And the way to avoid both sides of the peril is, in fact, to respond, to answer the text back (as Criseyde did *not*), so that, on the one hand, his instrumentality is always visible, to us as well as to himself, even as, on the other hand, his feelings are inscribed and tested.

But these are, in fact, the same phenomenon. A responsible audience—one that pays heed to what it hears rather than merely "printing" it off—is already an author, visible and true. Such an audience, in other words, by thinking about what it hears, contributes to the meaning of what it hears and thus authors it, in part. Just so, a visible, true author is visible because he is a responsible audience: he is trying to respond to the text, its inner life, in his own terms without at the same time merely imposing those terms on the text. Such is the kind of author-audience Chaucer wishes to be; such is the kind of author-audience he wishes us, his readers, also to be. Hence the strategy, here in the *Troylus* and supremely in *The Canterbury Tales*, of provoking the reader, of drawing him into the text and making him part of it (principally by means of the frame in *The Canterbury Tales*), thus problematizing his response and forcing him, in effect, to become coauthor of the text. This strategy will be my chief concern in the Introduction to Part Three. Here I want to emphasize that in Book 2 of the *Troylus* we already see Chaucer, in the character of the Narrator and in the (non)response of Criseyde to Antigone's lyric, articulating his theory of mediation. That theory, besides a position on the necessary morality of the author, also includes a position on the necessary responsibility of the audience. If the author is not a falsifier, if he and his desires are visible in the construction of his work, as in the case of the maker of Antigone's lyric, then the audience is resonsible for *its* construction of the work. Chaucer, throughout his career in poetry, sought to make himself as visible as possible. Indeed, we see him everywhere – he is no Pandarus with "wordes whyte" (3.1567) – and if his visibility often seems to hide him, that is only because we, the audience, are not doing our part.

The Narrator began in formulaic security from which he could presume omniscient certainty. By Book 2 he has abandoned the security and lost the certainty. Henceforth, he must feel his way. In Book 3, for example, he feels the might of Love and says as much in the Proem (3.8–11). And since he is now feeling his way, he further prays to Love: "Ye in my naked herte sentement / Inhielde, and do me shewe of thy swetnesse" (3.43–44). The Narrator is now completely open or exposed ("naked herte"), attempting no defenses, and he will interfere with his story, but interfere with it *openly*. His additions and comments will always be as visible as he can make them, for to conceal them or to let them lie hidden would be to falsify the text. Unlike Pandarus, whose words are "whyte" (3.1567), the Narrator will obviously color the text with his opinion: his rhetoric will always display its colors (cf. Serres 1982:160, 194, on the "white domino"). If Venus knows "al thilke covered qualitee / Of thynges" (3.31–32), he, as her "clerk," will attempt to share in, and to share, her knowledge. Since hers is the heaven of rhetoric in Dante's *Paradiso* – and Chaucer's word "covered" probably answers dialectically to Dante's insistence on Venus's "chiarezza" and its significance for rhetoric[9] – he the rhetorician will try to use rhetoric not only to "clarify" the covered but also to expose the covering. Rhetoric, like love (and cloudy Venus), fraught with desire, covers even as it uncovers; like love, also, it makes apparent incompatibles "jo" (3.33) – one thinks immediately of "concordia discors," for example.[10] The "clerk" of Venus, then, is in a peculiarly favorable position for exposition and composition of certain fundamental mysteries. But it is very much a position of desire – desire as trivial as curiosity, as vicious as voyeurism, or as profound as the thirst for Being. And because of his desire the Narrator is a Narcissus, but unlike Pandarus he is not narcissistic, because his desires are always visible in and separable from the "gold" of his text. If the Narrator colors the text with his rhetoric, so as to change its appearance of tragedy, the original hues nonetheless shine through, the original character asserts itself – this is not his "comedye." When the time comes, in fact, the Narrator will even expose Criseyde to infamy, much as he has come to love her. In the end, he *will* let the story tell itself.

The most compelling illustrations in Book 3 of the Narrator's openness, vulnerability, and growing pains are his last appearances in the book. The first of these may well be the Archimedean point of Chaucer's theory of mediation (3.1317–36):

> O blisful nyght, of hem so longe isought,
> How blithe unto hem bothe two thow weere!
> Why nad I swich oon with my soule ybought,
> Ye, or the leeste joie that was theere?
> Awey, thow foule daunger and thow feere,
> And lat hem in this hevene blisse dwelle,
> That is so heigh that al ne kan I telle!
>
> But soth is, though I kan nat tellen al,
> As kan myn auctour, of his excellence,
> Yet have I seyd, and God toforn, and shal
> In every thyng the grete of his sentence;
> And if that ich, at Loves reverence,
> Have any word in eched for the beste,
> Doth therwithal right as youreselven leste.
>
> For myne wordes, heere and every part,
> I speke hem alle under correccioun
> Of yow that felyng han in loves art,
> And putte it al in youre discrecioun
> To encresse or maken dymynucioun
> Of my langage, and that I yow biseche.

Note first of all the Narrator's incriminatory exclamation of desire at lines 1319–20; he is completely immersed in the text, seeing himself in it, and his narcissism borders on voyeurism. And yet, the spontaneity and innocence, perhaps naïveté, with which he exposes himself deflects cynical sneers and prudish remonstrances alike. He is certainly not trying to falsify or to betray. Quite the contrary, he goes on to confess his inadequacy to his original; and since there can be no more certain way to call attention to his interference with the text than to say that he is interfering with it, the reading of γ, which positions the two stanzas here at lines 1324 and 1331 rather than at lines 1401–14 seems to me to be much more likely the correct one (Root 1926:487). These stanzas in this position mark with a sure touch the growing awareness of the Narrator: that his instrumentality is necessarily narcissistic, that his translation is necessarily subjective and biased. He has already learned that he cannot translate faithfully or literally; he cannot re-create the "excellence" of the original and its author. Here and now, further, he openly admits that there will always be something omitted (see also 3.491–504). Hence the importance of β's reading, or "the grete of" (line 1327) as opposed to "al hooly his" of γ: in this reading, the Narrator insists that he expresses at least the essence or the important part of the original, and thus he acknowledges, as in his new awareness he must, *his change of* the original. His next remark also justifies β's reading, since it follows naturally from it. Not only does he do no more than say "the grete of his [the "auctour's"] sentence," he also "in eches" words. So far from an innocent instrument, then, he is guilty of direct addition to his text. And yet, "at Loves reverence." His addition is not "mondiglia"—he is not a Master Adam—because he openly confesses the addition. He is guilty, then—what translator is not?—but by putting his words "under correccioun" (line 1332) of his audience, he expiates the guilt, saying in effect: together we bear the burden of making the story and of making it new. Note, also, that Chaucer's words, "to encresse or maken dymynucioun / Of my langage" (lines 1335–36) obviously recall their technical Latin rhetorical counterparts, *amplificatio* and *abbreviatio*.[11] It is as if Chaucer assumed an audience of rhetoricians—an assumption he probably could, in fact, have made. Be that as it may, the consciousness of "art" here is deep and of sweeping consequence. Moreover, the Narrator is insisting on the public, communal structure of his medium. Language, like money, is public property, and in insisting on as much, the Narrator clears himself of the charge of private, self-seeking narcissism. In these stanzas, then, Chaucer involves his audience in his text, inviting them to participate in his authority, in such a way that we can already recognize what will be the mature authority of, say, "turne over the leef and chese another tale" (*GP* A 3177). Again, we know, the Narrator is no Pandarus or pandar.

But the difference between him and Pandarus is most visible at the end of the "blisful nyght," when he refuses to write what Pandarus, were the pen at that moment in his hand, would expansively indulge (3.1574–82; emphasis added):

> With that his arm al sodeynly he thriste
> Under hire nekke, and at the laste hire kyste.
>
> *I passe al that which chargeth nought to seye.*
> What! God foryaf his deth, and she al so
> Foryaf, and with here uncle gan to pleye,
> For other cause was ther noon than so.
> But of this thing right to the effect to go,
> Whan tyme was, hom to here hous she wente,
> *And Pandarus hath fully his entente.*

We do not know what the original, the "auctour's" text, said; the Narrator does not translate it. But we can guess, and, guessing, we know why he does not translate it. The Narrator does not translate here—he passes over, instead—because he chooses not to report Pandarus's and Criseyde's behavior. He does *not* suppress it—"And Pandarus hath fully his entente"—let us make no mistake about that. He communicates what happened, but he does not report or describe or detail what happened. He interferes consciously and purposefully with his original; so far from "whyte" (3.1567), his words are obviously colored. We *know* what he feels—something like a combination of reluctant love for Criseyde and open distaste for Pandarus—and we accept that feeling because the Narrator neither whitewashes nor indulges in lurid colors. Quite the contrary, he lets the story tell itself, even though it has most likely already begun to hurt him.

But this honesty—perhaps I can venture to say, authenticity—is costing him increasing amounts of pain. In the last two books of the poem the Narrator has gradually and to some extent tearingly to let go of his affection for Criseyde, even as he has to let go of the story. His affection for Criseyde *is* narcissistic: he desires so to exonerate her time and again because he desires to love her. But he cannot finally bring himself to *falsify* the text and the story which it tells. Hence his passionate hope that that story is the *truth* (4.13-21; emphasis added):

> And now my penne, allas! with which I write,
> Quaketh for drede of that I moste endite.
>
> For how Criseyde Troylus forsook,
> Or at the leeste, *how that she was unkynde,*
> Moot hennesforth ben matere of my book,
> *As writen folk thorugh which it is in mynde.*
> Allas! that they sholde evere cause fynde
> To speke hire harm, *and if they on hire lye,*
> *Iwis, hemself sholde han the vilanye.*

As important as the Narrator's narcissistic (but hardly unselfconscious) reservation—"or at the leeste, how that she was unkynde"—is his awareness that *auctoritas* is also on trial. It is a crucial measure of his growth and inchoate conversion that he will now challenge his "auctours." He is still following them—the challenge would make little sense were he not—but now he is a much more conscious instrument and no mere "rymer." Now he recognizes the possibilities of error and even of falsehood in his sources—"if they on hire lye"—and now, as he feels his way through the story, he is also sensitive to how easily he too could lapse into falsification.

The risk of such a lapse is very great midway through Book 4 when he attempts to convey Criseyde's sorrowful complaint (4.799–805; emphasis added):

> How myghte it evere yred ben or ysonge,
> The pleynte that she made in hire destresse?
> I not; but, as for me, my litel tonge,
> If I discryven wolde hire hevynesse,
> It sholde make hire sorwe seme lesse
> Than that it was, and childisshly *deface*
> Hire heigh compleynte, and therefore ich it pace.

It would be too much to claim that the Narrator anticipates Edgar's Law—"The worst is not / So long as we can say, 'This is the worst'" (*King Lear* 4.1.28–29)—but, at the same time, these lines must embarrass the theory of a stumble-footed Narrator. If he could describe her "hevynesse" it would not be her "hevynesse"; if he could utter it, he would obviously miss it. In fact, his description would "deface" her complaint. The connotation of falsification in "deface" attracts the Dantesque understanding of narcissism to the Narrator's speech; the Narrator's anxiety is the anxiety of one who desires to tell the truth. But the truth at this moment is slippery indeed, so slippery, in fact, that falsification or defacement—change of any sort for his own selfish ends—*is* an ominous threat for the Narrator. He can read, as well as we, the incriminatory duplicities in Criseyde's long complaint (4.757–98). "'How sholde a plaunte or lyves creature / Lyve withouten his kynde noriture'" (4.767–68)—but a plant or living creature can find food almost anywhere. "'Thanne shal no mete or drynke come in me / Til I my soule out of my breste unshethe'" (4.775–76)—and what kind of soul is a sword? Similar objections and/or questions could be raised of Criseyde's likening Troylus and herself to Orpheus and Erudice (4.789–91). But the most disturbing element of her complaint is the recourse to the language of religion (4.778–84; emphasis added):

> "And, Troylus, my clothes everychon
> *Shul blake ben in tokenyng*, herte swete,
> That I am as *out of this world agon*,
> That wont was yow to setten in quiete;
> And *of myn ordre*, ay til deth me mete,
> The *observaunce* evere, in youre absence,
> *Shal sorwe ben, compleynt, and abstinence.*"

It is a little, if just a little, too facile. She lapses back into the self-image of a nun or an anchoress with the kind of ease that suggests posturing or, at least, a rather superficial consideration of the implications of her words. And the Narrator as well as we can hear the potential for self-deception; he as well as we can see the potential for histrionics. Hence the rigor of his refusal to "discryven" her "hevynesse." If he described it, he would in fact "childisshly deface" it since he would almost certainly fall into excusing such excess with adolescent fervor.[12] He must be on guard, he knows, against his inclination to exonerate Criseyde—she is, after all, we know, very attractive, very dear. Therefore, he reports her complaint, complete with its incriminatory duplicities, acknowledges his own predicament, and in such a way as to involve us, his readers, in it and Criseyde's self-betrayal alike. Thus he manages to resist the narcissistic impulse, without pretending to pseudo-objectivity, by resisting falsification of his text—he manages, in short, to be objective by being thoroughly subjective. "Ars adeo latet arte sua" (Met. 10.252): just as art is hidden under art, concealed by its very appearance, so the Narrator's subjectivity is concealed by so obviously being subjectivity; and thus he achieves objectivity. We do see Criseyde for who and what she is.

After he has heard Criseyde's boast about how easily she will "converte" her father (4.1412), the Narrator's auctoritas— which is, of course, what we are experiencing—continues to increase (4.1415–21):

> And treweliche, as writen wel I fynde,
> That al this thyng was seyd of good entente;
> And that hire herte trewe was and kynde
> Towardes hym, and spak right as she mente,
> And that she starf for wo neigh, whan she wente,
> And was in purpos evere to be trewe:
> Thus writen they that of hire werkes knewe.

From the by now problematic "entente" to the crucial "thus writen they that of hire werkes knewe," this passage suggests the Narrator's increasing powers of interpretation and independent decision. He sees, and sees more than his own desires in the text. He sees Criseyde's fears (4.1363), her presumptuousness (4.1395), her doubts, her calculation (4.1373–79: like father, like daughter?), her love for Troylus (4.1414), her purpose (4.1420), which nevertheless proves little more than a pose; and seeing all this, showing it to us, he begins to let go, to decide where he stands, to take his position. He knows that otherwise he cannot finish the story. He is undeceived.

The undeceived, let us hasten to note, are not necessarily cynics, even if irony is the usual slant on the world in Chaucer's texts. In proof of which is the Narrator's conclusion of Book 4 (4.1695–1701):

> For mannes hed ymagynen ne kan,
> N'entendement considere, ne tonge telle
> The cruele peynes of this sorwful man,
> That passen every torment down in helle.
> For whan he saugh that she ne myghte dwelle,
> Which that his soule out of his herte rente,
> Withouten more, out of the chaumbre he wente.

The allusion to Saint Paul—"Quod oculus non vidit, nec auris audivit, nec in cor hominis ascendit, quae praeparavit Deus iis qui diligunt illum" (1 Cor. 2.9)—not even the most relentlessly secular of Chaucer's readers can reasonably deny. To my knowledge, it is the first overt quotation by the Narrator of a Christian authority in the poem.[13] As such, it signals the Narrator's assertion of his identity as a Christian poet who is translating a pagan text. He has almost broken now his narcissistic fascination with Criseyde and with the love between her and Troylus. He has clearly seen that, if they love each other very much, they also contain each within himself and herself the potential for tragedy—Troylus in the extremity of his idealism, Criseyde in the opaque complexity of her fear. He knows that, because of this tragic dimension to the story, he can no longer affirm the romance which Pandarus has written. Hence he chooses to speak with purposeful irony.

And his choice, his purpose, is as important as his irony. He has so taken his position as to make a choice. He chooses to invite us, thereupon, to look with him from his position, that of the Christian translator-poet, "over" or "behind" Troylus to the larger paradigm of Troylus's experience where we see the painful and indeed tragic discrepancy between experience and paradigm. The paradigm of Troylus's experience of love is something like the martyr's self-immolation in and for the love of God or the Good.[14] Troylus loves Criseyde, the Narrator's allusion to Saint Paul implies, as a man ought to love God. Hence—and this is very important—the Narrator's irony is as laudatory as it is vituperative. This typically complex Chaucerian irony suggests that, if the Narrator has taken his stand or position on the story, it is not one of facile or reductive moralism. Troylus's love may be directed to the wrong object, but it is still an extraordinary, a beautiful, and a meaningful love. If his love could be directed toward God (of course, it cannot be) it would be such as Saint Paul says is rewarded with things which exceed human comprehension. But directed toward Criseyde, Troylus's martyrlike love is rewarded with "peynes" which exceed human comprehension.[15] The irony points the discrepancy between the objects of love. At the same time, however, the allusion to Paul affirms the grandeur, the wholeness and martyrlike intensity of Troylus's love. The Narrator is no puritan scoffer at this world's love.

Unlike the puritan, he does not secretly love the world so much that he must vilify it. On the contrary, if he cannot affirm the romance which Pandarus has written, he can celebrate the love of Troylus for Criseyde; if he cannot excuse Criseyde, he can imagine salvation for Troylus. As he asserts his identity with his irony, as he takes the story into his own hands, the Narrator begins to find *his* meaning in it, but only because he has let the story tell itself, thus to discover in it, sometimes painfully, its independent meaningfulness. The story possesses a surplus of meaning which the Narrator knows now he can never circumscribe; he can only take his position.

This he does, without further reservation, throughout Book 5. A very good example is his "effictio" of Criseyde (5.813–26; emphasis added):[16]

> And, save hire browes joyneden yfere,
> Ther nas no lak, *in aught I ḳan espien*.
> But for to speken of hire eyen cleere,
> Lo, trewely, *they writen that hire syen*,
> That Paradis stood formed in hire yën.
> And with hire riche beaute evere more
> Strof love in hire ay, which of hem was more.
>
> She sobre was, ek symple, and wys withal,
> The best ynorisshed ek that myghte be,
> And goodly of hire speche in general,
> Charitable, estatlich, lusty, and fre;
> Ne nevere mo ne lakked hire pite;
> Tendre-herted, *slydynge of coràge*;
> But trewely, *I ḳan nat telle hire age*.

These justly famous lines are very important to understanding the whole poem. My only concern, a narrow one, is to point out how visible the Narrator is. Several passages in these two stanzas demonstrate that he has a position which he does not hesitate to take. There is, from his position, one "lak" in Criseyde's beauty anyway; it is a matter worth noting, from his position, that he (and we) do not know Criseyde's age; from his position, it is important to cite the authorities who saw Criseyde's paradisal eyes. Whatever the Narrator's precise position is, the effect of his taking it is that he becomes the measure by which or beside which we see Criseyde's beauty. Structurally, then, the effect is like that which Dante achieves in *Paradiso*: there he is the measure by which we see, and knowing that, we discount his measure in order to imagine the immeasurableness of Heaven. Now, Chaucer's Narrator is not trying, of course, to describe Heaven, but he is inviting us to discount his measure – to allow for the narcissism of his instrumentality – for only by doing so will we reach, each of us, his or her own position on Criseyde's beauty. Rather than provide an illusory verisimilitude, according to which we could assume "this *is* Criseyde," the Narrator positions the "effictio" relative to himself, insisting on his own eye, and thus he compels us to judge what is important *to us*, over against him, about Criseyde – eyebrows or "corage" or sobriety or what have you. In this way Criseyde remains a self always exceeding characterization – she remains, that is, irreducibly linguistic[17] – and her meaningfulness comes to derive from our position on the language of the story. Because we see the Narrator take his position, we know we must take ours. And we feel Criseyde to be a living self because we *have* taken each of us his or her position.[18] Criseyde is not the echo of any reader.

Unless, of course, his or her position is an imposition. In that case, Criseyde can do no more than echo what that reader says she is. As distinct from such a narcissistic reader, the Narrator has become someone who tries to interpret, to understand, to fathom Criseyde – all of which implies his willingness to treat her as more than his echo, as instead a living being. Extraordinary evidence of this willingness is found in his interpretation of why she decided to stay with Diomede (5.1021–29; emphasis added):

> Criseyde unto hire bedde wente
> Inwith hire fadres faire brighte tente,
>
> Retornyng in hire soule ay up and down
> The wordes of this sodeyn Diomede,
> His grete estat, and perel of the town,
> And that she was allone and hadde nede
> Of frendes help; and *thus bygan to brede
> The cause whi, the sothe for to telle,
> That she took fully purpos for to dwelle.*

If all this elaborate explaining incriminates Criseyde (as, I take it, Donaldson would argue),[19] note that it also posits every extenuating circumstance imaginable. The essential point is that the "cause whi" is complex, obscure, and in need of interpretation. Although the Narrator feels that he is telling the truth – "the sothe for to telle" – he could have it all wrong. He even leaves himself a margin of error in the verb "to brede": if the cause began to "spring" or to "bloom," then necessarily it had more growing and thus more changing to undergo, and this later growth and change may have complicated the cause beyond what the Narrator knows or can know. The cause, in fact, implies a human self which another human self must interpret. The Narrator has so far transcended his earlier narcissism that he no longer approaches Criseyde as an enshrined object of desire but as a human being who, like other human beings, is mysterious, obscure, mutable. On the one hand, this is to say that he is disillusioned, that he has suffered a loss; on the other hand, it is to say that he has matured, that he has come to a fuller measure of understanding about being human as well as human being.

Both the disillusionment and the maturity, the loss and the understanding, mark the Narrator's subsequent interpretations of Criseyde's behavior. Out of his experience he has come *to know himself*; and, I suppose, in a sense, like Narcissus, he has died. Certainly, he has changed—*converted*, I would say, from "unliklynesse" (1.16) to understanding of his "unliklynesse." Secure now in his knowledge of himself—with a security wholly different from that of the formulas with which he began the translation—he looks on Criseyde without deception of himself or of others. On the one hand, now he chastises her behavior when it is repugnant to him: "And ek a broche—*and that was litel nede*— / That Troylus was, she yaf this Diomede" (5.1040-41; emphasis added). [20] On the other hand, where it is possible, however remotely, to give her the benefit of the doubt, he does not hesitate to do so: "Men seyn—I not—that she yaf hym hire herte" (5.1050). The phrase "I not" is bittersweet: it is the most the Narrator can say or do—very little, in fact, but he does it anyway. Disillusioned and yet sympathetic, adult and yet concerned, he goes on finally to declare: (5.1093-99):

> Ne me ne list this sely womman chyde
> Forther than the storye wol devyse.
> Hire name, allas! is punysshed so wide,
> That for hire gilt it oughte ynough suffise.
> And if I myghte excuse hire any wise,
> For she so sory was for hire untrouthe,
> Iwis, I wolde excuse hire yet for routhe.

The maturity of the Narrator—how "likly" he is for understanding and for sympathy—is evident here. The full measure of his maturity can be taken by the delicate ambiguity of "sely": she is pitiable and unfortunate, yes, but just possibly, at some inscrutable level where we are not authorized to judge, she is innocent. [21] We will never know.

All we know for certain is that Criseyde betrayed Troylus: she "falsed" him (5.1053, 1056). "Thus goth the world. God shilde us fro meschaunce, / And every wight that meneth trouthe avaunce!" (5.1434-35). The Narrator's prayer is much to the point. God alone can advance the truth keeper, for God alone sees the human heart (1 Kings 16.7). The crux is "meneth." The word has surfaced a number of times in Book 5, and first in a couplet which almost summarizes the way of falsification in *Troylus and Criseyde*, the perversion of instrumentality, the introversion of Narcissus: "'I shal fynde a meene, / That she naught wite as yet shal what I mene'" (5.104–105). Diomede's words revel in the fact that means hide meaning, that words conceal even as they reveal, that language is the presence of an absence. When later we hear Criseyde tell him, "'I mene wel'" (5.1004), we can hardly avoid feeling crest-fallen and dismayed at the ominous reverberation. And when, finally, she writes to Troylus, "'Th'entente is al, and nat the lettres space'" (5.1630), we see, in all its ugly pettiness, the radical appropriation of instrument to self, such that the instrument no longer has any meaning apart from the self, empty of all communal value, perverted to a private intent – counterfeit: she is hardly Troylus's "frend" (5.1624). To mean not to mean is, the character of Diomede suggests, wicked; to mean well, the character of Criseyde suggests, is simply not enough; to mean the romance between two people, with all its rhetoric and metaphoricity, is, the character of Pandarus suggests, a dangerous presumption of superhuman authority; to mean truth, the character of Troylus suggests, is alone to be fully human – *what* one means as important as *how* one means. But, at the same time, to be fully human, the character of the Narrator suggests, is no guarantee of happiness, no warrant for peace, no deed for a home in this world.

Hence the cruel irony, from the Narrator's position, in Troylus's fate. Troylus is a pagan, whose highest god is an inadequate god, the god of philosophy and of philosophers. Consequently, as painful for the Narrator as his disillusion-ment with Criseyde is his regret for Troylus. Although Troylus apparently enjoys the "pleyn felicite / That is in hevene above" (5.1818–19), he does so at a cost of contempt for this world ("contemptus mundi") so exaggerated as to argue a failure of love *from a Christian position*.[22] And the Narrator's at this moment is a Christian position. The notorious difficulties with the end of the poem which all readers experience can in many, certainly not all, cases be re-solved by first recognizing that, at least in the fiction of the poem, a Christian translator is concluding a pagan and philosophical poem whose pagan and philosophical limits are all too clearly visible to him.[23] If the story which the Narrator translates is in the end a "tragedye" (5.1786), it is so because its pagan and philosophical vocabulary never transcends feigning (5.1848) to reach the truth of fiction.

Any one-sentence explanation of *Troylus and Criseyde*'s genre, such as I have just entered, is bound to distort the poem. But often we must distort, for a moment anyway, so as to see something which, under ordinary condi-tions, is invisible. The rest of what I have to say assumes that the ending of the *Troylus* is a case of such necessity.

The last six stanzas of the poem, I think we must assume, are a unit apart. They serve, I suggest, to articulate the Narrator's final position on the poem: he finishes his translation of the "Book of Lollius" at line 1827 – "Ther as Mercurye sorted him to dwelle" – and proceeds to speak in his own voice his own opinion. At this point the *Christian* translator assumes more importance than the Christian *translator*. His position, it is clear, is not an imposition on the story: he has so obviously separated these stanzas from the story that he is inviting us to take his position or leave it or, as some do, psychoanalyze it. Whatever we do, we know that we are now in the fourteenth century, where Gower and Strode are available for criticism of the work; that we are in the presence of a Christian, who to all appearances is a faithful one free of Pharisaism; and that, finally, we are listening to a personal voice unashamed of its own anxieties. These are the data with which to recover the theory of mediation which informs the Narrator's position. That theory, in turn, exposes the inadequacy of Troylus's philosophy and pagan aspirations since they lack precisely a theory of mediation – in particular, a theory which justifies the body as well as the spirit.

The terms of the theory are those Dantesque ones which we have already met in Book 4 (5.1835–48; emphasis added):

> O yonge, fresshe folkes, he or she,
> In which that love up groweth with youre age,
> Repeyreth hom fro worldly vanyte,
> And of youre herte up casteth *the visage*
> To thilke God that *after his ymage*
> Yow made, and thynketh al nys but a *faire*
> This world, that passeth soone as floures faire.
>
> And loveth hym, the which that right for love
> Upon a crois, oure soules for to *beye*,
> First starf, and roos, and sit in hevene above;
> For he nyl *falsen* no wight, *dar I seye*,
> That wol his herte al holly on hym leye.
> And syn he best to love is, and most meke,
> What nedeth *feynede* loves for to seke?

Here the Narrator, remembering the brief emergency of human love, repudiates the pandar's poetics of imposition and falsification. He calls the "yonge, fresshe folkes" away from the narcissism of the love which Pandarus "invents." Rather than see their reflections in such love, they should cast the faces of their hearts up toward the Image of God in which they are made.

They will then see their reflections, yes, but in a Mirror whose truth excludes all possibility of falsification. Hence, as in the case of Dante, so in
theirs: it is Narcissus who looks and must look into the Mirror, but it is not
Narcissus who sees himself. That the "yonge, fresshe folkes" can, in fact,
realize such reflection Chaucer further confirms by inflecting his exhortation
with a Dantesque emphasis on maturity: "In which that love up groweth with
youre age." As love grows with the age of the young, it will change, the text
intimates, toward a greater maturity; and that maturity will consist partly in
the recognition that, while each of us is a Narcissus, none of us ought or
needs to be a narcissist: the Narcissus in each of us seeks his image, but he is
not necessarily condemned to find his *own* image. On the contrary, if he casts
up the "visage" of his heart – and note well that Chaucer stresses the *face*,
"visage" – he will see his image but see that it is Other; and the *auctoritas* of
that Other certifies that the image is not a "vanyte" – not an emptiness as was
that of Narcissus (*Met.* 3.435, for example) – but rather "hom," the true and
abiding place of the heart. This it does because it is the *auctoritas* of the
greatest love there is, that of self-sacrifice, the opposite of narcissism. The
love of the Crucified Image does not "falsen" the image of any individual
human because He, Christ, already *owns* that image and, indeed, suffered
crucifixion to "beye" back or redeem it from the Devil.[24] Here emerges the
crucial importance of "faire" (5.1840) which, as Siegfried Wenzel amply
demonstrates (1976:150–51 nn. 42–46), must, in its primary sense, mean
"marketplace" – "and thynketh al nys but a marketplace / This world." The
young people should realize that in the marketplace of this world, where
everything is as evanescent as a flower, the negotiations of humankind inevitably involve falsification; and if they would spare themselves the pains of
this falsification, they must turn themselves to the One Merchant and the
One Moneyer who "nyl falsen no wight" because every "wight" is His. Why
should he falsify what He already owns?

Hence the logic of the exclamation, "What nedeth feynede loves for to
seke?" If one loves the Image of God first and foremost, one resigns oneself up
to Him. Owned by Him, one is free to be one's own authority in everything
else. "Love God and be your own authority" might be a fair paraphrase of
Chaucer's meaning. Become one's own authority, the love and the life one
then makes may be a fiction, but they need not be feigned. They need not, in
other words, be invented by some other authority – a Pandarus, for example – nor need they be invented from any prior code or set of rules, such as
fin'amors. Rather they may be made, in this event, after one's own image, the
Image of God, than which there is no greater Love (John 3.16). Then, unlike
the "tragedye" of the "feynede love" of Troylus and Criseyde, the fiction of

this love and this life can be a "comedye." Precisely where the Crucified and Resurrected Image is the source of Love, there can be no "tragedye," as Dante profoundly understood and as Chaucer with equal profundity but different style also understood. "Comedye," as *The Canterbury Tales* amply demonstrate, is the highest fiction because it embodies the highest truth of fiction, or Life, even life after death.

We see now that Chaucer's theory of mediation, which informs the Narrator's position on the book which he has just translated, assumes that there is only one Means which is also Its own End. This assumption Chaucer shares with Dante. This medium, the Verbum, will falsify no one because He is Alpha and Omega, Origin and Closure—the one Means that cannot be consumed by or for the End. Without Him the Narcissus in each man can only degenerate into narcissism, or the frantic and doomed search for the image of the self in *mortalia* and *visibilia*. But Troylus and Criseyde are precisely without Him. Instead of His mediation, they have only Pandarus—"'swich a meene / As maken wommen unto men to comen'" (3.254–55). To be sure, once he has brought them together, they find *in between them* a *meaning* which exceeds his *auctoritas* so far that he cannot understand it. But that meaning is immanent, condemned to presence, inseparable from the body and from the body's relentless metaphoricity (substitution), so much so that when Criseyde's body is translated from Trojan into Greek her "'name of trouthe / Is now fordon'" (5.1686–87), and she and Troylus lose the meaning which was between them. Everything is lost in translation. Without a Mediator and a theory of mediation that can redeem mutability and change—the body, in short—Troylus and Criseyde can invest their meaning only in what is bound to fail them—the body; without a permanent Image and an Image of Permanence, they impress their images upon impermanence with the inevitable results of loss and death. The Narrator does not condemn Troylus and Criseyde—he is far less damning than Troylus, in fact (see 5.1823)—he condemns rather "feynede loves," founded on and invented from the void and uncertainty. The Narrator finally pities Troylus and Criseyde: they looked to the human for what the human cannot give. Moreover, they had nowhere else to look.

Troylus fell in love—with a passion perhaps better reserved for God if also undeniably rooted in the flesh. He fell in love with an extraordinary and a beautiful woman and in effect proceeded to forget that she was a woman, stamping upon her the image of his deity, or love. But Criseyde cannot be the sign or the coin, the medium, for Troylus's idealizing passion because she is only Alpha and not also Omega: "But natheles, / Right as oure firste lettre is now an A, / In beaute first so stood she, makeles" (1.170–72). Criseyde is only Alpha and not also Omega because she is mortal and mutable – note well that Chaucer impressively insists on mutability with the temporal emphasis "Right as oure first lettre is *now* an A" – and she is therefore unable to bear such an imprint, unable to be so engraved and live. At most, she could be the image which "renders the promise whole"; but rather than spend her for the Good, Troylus enjoys her as the Good; and with that "mondiglia" of *as*, that addition of personal desire with no respect to that to which it was added, he falsifies Criseyde – feigns her as something she is not, renders her "irreferent" – with the all-too-predictable result that she "falses" him, betrays him when Diomede's touch restores her original character of fear and "slydynge corage." Falsifying Criseyde as the Good, Troylus condemns himself to being left with only the goods. And like all other goods, when Criseyde changes hands, she changes (compare 5.1634: "kalendes of chaunge" and 5.1683: "'that ye, Criseyde, koude han chaunged so'"). No *visibilia*, no "fiore" (flower or coin) is exempt from change; thus it can be trusted only to mediate the Good, never *to be* the Good. If someone trusts it to be the Good, his fate will be that of Troylus. When Criseyde changes, although he still loves her (5.1696–1701), Troylus has so far lost the "newe qualite," that he can only cry, "'From hennesforth, as ferforth as I may, / Myn owen deth in armes wol I seche'" (5.1717–18). Unable to exchange Criseyde for the "newe qualite," unable to own it through her, and this because he has no faith in such transactions, bound as he is in the immanence of the body, when he loses her, he loses it. Instead of spending, Troylus hoarded; and hoarded wealth, as the medieval horror of it suggests, is tainted with death (*Roman de la Rose* 195–234).

Troylus's error – almost it is not an error, but only almost – is the more comprehensible beside the Narrator's recognition and avoidance of it in the stanzas in which he sends his "litel bok" off. Troylus hoards Criseyde: having imposed his meaning on her, he cannot imagine letting her go; she is his money. And since she will not run away with him, he necessarily must risk her running away from him. It is proper to money to circulate, and if Troylus treats Criseyde as if she were money, he must expect her to behave as if she were money. Either she can be the End – a *fin'amors* goddess to be worshiped from afar – or she can be a means – a woman to satisfy Troylus's sexual yearnings; but, the human condition what it is, she cannot be both. "'Love has pitched his mansion / In the place of excrement / For nothing can be sole or whole / That has not been rent.'"[25] Marriage, which usually heals the rent, never really was a possibility for Troylus and Criseyde, and Troylus only deceives himself when he expects Criseyde to behave as if she were a wife.[26] If they had entered public space as husband and wife, the very publicity of their vow would have taken Criseyde out of circulation. But Priam's will as well as *fin'amors* precluded this possibility; then, too, Criseyde simply did not want to run away with Troylus and live as his wife; and so, necessarily, she remains in circulation—potentially money for someone else to spend.[27] Moreover, Troylus, we know, treats Criseyde not only as if she were a coin but also as if she were a sign. And it is as proper to a sign to circulate as it is to a coin—indeed, even more so, since signs cannot communicate if they are not shared in common.[28] Hence the Narrator, worker in signs, under at least equal compulsion, confronts the same problem that Troylus confronts. His relation to his text is analogous to that of Troylus to Criseyde: if he hoards it, he will falsify it; and so he lets it go (5.1779–98; emphasis added):

> N'y sey nat this al oonly for thise men,
> But moost for wommen that bitraised be
> Thorugh false folk; God yeve hem sorwe, amen!
> That *with hire grete wit and subtilte*
> Bytraise yow! And this commeveth me
> To speke, and in effect *yow alle I preye,*
> *Beth war of men, and herkneth what I seye!* —
>
> *Go, litel bok, go,* litel myn tragedye,
> Ther God thi makere yet, er that he dye,
> So sende mygt to make in som comedye!
> But litel book, no makyng thow n'envie,
> But subgit be to alle poesye,
> And kis the steppes, where as thow seest pace
> Virgile, Ovide, Omer, Lucan, and Stace.
>
> And for ther is so gret diversite
> In Englissh and in writyng of oure tonge,
> So prey I God that *non myswrite the,*
> *Ne the mysmetre for defaute of tonge.*
> And red wherso thow be, or elles songe,
> *That thow be understonde, God I biseche!*

The logic of the first two of these three stanzas is subtle but powerful. The Narrator sends the book off at just that moment in the text when he can intimate a similarity between women and books, that they are both subject to betrayal by "false folk" and "hire grete wit and subtilte." This intimation confirms what and how much the Narrator has learned about mediation from the story which he has translated. "Grete wit and subtilte" can falsify any and all media and will do so most assuredly when they preclude circulation of media by the imposition of their radically private will on them. "False folk" are folk who seek each his own private meaning to the exclusion of all other meanings: while the false coin is circulating, they are rubbing their hands over the gold in their coffers. In this sense Troylus, although he is almost innocent compared to Pandarus or Diomede, is nonetheless a falsifier because he sought his meaning in Criseyde to the exclusion of her very humanity: he did not know that she was "slydynge of corage" precisely because he did not know *her* very well at all; or, and this would be worse, if he did know this, or suspect it, then he ignored it, thus ignoring *her*, in favor of his own ideal figment of her.

And in just the same way as Troylus falsified Criseyde, the Narrator could falsify his book, betray it, by rendering it "irreferent," or falsely identical with its original. Just as Troylus, assuming that the *fin'amors* ideal fixed in his mind is her original, reduces Criseyde to identity with that "original," so the Narrator could assume that his conception of the Book of Lollius is the original and so reduce his translation to identity with it. He could claim that his translation is *the* version (already an oxymoron) and not just *a* version (however authoritative). He could add his desire for originality to the original—it would then be "mondiglia"—and thus falsify the original. The Narrator has already recognized this desire and its cruel consequences in Troylus's hapless realization that he has, in brute and brutal fact, become an original authority: "'O blisful lord Cupide, / Whan I the proces have in my memorie, / How thow me hast wereyed on every syde, / *Men myght a book make of it, lik a storie*'" (5.582–85; emphasis added). Troylus's desire for an ideal love, his desire that his be the "original" of loves, has realized itself in the only space possible, that of a book. The ideal can be spoken or written; it cannot be lived, as Troylus learns to his sorrow. Troylus has reduced his life to the contours and the limits of a fiction, a fiction which is regrettably feigned. And little wonder he rides out to kill or be killed: the meaning in his life is gone, the meaning of his life is finished—the book is written, and there is no more to say. The Narrator, on the other hand, can see the limits of fiction, and especially of fiction that is feigned, and opts for life instead. Rather than demand that the Book of Lollius cede its priority to his translation, he delivers up his translation to the original. Rather than hoard the original in the form of his book, he sends his book off, lets it go, and lets it go as *his*. The way to be original is not to be *the* original; be instead a version. Every version of the Image of God—every person, that is—is absolutely original; and the one creature who desired to be original by being *the* original succeeded, of course, only in damning himself (Lucifer). If you are going to be your own authority, love your original; proclaim that you are (*O felix paradoxa!*) a unique copy.

This the Narrator does when he sends the book off. Scholarship has long recognized that the "Go, litel bok" stanza fairly rocks with ambiguities. "Ther

God thi makere" is perhaps the most arresting one (Middleton 1980:55–56, especially n. 27). The "bank shot" (Kaske 1963:179), though, by which the Narrator suggests that his work belongs in the company of the great epic poets runs a close second (Donaldson 1972:95–96). The point of the ambiguities, however, is that they are part of the Narrator's *personal signature*. Like the adjective "litel," like the label "myn tragedye," like the desire for "myght to make in som comedye," these ambiguities serve to insist on the Narrator, his presence, and the hand of his instrumentality. But his signature is *not* an imposition, not a "mondiglia," not a metallic additive, not anything that hides or is to be hidden. Quite the contrary, a signature is a public testimony of responsibility, a public avowal of authorship. A signature is personal and manifestly *personal in* and *to the public*. The "Go, litel book" stanza, which serves in its position to suggest that books can suffer the same fate as women, also serves as the Narrator's acceptance of responsibility for his translation; and it does so first and foremost by insisting that the translation is his. This is not the original – it is not Virgile, Ovide, Omer, Lucan, or Stace – it is rather a copy, though a copy worthy, perhaps, to join their company.

If this stanza is the Narrator's signature, a mark of his personal relation to his book, the stanza that follows, in its first part, is a prayer that his signature not be effaced. This is not the original; this is the Narrator's version of the original; if it is to be judged, good or bad, then it must be judged *as* his version. Scribal error, then, would be catastrophic. Scribal error would be an addition of the personal to the book – an addition of the scribe's dialect, his personal accent – which would be immediately hidden: if the scribe writes "him" instead of "hem," then, in the absence (all too likely) of a holograph, "him" ("him") it remains forever (instead of "them"); and the text is falsified, though inadvertently and unintentionally.[29] The scribe, unlike the Narrator, does not expose his personal additions to the text because they are mistakes, errors, oversights. The Narrator *does* expose his additions in order that they *not* be mistakes. All the more reason, then, to see exactly what he wrote. If the text is not pure, then the Narrator's book cannot be judged. The graph must be fixed in order for the sign to be free (cf. Derrida 1976:34–37).

If the graph is fixed and the sign free, then the second petition of the Narrator's prayer can be realized: "And red wherso thow be, or elles songe, / That thow be understonde, God I biseche!" (5.1797–98). Liberated by the Narrator and, if not falsified by the scribe(s), whole and legible, the book can be read or sung – that is, entered into public space where its contents, the story which the Narrator has translated plus his position on that story, can be open to the process of understanding. That process, as the Narrator (and

we) have learned from his experience in translating, is arbitrary, random, for-
tuitous, selfish, and difficult. Understanding is rarely a once-and-for-all conclusion; it is much more frequently a groping toward a position which itself,
given the contingency and brevity of *mortalia*, must be resignable on short
notice. The Narrator's own position, in fact, is subject to circumscription by a
more inclusive one—indeed, an all-inclusive One, that of the "Uncircumscript" (5.1865). The Narrator's prayer, therefore, arises from his anxiety
about the very process of understanding; if he could assume that understanding would come naturally to all readers, he would feel the less compelled to
pray for it. Knowing that it will not, he intercedes with God for his book. He
also knows, even as he makes this intercession, that, if and when the book is
understood, what will be understood, in part, is the process of understanding
itself, or the increasingly self-conscious assumption of a position always
resignable because contingent upon mutable signs—signs fraught with
temporality.

Troylus, however—this, his tragedy—imagined that he could escape time
(and for a while, as he perceived it, perhaps he did) even as he was becoming
more and more bound in and by it (cf. Barney 1972: 445–58). He imagined an
absolute and unchanging love invented, however, by a very changeable
authority from equally changeable matter. He referred Criseyde to this imagined ideal, presuming that he had in that action found and founded truth
(both verity and loyalty).[30] He did not, nor probably could he, appreciate that
to refer is also to defer and that the very act of reference is thus grounded in
time (cf. Derrida 1967:302; trans. Bass 1978:203). To extend and modify the
coinage imagery: he invested everything in Criseyde's currency, unfor-
tunately innocent of the fact that currency "runs"—it changes.[31] Having made
this investment and in such innocence, Troylus would not exchange Criseyde
for any truth—he would not resign her in light of reality—rather he clung to
her body, the visible and receptive matter of his stamp. He could not imagine
any such exchange between *visibilia* and *invisibilia*, nor could he imagine any
such resignation of *visibilia* to *invisibilia*. He could not imagine such exchange
or resignation because he had no faith in such transactions. He had no faith in
such transactions because he had no faith. Troylus had no viable posture
toward the invisible. Troylus had only *fin'amors* and philosophy. And, to be
sure, while the constructs of reason are superior to a pseudo-religion, neither
in fact is adequate to human happiness which thirsts for, cries out for, truth.
Neither *fin'amors* nor philosophy can transcend feigning to reach the truth
which fiction knows because they have no adequate theory of mediation—such a theory as the Narrator posits when he takes his position on the
poem at the end. Vance (1979:293–337) has written persuasively of the in-

adequacy of *fin'amors* to the happiness of Troylus and Criseyde. I would like to complement his remarks by discussing the last appearance of pagan philosophy in the poem, in the three stanzas narrating Troylus's translation to Heaven (5.1807–27). Outstanding about these stanzas is the fact that no idea, sentiment, or statement in them is necessarily Christian. Everything in them could be found in some pagan source or *florilegia* of pagan sources.[32] To be sure, Chaucer used Christian sources—Dante, for one obvious example (*Par.* 22.151 at 5.1815)—but, even so, he writes nothing in these three stanzas that *must* be read as Christian. And this fact is crucial. These stanzas conclude the pagan original which the Narrator is translating, and they represent the highest or sublimest vision which pagan *auctoritas* can reach. That vision is indeed sublime, but note how much it depends on despising and on condemnation: "and fully gan despise / This wrecched world," for example (5.1816–17). In contrast, the Narrator urges the "yonge, fresshe folkes" to think that "al nys but a faire / This world, that passeth soone as floures faire" (5.1840–41). This sentiment, though obviously contemptuous of the world, is a good deal softer and calmer than Troylus's—he "dampned al oure werk that foloweth so / The blynde lust" (5.1823–24). Note also that where Troylus "lough" (5.1821) Dante only smiles (*Par.* 22.135).[33] Finally, all the claims of Troylus's felicity and bliss are slightly, if only slightly, embarrassed by the silence about *where* "Mercurye sorted hym to dwelle" (5.1827). In short, Troylus's Heaven, though Heaven, is not necessarily the happiest of all possible heavens. The Narrator (and we) have good reason to doubt the value of this sublime, even as we recognize that it *is* a sublime.

And just such doubt goads the Narrator in stanzas 1 and 4 of *his* conclusion to the story. In these stanzas, because of his doubt, the Narrator does contemn and he does reject, but he does not reject love or life or even this world (flowers, after all, *are* fair); rather, he rejects a false sublimity and a severely restricted form of speech ("the forme of olde clerkis speche / In poetrie"; 5.1854–55). The former, false sublimity, he never bothers with again; the latter, of course, he transcends in *The Canterbury Tales.* In short, these stanzas tell us why Chaucer turned to the "comedye" which proved to be the major work of his life.

The first five lines of the first stanza express the Narrator's dismay at the "fyn" of the original text (5.1828–32):

> Swich fyn hath, lo, this Troylus for love!
> Swich fyn hath al his grete worthynesse!
> Swich fyn hath his estat real above,
> Swich fyn his lust, swich fyn hath his noblesse!
> Swich fyn hath false worldes brotelnesse!

Most significant about these lines is their reduction of "love," "worthynesse," "estat real," "lust," "noblesse," and "false worldes brotelnesse" to the one "fyn." "Love" and "worthynesse," etc., all come to the same "fyn" as "false worldes brotelnesse," and this suggests not that "love" and "worthynesse," etc., are wicked or disgusting but that and only that they are equal to or bound within the "brotelnesse" of the false world. The "brotelnesse" of the false world is under attack – it has the culminating line – and not the other qualities or experiences. The Narrator does not reject anything here; he laments that in the pagan sublime such qualities and experiences are so radically world-bound. The pagan sublime, which includes *fin'amors* and philosophy and epic grandeur (in Chaucer's conception), cannot imagine transcendence of the *false* world and its "brotelnesse." If the world is false, its falsity is its "frangibility" ("brotelnesse"; Davis 1979:19) – its mutability and insecurity. Nothing remains true to its name (5.1686); everything is "slydynge of corage." Philosophy can imagine the enduring identity of the name (Platonism), but it cannot redeem or forgive or recover the flesh and the things of the world that necessarily change under the name. Only a theory of mediation that finds meaning in decay, decline, and death can transcend the falsity of the world because, in addition to imagining the enduring identity of the name, it also imagines the perfection and glorification of the body through change – decay, decline, and death. When Chaucer translates *Paradiso* 14, 28–30, in the very last stanza of the poem, as the opening to his prayer to the Trinity (5.1863–65), he is also quoting that section of the *Paradiso* in which Solomon explains to Dante how the bodies of the blessed will return to them in the day of judgment (*Par.* 14.37–60). Thus he supplies what the pagan sublime lacks: a sense of the body's change as part of the Good, not inimical to the Good. Philosophy's posture is to revile the body; *fin'amors'*, to idealize it; the epic's, to politicize it (especially in Virgil). Chaucer's Christian, comic poetics, on the other hand, imagines the body as one more good of God's plenty – to be referred, therefore, to Him, and if referred to Him, then to be enjoyed in the fiction of one's life and love. Without this reference, however, the world will prove false because the body cannot endure its "brotelnesse": the body will *break*. Without this reference men and women will impose upon the body or add to it what it cannot bear – be it desire or "Daunger" or a "newe qualite" or what have you. But a theory of mediation, such as that embraced by Chaucer's Christian, comic poetics, which does refer the body to God, will always detect and expose any attempt to impose on the body a meaning it cannot bear. Such a theory is intolerant of falsification and feigning: in its view – in a work, that is, obeying such a poetics – the coining of Criseyde would (and does) appear as the coining of "Alisoun fra biside Bath" where no *fin'amors* idealism obscures the basic narcissism and commercialism of the coiners—namely, men in general and her husbands in particular. Without such a theory, the pagan sublime sees the body as both a necessity for and an impediment to the expression of meaning—a necessity because without it there is no communication of any sort; an impediment because its changeableness is unpredictable and threatening. The Stoic, for example, must have the body to practice his heroism, but he practices his heroism against the body's weakness. The pagan sublime, as a consequence of its blurred understanding of the body, imposes on the body meanings which can only exacerbate its already frangible "brotelnesse." Human beings were not meant to be Stoics (or Epicureans, for that matter). Unable to refer the body beyond the world, the pagan sublime, which can refer only the soul beyond the world,[34] submits the body to the world, with the result that all the goods of the body—love, worthiness, royal estate, lust, pleasure, and nobility, for examples—have the same "fyn" as "false worldes brotelnesse." The pagan sublime cannot transcend falsity because it cannot imagine a Permanent Image or an Image of Permanence which circumscribes and protects the body from falsification.

If Troylus and Criseyde, with Pandarus's complicity, look to the human for what the human cannot give, it is because they cannot imagine the transhuman. The Love which Troylus hymns in 3.1254–74 has no transhuman body (the Resurrected Christ), and consequently its images reduce to violence—for example: "'And if that Love aught lete his bridel go, / Al that now loveth asondre sholde lepe, / And lost were al that Love halt now tohepe'" (3.1762–64). Little matter that the same idea is found in Boethius or Dante (*De cons.* 2, m. 8; *Par.* 33.85–87). Of greater moment by far is the fact that they, unlike Troylus, *also* know this Love as a *personal* God, Jesus the Christ. For Troylus this Love is only gravity—worship it and receive silence in reply; defy it and die. This Love does not transhumanize; it does not redeem the time.

The concluding couplet, "And thus bigan his lovyng of Criseyde, / As I have told, and in this wise he deyde" (5.1833–34), follows naturally, without disjunction, upon the preceding five lines. It emphasizes the limits of the story, beginning and end, which the Narrator has translated. If "swich" is the "fyn" of Troylus's love, it began thus as the Narrator has told and he died in this wise. "In this wise he deyde" is by far the most important part of the couplet: in *this* and no other wise Troylus died. There are, that is to say, other ways to die and, by implication, other ways to love. If the Narrator is sad, and I believe he is, it is because there are other, better ways which, lamentably, Troylus and Criseyde did not know. And thus he proceeds, naturally and compellingly, in the following stanzas addressed to the "yonge, fresshe folkes," to name the origin of these better ways—God. The coherence of the first three stanzas of the Narrator's conclusion is palpable and inspiring.

As much can be said for the coherence of the last three stanzas of his conclusion, though here the issues are even more complex than in the first three. Stanza 4 itself presents the severest problems (5.1849–55):

> Lo here, of payens corsed olde rites,
> Lo here, what alle hire goddes may availle;
> Lo here, thise wrecched worldes appetites;
> Lo here, the fyn and guerdoun for travaille
> Of Jove, Appollo, of Mars, of swich rascaille!
> Lo here, the forme of olde clerkis speche
> In poetrie, if ye hire bokes seche.

More than one critic has come to grief over these lines, I know, and I have no special formula against a similar fate; but I do think I can contribute some helpful observations on some of the problems involved. And, first of all, note that four of the seven lines (the first two and the fourth and the fifth) directly attack paganism and especially the pagan gods. While the pagan gods and pagan rites have certainly played a role in the story, that role does not seem so important, upon reflection, as to merit such a formidable attack. If we want to make sense of the stanza, then, I feel we must account for the apparent imbalance which it expresses.

This we can do by first interpreting the concluding couplet, certainly the most vexed part of the stanza. Most arresting in the couplet is the mention of two orders of discourse, "speche" and "poetrie." "Speche" and "poetrie" are discontinuous: the one must be cast in the other; the one is a stylization of the other. Although many distinctions among kinds can be made within the broad category of "poetrie," I think that the distinction between speech and poetry is sufficiently basic as to arouse no quarrel. Because "speche" and "poetrie" are discontinuous, there are at least two ways of reading "Lo here, the forme of olde clerkis speche / In poetrie": either "this is how old clerks spoke in poetry when they were speaking in poetry"; or "here is the speech of old clerks cast in poetry." The former reading would refer the phrase to the whole poem with the consequence that the phrase would contemn the whole poem. The latter reading, on the other hand, would suggest that somewhere is a piece of speech which has just been cast in poetry. In either reading, "forme" retains the meaning of "substance" or "informing principle": the matter of "olde clerkis speche"—the original version, that is—necessarily cannot be "here" because here the matter is Englished, converted into the Narrator's own mother tongue.[35]

Now the latter reading would conveniently eliminate the problem of contempt of the whole poem, and do so without asserting that the couplet means the opposite of what it says. However, the question remains: What is the "forme of olde clerkis speche" just cast "in poetrie"? The answer, I think, is not far to seek. It is the pagan and philosophical sublime which translates Troylus to Heaven; and thus, the piece of speech, of which this sublime is the "forme" or substance, consists in the three stanzas which narrate that translation. The text then says, I am suggesting, "Lo, here, cast into modern (i.e., fourteenth-century) English poetry, is the substance of the way old clerks, such as Cicero or Seneca or Macrobius, spoke about the reward in heaven for pious pagan souls." In this reading, and to its credit, "olde clerkis" has a specific referent; "Lo here" points in a specific direction and to a recent utterance; "speche" and "poetrie" remain separate orders of discourse, as in fact they are; and, finally, the phrase "if ye hire bokes seche," which has about it already the scholar's punctiliousness, follows naturally from what precedes it—if you go to the pagan philosophers on this subject, such is the form of speech you will find.

This reading of the couplet possesses an attractive economy. In addition to eliminating the problem of contempt of the whole poem, it also goes far toward accounting for those four lines in contempt of paganism and the pagan gods. In this reading of the concluding couplet, those lines would suggest, with understandable sarcasm, that Troylus's translation to Heaven is the most the righteous pagan receives for his piety toward the gods: "Lo here, the fyn and *guerdoun* for travaille / Of Jove, Appollo, of Mars, of swich rascaille" (emphasis added). The Narrator's contempt, then, would be contempt only for paganism and the pagan gods—understandable, in the case of one who is a confessed Christian (5.1845; and note the "dar I seye").

This reading, of course, has so far omitted the third line of the stanza: "Lo here, thise wrecched worldes appetites." This line is obviously more sweeping in its reference; it obviously points with a gesture of anger as well as contempt. But two observations can and should be made. First, the "appetites" are "wrecched" and not the world itself; since it would be folly to reduce the world to one of its contents (however awfully powerful that one might be), the phrase does leave open the possibility that there is something in the world not "wrecched." Second, and to my mind more important, is the word "wrecched" itself: we should not, I feel, forget that in addition to "despicable" it also means "pitiable" (Davis 1979:176). I doubt that Chaucer forgot it, and if I cannot name the referent of this line, I do not, at the same time, feel that it is "irreferent."

The last two stanzas of the conclusion form a unit to themselves (5.1856–70):

> O moral Gower, this book I directe
> To the and to the, philosophical Strode,
> To vouchen sauf, there nede is, to correcte,
> Of youre benignites and zeles goode.
> And to that sothefast Crist, that starf on rode,
> With al myn herte of mercy evere I preye,
> And to the Lord right thus I speke and seye:
>
> Thow oon, and two, and thre, eterne on lyve,
> That regnest ay in thre, and two, and oon,
> Uncircumscript, and al maist circumscrive,
> Us from visible and invisible foon
> Defende, and to thy mercy, everichon,
> So make us, Jesus, for thi mercy digne,
> For love of mayde and moder thyn benigne
>   Amen.

Once again the Narrator invites correction of his book, this time, however, from a different audience. As a result of confronting and purging the narcissist in himself, the Narrator has discovered the moral and philosophical implica-tions of his "tragedye"; and he turns to the audiences who can best judge of those implications.[36] Gower and Strode he invites to *consent* where there is need to correct: "vouchen sauf" is a curious locution since it implies consulta-tion and agreement but also a taking responsibility for (Davis 1979:165). If they consult together or with the Narrator or both, they also vouch with him for the corrections which they enter and for the text which they thus pro-duce. Hence the Narrator affirms and even underscores the communal and perhaps covenantal nature of understanding and textual production and of understanding as textual production. Understanding is not singular, nor is it final; rather, it is plural (political, in the profoundest sense of the word), posi-tional, and ideally seminal.[37] Beyond understanding, however, is mercy; and the Narrator finally leaves behind morality and philosophy to seek that mercy.

He turns to Christ, the Image of God, and specifically to Jesus the man, born of Mary the maiden. He turns to the divine but—and here Donaldson is profoundly right (1972:100–101)—only in such a way as to affirm the human. The Mother of God was a human woman also, like Criseyde, and in Mary all

156

women are redeemed. Moreover, no one comes to the Father except by the Son (John 6.35–59). In addition, the Narrator prays for protection from visible and invisible foes. The relevance of this petition at first seems obscure until we recognize, with Dante's help, that Troylus had no viable posture toward the invisible—he had no faith. Without faith Troylus had no defense against the invisible foes of pride and idolatry and—formidable foe, indeed—the vanity of idealism. The Christian, however, does have faith and faith in precisely protection from such foes—against which no man, as man, is proof.

Finally, the Narrator begins his prayer with an address to the supreme paradox of Christianity, or the Trinity—an address which is a translation from Dante (*Par.* 14.28–30). This translation at this moment affirms, every bit as much as the peititon to Jesus the man, the Narrator's and our humanity. For, to address the divine Authority, the Narrator goes to and through another *human* authority, or Dante, who is neither more nor less fallible than he is himself; and thus he historicizes and humanizes his own authority—inserts it into the seminality of history, the ongoing interpretative labor which inscribes man in time and the world, which marks him as man. Even in a moment of prayer and "sincerity," the Narrator's authority and the position it assumes are derivative, belated, secondary—very human, in short—but wholly free of anxiety. The Narrator's position is itself in part a version of someone else and of someone else's. Hence the absence of anxiety—in the very assumption and display of the human condition of derivativeness (creatureliness). Roles remain. Humans have only roles—faith being the ultimate and most difficult role to play. And playing that role, the Narrator is content with the role of translator, even here in his personal prayer. That role, his faith has helped him see, is the role which most becomes the human author since it is farthest from usurping the Authority of God. God is "uncircumscript and al maist circumscrive"; a translator, however, is "circumscript"—by his original—and his only hope is to break the circle of writing and thus break out of the circle of writing to a position, not the only position, from which to see the point which encircles all the circles. And so Chaucer did, with Dante's help, in the *Troylus.*

PART THREE

The *Canterbury Tales*
and the
Ethics of Reference

Value is the quality a thing can never possess in privacy
but acquires automatically the moment it appears in public.
(Hannah Arendt)

A poem does not come into existence by accident. The
words of a poem, as Professor Stoll has remarked, come out
of a head, not out of a hat. Yet to insist on the designing intellect as a *cause* of a poem is not to grant the design or intention as a *standard* by which the critic is to judge the
worth of the poet's performance.
(William K. Wimsatt, Jr., and Monroe C. Beardsley)

So far as rewards and punishments are concerned—and
they are a great concern in tragedy—distributive justice, to
each according to his desert, is a weak dramatic form, a con-
cession to the audience. It appears in comedy.
(William K. Wimsatt, Jr.)

The juxtaposition of tales to each other and to the dramatic
frame of the pilgrimage is the largest counter of Chaucer's
style. It is the largest manifestation of what we can see in
The Canterbury Tales from the mixed idiom up: Chaucer's
endless interest in comparisons and relationships.
(Charles Muscatine)

A poet is called a "fictor" or "formator" because for true
things he says false things or at least he from time to time
mixes true things with false.
(Conrad of Hirsau)

Chapter 10
Introduction: Fragment A
and the Versions of the Household

T THE END of the *Prologue* to *The Miller's Tale*, Chaucer addresses his audience in the voice which he discovered in the process of translating *Troylus and Criseyde* (MilP A 3167–86; emphasis added):

> What sholde I moore seyn, but this Millere
> He nolde his wordes for no man forbere,
> But tolde his cherles tale *in his manere.*
> M'athynketh that I shal reherce it heere.
> And therfore every gentil wight I preye,
> For Goddes love, *demeth nat that I seye*
> *Of yvel entente,* but for I moot reherce
> Hir tales alle, be they bettre or werse,
> Or elles *falsen* som of my mateere.
> And therfore, whoso list it nat yheere,
> *Turne over the leef and chese another tale;*
> For he shal fynde ynowe, grete and smale,
> Of *storial thyng* that toucheth *gentillesse,*
> And eek *moralitee* and *hoolynesse.*
> *Blameth nat me if that ye chese amys.*
> The Millere is a cherl, ye knowe wel this;
> So was the Reve eek and othere mo,
> And harlotrie they tolden bothe two.
> Avyseth yow, and put me out of blame;
> And eek men shal nat maken ernest of game.

Here Chaucer successfully applies the theory of mediation which he arrived at in the *Troylus*. And the Dantesque elements of the theory are relevant building blocks. Chaucer is going to make a copy of original "mateere." The "mateere" in this case is that of the Miller. The Miller, Chaucer is quick to point out, has his own position, too, his "manere" as well as his "mateere," that of a "cherl," and Chaucer must respect that position, "reherce" that "manere" as well as the "mateere." But his copy, while faithful to the original, must *not* be identical with it. His copy must be a copy in order to posit the illusion of an original and thus the illusion of a Miller in all his distinctive individuality. If there is to be a Miller, he must be copied. If Chaucer does not *copy* the Miller, thus negating possible identification of himself with his character, there will be no (illusion of a) Miller, only a *false* image of a Miller. He must copy the Miller to put the Miller "off there" where distance helps generate the illusion of reality. To bring Dante to bear directly on the text: if Chaucer *subtracts from* and then *adds to* his "mateere" (like a Master Adam), he will reduce "mateere" and "manere" to identity with his own version of them, and he will render them thus "irreferent," counterfeit, false. He will—and the word is big with significance for *The Canterbury Tales*—*falsen* his "mateere" if he does not copy it as faithfully as possible. But this means he must insist *on the copy* as much as on the fidelity. If he is copying and not masking the fact that he is copying, then the likelihood is greater than it would otherwise be that he is not falsifying. The fact of copying is as important to the illusion as the fidelity of the copy. Now, at the same time, it is true—and this truth is important to Chaucer's poetics—that, even as he insists on the copy and its fidelity, he *censors* the Miller, every bit as much as the Narrator in Book 3 of *Troylus and Criseyde* censors the play of Pandarus with Criseyde after Troylus's departure from the "stewe" (lines 1576–82). For Chaucer to inform us that he "moot reherce / Hir tales alle... / Or elles falsen som of [his] mateere," is also to inform us, inevitably, that the Miller's "tale" is a "cherles"; and that is, without question, to censor. However, it is to censor without subsequent ban. Moreover—and this is essential Chaucer—it is to censor in such a way as *to enlist* the censorship *in support of* (the illusion of) the reality of the Miller. In other words, by following Dante's lead and insisting on himself as mediator of what his audience reads, Chaucer has it both ways: he censors the Miller and tells us in the process exactly what kind of tale and language we are about to read, while at the same time and in just this way, he insists on the autonomy, the independence, and the reality of the Miller as character and free agent—one does not censor a mannequin. And all this he achieves, first and foremost, by *intruding* into the text *to tell us* "I moot reherce / Hir tales alle." His very visibility in the text is a guarantee that he is not a Master Adam or a Pandarus forging a false image, in this case, of a Miller. His very subjectivity—the emphasis on "I" and "me" (lines 3167, 3170–73, 3175, 3181, 3185)—generates the true image of a Miller, wholly other (in the illusion) than the signs which refer to him.[1] Chaucer's very mediation or instrumentality posits a personality. Although every pilgrim is Chaucer's version of or position on that pilgrim, his theory of mediation enables him to discount the narcissism of his instrumentality, thus to posit, precisely through the dialectic with his position, the (illusion of the) reality of each pilgrim and his or her position.[2] Every time Chaucer speaks, our position changes—we have to take our bearings again. And by keeping us on the move, he keeps us moved. Finally, there is only Chaucer, only writing his text (Leicester 1980:220–21). There is no naïve Narrator; there are not three Chaucers (cf. Donaldson 1972:1–12). There is only the one, extraordinarily sophisticated Chaucer—so self-conscious of his poses that he will never falsify his text. For six centuries now we have believed in his character(s).

Chaucer's position, so clearly visible if often difficult to construe,[3] prevents his imposition upon the Miller. His own position, moreover, opposes not only the Miller's ("M'athynketh that I shal reherce it heere") but also that of "every gentil wight." The "gentils" such as those who so unanimously approved of The Knight's Tale (A 3113) have their position, their "manere," their version of the truth, too; and Chaucer's differs from, is op-posed to, that position, again in order for him to posit the illusion of reality. When Chaucer enters his anti-Pandaric plea—"demeth nat that I seye / Of yvel entente"—he is establishing the (illusion of the) reality of the "gentils"—not only those who are on the pilgrimage with him but also those who are (in the fiction) in the audience which he is this moment addressing. When Chaucer takes his position, he adopts the pose of one who finds drunken millers slightly abhorrent and certainly churlish in their manners, though fascinating in their vitality, and this is also the pose of one who defers to "gentils." The net result of his pose is to compel his audience to declare their own positions by the choices which they make.[4] If the audience choose not to hear a "cherles tale," then they may "turne over the leef and chese another tale." But this choice makes them responsible for what they read. Indeed, reading ("legenda") always carries with it the responsibility of choice ("legenda").[5] To read is to choose, and it is to choose necessarily versions of the truth, such as "gentillesse" or "moralitee" or "hoolynesse" or "harlotrie." All these versions of the truth have each its legitimacy but, at the same time, each its limitations, too. Indeed, truth is inversely proportional to the limitedness of the given version of it—almost that is an epigraph, if a bit clumsy, for The Canterbury Tales. And if the audience choose their truth "amys" (although it may well be the truth about them), they cannot blame Chaucer since he only rehearses the numerous versions or positions. His pose is necessarily a "game," a play or a fiction,[6] since only in fiction can he copy a Miller or anyone else and remain himself, not falsified nor falsifying. "And men shal nat maken ernest of game" by imposing their versions of reality or of truth on a poet's fictional positions, his poses in "game." In the *Prologue* to *The Cook's Tale* Herry Bailly is right that "'a man may seye ful sooth in game and pley'" (*CkP* A 4355), but Hogge of Ware is also right, and perhaps nearer to Chaucer's own position, when he rejoins, ""'sooth pley, quaad pley," as the Flemyng seith'" (line 4357). If a "true joke" (one could almost say, "earnest joke") is a "bad joke" (Davis 1979:110), so is a true fiction, already a monstrous hybrid, a bad fiction because it is a false or "ir-referent" fiction. I am here extending (I hope not stretching) the proverb into Chaucer's poetics of reference, and I am following the proverb's lead in com-plicating the everyday, received senses of "true." A true fiction is a bad fic-tion because, like a false coin, it looks like its original, or fiction, but is, in fact, tainted with a dross of personal desire—desire which has designs on others. A true fiction, as in the case of Herry and Hogge, has it in for someone or some-thing—innkeepers and cooks, of course, would be natural enemies (*CkP* A 4358–61); as Hogge says to Herry: "'But er we parte, ywis, thou shalt be *quit*'" (line 4362; emphasis added). Such fiction is in deadly earnest: I will call it, this true fiction, *designing* (on others); the other sort, "true" fiction, I will call *designed*. The former, earnest and designing fiction, is fiction which serves "commoda privata" when, in fact, fiction should serve "commoda publica."[7] True fiction, then, serves a "private interest" and is corrupt; "true" fiction serves a "public interest" (where "public" must not be assumed to be tainted with modern senses of "government" or "the state") and is a kind of universal vow and vowing which binds together community.

True or designing fiction and its consequences Chaucer brilliantly illus-trates in *The Miller's Tale* with "hende" Nicholas's fiction of the flood.[8] Like a coarser Pandarus, "hende" Nicholas—"handy" at all sorts of artifice as he is—"engineers" a plot (fiction) to be his "meene" to Alisoun and her favors. It is a false fiction, true in the perverse sense, and very earnest, because it designs upon "sely John" the carpenter and indeed finally harms him bodily. At the same time (Chaucer never rests with one position when he can maneuver from two or more) a true or designing or earnest fiction depends for its success upon the impressionability of imagination (*MilT* A 3611–13):

> Lo, which a greet thyng is affeccioun!
> Men may dyen of ymaginacioun,
> So depe the impressioun be take.

Here "ymaginacioun" may mean "plot" or "scheme" as well as "imagination" (Davis 1979:79). But these meanings only enhance Chaucer's point. Imagina-tion and the products of imagination, such as fictions, may be anything but disinterested (they may be designing), and one had best be careful of "affeccioun." The reader, we already know from Antigone's lyric (see Chap. 9), is as responsible as the author; and gullibility *will* bring forth true or designing fictions: "Never give a sucker an even break," as the saw has it. Different as they are, Criseyde and John are one in their failure to detect the falsifications perpetrated upon them. "They that have ears to hear, let them hear" (Matt. 11.15). But at the same time, the Father of lies, "when he speaks a lie, speaks his own and from his own" (John 8.44), and indeed, every liar, such as "hende" Nicholas or Pandarus, speaks his "own" or "from his own" when he lies—that is why he is so hard to hear. Even the poet speaks his "own" or "from his own" if he is not careful, for when he "lies"—that is, makes a fiction—in the process of his "lie" he is gazing intently at himself (else he could not write), and thus he risks being another Narcissus, artificer of the consummate true (that is to say, false and "irreferent") fiction—so true, so earnestly true, that it killed him.

Chaucer's theory of mediation saved him from the fate of Narcissus. With this assertion we reach a crucial juncture, and it will be of help to summarize briefly before taking the next step. The theory accounts for the instrumentality by which Chaucer posits the characters of his pilgrims. By insisting on himself, by interposing himself between, say, the Miller and us, Chaucer compels us to ask why he is complicating our perception of his narratives in this way (cf. Leicester 1980:221). And once we have asked that question, we are no longer innocent audiences but active participants in the text—readers in the double sense of "legenda." Moreover, the theory reveals that if we are not such self-conscious readers and choosers we may well wind up being counterfeiters or falsifiers of fiction—we may well try to "quite" others with fiction, spending fiction as if it were coin.

We are poised here, I think, for a major breakthrough into the structure of *The Canterbury Tales*. In fact, every pilgrim "quites" someone or something with the tale he or she tells (even the Knight, who "quites" his version of disorder in the world). Every pilgrim is an unredeemed, unself-conscious narcissist. Selfhood depends on taking a position, but if one's position is only in opposition to. . . , then one's opponent radically circumscribes one's self. Not in opposition, then, but in relationship, in mutual and just exchange, is freedom of the self posited. The Canterbury pilgrims repeatedly fail in such relationship, fail in community, because they are forever opposing or "quiting" someone or something; even though we occasionally hear some such formula as "God save al this faire compaignye" (*KnT* A 3108), we are never allowed to forget at the same time that, for example, the Friar and the Summoner cannot stand each other (*FrP* D 1265-68). And since the sphere of economics, the marketplace, is the space where community, mutual and just exchange, is most visible and strenuously tested, Chaucer posits economics, "quiting," as the structure of relations in *The Canterbury Tales*.[9] Economics is their genetic origin—economics understood, by Chaucer and his contemporaries, probably under the category of ethics from the perspective of positive justice.[10]

Opposition is indisputably one of the most basic phenomena of *The Canterbury Tales*, if not the most basic phenomenon.[11] Indeed, recent scholarship has argued that binary oppositions are the organizing principle of the poem as a whole (Patterson 1978:375–76). In addition to the exchange between Herry Bailly and Hogge of Ware, consider, for example, the Miller once again (*MilP* 3126–27):

> "I kan a noble tale for the nones,
> With which I wol now quite the Knyghtes tale."

Not only does the Miller obviously oppose the Knight; he does so in terms of "quiting" too. He actually repeats the word "quite" from Herry (line 3119), who uses it because of the contest of taletelling which he is conducting. The Monk should "quite" or *repay* the Knight, Herry insists, because he is in competition with him; they should exchange tales to see who tells the superior one; theirs is a game of exchanges. The Miller interrupts Herry and (within the game of the fiction) interrupts the game, too, to take it all very earnestly, in his drunken sort of way (he does threaten to leave; line 3133); and in doing so, he adds a much sharper edge to the economics of "quite"—as if he were retaliating for some higher stakes. The Miller, in fact, wants something, wants to own something, and to that end he will *pay* the Knight back. The Miller behaves here, on the road to Canterbury, just as if he had never left his mill.

Status, perhaps, is what he wants, or perhaps only a good time, or perhaps recognition of the rightness in love of vitality, such vitality as he certainly already possesses. But whatever it is precisely that he wants, it cannot be denied that he pays the Knight back, "quites" him, by almost retelling *The Knight's Tale*. This scholarship has long recognized (Donaldson 1958:1066–70). In light of the theory of mediation, however, it is possible to go further and say: the Miller tells *his version* of *The Knight's Tale*, the Miller takes *his position* on *The Knight's Tale*, the Miller betrays who he is by his carefully *instrumented opposition* to *The Knight's Tale*. But this is hardly all we can say. Chaucer almost certainly knew the etymology of "yconomique" offered by the great French translator of Aristotle, Nicole Oresme (d. 1382), and that etymology enables us to retrieve an even deeper understanding of the relation between the Miller's and the Knight's tales. Oresme writes (ed. Menut 1957:807–808):

The second division is called economics, from Greek *ycon*, meaning image or conventional sign; and from *nomos* meaning rule or law; and from *ycos*, meaning science. For by means of economics the master of the house is able to establish conventions and rules or ordinances for governing his family and himself with respect to his family.

If economics is, then as now, the science of rules and signs because ultimately it is the science of money, *the* referential sign, then we can say that in the *economic* structure of *The Canterbury Tales* the Miller exchanges the Knight's conventions and rules and signs for his and thus converts the latter's tale into his own. If you tell *The Knight's Tale* with a slightly different set of conventions and rules (fabliaux) you get *The Miller's Tale*. Here Dante is profoundly instructive. The Miller has *falsified The Knight's Tale* by subtracting from it its own reference and adding to it his. His tale, as Chaucer's, I hasten to say, finally transcends falsity; it is, as Chaucer's, more than a counterfeit *Knight's Tale*. But, all the same, Chaucer is asking us to see, in the economic structure of the poem as a whole, how the Miller fails in community, in mutual and just exchange, because of his designs, very selfish designs, on the Knight's version of the world. Chaucer achieves a great poem in *The Miller's Tale*. The Miller's falsification is Chaucer's true coin and coin of truth. The Miller himself, however, manages only to betray the limits of his self-consciousness. The Miller, to put it bluntly, does not like "gentils."

Here is, one can hardly deny, a powerful tool of analysis. We can use it to go further. We can say that *The Reeve's Tale* and *The Cook's Tale* are also versions of *The Knight's Tale*, and, in the Reeve's case, of the *Miller's*, too. So much, note, the Reeve himself makes explicit: "'I shal hym [the Miller] *quite anoon;* / *Right in his cherles termes wol I speke*'" (RvP A 3916–17; emphasis added). We can continue and say that all four tales of fragment A are versions of the household. In the strict sense, each is a version of the ways in which a master, by conventions and rules, controls or fails to control his household.[12] In a wider sense, each is a version of the truth of the "political animal": man must and does, by ethical norms, form communities (households) which succeed or fail according as those norms are just or unjust. In this wider sense, it is possible to affirm that every Canterbury tale is a version of the household – some directly, as the *Wife's*, the *Merchant's*, and the *Nun's Priest's*; some less directly, as the *Prioress's* or the *Second Nun's*, where the household is ultimately the Kingdom of God. Hence in addition to binarism or opposition between pairs of tales, within each tale economics, in the wider sense, is also structurally relevant. Just as economics, or "quiting," structures the relations between tales, so economics structures the relations between a tale and its manifest content. Just as the Wife of Bath "quites" the Man of Law, so she also "quites" men and marriage; just as the Merchant

"quites" the Clerk and the Wife of Bath, he also "quites" women and marriage; just as the Prioress "quites" the Shipman (especially his view of
feminine virtue), she also "quites" Jews; and so forth.[13] We have, so to speak,
horizontal "quiting" (between the pairs of tales) and vertical "quiting" (within
each tale). The vertical "quiting" derives from conflicts between an individual
and various norms, hence also communities, even as the horizontal "quiting"
derives from conflicts between two individual positions. From an analysis of
each and of both combined, we can proceed to recover the characters of the
pilgrims and, ultimately, the character of Chaucer. If we determine, in the
case of each pilgrim and his or her tale, why community (the household) fails,
we can deduce the basic injustice of that community's ethical norms; then,
from his or her opposition to that injustice, we can infer the personal blindness, or the gap of self-consciousness, of each pilgrim; and we can assume that
where a link is available, or some interaction or opposition between pilgrims,
it will confirm our inferences about the characters of the pilgrims involved.
Hence, in the exchange between the Wife of Bath and the Pardoner (WBP D
163-87) we will surmise that she wants what he has—or consummate verbal
skills winning him public status as a preacher—and that he wants what she
has—or indisputable sexual prowess. We will be defining character thus from
the incompleteness of each character's position, from the partiality of his or
her version of the truth. We will be isolating in each pilgrim the desire which
makes him or her so individual, so very real. We will be identifying the narcissism of each pilgrim's instrumentality: each tells his tale according to how
he loves himself, and how someone loves himself is the most certain betrayal
of who and what that self is. Chaucer was wise, as we have known all along,
in the ways people hide from themselves the desires which most determine
their characters. And now we know that his theory of mediation serves that
wisdom.

"Quiting" is, to conclude the argument now, an instance of reference. The
Miller refers to the Knight, the Merchant refers to the Clerk and the Wife,
the Franklin refers to the Squire, and the Parson refers to everyone.
Moreover, "quiting" exposes instrumentality. We can see the workings of
each pilgrim's language as he or she tries to persuade the world of his or her
truth. We can weigh the self-aggrandizing exordium—"'Experience, though
noon auctoritee / Were in this world, is right ynogh for me / To speke of wo
that is in mariage'" (WBP D 1-3)—we can judge the self-masking attempt
upon our pity—"'but of myn owene soore, / For soory herte, I telle may
namoore'" (MerP E 1243-44)—we can take the measure of self-doubting
rhetorical gambits—"'And Jhesu Crist, that is oure soules leche, / So graunte

yow his pardoun to receyve, / For that is best; I wol yow nat deceyve'"
(*PardT* C 916–18). Chaucer structured his text with the economics of
"quiting," vertical as well as horizontal, precisely in order that we might see
the instrumentality, in order that we might see the Narcissus in each pilgrim.
The tentativeness, the contingency, the uncertainty, the unpredictableness
of the Canterbury tales and the Canterbury pilgrims derive, just as they do in
real life, from the randomness of personal and often passionate relationships in
a nonetheless strongly if also mysteriously boundaried world. Of such a world
the marketplace is perhaps the most fitting microcosm. And of the marketplace an inn is perhaps the truest center ("At nyght was come into that
hostelrye / Wel nyne and twenty in a compaignye, / Of sondry folk, *by aven-
ture* yfalle / In *felaweshipe*" (*GP* A 23–26; emphasis added). And the Tabard
is where it all would have ended, in the fellowship of a meal, had it not ended
in a different Economy – the Economy that transumes even pilgrimages since
it is their reason for being (Judgment; Salvation).[14]

The economic structure of *The Canterbury Tales*, in which reference appears
as "quiting" (consider the Wife of Bath's "'I ne owe hem nat a *word* that it nys
quit'" (*WBP* D 425; emphasis added), enables Chaucer to explore the ethics of
reference. Reference is not only verbal nor only literary but also personal and
behavioral. The ways in which people connect words and things reflect the
ways in which people love. The Wife of Bath, for example, is more loving than
the Merchant because, in spite of herself, she does not tyrannize the relation
between words and things, as he certainly does when, for example, he reduces
the Song of Songs to "olde lewed wordes" (*MerT* E 2149), assuming and hoping
that we too will assume that the song means no more than January's lust. At
the same time, the Wife is insufficiently self-conscious of the fact that the
ways in which she connects words and things involve the publication of her
"privitee" – "'I hadde the beste *quoniam* myghte be'" (*WBP* D 608). As the
pilgrims speak, so they behave; as they behave, so they speak. Indeed, their
speech is their behavior. Hence our understanding of their speech must be
ethical understanding. Ethics is the science best suited to helping us understand *The Canterbury Tales*, for ethics is "the science which treats of
behavior."[15] Ethics, the system of ways in which people behave and especially
behave verbally, will recover Chaucer's poem for our understanding.

And this because Chaucer, the one Chaucer in his many poses, desires a
world of justice, where each is rendered his due.[16] But if a man is to render
each his due, he must know and understand and sympathize with the due of
each. He must be able to recognize the various masks of desire, be able to
distinguish each man and woman from his and her Narcissus. He must appreciate that Narcissus is necessary to every man and woman, for without

self-love there is no life, but he must also be able to distinguish person from image—"And I seyde his opinion was good" (GP A 183), and we know instantly that his opinion was not very good at all, we know, and know there is, a gap between the Monk's person and his image, between his position and his pose (Leicester 1980:220). So that he might distinguish the many persons in life from the many images of themselves they pretend to others, Chaucer invented his (potentially vast) "distinctio" collection of pilgrims.[17] In a kind of daringly tentative synecdoche, they add up, and the effect is consciously additive, to the whole creature Man, as the many distinctions of a scriptural term add up to its whole meaning.[18] The fictions they tell, in the same daringly tentative synecdoche, add up to all the fictions of Man. And this is Chaucer's vision. If he embraces Man, he can understand and sympathize with men. If he understands and sympathizes with men, he can embrace Man. Obeying this vision, he can be the poet of each pilgrim without being the sort of poet that each pilgrim represents. He can manage to avoid by fictionally indulging the narcissism of each. Thus he can render each his due. He wears the mask of each in order to discover his or her person; he endures the errors of each in order to learn his or her truths; he pays each of them homage even as he laughs at the follies of each. He renders them each his or her due. Poetry its method, economics its structure, Man its Content, justice its end—such is the poem we call The Canterbury Tales.

In the next three chapters I attempt to analyze the tales of the Wife of Bath, the Merchant, and the Pardoner from the perspective of Chaucer's theory of mediation. These three are tales in which money and exchange and falsification of one sort or another dominate. They are thus ideal test cases since not only is their structure economic but also their content is economics and, in the strict sense, commercial. Each chapter proceeds with an introductory summary of the contemporary economic data and developments significant to an understanding of that pilgrim and his or her tale; it continues with a close reading of the tale and concludes with an attempt to illuminate the character of each pilgrim—in particular, what in that character makes him or her the sort of poet Chaucer wishes not to be. Finally, the Epilogue surveys the entire argument of the book and enters some reflections on the "Retracciouns" and reference.

Chapter 11
The Wife of Bath and the Mediation of "Privitee"

LL ECONOMIC exchange, from the most primitive barter to the most sophisticated credit transaction, involves signs, as universal as the grunt of agreement and as nominal as "money of account."[1] Economic exchanges are, as it were, a laboratory of signs in action. And in this laboratory, where Chaucer posed the question "How shall the world be served?" he also posed the question, "How shall the word be served?" If, for many, language too is money, one more item to spend, what can we learn about them from the ways in which they spend it?

Chaucer's concern with such questions as this should come as no surprise. His age was a period of continuous economic upheaval—owing chiefly, after midcentury, to the Black Plague.[2] The changes in the economy of Europe and England resulting from the plague were many and vast,[3] but the changes crucial to Chaucer's vision of England and human life are relatively easy to catalogue. Most important among them was the emancipation effected in the middle class and among the peasantry by greater wealth. This greater wealth was due, almost paradoxically, to the most drastic effect of the plague, the reduction in population. For if the population of England dropped by about one-third, the "gross national product," to speak anachronistically (Du Boulay 1970:30, 40), while it declined, did not plummet and, in fact, in some areas even flourished (Bridbury 1962:36). Hence the fewer people had a larger share of the available wealth (Postan 1973:47, 194). As Bridbury expresses it (1962:103):

> Undistracted by politics and enriched by a prodigious transfer of control over the resources of the economic system, the middle classes and the peasantry, during the later Middle Ages, entered upon a period of domestic comfort so astonishing by the standards of the time as to rouse passionate expressions of enthusiasm and disgust.

So significant is this increase in personal wealth during the later fourteenth century and most of the fifteenth that Du Boulay (1970:70, 73) has characterized this period as the age in which "to be meant to have." Little wonder contemporary reactions were so mixed and often so extreme.

During the same period of problematic affluence, however, another economic factor, ultimately at odds with it, was also prevalent—namely, a serious monetary shortage (Miskimin 1964:490). This monetary shortage had many crucial repercussions. For example: "Shortage of bullion led to hoarding, either by hiding precious metal in treasuries or by using it in the form of fine gold and silver utensils and jewelled settings, and thus by a vicious circle the hoarding was perpetuated and aggravated" (Du Boulay 1970:37). Hence the peculiar situation in later-fourteenth-century England: more wealth, less coinage; more to exchange, but fewer media of exchange. In such a situation the available media become dear, and as they are hoarded, substitutes for them are sought. But the most noticeable and the most far-reaching consequence of such a situation is the increased desire for "real" property (Du Boulay 1970:93). To be now means to own the real. And in this situation the fate of linguistic media is rather the opposite of that of economic media. Words become cheap, since in the dearth of other media they are the most obvious and the most available substitutes, and credibility—or, as Chaucer would have put it, "trouthe"—everywhere is strained. To speak now means to traffic in the meanings of words. People now appropriate the word to aggrandize their fame.[4] And Chaucer tells us as much about this situation as any history can (cf. Leicester 1980:218). There was little that people would not say or do to gain fame. And surely one of the loudest denizens of the House of Fame is Dame Alisoun, the "good Wif of biside Bathe," who earned her place in that notorious house precisely by trafficking in the meanings of words. In her particular case, the traffic is for sexual aggrandizement and a woman's place in a man's world and in man's language. Other pilgrims traffic for other "goods." But the Wife, with her unusually long prologue, is the central example of such traffic in the meanings of words, and hence she is crucial to an understanding of Chaucer's concern with the ethics of reference.

The commercialism of the Wife of Bath pervades her idiom and her very imagination. Consider, for example (WBP D 477–78):

> "The flour is goon, ther is namoore to telle;
> The bren, as I best kan, now moste I selle."

or, even more blatant (lines 413–14):

> "And therfore every man this tale I telle:
> Wynne whoso may, for al is for to selle."

Further, in the portrait of her in *The General Prologue*, she is said to be a cloth maker, and thus a member of the dominant industry of fourteenth-century England.[5] By describing the Wife as a figure of the commercial idiom and the commercial imagination, Chaucer problematizes in her three of the most volatile issues of human experience: economics, sexuality, and semiotics. Common to all three is the necessity of mediation and hence the risk of injustice.

Because she is a commercial being, the Wife herself is obsessed with media – money, clothes, church doors, and phalluses. But in her, commer-cialism has reduced media to commodities. The Wife consumes signs and their significances in the same way she consumes money and phalluses: they serve her pleasure – "'Of fyve husbondes scoleiyng am I'" (line 44f). The Wife of Bath renders "scoleiyng" *irreferent*: it refers to "scholarship" or "teaching" but it has very little reverence for either. For the Wife of Bath, scholarship is very much "explication de sexe," while sex is very much a business transac-tion (lines 154–55; emphasis added):

> "An housbonde I wol have, I wol nat lette,
> Which shal be bothe *my dettour and my thral* . . ."

The Wife means to collect on the letter: she glosses the church's metaphor (of the "marriage debt") *stricte*.

This gloss introduces us to the Wife's pose, that of an exegete, and hence to her highly promiscuous exegesis (lines 346–47; cf. Robertson 1962:317–21):

> "After thy text, ne after thy rubriche,
> I wol nat wirche as muchel as a gnat."

The Wife, of course, declares that experience is the equal of authority (lines 1–3) and thus very neatly sets herself up as an authority. Indeed, her challenge to authority is not that she will replace it. Rather it is that her posi-tion is just as authoritative as authority's. Hence her position convicts her of narcissism, but, at the same time, of a narcissism significantly different from any we have seen before. To be sure, for the Wife all media are mirrors: she sees herself in them, especially her body, and they are to be referred to her pleasure ("ad placitum"). For her, "le plaisir du texte" is "le texte du' plaisir" – and that is her "écriture." But narcissist though she be, the Wife is not a falsifier, she is not a counterfeiter, she is not a liar.

Although it will seem to many heretical that I say so, the Wife of Bath is a heretic. I do not mean, I hasten to say, that she utters this or that heretical doctrine (though, in fact, she may do so) nor do I mean to initiate an inquisition of her prologue. I mean rather that the structure of her peculiar exegesis is that of heresy. Medieval theology understood the word "heresy" to derive from Greek *haeresis*, meaning "to choose"; and it then reasoned that the heretic is he who chooses willfully to disobey orthodoxy or to supplant orthodoxy or to set himself up as an independent orthodoxy.[6] And, we can readily agree, the Wife of Bath's reading of texts ("legenda") is certainly willful choosing ("legenda"-*haeresis*) of the meaning of those texts. Moreover, among the various labels for heretical construction of Scripture current in the Middle Ages one in particular seems almost designed for the Wife of Bath—"peregrinus sensus."[7] Alisoun of the many pilgrimages (*GP* A 463–67) is also Alisoun of the "pilgrimaging sense." Indeed, not only her sense but also her story wanders: "'But now, sire, lat me se, what I shal seyn? / A ha! by God, I have my tale ageyn'" (*WBP* D 585–86). Precisely because the Wife is very well versed in "wandrynge by the weye" (*GP* A 467), she does tend to stray, whether from orthodoxy or from one husband to the next.

If the Wife of Bath's exegesis is heretical, it is not necessarily false or lying. This is the crucial distinction, between her and, say, the Pardoner, which the structure of heresy introduces. The Pardoner, of course, is exceedingly orthodox, and a consummate liar; the Wife is heretical, but she is not a liar. While heresy may be the "proprius sensus" or the "propria pravitas" or the "sensus perfidus," it is not necessarily the "sensus falsus." And indeed, the Wife of Bath accurately quotes "wexe and multiplye" (*WBP* D 28), and she accurately quotes Saint Paul on marriage (lines 63–94). She is even scrupulous with these positions (lines 95–104). She just does not buy them, though. She has her own position, which is good enough for her. Hence she is not guilty of appropriation in the same way as Master Adam or the Pardoner is. She does not seek to deceive. Her will is good, though she may have lost her way.

Although the Wife, like all the other pilgrims, refers to "quiting" (line 422, for example), she "quites" less to own language than to make a place for herself in language. She spends words as if she owned them (so do we all), but she would really prefer to share them. "'Taak al my good, and lat my body go'" (line 1061), cries the young knight, in her tale, when the Loathly Lady requests to become his wife. And just so, if the Wife's body were free—if there were a place in language where her body were not a commodity, to be sold to the highest bidder—she would, I suspect, happily give up all her goods, including language, since she would no longer *need* to own it. As it is, however, no such place exists for her or for women generally, and so she continues to assert her position in opposition to that of her male-dominated society. At the end of her tale, as if (ever the exegete) interpreting it for us, the Wife reduces its meaning to her very predictable position (*WBT* D 1258–64):

> ...and Jhesu Crist us sende
> Housbondes meeke, yonge, and fressh abedde,
> And grace t'overbyde hem that we wedde;
> And eek I praye Jhesu shorte hir lyves
> That wol nat be governed by hir wyves,
> And olde and angry nygardes of dispence—
> God sende hem soone verray pestilence!

And yet so much more than this transpires in her tale, her tale exposes a temperament and a vision so much finer than this, that we are left wondering whether the Wife felt compelled to cover herself—to lapse back into that pose of bitchy exegete in which she is, at least, safe from the prodding eyes of those who deal in women and wives. This wonderment is not as fanciful as it seems. All her life Alisoun has had to expose her "privitee." From the age of twelve, she has been a commodity for sale, a wife, and she has had to advertise herself. Indeed, she has not stopped yet: "'Welcome the sixte, whan that evere he shal'" (*WBP* D 45). Handled like a commodity all her life, the Wife of Bath handles all other media like commodities too.

In an economic environment like that of the late fourteenth century in England, the phenomenon of a Wife of Bath—of a woman of means, of independence and outspokenness, and of wide traveling—was not an isolated or unusual phenomenon. The means which liberated such a woman into public space did *not*, however, at the same time provide for her a status—a public posture transcending the contingency of her empirical self—in a society which despite spreading affluence was still male-dominated.[8] Alisoun was liberated into public space in a society which actively sought to dictate the lives of women. Hence the media available to the Wife for her self-expression in public space were radically circumscribed by the male population. She did not have a blazoned shield, an Oxford degree, or an ecclesiastical privilege. She had at most her trade, her funds, and her sex and its numerous modes of appearance.[9] Accordingly, in contradistinction to the media available to the men in her society—which were resoundingly public—the media available to the Wife of Bath, if she was going to be more than just an "everyday" wife, involved the exposure of her "privitee" (lines 531, 620). If she would be seen, she had to sell herself.

Both male and female media functioned as commodities, to be sure. The ecclesiastical privilege was bought and sold, we know. But it was bought and sold as a commodity with a public value which was recognized as transcendent of the individuals who entered into the transaction. The Wife's sex and its modes of appearance, however, were so proper to her individual self that when they emerged in the public sphere, where women were only beginning to appear, they emerged inevitably as her "privitee." That is why, for example, the Wife's admirers for the past six centuries have known practically everything there is to know about her, from the position of the stars at her birth to the quality of her "quoniam" (lines 603–20); that is why there are very few secrets about the Wife of Bath. The more public the Wife became, the more private she appeared—that is, the more her "privitee" was exposed and the more she was deprived of a conventional public role.[10] Instead of a role, publicly recognized and publicly validated, the Wife, in fact, had only poses. Everyone has sensed the feeling of frustration Alisoun suffers deep within her: "'Allas! allas! that evere love was synne'" (line 614). She may have had her world in her time (line 473), but she has had to pay for it with a certain lack of definition. The only medium of exchange which her society assigned Alisoun once she had entered public space was her body, and in order to express herself in public space, she had to sell herself, her sexuality—she had to become a commodity if she was to remain visible in public space. From the first husband who bought her (lines 197, 204–206) to the last, the Wife of Bath was a commodity, and the essence of a commodity is *to appear* on the market there to have others handle all its hidden parts. Little wonder, then, that the Wife of Bath handles all other media, such as language, like commodities. She does unto them as others have done unto her.

The basic injustice of the community in which the Wife of Bath lives is the reification and commoditization of human beings. She opposes this injustice from her pose as heretical exegete of the feminist position. But in doing so, she becomes herself guilty of it. She reduces media of all sorts to commodities. They become servants of her "commoda privata." Evidence of this actually bitter irony comes from one of the most brilliant scenes which Chaucer ever wrote—the burning of Janekin's book.

The Wife's fifth husband, the one she loved best of all, "'was of his love daungerous'" (line 514) to her. The Wife elaborates on his behavior and its meaning in an image ultimately commercialistic (lines 515–23):

> "We wommen han, if that I shal nat lye,
> In this matere a queynte fantasye:
> Wayte what thyng we may nat lightly have,

Therafter wol we crie al day and crave.
Forbede us thyng, and that desiren we;
Preesse on us faste, and thanne wol we flee.
With daunger oute we al oure chaffare;
Greet prees at market maketh deere ware,
And to greet cheep is holde at litel prys."

Alisoun begins in conventional *fin'amors* rhetoric, but this rhetoric mutates under the pressure of the commercial idiom, and this mutation is part of Chaucer's concern: "daunger" has become an advertising gimmick. As any good advertiser knows, persuade many people to desire a commodity, and each of them will pay dearly for it. The Wife will spend herself recklessly for "daungerous" love. The obverse of this advertising gimmick is crucial to an understanding of Chaucer's exposition of the Wife: hoarding appreciates value.[11] The desirable item which is absent, or in danger of becoming absent, constantly escalates in price. Janekin hoarded his affection for and attention to the Wife, and consequently, she swears that she "loved hym best." She paid the highest price for him: not only did she take him "for love and no richesse" (line 526), but in addition she made over to him all her "winnings" from her previous four marriages (lines 630–31).

Janekin's hoarding took the form of reading. He invested all his attention and affection in reading books, old books, that dealt chiefly with the hallowed profession of misogyny.[12] This form of hoarding resulted, as we all know, in the Wife's deaf ear and Janekin's burned book—after, of course, the Wife had torn a few pages out of it. Since Janekin's book is a hoard of affection and attention, it is the presence of an absence which in the commercial idiom constitutes dearness. His book is the medium of—it emerges as and it interrupts—an absence always on the margin of presence: the Wife knows there is affection and attention absent in the book; all she has to do is burn the book—somehow consume the medium—and the affection and the attention will be present.

Not only commercially but also metaphysically speaking, a book is the presence of an absence. Metaphysically, such is every sign: something present in phonic substance which imports something else in its own substance absent.[13] Hence, commercially speaking, Janekin's book "presents" the affection and the attention which is "absent" to the Wife: present in his book as hoard is that absence. But the book speaks also metaphysically as a sign. And as a sign it mediates a most unflattering, or—from the Wife of Bath's position—improper meaning of womankind: for her, the book is a lie. Present in it as sign is the absence of a meaning of woman which she desperately wants to materialize, to reify, so that she can consume it and destroy it. Thus Chaucer exploits the analogy between commercialism and the metaphysics of the sign. By selecting a book, which is already a sign, to be also the locus of a hoard and the focus of sexual desire, Chaucer centers in the one object all those vectors — economic, sexual, and semiotic — which subtend the pose of the Wife of Bath. When the Wife tears pages out of Janekin's book and forces him ultimately to burn it, Chaucer exposes her fabulous mixture of narcissistic and heretical exegesis and commercial and sexual savvy. The Wife of Bath consumes the sign, the presence of an absence: as she will not permit the absence of Janekin's affections and attention, but consumes his book, so as to own them, so she will not permit the absence of the sign, but consumes it, too, in her own desire, so as to dictate its reference. As the archetypal consumer — of sex, money, and signs — the Wife poses the fate of the sign in a commercial world: it belongs to the customer who is always right.

But at the same time the consumer is consumed by what he consumes. If the Wife of Bath reduces media to commodities which she then consumes, she only reinforces the tendency of men to do the same to her. Moreover, and more precisely, in the act of consuming signs, she becomes herself a sign and is consumed in signs. It is her doom that every refutation she enters against the misogyny of men — such as informs Janekin's book, for example — immediately incriminates her as a living example of the women whom the misogynists so prolifically attack. Every time she opens her mouth the Wife becomes an exemplum in a "Legend of Bad Women." She becomes, that is, a sign of all that is bad in women. Reduced to a sign, partly by her own doing, she is treated like a sign: Janekin is said to "glose" her (line 509). Of course, "glose" means "cajole" primarily, but it also means "gloss." Janekin had the Wife by her "gloss," her significance. He already "owned" her significance, or so it seemed from the perspective of the male position. A wife "means" lust, or, we might say — "*quoniam* (line 608) mulier est, lussuria est": "*since* she is a woman, she is lust" but also "*pudendum* is woman, and she is lust." The double meaning of "quoniam" connects logic (a traditionally male prerogative) and sex in a devastating reduction of the person of woman to the status of an abstraction. Once she is reduced to a sign, the Wife's predicament is one with the predicament of the sign. Every sign mediates an inevitable anteriority: someone has always already enunciated the sign. So much the Middle Ages acknowledged in the theory of "impositio ad placitum." From the perspective of the Wife's position, the opposition has contaminated the words available to her self-expression. Hence, to purge the words, she must gloss them according to her exegesis. For example (lines 440–42):

"Oon of us two moste bowen, doutelees;

And sith a man is moore resonable
Than womman is, ye moste been suffrable."

Note the intricacy and the deftness of the heresy. Man is, in fact, throughout medieval thought, understood to be more reasonable than woman. This the Wife concedes. But in conceding the point, the Wife has let it "wander by the weye" into a context which is false to it. This "peregrination" of the reasonableness of man ends in the *un*reasonable result of female "soveraynetee." In fact, the Wife of Bath has counterfeited the reasonableness of man: her argument looks eminently reasonable, but it is not—it is false (from the male point of view).

And yet, she is not a counterfeiter in the same sense in which Master Adam is. She does not seek to conceal a crime; she does not even seek to deceive. She, in fact, seeks to persuade. But the attempt to persuade is carried out in male terms and male arguments: the Wife opposes men with their own arguments—"'a man is moore resonable / Than womman is'"—and ipso facto her position can only be an imposition on their position. Hence, the Wife willy-nilly concedes the opposition's position—her shrewishness. Any assertion of individuality by the Wife issues in a proof of the hated generality. The sign as the presence of the type inscribes the absence of the individual. And the Wife's identity is only an illusion maintained, as on a life-support system, by constant opposition to men.

So it is that the burning of Janekin's book is so disturbing (and so successful a poetic structure): in that act of scandalous consumerism the Wife only condemns herself to the meanings she would rather dictate, becomes a falsifier when she would be an authority, a shrew when she would be a lover. When Janekin finally capitulates (lines 804–22), the Wife, to be sure, has "won" (i.e., bought) her "soveraynetee," but she has sold her sovereign privilege to be loved for herself. Janekin's love for her will never again be free of guilt and obsequiousness. He may be kind and true to her (lines 823–25), but he is also beaten. The customer, yes, is always right, but the consumer is consumed by what he consumes—be it sex, signs, or money. Little wonder the legend of Midas so appealed to the Wife of Bath, though for reasons other than those she consciously assumed: everything she touches turns to sex. Everything the Wife of Bath touches turns to sex, the principal commodity to which the male world reduces her. Because a commodity once in public space, the Wife attempts to control media, especially signs, as if they too were commodities, or private property—in order, as it were, to "feminize" them. In fact, however, signs in her world, meanings generally, were almost the exclusive "property" of men—just as, in fact, women were too. In regard to marriage, men bought

DANTE, CHAUCER, AND THE CURRENCY OF THE WORD

and sold women regularly, with often drastic results (Margulies 1962: 210–16). In a passage which would be gruesome were it not for the breathless energy of her vituperation, the Wife castigates the alleged "property" rights of men (lines 285–92). The array of goods which she lists during this out-burst—in which, by implication, from the masculine perspective, women should belong since, after all, they too are "housbondrye" (line 288)—is cer-tainly less than flattering to women. More troubling, however, is the poverty of the Wife's response to the "property" rights of men: she can do no more than vituperate; she cannot offer an authentic, workable alternative to the masculine attitude. Similarly, in regard to the alleged "property" rights of men over signs and meanings, the Wife cannot offer an authentic, workable alter-native. For example, in a passage where she effectively acknowledges these rights, she exclaims (lines 368–70):

> "Been ther none othere maner resemblances
> That ye may likne youre parables to,
> But if a sely wyf be oon of tho?"

If the trope or metaphor ("resemblance") is a "turning" or violent ex-propr-iation of a word or thing in favor of an alien sense, then—so the Wife is com-plaining—men have subjected wives to this violence by "troping" them—turn-ing them into "resemblances" and hence turning them out of themselves.[14] It follows that if wives are to escape this violence they must somehow circum-vent the dominant tropes of the male culture. The Wife of Bath herself peregrinates around these tropes, or tries to do so, by means of her heretical exegesis, whose "auctoritee" is her "experience." But in the attempt, as we have seen, she becomes herself as guilty as the men in her world.

In fact, there is very little difference between them. She herself confesses as much when she asserts *her* "property" rights—and by extension those of women generally—over signs and their meanings (lines 693–96):

> "By God! if wommen hadde writen stories,
> As clerkes han withinne hire oratories,
> They wolde han writen of men moore wikkednesse
> Than al the mark of Adam may redresse."

In other words, women would write tropes in the same way and to the same end as men have done. But the word they thus usurp can only usurp in turn their womanhood. If women ex-propr-iate words and things as men have done with their institutionalized tropes, they must suffer the painful and immediate consequence of coming to resemble men. This is, in fact, what has happened to the Wife of Bath. Not only does she argue like a man, drink like a man, and

ride like a man, she also even fights like a man (lines 788–93; 808) – with per-
niciously ironic results. Her blows on Janekin's cheek assert, "I am a woman!
How dare you treat me this way!" – and yet, how like a man to Janekin must
Alisoun have looked when she landed her punches. The Wife, because she
seeks power *over* men, also, inevitably, seeks the power *of* men, with the
equally inevitable result that she resumes her identity, sexual and otherwise,
from her opponent – not that it is improper for a woman to argue, drink, ride,
or fight, but that it is a crime that reverse bondage should determine the identity of a woman. And yet to justify herself and to found her identity, the
Wife of Bath must resort to the works of man: at the extreme of this snarled
predicament, she must plunder the literary works of men for arguments in
defense of her position. As long as the "proper" of words falls to the "property" of discrete positions, the movements of ap-propr-iation and ex-propr-
iation will determine human relationships – reduce them to oppositions, in
effect. Only fiction, "true" or designed *not* true or designing, fiction, can prevent this fall or reverse it. The universalizing power of fiction, the power to
make whole and hale, unifies positions and pacifies oppositions in its beauty
and truth. Great beauty and no little truth occupy *The Wife of Bath's Tale*. If
we leave to one side, for the moment, her exegesis and interpretative ap-
propriations, her "quiting" the Friar (*WBT* D 864–81), and her asides on
"'What thyng [it is] that wommen moost desiren'" (line 905), we can agree on
the beauty of "gentilesse," on the truth of mercy, and on the value of poverty;
we can agree that there is a beauty in the Wife's fiction which transcends her
and her exegesis and us and our exegesis – a beauty which is no one's
"property."

Ultimately, no one, man or woman, "owns" language; if anything, it is far
truer to say that language "owns" us. To be sure, men have demanded – and
still do demand – unreasonable rights over language. Perhaps the modern
feminist movement will correct their error. But if it is to do so, its members
will have to remember what, in the end, Alisoun forgot (despite the beauty of
her tale) that two wrongs do not make a right. If I have understood her
predicament in any way fairly, the Wife of Bath confronted massive societal
pressure which she could not bear but which she in part brought on herself.
Yet she is not a victim to be pitied so much as a natural force to be wondered
at. Loud, ostentatious, selfish, avaricious, and promiscuous, she nonetheless
commands energy so extraordinary that if our life on this planet were the
highest good in creation we would probably be forced to swear by her and
others like her. Such prodigious openness to life is in its way possibly humble,
certainly humbling. Alisoun will survive what W. H. Auden calls "the

treason of all clerks" ("At the Grave of Henry James") precisely because she is always reaching out, demanding to be understood.

But energy and our life on this planet have their limits. And if "'the children of Mercurie and of Venus / Been in hir wirkyng ful contrarius'" (*WBP* D 697–98), it may be because Mercury is closer to the sun. In a sense, the Wife of Bath has traded the light of understanding for the beautiful but murky clouds of passion. And so she goes "wandrynge by the weye," lost in the fabulous and fabular if obscure side paths of her exegesis, looking for the world she did *not* have in her time (cf. line 473).

She will not find it—though in her missing it Chaucer finds a poetry very close to it. She will not find it because she cannot escape the relentless pro-cess of opposition. She depends on it for her very identity. When the Wife of Bath "privatized" signs and meanings, such as "scoleiyng," so as to open for herself a place in language, she had to load them with her "privitee." Her own "privitee" had to come "in between" her and her world. Her only publicity is her privacy (and that reads two ways). From her "bele chose" (line 510) and its "Martes mark" (line 619) to her doubts about the Judgment Day ("'Allas! allas! that ever love was synne!'") the publication of the Wife's "privitee" is the very ex-propr-iation she so resents in men. She expropriates herself: she makes of herself a sign, she publishes herself, as if she were a piece of writing—a peregrinating commercial, looking for a buyer. If the Wife of Bath seems to us so delightful, so energetic, so saucy, so very individual and yet so disturbingly unfinished and unhappy, that is because, as a woman who chose to be, and even reveled in being, for sale, she still is.

Chapter 12
The Merchant and the Parody of Creation

ITHOUT FEAR of exaggeration *The Merchant's Tale* can be said to be one of Chaucer's most complex poems and possibly one of his highest achievements. For a long time its surface brilliance, its comedy and wit, and its carefully crafted plot have received high praise. The poem is a delight to read. In recent years scholarship has begun to realize that, in addition to all these features, the poem has unusual philosophical heft and that it possesses wide-ranging implications for the whole of *The Canterbury Tales*. Brown (1978:141–56, 247–62) has argued that the poem is a kind of confession, for example, a position I have assumed for some time now, and that as such it suggests how the whole of *The Canterbury Tales* might be confessional, a suggestion we ought not to take lightly. Smarr, to take another example, has demonstrated the extraordinary care with which Chaucer has shaped his sources in the poem, one of which might have been the *Decameron*.[1] My own researches into the sources, which I am about to report, will support her approach even as they extend the range and type of sources we assume to be relevant to the poem. At the same time I will make a conscious effort to isolate and articulate the philosophical position of the poem. My remarks are necessarily incomplete, but I do hope to suggest that in the Merchant and his tale Chaucer explores the position of nihilism and in particular a nihilism of the sign and that he does this by assigning the Merchant a style best described as "usurious"; moreover, I will argue that the tale is the work in which Chaucer most successfully exposes the nature of allegory. Finally, I will suggest that, if the Merchant claims that "craft is al, whoso that do it kan" (MerT E 2016), Chaucer, consummate craftsman though he be, repudiates this position of malicious instrumentality and repudiates it in favor of a poetry whose content is not the victim of its craft.

Donaldson (1958:1083–84) has noted that "there is no more startling disclosure of character in *The Canterbury Tales* than the one that follows the telling of the tale of Griselda. . . . While in his tale the Merchant does not tell us of his unhappy marital experience, the attitudes he assumes toward the plot and its people are conditioned by what has happened to him." In other words, Narrator identification with narrative matter is extreme in *The Merchant's Tale*. This is crucial. It helps us to reason that the Merchant is a usurer. At the beginning of his tale the Merchant tells us that January dwelt "in Lumbardye" (line 1245). A prosperous Lombard to Chaucer's audience would have meant, instantly, "usurer." Along with Jews, Lombards formed the largest class of usurers in medieval Europe, and they were extremely active in London in the fourteenth century.[2] January has almost certainly made part of his fortune through usury. Now given the extreme of Narrator identification with narrative matter in this tale, if January is a usurer, the Merchant probably is, too. And this probability approaches certainty once the tale is analyzed as if its teller were a usurer.[3]

As understood in the Middle Ages, usury is the taking of any interest whatsoever on a fungible commodity—that is, a commodity replaceable by another of the same definition—which is also consumptible.[4] Such a commodity, for example, is wine or grain, which can be replaced by other wine or grain and which cannot be used without also being consumed. The teaching that money also is a fungible consumptible derives from Aristotle. Aquinas, for example, quoting Aristotle, argues that "money, however, was invented chiefly for exchanges to be made, so that the prime and proper use of money is its use and disbursement in the way of ordinary transactions."[5] Hence, as Aquinas goes on to insist in the same response: "It follows that it is in principle wrong to make a charge for money lent, which is what usury consists in." Since a loan is a "mutuum," where "mine {meum} becomes yours {tuum}," to charge for the use of money in a loan is to demand that yours remain mine, although mine was consumed in becoming yours.[6]

Not only is money a fungible consumptible, it is also, according to ideas current in the Middle Ages, sterile ("money does not give birth to money") because, once it is consumed by being alienated to another in a transaction, its original possessor can no longer profit from it.[7] Hence usury, or the generation of more money from alienated money, is not only illicit but also unnatural (Oresme *Politiques* 1.12) and, indeed, illicit because unnatural. Usury is not only against the law, or a conventional human code, but also against nature, or the divinely established order; moreover, it is against nature also because, to employ Dante's argument, it perverts art which "follows" nature (*Inf.* 11.97–111; Reade 1909:429). Hence the usurer, properly speaking, abuses nature, society, and art alike. Finally, since the origin of money, according to

Aristotle, is need, the usurer exploits and violates the greatest human vulnerability, or that insufficiency of the discrete individual because of which he must enter into society and public space—the usurer, in short, is a cor-rupter of relationships and of relationship.

Before he is a usurer, the Merchant is, of course, a merchant, or someone who, according to the scholastic definition, buys goods only to sell them again, just as he received them, at a higher price.[8] Hence a merchant, by definition, is rarely interested in the thing itself but only in what it will bring—what it is worth. Such is the mental attitude of January as he literally "shops" for the girl who will be fortunate enough to become his bride (*MerT* E 1577–85; emphasis added):

> Heigh fantasye and curious bisynesse
> Fro day to day gan in the soule impresse
> Of Januarie aboute his mariage.
> Many fair shap and many a fair visage
> Ther passeth thurgh his herte nyght by nyght,
> As whoso tooke a mirour, polisshed bryght,
> And sette it in a *commune market-place*,
> Thanne sholde he se ful many a figure pace
> By his mirour.

This passage and its context are remarkable for a number of reasons. First and foremost is the emphasis on "fantasye." This emphasis responds to the issue of subjectivity in valuation and pricing, an issue crucial to late-medieval economic theorists. For example, Peter John Olivi—as I have already remark-ed (Chap. 9 n. 2), perhaps the most important of the scholastic theorists—argues that three factors are at work in valuation. In the terms invented by San Bernardino of Siena (1380–1444), who uses Olivi's theory without acknowledgment, these are *virtuositas*, or the intrinsic worth or "virtue" of the object, *raritas*, or the abundance or scarcity of the object, and *com-placibilitas*, or what we might call simply personal preference.[9] It is here, with this last factor, that Olivi and subsequent theorists like San Bernardino recognize the element of subjectivity in valuation. But what for the theorists is a necessary step in valuation, or just a part of it, for January is rather the whole process. To be sure, he pays some attention to *virtuositas*, at least after his own fashion, and in this regard he is willing to listen, for a while at least, to the valuations of others (lines 1478–1565); but finally *complacibilitas* is his main criterion for girl-flesh—his girl must, quite literally, suit his "fantasye" (lines 1597, 1608–10):

> And [he] chees hire of his owene auctoritee;
> . . . .
>
> Hym thoughte ech oother mannes wit so badde
> That inpossible it were to repplye
> Agayn his choys, this was his fantasye.

Most incriminating here of January's economic sense, not to mention his moral fiber, is his solipsistic certitude in the matter of wife pricing. Under the second item of *complacibilitas*, Olivi notes:

> We must understand that such deliberation we rarely or never perform *except through conjectural or probable opinion*. And even then, we are not precise or rational or using absolute measurement which is not further divisible into more and less. Quite the contrary, *we are working then with a certain latitude or play in estimation about which various opinions and judgments might differ*. And so it is that *such estimation or valuation includes various degrees of precision and little certainty and a lot of ambiguity*, which is only in keeping with judgments by opinion—even as in some cases, it is a question of more, in others, of less (Ed. Spicciani 1977:255–56; emphasis added).

January chooses a wife according to his and no one else's "good pleasure," but at the same time he insists that his choice is absolutely the best, full of certitude and lacking in ambiguity (just the opposite of Olivi's "little certitude and a lot of ambiguity"). And so it is that medieval economics exposes January's "fantasye" for the extremism of its subjectivity.

Chaucer stresses January's "fantasye," of course, in the context of a "commune market-place." He complicates the context and deepens its import by adding the image of the "mirour" (line 1582). Had Chaucer left us with only the "fantasye" on a shopping spree, the image would have been pertly ironic, eliciting the calculated effect, and we would have gone on to the next image of January's high foolishness. But Chaucer is about a more serious game than irony here. Ultimately the girls whom January sees are projections of his own fantasy. And of all Chaucer's characters, perhaps, he is the nearest equivalent to Dante's Master Adam: an obvious narcissist, he is also counterfeiter and falsifier. And this because he is a (very perverse) maker of images.

January's image-making the text insists on through the trope of wax. At one point in his harangue about the best way to dicker for a good marriage, January observes: "'But certeynly, a yong thyng may men gye, / Right as men may warm wex with handes plye'" (lines 1429–30). January has delusions of Pygmalionism, on top of his relentless narcissism.[10] The girl he marries, rather than be a person in her own right, must be his manufacture. This lust, of course, backfires on January when May takes "swich impression" (line 1978) of Damyan that she desires "to doon hym ese" (line 1981). Having treated May like wax, January discovers to his dismay that she *is* wax in Damyan's hands. Moreover, when May "In warm wex hath emprented the clyket / That Januarie bar of the smale wyket" (lines 2117–18), the impressionability of wax must once again dismay January. Finally, perhaps the most telling instance of the reversal of January's delusions of Pygmalionism occurs in his garden when he is, to all appearances, "sweet-talking" May and actually admits: "'Ye been so depe *enprented* in my thoght'" (line 2178; emphasis added). He who would "enprent" his "fantasye" on another person reduced to a lump of wax is forced to admit, doubtless with no sense himself whatsoever of the irony at work, that she is "enprented in [his] thoght." It is as if the wax to which January reduces reality is continuous with and extends into his own brain; and here he unwittingly confesses that, so far from being a creative authority impressing an Idea or an Archetype upon chaos, he is himself, in his own thought, a lump of wax impressed or imprinted by the "fantasye" of lust.

If the false coiner is here himself coined, more than local irony motivates this reversal. The Merchant doubtless remembers the Clerk's lament about the scarcity of "Grisildis" in the modern world (ClT E 1163–69; emphasis added):

> But o word, lordynges, herkneth er I go:
> It were ful hard to fynde now-a-dayes
> In al a toun Grisildis thre or two;
> For if that they were put to swiche *assayes*,
> The *gold* of hem hath now so badde *alayes*
> With *bras*, that thogh the *coyne* be *fair at ye*,
> It wolde rather breste a-two than plye.

It is as if, to "quite" the Clerk, the Merchant went out of his way to corroborate his lament. Wives "now-a-dayes," the Merchant implies through May, have so far degenerated that they are wax, hardly even brass, and, so far from being able to hold the print or stamp of those who "coin" them, they on the contrary turn on the coiners and coin them, "enprent" them, as if having reduced them to wax.

If May is what the Merchant thinks of Griselda, January is what he thinks of any man fool enough to get married (including, I suppose, himself). Such a man presents the sorry figure of a Narcissus complete with mirror, wax, and porno-mint in his brain. Moreover, and what can only be worse foolishness in the Merchant's eyes, such a man actually spends money to fulfill his "fantasye." Indeed, if January finally condescends to buy May, she does not come cheap—the Merchant makes that abundantly clear (*MerT* E 1696–99). But, in return, January is expecting her to fetch him no less a "good" than Heaven: "'I shal have myn hevene in erthe heere'" (line 1647). We can almost hear the Merchant muttering "a fool and his money are soon parted." Be that as it may, his relentless scorn for January does succeed in insisting on the latter's strictly mercantile interest in May. January buys May only to spend her for Heaven on earth. Just like a merchant, he is interested not in her but in what she will fetch. Hence when he treats her like wax, he is, in effect, trying also to convert her into coin, so as to spend her, the living girl, on his "fantasye," thus littling her to a thing. Confirming this reasoning, Aquinas, who is follow-ing Aristotle (*Ethics* 4.1.1119b26), declares that "anything whose price can be measured in money is deemed to be money" (*ST* 2a. 2ae. 78, 2 resp.). If May can be bought for money, she is money—"can be measured in money." And in what is a chillingly precise "quiting," when Damyan comes, as it were, to bor-row May, just like money, she will be ready to change hands. Coined by January's "fantasye"—falsified for his pleasure—she will, in fact, be spent by another man, who seeks to deposit his "interest" on this "loan" in the mint, where, according to Macrobius, the human "coin" is fashioned, or "hire wombe [that January] stroketh...ful softe" (line 2414).[11]

January's marriage arises from and presupposes exchange of property. So in fact did most if not all marriages of the Middle Ages.[12] No sentimentality should obscure our understanding of the role of property in medieval mar-riage. But the mercantilism attending the sacrament did not necessarily reduce it to merchandise. In 1374, Oresme finished translating and glossing for Charles V of France the Latin version by William of Moerbeke of the Pseudo-Aristotelian *Oeconimica* (Menut 1957:791). The bulk of *Le Livre de yconomique* is concerned with marital relations within the household, which is the space of "yconomique." Now Oresme recognizes the mercantilism attend-ing the sacrament of marriage, but he does so in a wholly different spirit from that of January and the Merchant:

> Text: For she [the wife] has been bought at great price, that is, as his life's
> companion....
> Gloss: Until death without separation and not for a period of time like a
> hired woman or like a slave who can be sold again (Ed. Menut 1957:830).

A man may have bought his wife, yes, but the price which he paid is, or should have been, "societé de vie"—obviously a price January cannot and will not afford. Hence, without sentimentality, and in full recognition of the role

of property in medieval marriage, it is possible to censure January's mercantilism in marriage as a literal practice of "yconomique" devoid of the spirit of
"yconomique."

Aristotle, and after him medieval economists, distinguish between
oikonomía and *kapēlikḗs* – the former being the art of wealth getting for the individual household and for the *polis* inasmuch as it consists of a collection of
households, the latter being the art of wealth getting for its own sake, or
trade or merchandising.[13] "Yconomique" is, then, in Oresme's terms – and
here I allude to the etymology cited earlier – the science or "ycos" of
establishing "icons" and "nomoi" for the successful and beneficial conduct of
the family within the household. The implications of "symbol depositing" and
of "convention depositing" in Oresme's etymology of "yconomique" will re-
quire further discussion in a moment. Here I am chiefly interested in the
norms of marital behavior within the household which the treatise
establishes, since these are the norms which define the enormity of January
and May's travesty of marriage. For example, the treatise declares:

> Text: What Hesiod says is correct: namely, that it is fitting and expedient
> for a man to marry a young maiden, tender in years, so that he may in-
> struct her in good behavior. . . .
> Gloss: For affection cannot exist between persons of contrary wills. And
> such are those couples whose habits are unevenly matched and discor-
> dant. And when the wife is young, the husband can better bend her to
> his will than when she is older (Ed. Menut 1957:816).

The position expressed by "can better bend her to his will" is mitigated elsewhere in the treatise on those many occasions when it insists that a husband
must treat his wife not like a slave or a hired woman but precisely like his
mate (Menut 1957:816, 333c; 837, 344b; 839, 344d; etc.). All the more
ironic, then, is January's immoderately literal practice of "yconomique" in
regard to the difference between the ages of husband and wife. His desire for
a wax doll who "'shal nat passe twenty yeer'" (*MerT* E 1417) argues a certain
nonchalance about making ends meet. "Whan tendre youthe hath wedded
stoupyng age" (line 1738), the irony is not only literary (the topos of the
"senex amans"; Brown 1973:97) but also "economic."

January's literal practice of "yconomique" (which, note, is quite *un-*
economical) continues when he prepares May for her initiation into the
mysteries of the connubial couch. For such a moment, *Le Livre de yconomique*
gives the following prescription:

> Text: It is a decent, proper and fitting procedure that the husband should
> approach his wife when she is calm and composed. . . .

Text: With great courtesy and modesty or self-restraint and also with awe and humility, speaking to her such words concerning carnal union as are fitting and suitable to the lawful and honorable performance of the sexual act.

Gloss: For should he approach her too roughly and shamelessly and use indecent language and behave in a dissolute manner, he would make her too brazen and incline her to incontinence and to lust after another man. And this is not the way chaste persons act but rather the manner of incontinent men toward wanton women (Ed. Menut 1957:837).

Now January's compliance with this prescription is enough to make one wonder whether such a prescription should even be allowed to stand, so contrary a result it produces (MerT E 1828-34):

> "Allas! I moot trespace
> To yow, my spouse, and yow greetly offende,
> Er tyme come that I wil doun descende.
> But nathelees, considereth this," quod he,
> "Ther nys no werkman, whatsoevere he be,
> That may bothe werke wel and hastily;
> This wol be doon at leyser parfitly."

Again it is a case of immoderately literal practice of "yconomique." January's approach is and is not the one which the treatise prescribes. He would comfort May regarding her imminent deflowering but succeeds, one strongly suspects, only in disgusting her – and it is certainly true that hereafter she is inclined to "incontinence and to lust after another man." January adopts the manner which the treatise recommends, but he adapts it to utterly incongruent matter. At "economizing" as at love making, one suspects that May "preyseth nat his pleyyng worth a bene" (line 1854).

If January's literal practice of "yconomique" succeeds in being uneconomical, May's is hardly less self-contradictory. In the course of discussing the friendship in marriage, Le Livre de yconomique notes that

nature granted carnal pleasures to the animals only for the purpose of reproduction; but it accorded the human species this pleasure not only for reproduction of its kind but also to enhance and maintain friendship between man and woman. This is implied in Pliny's statement that no female, after she has become pregnant, seeks sexual union, except woman only (Ed. Menut 1957:813).

Now here is May worming her way through January into the tree (MerT E 2335-37; emphasis added):

"I telle yow wel, a womman *in my plit*
May han to fruyt so greet an appetit
That she may dyen, but she of it have."

"In my plit," of course, refers "irreferently" to pregnancy, and so it is that
May "re-presents" one of the "signs" of the "yconomique" of married friendship in the moment just before her adultery, or the opposite of married friendship. Moreover, note the literalism of her practice of "yconomique": the
pregnancy (*res*) is only literal, only in the letter (*vox*), "in my plit" – it is literally the presence of an absence – and the "re-presentation" is a falsification
(though, as we shall see, much like a trope or metaphor too).

These ironies, dazzling though they be, pale beside May's intricately
straight compliance with the treatise's prescription that a wife should help
her husband "when he is the victim of his own faulty judgment" (Ed. Menut
1957:829): "'Ye maze, maze, goode sire,' quod she; / 'This thank have I for I
have maad yow see.' / . . . 'He that mysconceyveth, he mysdemeth.'" (*MerT*
E 2387–88; 2410). May does, indeed, minister to her husband's "faulty judgment" – only to make it more manifest. Here, as in the other cases, the right
thing to do, the good thing to do, the "economical" thing to do, is done – but
to ends diametrically opposite those intended by the spirit of "yconomique."

The culmination of this literalism is the "yconomique" of January's marriage
itself: it answers almost literally to Oresme's etymology of the term. For May,
in January's mind, resembles an "ycon" in wax; and January himself, solipsistic valuator of girl-flesh, is full of "nomoi" (private laws for ruling his household); and his "ycos" is carnal knowledge ("scientia"). January's "yconomique"
is a concupiscible science predicated on private conventionality and fantastic
signs. Hence the failure of his household. His "yconomique" is another extension of his "fantasye," and the signs he deposits refer only to their insistence
in his "fantasye." His marriage and his bride alike are products of his peculiar
and pecuniary art through which he disposes of his private conventions and
his fantastic signs. Such a fantastic product, too, is his garden, which is so
much his "work of art" that it excludes Nature herself from her proper realm,
and is thus a counterfeit or false garden whose "irreference" defines a new
depth of reference without reverence.

January's garden, one of the most famous in English literature, is both pudendum and paradise, which he fashioned, doubtless at great cost, because, the
Merchant notes, he agreed with those clerks who "holden that felicitee /
Stant in delit" (lines 2021–22); and, therefore, "with al his myght, / In honest
wyse, as longeth to a knyght. / [He] shoop hym to lyve ful deliciously" (lines

2023-25). Betrayed in the Merchant's observations is January's conviction that the Lord of creation is inadequate to see to his, January's, felicity, either in this world or, one may assume, in the next. Hence January supplements creation with his garden wherein "thynges whiche that were nat doon abedde, / He...parfourned hem and spedde" (lines 2051-52), in what we might call a physical or carnal parody of creation. But in addition to this parody and concurrent with it is the far vaster parody, at the Merchant's will, of God's creative Word itself, for January's pudendum-paradise—complete with tree, fruit, serpent, and deities, even if Pluto and Proserpine are hardly Christian—fairly boasts its emulation of the original home of man east in Eden. In effect, January has bought his own Eden, as a merchant would do, and conducts therein his fantastic business. At the same time, in narrating this business in Eden, the Merchant imposes his will on a constellation of signs crucial to Christianity, *the* source of meaning in his world, in an effort to make the meaningful meaningless—in an effort to make the real (*res*) merely vocal (*vox*), so that, by commanding the voices, he might dictate the real.

The Merchant goes out of his way to observe that the garden which January's money buys and his "fantasye" constructs, to enclose his "hevene on erthe," would tax the descriptive resources of the author who "wroot the Romance of the Rose / [Who] ne koude of it the beautee wel devyse" (lines 2032-33).[14] The emergence of the *Roman de la Rose* at this moment in *The Merchant's Tale* is significant since, in Jean de Meun's, as in Alain de Lille's, figure of the goddess Nature, the three mediations which we have met before—sexuality, language, and coinage—are assimilated and articulated as reflexes each of the other. For example, Jean observes (lines 15975-86):

> But when Nature, sweet and compassionate, sees that envious Death and Corruption come together to put to destruction whatever they find within her forge, she continues always to hammer and to forge and always to renew the individuals by means of a new generation. When she can bring no other counsel to her work, she cuts copies in such letters that she gives them true forms in coins of different monies (Trans. Dahlberg 1971:271-72).

Sexuality, as Nature's instrument against Death and Corruption, is both a writing ("letre") and a coining ("quoinz"). January in his garden, practicing his fantastic sexuality (all those "thynges whiche that were nat doon abedde"), is thus Nature's deformed double, perverting not only sexuality but also the art of writing and that of coining as well. And as goes January, so goes the Merchant: if January forges paradise into something as material and carnal as

Dante's Hell, the Merchant falsifies the sacrament of marriage, the story of Adam and Eve, the *Roman de la Rose*, the *Marriage of Mercury and Philology*, and many other texts and tropes into a tale just as material and carnal. In doing so, he proves himself unnatural, too, a corrupter of mediations.

But if January and the Merchant both corrupt mediation, the process is more easily and quickly grasped, initially anyway, in the former. When January approaches May in his garden, his labors upon her body are an all too easily imagined mockery of Nature's labors at her forge or in her mint. In the iconography as well as the written tradition of the goddess, her forge is both implicitly and explicitly assimilated to the pudendum, and her hammers are the male genitalia.[15] Hence when January hammers on May's anvil inside his pudendum-paradise, from one perspective he is simply a man (hammers) coupling with a woman (anvil or forge) as Nature dictates; from another perspective, however, one which sees his arrogance in fashioning the garden and his attempted usurpation of Nature, he looks like nothing so much as a puny smith, trying to assume Nature's powers, imagining himself her substitute while in fact he can only corrupt her work.

The case is similar with his coining or moneying. January coins upon May, whom he has already coined in his "fantasye." And he perverts Nature as much in the former act as in the latter. Not only is the womb a mint (Macrobius; see above), but Nature, we know, is a moneyer.[16] Alain de Lille, for example, insists on Nature coining or moneying creatures; this insistence begins as a fascination with the stamping or imprinting of the Ideas upon chaos—a fascination which he shares with Bernard Silvestris and other medieval Platonists.[17] Similarly, in Jean de Meun, the image of Nature as moneyer is a serious trope for the providential ordering of the natural world. Nature's forge, or anvil, and her mint are images of the organs of generation without which the natural world must fail. Hence, when Chaucer's text suggests that January would arrogate to himself Nature's dominion, it is underlining his *un*naturalness. January the merchant at the mint of May corrupts natural mediation.

January's corruption of natural mediation is also evident from his perversion of writing. Immediately after May and he enter the garden and just before the climactic scene in and beneath the tree, January appeals to his wife to be true to him (*MerT* E 2169). If she is, she shall have, he says, "'al myn heritage, toun and tour; I yeve it yow, *maketh chartres as yow leste*'" (lines 2172–73; emphasis added). Apparently January held something back when by many a "scrit and bond...[May] was feffed in his lond" (lines 1697–98), and now he uses his "heritage, toun and tour" as a bargaining item. He encourages May to make charters in witness of her ownership of this "heritage"; it is crucial to remember, however, that such charters would bind May also—to complete fidelity to January. Hence January encourages writing—charters are very much written documents—in order to make a contract which, none too subtle, really, would bind May to him legally, where the bond of partnership ought first to be amorous, spiritual, and sacramental and only then legal. January is blind, indeed, and blind most of all to the spirit behind the letter.

If January displaces and perverts Nature, corrupting mediation, it is because he subsumes discourse and intercourse under currency: for him, money is the measure of all other mediations. Whereas the Wife of Bath would spend language but only for her own kind of freedom, January spends language and spends May just to spend. Here as elsewhere the letter rules: language and sex are literally money for January. And when money measures discourse and intercourse, creativity, or the generation of the Other in speech and in nature, falls victim to replication, or the reduction of the Other to the Same. January perverts Nature ultimately because he frustrates difference.

This last sentence is much less cryptic than it might seem at first. January frustrates difference, producing the Same, because he is incapable of pretense and therefore, by implication, incapable also of that alienation of self through media into the Other (sympathy, empathy) which initiates definition of the self. January's incapacity for pretense is most obvious at the moment in the garden when he stands beneath the tree. Here the *Roman de la Rose* is of great help. In Amis's advice to Amans in Jean's continuation, at one point he declares (lines 9666–72; emphasis added):

> "Moreover, the less to estrange her, *if he [the young lover] finds her even in the act*, he should take care not to open his eyes in that direction. *He should pretend [senblant doit fere] to be blind* or more stupid than a buffalo, so that she may think it entirely true that he could detect nothing" (Trans. Dahlberg 1971:173).

Now it would be hard to deny the relevance of this passage to January's behavior in his garden and beneath the tree. But its precise application is tricky, principally because of the multiple layers of irony in Jean's text. However, we can rely on what seems the Merchant's typical ploy: wherever a standard of any sort seems relevant, we should adduce it because the Merchant consistently and obsessively seeks to destroy standards—to set them up in contexts where they must inevitably fail. Hence we can and should assume that January should be judged according as he actually follows the *fin'amors* directives which Amis gives Amans; and we should not be surprised to discover that he follows them in such a way as not to follow them at all.

Hence, for example, he is blind when May and Damian are coupling in the tree, but literally so, and therefore he cannot *pretend* to be blind as a good *fin amant* should. Subsequently his eyes are opened, but at that point he screams in rage at what he sees above him in the tree; and obviously he does not pretend to be blind or "simple" in this situation. Finally, with his eyes open, January is in fact blind, as Amis advises precisely, but not out of pretense or of his own will, but rather because May has deceived him with her impromptu justification of struggling in trees. Hence on each of the occasions when Amis's advice might be taken, January repeatedly fails to pretend, a "fere senblant." He fails to be the *fin amant* because he remains the same as he has always been—rigorously and laboriously himself.

Although replete with "fantasye," January lacks invention; he is incapable even of pretense. Pretense is not, of course, a consummation devoutly to be wished, and I am hardly advocating that January become the Pardoner. The failure to pretend is not important because pretense is desirable but rather because it suggests the stultifying uniformity of January's character. He can participate in no Other; he can only replicate himself. If he is Pygmalion, he is Pygmalion in reverse: whereas Pygmalion (who could both pretend and empathize) would make the naturally dead unnaturally alive, January would make the naturally alive unnaturally dead. Incapable of pretense, sterile of invention, January parodies and subverts Nature, who incessantly generates difference and differences.[18]

If January would replace Nature in the garden, she is nonetheless present though in a guise she is not wont to wear. In her confession to Genius in the *Roman de la Rose*, Nature at one point exclaims: "'I am a woman and cannot keep silent; from now on I want to reveal everything, for a woman can hide nothing'" (lines 19188–90; trans. Dahlberg 1971:317). Now in January's garden, Proserpyna makes a very similar exclamation: "'I am a womman, nedes moot I speke, / Or elles swelle til myn herte breke'" (MerT E 2305–2306). Chaucer's strategy is that Proserpyna should speak in Nature's voice. Previous scholarship has long recognized the mercantile-monetary relevance of Proserpyna to *The Merchant's Tale*; according to one gloss, for example, "Proserpina significat pecuniam" (Olson 1961:212). Complementing this relevance is her role as natural or chthonic power. And, it must be emphasized, it is this power which enables her through May to deceive January with a fiction or pretense (lines 2265–66, 2272–74; emphasis added):

> "Now by my moodres sires soule I swere
> That I shal yeven hire suffisant answere
> . . . .

Al hadde man seyn a thyng with bothe his yen,
Yit shul we wommen *visage* it hardily,
And wepe, and swere, and chyde subtilly."

Proserpyna it is who enables May (and all other women, too, we note) to "fere senblant"; and she suggests, therefore, that pretense or invention is a natural power, a power of the earth. More pertinent, perhaps, she suggests that imagination or fantasy, which is ultimately the faculty May employs (if to very dubious ends), is also a natural power—one which, if suppressed or perverted, as January perverts it, can and will reassert itself indiscriminately. It is as if, in the figure of Proserpyna, imagination or fantasy, continuous with Nature in man's person, rises up to claim its due.

Because of Proserpyna, May proves more than an "ycon" of January's "fantasye"; because of the power which she shares with Proserpyna, she proves more than the dead thing which January would make her. On the contrary, she is very much alive and capable of signification or mediation. She can *at least* make a fiction, even if that fiction, regrettably, should be only a lie. We can hardly approve of May, but we can hardly deny either that she is more imaginative and more alive than January. Through Proserpyna, May is the fiction maker in January's garden, to his great chagrin and despite his will to the contrary.

May's extraordinary capacity for signification or mediation actually emerges earlier in the tale, though without Proserpyna's vow we probably would not recognize the pattern. Repeatedly May is said to make or to give signs to Damyan and to write to him. For example: "But nathelees, by *writyng* to and fro, / And privee *signes*, wiste he what she mente" (lines 2104–2105; emphasis added; see further, lines 2150–51, 2209, 2213). One or two instances might be too few to justify suggesting a pattern; five are too many to excuse not suggesting a pattern. The text definitely insists on May's capacity for signification. In spite of January's concupiscible science of private conventionality and fantastic signs, May makes signs of her own. January's household and his garden are definitely not without signification, though he wishes they were. And wishes they were for good reason, given his position. Writing, the *Roman de la Rose* makes clear, is a trope for intercourse (see lines 19599–606), and in May's actions this trope has been almost literalized. Her signs and writings to Damyan not only anticipate her adultery but in fact *are* the early stages of her adultery. The mediation which they achieve is, in more senses than one, a false copula. It looks like communication, but there is in fact little community in it—at most, it is "irreferent" exchange of sexual pleasure. May the "visager" is indeed full of mediation or signification, but she is devoid of significance—much like a puppet whose strings are of sex.

So, too, with January's garden. He "shoop" it as a reification of his own desire—as a thing fixed in one meaning, his own. The last appearance he wants in his garden is the appearance of significance. He much prefers instead his carnal satisfaction. He could care less about the *sponsa* of the Cantica Canticorum when he addresses May in the language of that poem (MerT E 2138–48): he is only interested in the "dowve" spreading her wings. And yet the garden which he "shoop," precisely because it is a garden, is full of signification; it bristles with signs—of Paradise, of the genitalia, of classical mythology, etc. As he sees it, though, "for love is blynde alday, and may nat see," they signify only his desire and its satisfaction. As the Merchant sees it, however, the garden with its signs, like the tale itself, is not yet devoid of significance. Not until he annihilates the plenitude of signification, for evil is blind always and blindly sees, will the threat of significance pass from him—"irreference" become the only reverence.

The most ostentatious stylistic quirk which the Merchant displays in his narrative is disregard—indeed, disrespect—for the boundaries of his fiction. Not only does Justinus, supposedly in Pavia supposedly in fictional time, refer January to the Wife of Bath's recent sermonizing about marriage (lines 1685–87), but the Merchant himself also trespasses the boundaries of his fiction to apostrophize his character Damyan (lines 1866–69):

> Now wol I speke of woful Damyan,
> That langwissheth for love, as ye shul heere;
> Therfore I speke to hym in this manere:
> I seye, "O sely Damyan, allas!"

If we couple this trespass with the Merchant's obvious manipulation of personifications—January, May, Placebo, Justinus—in all but one of his major characters, and if we add to both Justinus's simultaneous existence (so to speak) in Pavia and on the road to Canterbury, we have an evident case, within a fiction, of someone reducing media to a mirror.[19] The Merchant, in this like his character January, rather than reality sees the images of his "fantasye" which he has projected onto media. He too is a moneyer of imagination; he too suffers from delusions of Pygmalionism; he too desires that reality be wax to bear the stamp of his die. Hence, for example, the Wife of Bath (who is, within the fiction, part of his reality) is reducible to material for his fiction. Unlike his character January, however, the Merchant perverts media with conscious malice. Where January moneys imagination or "fantasye" only for his sensual pleasure, the Merchant moneys imagination out of spite and envy. It is important to note here that the medieval etymology of "invidia" (envy) is "in-videre," or "not to see."[20] If there is such emphasis on blindness in *The Merchant's Tale*, it is owing in part to the blindness of envy which the Merchant suffers. He envies all those who are sexually and maritally happy, and his tale is an eruption out of that envy. Like all other envious, he does not want others to be happy. Indeed, he prefers that they share his hell. And so it is that the Merchant tries to stamp the wills of his audience, to impose his stamp upon them, so that they will become coins of his "fantasye": if they become such coins, he can spend them, use them, to validate and valuate his poisoned view of human sexuality and, indeed, of human creativity itself.

We are in a position here to grasp the peculiar effect of *The Merchant's Prologue*, discussion of which I have purposely delayed until this moment. After twenty-six lines of misogamy delivered in a tone of near hysteria, the Merchant agrees to begin his tale, "'but of my owene soore, / For soory herte, I telle may namoore'" (*MerP* 1243–44). By now we should be able to see through the falsification, the lie, which the Merchant has just uttered – of course, he is going to tell us of "his owene soore." His claim to the contrary, an attempt to throw his audience off the track, almost protests too much to succeed, though our common and natural tendency to believe someone until we have reason not to believe him probably works in his favor at first. But by the time we hear the allusion to the Wife of Bath, if not before, we are aware of a design upon us. And with *this* Narrator we may indeed die of imagination, if we are not careful of the impression we take. For he means to take out on his audience his bleak disappointment with his wife and his marriage, and he means to take out of his audience some compensation. The Merchant's furious indignation at his wife only exacerbates his desire for property. Because his private property has betrayed him – one gathers that his wife was something more than wax – he desires more property all the more vehemently, property which, because he owns it, will reinforce his sense of self. And the property which answers most expediently to this desire is the will of each member of his audience. If they consent to his view of sex and marriage, then he "owns" them, and the ruins of his ego are shored up by this "property." And he almost succeeds in his design. Listen to how like the Merchant Herry Bailly sounds at the end of the tale (lines 2421–40; emphasis added):

> "Lo, whiche sleightes and subtilitees
> In wommen been! for ay as bisy as bees
> Been they, us sely men for to deceyve,
> And from the soothe evere wol they weyve;

> By this Marchauntes tale it preveth weel.
> But doutelees, as trewe as any steel
> I have a wyf, though that she povre be,
> But of hir tonge, a labbyng shrewe is she,
> And yet she hath an heep of vices mo;
> Therof no fors! lat alle swiche thynges go.
> But wyte ye what? In conseil be it seyd,
> Me reweth soore I am unto hire teyd.
> For, and I sholde rekenen every vice
> Which that she hath, ywis I were to nyce;
> And cause why, it sholde reported be
> And toold to hire of somme of this meynee, –
> Of whom, it nedeth nat for to declare,
> Syn wommen konnen outen swich chaffare;
> And eek my wit suffiseth nat therto,
> To tellen al, wherfore *my tale* is do."

Herry's words, of course, are not the same as the Merchant's; Herry, thank God, is not the Merchant's replica. But this is the only *tale* which Herry tells, and it is, for a moment, a playback of the Merchant's, at least in vitriol and violence.[21] For a perilous moment Herry is a coin stamped by the Merchant, made in his image – unable to see anything but vice in women – and for that moment, before Herry's innate good humor reasserts itself, we see the cruel and ugly result of a narrative style that can only be called "usurious."

To understand the usury of the Merchant's narrative style, we must first see that his inflation of self, his self-aggrandizement, appears rhetorically as *amplificatio*. For example, he practices "astrological" inflation by means of the *amplificatio* of *circuitio* or *circumlocutio* (periphrasis) at lines 1795–99.[22] Then, too, he inflates through the *amplificatio* of apostrophe, as at lines 2057–61.[23] Finally, he indulges for amplification the "outdoing" topos, as at lines 1715–21.[24] It is as if the Merchant has memorized his Geoffrey of Vinsauf. This supposition is all the more attractive, if not compelling, when we recall how Geoffrey finishes the introduction to his section on *amplificatio*. Telling the novice poet to "reflect upon the precepts below," because "they will guide your pen and teach the essentials," Geoffrey continues: "The material to be moulded, *like the moulding of wax*, is at first hard to the touch" (Ed. Faral 1971:203; trans. Nims 1967:23; emphasis added). The Merchant's inflationary or amplificatory rhetoric is itself a sign of his delusions of Pygmalionism: he would follow Geoffrey almost literally in treating the material of his "fantasye" (or his tale) like wax, just as his character January treats the material of his "fantasye" (or May) like wax. But the Merchant's inflationary rhetoric does not stop with *amplificatio*; it also runs to what we might call brazenly literal *captatio benevolentiae* (Arbusow 1963:98). He says (lines 2350–53):

> Ladyes, I preye yow that ye be nat wrooth;
> I kan nat glose, I am a rude man –
> And sodeynly anon this Damyan
> Gan pullen up the smok, and in he throng.

We might want to strike the *bene* from *benevolentiae*; but still the Merchant has "*seized* the will" of his audience all right, and by as prim a turn of reverse pornography as we might hope to read.

In his darkness visible of human sexuality and creativity, after May has cast Damyan's letter in the privy and privily informed him of her availability, the Merchant describes Damyan's behavior as "so plesant unto every man / (For craft is al, whoso that do it kan) / That every wight is fayn to speke hym good" (lines 2015–17). For the Merchant too, craft is all – content, or that which is crafted, merely wax, passive and defenseless – and his position is one of constant imposition of his craft upon others. He is, after all, a merchant, hence a salesman. Selling is his craft, and selling is endless. Endlessly and relentlessly, the Merchant sells his craft of selling. If his audience buys it, they too become salesmen, just like him, for whom the craft of selling is all; and whether they sell the "wax" of misogamy or sell "sheeldes" (*GP* A 278) or sell the sacrament of marriage, they are his replicas and his property. They have, in fact, paid *interest on* as well as had *interest in* his surreptitious autobiography, his "irreferent" fiction.

I am moving here, tentatively but seriously, toward a description of exactly how the Merchant's narrative style is usurious. At this point the technical term during the Middle Ages for monetary exchange, or *cambium*, will, I believe, be helpful. Human communication, I would like to suggest, resembles a *cambium* because in communication we *exchange* our words of *different value*: we exchange difference as and because we are different. Even if, upon occasion, our words happen to be the "same," in reality they are not because they are, on the one hand, mine and, on the other, yours (cf. Deleuze 1968:35). Now if, on the contrary, I stand before you and demand that you consume my words exactly as mine – my words as money to buy your assent – you can become only my replica, not my mate in the exchanges of humanity. In this event the *cambium* of communication has become a usurious *mutuum* where, with no exchange from you, mine "becomes" yours – you consume what I want you to hear – while, just so, I insist that mine remain mine and return to me with more of mine, or the same. Where a *cambium* conceals a usurious *mutuum*, community dies.[25]

To preserve community, usury must be rejected. Even if it should happen that a *cambium* is impossible and a *mutuum* necessary, then the *mutuum* should flow from "caritas," as indeed the church taught (Noonan 1957:42, 64–65, 72–73). Hence, for example, because (but only because) my students are younger than I, often I lend them my words when they do not have their own to return, and they credit me: they believe me. But this is only in order that they may return their words to me, not mine but theirs, equally as equals, when their understanding has matured. "And unlike money, the word gives birth to the word," but only when my word is consumed and bears new fruit. And I can only ask in exchange an equal return. Not a return of the same, but an "equal return": "The Roman law said that the matter of loans was goods consisting in number, weight, or measure, that is, goods which were fungibles; since 'by giving them we contract a credit; for they can be repaid by being returned in their species rather than individually'" (Noonan 1957:40). Just as the "same" money hardly ever returns "individually" to the hands of the lender, so the "same" words should not return "individually" to either party in the *cambium*, or the occasional *mutuum*, of communication. Return of the "same" is replication merely and reification of the self demanding the "same." To be sure, my meaning may return; you and I may agree with each other; you and I may understand each other; you and I may communicate with each other. But, in this case, even when our words happen to be the "same," they are not because they are mine *and* yours. True "inter esse" is the celebration of difference without which life itself is impossible.

But the fertility of the word is ruined to sterility when the word is transumed into money—when it is used to buy replication of the self rather than to facilitate exchanges of self with the Other. When the word is confounded with money, the *cambium* of communication becomes a usurious *mutuum*. The usurer of the word demands not interest in himself calling to the Other but interest on his word such that it will return to him laden with more of himself. This unnatural increase of self dissolves the "inter esse" of human society. And this dissolution exposes the crime of the usurer, or his violation of humanity in trading on the necessity of togetherness to human being.

For the Merchant, usurer of words, as for January, the only "real" audience, the only audience he deems worthy of his performance, is such an audience as will acquiesce in his version of the world. To such an audience the Merchant would sell his fantasy and thus reinforce it. It is as if, to this end, he empties words of their living mediation—"Swiche olde lewed wordes used he" (*MerT* E 2149) – until they become dead matter which he can then quicken with his own insistent sexual and marital trauma. Where Geoffrey of Vinsauf *likens* the poet's material to wax, the Merchant wants words (and probably reality itself) *to be* wax, to be malleable to his will. He would prefer that words have no independent life of their own, no freedom to generate new forms (though, of course, they do, in spite of him). Rather than media which facilitate exchanges of self and Other, he would prefer that they be things which his craft of selling could consume. For if sold, they would return to him, or so he wants to believe, the Same. This is his desire. He does not want credit; he wants replication. He wants Herry Bailly to sound just the way he himself sounds. And at the core of this desire is the axiom, the frightening axiom, that everyone is just as unhappy, just as depraved, just as sorry as he is. Everyone desires the Same; there is no desire for Difference. These are axioms of the Merchant (and, if we stop to consider the matter, of the mercantile world too – think only of the assembly line). Without an iden-tity of his own, possessed only of craft, the Merchant must try to eliminate the differences of others so that they will want only what he wants. He must try to reduce everyone to the same desire and to the desire for the Same. Hence he invests the money of his imagination in the wills of his audience, hoping for a yield of the Same. The Merchant must have more and more of the Same (we are all, I suspect, fairly tired by the end of his tale of his relentless pursuit of the Same). Aristotle taught the Middle Ages that the curse on "campsoria" (traffic in money) was precisely the infinite desire which it unleashes (Noonan 1957:46–47).

The Merchant's lust for the Same is a will to level creation into destruction. It is a will to eradicate difference whose ultimate perversion is that creation "means" destruction or that good "means" evil or that, as Donaldson would express it (1958:1086), the positive "means" the negative. It is, in fact, creativity itself which the Merchant hates, and so death is his consuming desire. Because January claims that he is a green tree (*MerT* E 1461–66), we know that (the Merchant "means" that) he is rather a "lignum aridum," or a sterile or dead tree (Miller 1955:182–91). Because January claims that "'mariage is a ful greet sacrement'" (line 1319), we know that (the Merchant "means" that) marriage is a curse, a dead thing, bearing death. Because January's eyes are opened, we know that (the Merchant "means" that) he is in that moment most utterly blind. And so on, again and again, that which is life and creative is for the Merchant death and deadly.

The Merchant's desire for death is a reflex of his lust for the Same. The rhetorical appearance of this desire, this lust, is the opposite of allegory – hence the presence of so many potential allegories in *The Merchant's*

Tale—and since the medieval manuals universally define allegory as "alieniloquium," I propose here to call its opposite "proprioloquium."[26] If allegory and irony, which is one of the tropes of allegory, are an "other-speaking," then the Merchant's version of allegory, his falsification of it, is "self-speaking." Note well that, as with all of the falsification or counterfeiting, the original appears to be present—we have in the tale what looks like an abundance of allegory—but it is in reality false—the various allegories are actually "self-speakings" of the Merchant. Hence, the green tree "means" as if it were an allegorical image, but it "means" dead tree in the Merchant's coinage. Hence, again, the garden "means" as if it were an allegorical image—it is so near a duplication of the one in Genesis that it could hardly fail to do so—but it "means" the duping of an old fool by a young slut in the Merchant's coinage. We are, I must hasten to insist, talking now exclusively about the Merchant's, not Chaucer's, narration; Chaucer's narration is another matter altogether. In the Merchant's narration, with its usurious style, we confront again and again the structure of "other-speaking" (allegory), but what we hear is "self-speaking," or "proprioloquium." In the Merchant's narration, with its usurious style, we have false or counterfeit allegory. The Merchant doles out words and images fully intending that they "mean," or bear fruit, but also fully intending that their meaning, their fruit, remains exclusively his to profit from as he pleases.[27] The fungible word, we have seen, is fertile if it is consumed and then reborn in the Other, but for the Merchant the word is a coin whose ownership he retains after it has left him, with the result that when it is consumed by his audience the only fruit it can bear is his and himself. Counterfeit allegory, these arguments suggest, looks like plenitude of meaning, but, in fact, it is impoverishment of meaning (green tree = dead tree) for aggrandizement of the self.

As May is to January, so is his tale to the Merchant: devoid of signficance, except for the expression of lust, it is full of signification, despite the Merchant's will. And as May overwhelms January with her pretense or "lie," so his tale overwhelms the Merchant with its allegorical resonances. These resonances, in Chaucer's gift and control, are more than pretense, I should hasten to add, and they are "lies" only in the structural sense in which all fiction is a "lie." In Chaucer's narration they are not false but true "alieniloquium" (i.e., "true" or designed fiction). And this we know, first and foremost, because we sense the living mediation in his narration: we are not melting a lump of wax, we are not being duped by counterfeit coin, when we read and interpret Chaucer's poem. Hence it is a fair question to ask, What exactly is the difference between Chaucer and the Merchant?

At its simplest and before nuancing, the difference is this: the one is blind, the other can see. In media the Merchant can see only himself; Chaucer, we know, can see the Other, can see differences and Difference, can see the many ways in which people love themselves, define themselves, rule and fail to rule themselves. Chaucer is a love poet; the Merchant is a hate poet. And it is the measure of the love poet's love that he tried to see matters from the perspective of the hate poet's position.

We can nuance the difference between Chaucer's and the Merchant's visions with the help of Saint Augustine. He himself was a merchant, a "venditor verborum," or merchant of words, as he tells us.[28] And he wrote an autobiography, just as Chaucer's Merchant did. He and the Merchant both *confess* through *literary form* (cf. Shoaf 1981:175–85). In the eighth book of the *Confessions*, Augustine describes the consummation of his conversion, which took place beneath a tree in the garden of a friend. The tree strongly resembles the one which stands in January's garden, since both recall that "original" tree east in Eden; indeed, Augustine probably means to assimilate this tree to the earlier *pear* tree, where he first saw the fruits of his concupiscence (2.4), and by way of that tree to the Tree of Knowledge of Good and Evil. Now the conversion beneath the tree in his friend's garden was immediately preceded by the narration of the life of Saint Anthony (8.6). And as Augustine prepares to relate the events of his own momentous response to that story, he writes:

> This was what Ponticianus told us. But while he was speaking, O Lord, you were turning me around to look at myself. For I had placed myself behind my own back, refusing to see myself. You were setting me before my own eyes so that I could see how sordid I was, how deformed and squalid, how tainted with ulcers and sores. I saw it all and stood aghast, but there was no place where I could escape from myself. If I tried to turn my eyes away they fell on Ponticianus, still telling his tale, and in this way, you brought me face to face with myself once more, forcing me upon my own sight so that I should see my wickedness and loathe it. I had known it all along, but I had always pretended that it was something different. I had turned a blind eye and forgotten it (8.7; trans. Pine-Coffin 1961:169).

Augustine tries to turn from what he sees, but Ponticianus is "still telling his tale," and he cannot avoid the impingement of himself upon his eyes. He sees himself in and through the story of Saint Anthony—and cannot endure the self he sees. Hence, the story of Saint Anthony is a mirror, but it is a very special kind of mirror. Instead of the self which he desires to see, Augustine sees the self and its iniquity which he has known all along but avoided through dissimulation. And so, if the story of Saint Anthony is a mirror, we must say that it is a mirror of Difference. In it Augustine sees a man so different from himself that the difference throws into relief his own iniquitous self. Augustine sees Difference, or, sees the Other, and the Other tells him who and what he is. It turns him and twists him until it makes two of him, the one seeing and the one seen. This, we know, is self-consciousness. And Augustine is self-conscious—what rhetorician is not?—and becoming so much more self-conscious that he can no longer dissimulate and hide himself from himself; rather, seeing the truth, he must confess it. When he looks into the story of Saint Anthony, Augustine sees through the medium to the Other, and its Difference tells him who he is. We might think of Dante once more: it *is* Narcissus who looks into the mirror, but it is *not* Narcissus who sees himself.

Nor does Narcissus see himself when Chaucer looks into the mirror, whether the mirror of *The Merchant's Tale* or the mirror of any of his other poems. Chaucer, too, sees Difference even as he always celebrates differences. The Merchant, however, sees only the Same. Condemned to presence—to the hard, carnal materiality of his mercantile imagination—the Merchant is blind to the "alien-ness" of allegory. His "proprioloquium," a kind of verbal usury, so far from turning him to make two of him (self-consciousness), re-turns him the "turning" of the trope so that "meaning" may be *his* meaninglessness. The trope is ex-propri-ation, or the alienation of the proper of the word into the Other and new meaning—"pratum ridet" ("the meadow smiles")—and the whole community of the language is the richer for this "transfer" of "property" between meadows and smiles.[29] But this turn or transfer or alienation the Merchant assiduously attempts to direct toward himself and into his own possession, so that he might control it or dictate it. Do not ask for whom the meadow smiles or for whom the tree is green; it "smiles" for him; it is "green" for him.

Perhaps the single most revealing example of this perversion is the Merchant's gloss on January's paraphrase of Solomon's song of love—namely, "swiche olde lewed wordes used he" (*MerT* E 2149). January sings the song to entice the "columbyn" to spread her wings in his garden. Very well, this is lust, and bad though it be, it is only lust, least criminal of the seven deadly sins.[30] The Merchant, however, much more terrifying than January, is guilty of envy (not to mention other sins), and he utters the song *cum* gloss to annihilate its allegorical plenitude. The key here—it is one of the most brilliant word choices in Chaucer's poetry, as brilliant as "taille"—is "lewed." In glossing January's words as "lascivious," the Merchant is also trying to suggest that they are "unlearned" and "simplistic," the other and possibly more dominant meanings of Middle English "lewed."[31] In fact, however, words are "learned," and they are "knowledgeable" (cf. Payne 1981:36). They have a life of their own which is their property. This is not merely a way of speaking. Or if it is a way of speaking, it is such a way as Heidegger follows (1971:213–29) when he affirms with Hölderin that "dichterisch wohnet der Mensch" ("poetically man dwells"). Language speaks man at least as much as man speaks language. And this because words have a life of their own. They have their life in the "in-between" (the "inter-esse") not only through the power of convention, or that agreement or concordance by means of which men form communities of meaning, but also through their power to ex-propriate themselves. The church, the body of the faithful, had agreed that Solomon's Song was "learned" in the relationship between Christ and His Bride; but if the community of the church celebrated that significance as real, it is because that significance "turned" from the property of Solomon's words.[32] The agreement and the trope are simultaneously cause and effect each of the other. But January will sing Solomon's Song only if his carnality is its "allegory": the trope "turns" but it is privatized; January's satisfaction, alone in his world, signifies – "this [is] his fantasye." But as the Merchant sees it, allegory itself, the plenitude of signification, must be "lewed": unlearned and unknowledgeable, the trope is not not "turned" but "turned" not to "turn" ("propriology": counterfeit allegory) – "this [is] his fantasye." Finally, January is an idolatrous old fool. The Merchant, on the other hand, is a nihilist of the sign: for him, meaninglessness is the only meaning.

Because he is a nihilist of the sign, because he would annihilate significance in the world, the Merchant is most fittingly seen as, so to speak, an escapee from Dante's *Inferno*. Characteristic of the damned is their reduction of all media to the carnal and the literal: in addition to Master Adam, we may think of the Medusa as the type of authority in Hell (Freccero 1972:1–18). As Master Adam almost turns Dante into a falsifier and narcissist, so Medusa would turn him into stone. Their false authority carnalizes or hardens those who are exposed to it. Just so, to look at the Merchant and his tale directly – without any protection, without any mediation, such as Virgil provides Dante (*Inf.* 9.55–63) – would be to turn to stone, one's will reduced to the Merchant's property without any further vocation, the fate which Herry Bailly almost suffers. The Merchant utters, breeds, and sells death. The creativity of media, of words especially, he must kill to satiate his envy. This he attempts by the supreme usury of insisting that he alone determine their structure and their meaning – "swiche olde lewed wordes used he." The Merchant would have it that conventionality, or the creative concord of the community, and expropriation, or the creative "turn" of words, be replaced by his counterfeit allegory. The words which he uses, alive with meaning, he tries to reduce to wax or to stone, so as, once they are dead, to quicken them with his own character; the coin of his imagination, they will return to him, having bought the wills of his audience—an infinity of the increase of the Same were he to succeed. The Merchant, usurer and "proprioloquist," disposes of a narrative style which would reduce the community of meanings to a soliloquy in Hell.

But this in fact does not happen. And this because of Chaucer, the other voice if not the voice of Other. I am not here invoking tale-teller irony, that old if not wearied dogma of Chaucer criticism. I am speaking rather to the phenomenon of a text which revels in disclosure, which plays with the profoundest of all paradoxes of mediation, or the concealment simultaneous with every revelation. As the Merchant tries to close (as he "sees" it, *reveal*) the reality of romance and marriage within his own blind view, darkened by usury and a bankruptcy not monetary only, his words disclose his malice and his suffering. As the Merchant tries to impress upon the wax of his material the dies of his "fantasye," his words prove more than wax, and as living mediation, they succeed in implying that he is a copy of a very old Hater of life. What the Merchant would close, materialize, and reify, Chaucer opens, spiritualizes, and personalizes. He does so by giving the Merchant what the merchant would destroy: significance. Chaucer protects us from the Merchant and his tale just as Virgil protects Dante from the Medusa, but not in the same way. Whereas Virgil covers Dante's eyes, Chaucer is rather the light by *means* of which we *see through* the Merchant and his tale to the *significance beyond.*

Chapter 13
The Pardoner and the Word of Death

HIS BOOK concludes with an analysis of *The Pardoner's Prologue and Tale*, for several reasons, some more obvious than others. Most obvious is that the Pardoner of all Chaucer's posers is the most skillful, theatrical, and elusive. Only slightly less obvious is the connection in the Pardoner and his discourse between language and money. He is obsessed with both and uses the one as a magnet for the other: "'Of avarice and of swich cursednesse / Is al my *prechyng*, for to make hem free / To yeven hir *pens*'" (*PardP* C 400–402; emphasis added). Then there is the emphasis on "entente," this word so insistent in Chaucer's vocabulary: not only does it occur three times (lines 403, 423, 432), but the problem which revolves around it is vivid in the Pardoner's claim that "'though myself be a ful vicious man / A moral tale yet I yow telle kan'" (lines 459–60). Here is an open breach between intent and content, and the emergent crisis of reference demands attention and scrutiny. Next, less obvious but no less important than these other reasons, is the insistence on buying and especially on the buying of the Redemption. On three occasions the Pardoner recurs to the "buying again" which Christ's sacrifice effected, and twice he uses the exact phrase "boght agayn," as if the etymology of "redemptio" held some sort of magical power for his own personal redemption (*PardT* C 501, 766, 902). Answering to this insistence on the Redemption is Herry Bailly's pointed remark, just before he calls on the Pardoner, about Virginia of the *Physician's Tale*: "'Allas, to deere *boughte* she beautee!'" (*Phy-PardL* C 293; emphasis added). In addition, there is the large and almost oppressive fact, if also usually implicit, that the Pardoner's audiences as a rule "buy" his words—his, so to speak, "pitch"—when he wins pence from them (see *PardP* C 403–404). The Pardoner's desire for personal redemption, I think we can suggest, is, in fact, displaced and materialized in the purchase of him which his audiences make when they buy his words.

The manner of this displacement is crucial to understanding the Pardoner and the crisis of reference; in fact, it relates to the final and perhaps most important reason for concluding this book with the Pardoner, or the agon in his prologue and tale between the literal and the allegorical. Commentary on this and related matters is by now very extensive.[1] Here I make no pretense to the last word and certainly no attempt at a summary of all the previous words. I do propose, however, to open the question of the letter and the spirit from the position which this book has so far mapped out. In particular, I will argue that, if the Merchant's allegory is counterfeit, the Pardoner's is, on the contrary, true; and the truth in which he deals, I will go on to argue, is what makes him so dark and ominous a figure. He is a liar, a consummate liar, who nonetheless deals in the truth, and deals in it even to the point of truly confessing that he lies. This mixture of truth and lies resembles the mixture of life and death in the Pardoner. For a lie is the word of death. Recall that the Father of lies (John 8.44) brought death into the world (Sap. 2.24); and "when the Devil speaks a lie, he speaks from his own" (John 8.44), and just so the Pardoner "from his own speaks" (from his own "proper") when he lies. But when he lies, his word of death is a very live word, having its own strange efficacy. Hence the word of death (a lie) is the death of the word—but while it still lives. And is this not the Pardoner? A living death?

The Pardoner recurs to the Redemption twice in his own voice, once in that of the Old Man. The first time he is castigating gluttony (PardT 500–504):

> O original of oure dampnacioun,
> Til Crist hadde boght us with his blood agayn!
> Lo, how deere, shortly for to sayn,
> Aboght was thilke cursed vileynye!
> Corrupt was al this world for glotonye.

The second time, at the end of the tale, he is attacking the "cursed synne of alle cursednesse" (lines 900–903):

> Allas! mankynde, how may it bitide
> That to thy creatour, which that the wroghte
> And with his precious herte-blood thee boghte,
> Thou art so fals and so unkynde, allas?

Finally, the Old Man, as he directs the revelers to Death says (lines 765–67):

> "Se ye that ook? Right there ye shal hym fynde.
> God save yow, that boghte agayn mankynde,
> And yow amende."

Note in passing that in the first example the Pardoner uses "bought" twice ("Aboght was thilke cursed vileynye"); and I suspect that the point he is suggesting is that, as Adam dearly bought damnation, so Christ in turn bought us back from damnation, just as dearly. In good homilectic fashion he is alluding to the doctrine of first and second Adam, so emphasized by Saint Paul.[2] But whether or not he is, in fact, flourishing his preacher's skill in this way, certainly the notion of buying holds some special importance for him. And we can trace this importance to its source in his longing for personal redemption, a longing which is part of a personality at once desperately incomplete and unbearably brilliant.

That the Pardoner's personality is incomplete should need no arguing: he is a "geldyng" or a "mare" (GP A 691). But the amount of ink spilled in arguing anyway over these words and their implications cannot go unnoticed. Some say that the Pardoner is a *eunuchus ex nativitate*; some say that he is a homosexual; some say that he is a hermaphrodite; some say that the question is open; and Donaldson says that "the fact seems to be that there is good evidence that the Pardoner is and is not homosexual, and you may read him either way you please, with perfect confidence that you are probably wrong."[3] I say that all this is beside the point, the point being that the Pardoner's identity is a question to others, such as Chaucer the pilgrim, and therefore almost certainly a question to himself. To this extent, then, he is incomplete.

That the Pardoner is also an unusually brilliant man would seem evident from his skill with words: he delivers a sermon which is a model of rhetorical finesse.[4] An incomplete but brilliant man is likely to suffer wrenching emotions and as a consequence to be abnormally sensitive. Chaucer has a number of ways of suggesting this abnormal sensitivity. At this point I want to call attention to the one which I consider most important, the Pardoner's position in *The General Prologue*.

He comes last among the portraits. To be sure, Herry is described after the Pardoner (at lines 751–57), but in introducing the last five of his "compaignye," the last of whom is the Pardoner, Chaucer goes out of his way to remark, "there were namo" (line 544). Hence, obviously, Chaucer must have consciously placed the Pardoner last. Now in itself the Pardoner's position might indicate some special emphasis but no more. In opposition to the first position, however, and the figure who holds it, the Knight, it does considerably more than that. The Knight and the Pardoner form a polarity of far-reaching significance, especially since it is the Knight who attempts to reconcile Herry and the Pardoner at the end of the latter's sermon.[5] The Knight, in contrast to the Pardoner, enjoys the highest social status of the pilgrims;

moreover, as a crusader, he is a valuable servant of the church, though he has taken no orders as far as we know and obeys no direct mandate from Rome; his great piety seems obvious from his haste to go on the pilgrimage; and he is definitely masculine since he has fathered a son—no question about his identity. All these characteristics, and doubtless others one could name, suggest a positive to which the Pardoner is a negative. And yet Chaucer never leaves anything so simple as all that. From the tale which the Knight tells—where order is so stifling it is a kind of disorder, where a soldierly Stoicism fills out an ostensibly Christian mold, where an old man's weary wisdom disconcertingly recommends a bloodless and a dubiously Christian resignation, where the highest human achievement is the pagan and heroic, hardly Christian, ideal of good fame after death (KnT A 3047–49), and where passion is cynically laughed at (KnT A 1785–1814)—from all this it is possible to conclude that the Knight is one of the least passionate and most rigid men whom Chaucer ever imagined.[6] To *this* negative the Pardoner is a certain though highly problematic positive, and this is principally why Chaucer positions his portrait last. With his vivid imagination, powers of projection, and ability to identify with roles, the Pardoner could never, for example, take such a mechanical and coldly matter-of-fact position on Arcite's death as does the Knight when he describes the dissolution of the latter's body (KnT A 2743–60, especially 2759–60: "And certeinly, ther Nature wol nat wirche, / Fare wel phisik! go ber the man to chirche!"). The Pardoner would give as vivid a description, if not one more vivid; but he would entertain none of the Knight's clinical pedantry or any of his soldierly brusqueness—he would feel more of what he was saying and communicate more of that feeling. Thus he and his position counterpoise the Knight and his in order to suggest the significant difference between them, or the Pardoner's capacity for feeling.

The Pardoner's capacity for feeling, I perhaps should note, is hardly the same thing as sympathy; it is, quite the contrary, more like abnormal sensitivity. And in this condition the Pardoner suffers his mutilated personality morbidly. He is not whole, and he knows it; moreover, the community in which he must live can include him only by ostracizing him.[7] And yet, brilliant as he is, he must have an abstract appreciation of what it would be like to be whole and to belong—he can imagine it, for imagination is supremely if also pervertedly his gift. And in his imagination would be borne the longing for personal redemption, such as Christ holds out to man, and thence would arise the obsession with buying. He keeps coming back to that possibility which he knows he can never enjoy (cf. Patterson 1976:153–73).

It is important to this argument that Christianity, both before and during Chaucer's day, emphasized the element of "purchase" in the Redemption.[8]

Saint Augustine may be considered representative: "Behold, Christ has suffered; behold, the Merchant shows us the payment; behold the price which he paid: his blood is poured out."[9]

This example could be supplemented by many others from the patristic and later medieval periods.[10] More important for the moment, however, is to set the emphasis on purchase and debt in its wider scriptural context. It goes back to Paul (1 Cor. 6.20, for example) and ultimately to Christ himself (Matt. 13.44–46, for example). Christ and Paul are also responsible, in different ways, for the fundamental notion supporting the Pardoner's vocation, or the selling of pardons. For these pardons derive ultimately from the treasury of merit which Christ's sacrifice and that of his saints established in and for the church.[11] Strictly speaking, the church dispenses to the Pardoner merit from its superabundant store, and he, in turn, sells this merit in the form of pardons for a profit which is indisputably illicit in his case. Buying and selling, credit and debit, merchandising, are structured into everything the Pardoner says and does (Scheps 1977:107–23); and they are as much a part of the legitimate church as they are a part of his illegitimate desires and deeds.

A ravaged personality, mutilated; a brilliant mind, unbalanced; abnormal sensitivity; a probable desire to be saved, to be redeemed, precisely because of such deformity; a profession which involves merchandising out of the store of the Redemption and the treasury of Christ. The pattern of the obsession should be clear by now.

According to Saint Augustine, men "were able to sell themselves, but they were not able to redeem themselves."[12] The Pardoner, I am suggesting, is well aware of this. He sells himself, his act, every day in his profession; but, to judge from the pattern of his obsession, he knows because he regrets that he cannot buy himself back. Only the Other can redeem. Hence his unmistakable but also nervous delight in duping his audiences: by means of his poses and impostures he wins their pence. In a very "literal" or "carnal" or material sense, they purchase him, and this purchase is a surrogate for the Redemption he can never otherwise have. Although I have used the word "literal" here, its precise application is problematical; and we will need to return again and again to the problematic of the "literal." Already we can see one element in it. If the Merchant is a "propriofoquist," always seeking his own meaning of meaninglessness, the Pardoner, on the contrary, is an "alieniloquist" because he needs and he craves the Other and others:

> What results is the "vertige du même," the fear or the blank awareness that
> comes when you realize that you are only one, that you do not have the

colorful interest of variety about you, that there was only yourself to deal with all the time. With this recognition, with the lack of a genuine "other," you collapse into nothingness. Hence the myth of the suicide of Narcissus, the meeting in sameness that extinguishes the tautological consciousness (Massey 1976:116).

In order to escape his "tautological consciousness," the Pardoner desperately seeks the Other: hence the coruscation, the torrent, of meanings he releases in his prologue and tale—he never stops talking until Herry shuts him up.

But at the same time, all the meanings, we suspect, do somehow serve the letter; somehow they are carnal and material. Instead of the blood with which Christ redeemed man, the Pardoner desires the coin of his audiences. Instead of the sacrament which "effects what it signifies" because the blood of Christ instituted it,[13] the Pardoner desires "real" money whose tangibility and materiality solace him and whose efficacy is visible and present. For the efficacy that is invisible and intangible, the Pardoner substitutes the materiality of purchasing power. Where the pardon he preaches is sacramental, immaterial, and invisible, but efficacious for the faithful, the Pardoner himself is relentlessly carnal and material. And this because his faith, like his body, is sterile: it exists, but it bears no fruit.

My concern here is the connection between the Pardoner's sexual and spiritual conditions. Whatever the former is said to be, there can be no doubt that the Pardoner is physically sterile. Now from this condition, some have reasoned that he is also spiritually sterile.[14] And I agree that he is, even as I also doubt such reasoning. I doubt it because the Pardoner does in fact produce (*PardP* C 429–34; emphasis added):

> "But though myself be gilty in that synne,
> *Yet kan I maken oother folk to twynne*
> *From avarice*, and soore to repente.
> But that is nat my principal entente;
> I preche nothyng but for coveitise."

The Pardoner saves souls, or at least he claims that he does. He is doubtless boasting, but boasting is usually an exaggeration of fact, and given the Pardoner's powers at preaching, it is not difficult to concede the probable fact that he has saved *some* people from avarice. The Pardoner does, then, probably produce fruit, or good works, through the seminal power of his verbal art. But he is himself, as has rightly been said, sterile because he does not believe in this fruit; he has no faith in its efficacy—he has, as he says, a different intent. The Pardoner has no faith, though he certainly knows in the abstract what faith is, because his intent is "nothyng but for coveitise." Between him and the efficacy of the word, blocking that efficacy for him, is a covetous intent, like a dead body across the way.

The Pardoner *does* good works; he *is* sterile and faithless. So much is in keeping with his role of actor or poser or impostor: nothing in himself, he can play anyone or anything. Between his act and his "self" falls his "yvel entencioun" (line 408) to "wynne gold and silver" (line 440). Hence, of any simplistic theory of the instrumentality of words the Pardoner will make a mockery. His words are almost always duplicitous. And in the "yvel entencioun" where this duplicity arises is the failed reference of the Pardoner's "dead" or sterile body.

The Pardoner lives in a body that has no referent. He is not really a man, not really a woman, and if he is both, he is neither—in fact, as we say of animals, he is *neutrum*, or neuter. And this I take to be the importance of Chaucer the pilgrim's doubt, "geldyng *or a mare*" (*GP* A 691; emphasis added)—the Pardoner is *neither* this *nor* that. *In* his body, consequently, the Pardoner can refer to all sorts of things; *with* his body, however, he can refer to nothing (not even to pleasure, I suspect, since a man who could enjoy pleasure would not dirty it the way the Pardoner does). Sterile and thus without reference with his body, the Pardoner must rely on the surrogate seed of language, in something like the same way an actor relies on the costumes and props attending a role. This surrogate seed is obviously as much a fishwife's or a sailor's or Herry Bailly's as it is the Pardoner's; and this must gall him, wound his pride. Nevertheless, it is fertile; it does produce. It produces, however, not the Pardoner's property but the converted souls of others. And the Pardoner is dependent on this creativity. Without it, he could not fulfill his "yvel entencioun." With it, he works roughly as follows. He lets the seed of language (or the seed of the signs which are his relics) inseminate others with conversion, but he charges them for it so that, as language converts them, they convert language or seed into money which then "inseminates" and "fertilizes" as it "redeems" the Pardoner and his "dead" body.[15] Words become seeds, seeds become money, and money becomes seeds to fill the Pardoner with the sexuality and fertility which he otherwise lacks. Hence the "yvel entencioun" and duplicitous reference can accurately be said to originate in the Pardoner's "dead" body. The desire to "quicken" that body gives rise to them both.

Because of his sexual deformity, the Pardoner indulges an "yvel entencioun" which eventuates in a "literal" or "carnal" acceptation of signs. Instead of spiritual redemption, he desires the "literal" purchase which audiences make when they pay him for preaching. But this "literalism," we can see, is peculiar: it depends, in fact, on metaphoricity. We must never forget the Pardoner's manifest intelligence. He knows that he cannot be spiritually redeemed because he is in a state of sin. He also knows (he is too self-conscious a poser not to know) that he is playing a game with his audiences and their pence. Hence he probably also knows that he wants and accepts their hard cash because metaphorically as well as literally it is redemptive. The Pardoner knows his metaphors—every poser must. And if he takes Christ's redemption "literally," reducing it to "real" coins, he covets "real" coins in part because of their metaphoricity in the theology of Redemption: their lure for him in part is that metaphoricity. Because Christ's saving work is understood in terms of purchase, merit, treasury, wealth, and so on, these and related concepts and objects hold a special appeal for the Pardoner, who desires even as he resents and resists Christ's saving work. The Pardoner is a "literalist," yes, but to be a "literalist" in his case is to take metaphors very seriously. The word of death, to repeat, is a very live word.

Hence, one can argue that the Pardoner has a sort of faith—he takes metaphors seriously, and he believes that words are creative—and one can argue that he produces good works. But, and this is at the center of the tragedy he suffers and the terror he inspires, the works are not the product of the faith—they are the product rather of his "yvel entencioun" to "wynne gold and silver." Hence the Pardoner's faith is without works, and "even as the body without the spirit is dead, so also faith without works is dead" (James 2.26). The Pardoner's faith is like his body, his body like his faith—there but sterile, alive but dead, neuter and ready for any position. Neuter and ready for any position, the Pardoner obviously has no position of his own. Rather, he takes his position from the available cue. And in the present case, Herry Bailly provides the cue. He not only anticipates the Pardoner's obsession with buying but also suggests to him the two fundamental themes of his sermon, or Fortune and Nature (Bartholomew 1966:9–57). In "the wordes of the Hoost to the Phisicien and the Pardoner," Herry exclaims of Virginia, "'Allas, to deere boughte she beautee!'" and then proceeds immediately to pontificate (*Phy-PardL* C 293–96; emphasis added):

> "Wherfore I seye al day that men may see
> That yiftes of *Fortune* and of *Nature*
> Been cause of deeth to many a creature."

Just so, the Pardoner proceeds to deliver a sermon whose central exemplum is a story very much involving the "yiftes of Fortune and of Nature." Moreover, and this is as important though perhaps less noticeable, these "wordes of the Hoost" begin with the statement that "Oure Hooste gan to swere as he were wood" (line 287), and, of course, the Pardoner goes on to attack the sin of swearing in his sermon. Then, too, Herry introduces the "'draughte of moyste and corny ale'" (line 315), which spurs the Pardoner to abominate drunkenness. Finally, and of fundamental importance, Herry jargonizes with the Physician's profession (lines 304–306):

> "I pray to God so save thy gentil cors,
> And eek thyne urynals and thy jurdones,
> Thyn ypocras, and eek thy galiones."

As Herry himself says, only too truly, he "'kan nat speke in terme'" (line 311). But by the attempt he inspires the Pardoner to pull out all the stops in his own jargon engine of preaching. Hence, when the "gentils" (line 323) protest: "'Nay, lat hym telle us of no ribaudye! / Telle us som moral thyng'" (lines 324–25), the Pardoner obliges them by drawing, like the parasite he is, on their Host.

A parasite, with no position of his own, an actor and an impostor ready for any role, a neuter who is sterile, the Pardoner is both alive and dead. In fact, this is the way in which the very theology he exploits would characterize and analyze him. He himself shows us the way (lines 542–43, 547–48; emphasis added):

> for they [cooks] caste noght awey
> That may go thurgh the golet softe and swoote.
> . . . .
> But, certes, *he that haunteth swiche delices*
> *Is deed, whil that he lyveth in tho vices.*

Every sinner, like the glutton, is dead while he lives in his vices (cf. Rom. 6.23). Of the Pardoner this is especially true since his body is "literally" dead as far as fertility is concerned. Hence theological analysis of the sinner and his condition realizes itself "literally" in the Pardoner: the *metaphor*, no less actual for that, of the sinner's living death is *literal* in the Pardoner. The Pardoner is literally a metaphor, the living death of sin—he is himself the word of death. At the same time, because the letter is not only dead but also "killeth" (2 Cor. 3.6), the Pardoner is metaphorically a letter: he figures in his body and in the use of his body the literalism which kills—he is also the death of the word. He is (once again the text draws us back to this formula) neuter: he is neither a metaphor nor a letter but a positionless mixture of both. He can pose as either and poses either as he will.

In fact, this—posing either indiscriminately—is the way in which he generates his sermon exemplum. It is a way much like the way in which cooks provide for a glutton's "wombe" (*PardT* C 534). He says (lines 538–39):

> Thise cookes, how they stampe, and streyne, and grynde,
> And turnen substaunce into accident.

The Pardoner is himself a kind of cook: he boasts to the pilgrims that "'in Latyn I speke a wordes fewe, / To *saffron* with my predicacioun'" (PardP C 344–45; emphasis added).[16] His preaching is indeed a kind of stew of rhetorical sleights-of-hand. And he, like his culinary "scholastics," turns substance into accident: he reduces the substance of meaning into the accident of the letter or its carnal, material manifestation. The best brief example is his conversion of the Eucharist into its literal and material elements: "'But first...heere at this alestake / I wol bothe *drynke*, and *eten* of a cake'" (Phy–PardL C 321–22; emphasis added). Although ale is not wine, eating and drinking just before preaching are obviously gestures reminiscent of the Eucharist.[17] And the Pardoner doubtless intends to pose the *materials* of the sacrament (anything to eat and drink) as the *meaning* of the sacrament which most interests him.

So also with his exemplum. Here the best illustration is the revelers' boast that "this false traytour Deeth / ...shal be slayn, he that so manye sleeth" (PardT C 699–700). While the text hardly needs scriptural exegesis to be interpreted, once interpreted, it profits from the context which exegesis provides. The revelers' words allude, of course, to Hosea 13.14, to which Saint Paul himself alludes in 1 Corinthians 15.55: "I will deliver them out of the hand of death. I will redeem them from death. O death, I will be thy death; O hell, I will be thy bite." The cry of the prophet, "O death, I will be thy death," exegesis consistently understands as the triumphant claim of Christ the Redeemer.[18] It is He who will conquer Death or Hell or the Devil (ultimately one from the theological perspective) during his "descensus ad inferos" when He will liberate all those whom Death or Hell or the Devil think to hold in their power.[19] The revelers, who number three probably in deliberate mockery of the Holy Trinity, are a drastically carnal version of the Triune Lord, and they are hardly likely to equal His victory in the struggle with Death. Indeed, they become the victims of Death instead of the victors precisely because they are so carnal. Scripture and its exegesis predict as much. In Hosea, after the outcry against death, the voice goes on: "Because he shall make a separation between brothers. The Lord will bring a burning wind that shall rise from the desert, and it shall dry up his springs, and shall make his fountain desolate; and he shall carry off the treasure of every desirable vessel." According to the commentaries, the one who "makes division among brothers" is the Devil or Hell or Death.[20] Just so, when the three revelers were four, Death divided them by taking their "old felawe" (PardT C

672), whereupon the remaining three swore an oath of brotherhood together (as though each were the other's "owene ybore brother"; line 704). But this brotherhood is destroyed in just the way in which Scripture and its commentaries suggest that it would be. When the youngest reveler decides to betray the other two, "*the feend*, oure enemy, / Putte in his thought that he sholde poyson beye" (lines 844–45; emphasis added), and the result is precisely "division among brothers." The text consistently accords with what a contemporary would have expected from exegesis of this famous verse in Hosea. The Pardoner's allegory – almost, we might say, his allegorical method – is very neat and prim.

But he continues to serve the word of death. If his allegory reveals the fate of carnal men – of gluttons, gamblers, and oathtakers – it is, just so, an allegory about the carnal, about all those acts and features of carnality which so obsess the carnally frustrated Pardoner. Moreover, if his allegory is creative and fruitful, it nonetheless allows him once again to literalize the Redemption – if Christ's Redemptive work is the death of Death, the Pardoner's version of this work is the story of three youths who would literally kill Death. Once again the Pardoner has posed the metaphor of Redemption as literal: all the materials of the Redemption are here – a trinity, a tree, money (gold), death – to serve as the meaning of Redemption. And this pose is explicable, once again, in terms of his deformity and obsession. Himself "dead" and spiritually an "old man" (Rom. 6.6; Miller 1955:188–93), he longs precisely for the death of Death, but for the literal death of Death. If Death literally died, then the "death" (of sterility) in his body might also die. He knows full well, I hasten to add, that this cannot be, but once again he takes the metaphor seriously. And he mixes metaphor and letter indiscriminately in a story about the death of death. The death of Death *is* the promise to spiritual man: if a man dies to sin and the flesh, then he shall live (Rom. 6.3–11) – the life of the spirit. But the Pardoner does not want this life: he does not want to die – he is already dead. He wants rather the life of a virile, fertile body, and he wants the renewal of youth. Hence, necessarily, he longs for the literal death of Death. Just as his desire carnalizes or materializes the benefits of the Redemption, so it must also carnalize or materialize, literalize, the work of the Redemption, or the death of Death.

One other illustration of the Pardoner's "stew" of metaphor and letter will perhaps be of help. The Old Man directs the three revelers up a "croked wey" (*PardT* C 761) to a grove where he left Death "under a tree" (line 763). Now it was under a tree that sin entered the world – the Tree of Knowledge of Good and Evil. It was *on* a tree – typologically and according to legend, the same tree (Quinn 1962:76–78) – that Christ by His sacrifice conquered sin and destroyed Death. The metaphoricity of the tree where the three revelers, carnal parody of the Lord, will struggle with Death is manifest, even ostentatious. But this ostentatious metaphoricity only serves the greater triumph of the letter. For when this unholy trinity dies under/on the tree, Death—which is to be equated with the letter—consumes the metaphoricity itself as well as three foolish mortals. Death and its letter not only win the unholy trinity, they also win the *holy Trinity*. Death and its letter do not merely kill three men; they subvert the Crucifixion and the Redemption, "turning" their spiritual "substance" into the "accident" of three ordinary greedy men killing each other over "eighte busshels" (line 771) of gold florins. Even as the event sets up the meanings, the very banality of the event undermines the meanings. and this is the way the Pardoner *intends* it: for him, the closest men get to redemption is a brief glorying over gold, then daggers and poison.

And this because he has himself failed of redemption. It is probably obvious by now that in the debate over the Pardoner's sudden *volte face* at the end of his sermon, I will incline to the old—and, I suppose, most would say, sentimentalized—view of Kittredge (1939:217) that he suffers a "paroxysm of agonized sincerity." While I disavow the late-nineteenth-century characterology implicit in this evaluation, and while I am sympathetic with the more modern position that the Pardoner is not a character at all but an instance of the illusoriness of self, I still maintain that the text asks us to hear a sudden reversal of positions. The crux is the word "leche" (*PardT* C 915–18; emphasis added):

> —And lo, sires, thus I preche.
> And Jhesu Crist, that is *oure soules leche*,
> So graunte yow his pardoun to receyve,
> For that is best; I wol yow nat deceyve.

Of course, the first problem is the "I wol yow nat deceyve": given his "yvel entencioun" to "wynne gold and silver" and his confession of hypocrisy—"'Thus spitte I out my venym under hewe / Of hoolynesse, to semen hooly and trewe'" (*PardP* C 421–22)—it is difficult to believe that the Pardoner would ever will not to "deceyve"; it is difficult to believe that he would ever *take a position*—would ever expose himself as "himself" rather than as some imposture. But the same evidence—evidence of the lack of a self—can suggest, quite humanly and understandably so, the opposite conclusion. For a man of "yvel entencioun" and gross hypocrisy who "'wol noon of the apostles countrefete'" (line 447) is necessarily a man of acute self-consciousness. A poser always knows he is in a pose—that is the definition of a poser. And because of such knowledge, because of such self-consciousness, the Pardoner cannot but realize that he is sick, that he is moribund. His very obsession with Death and the Redemption also argues the same conclusion. Hence it only makes sense that he would at some point take that position, of all the positions in his neutrality he might take, which is the least possible, most tenuous, and yet desperately attractive to him—the position of "I want to be whole." So, for a moment, he admits, he poses (and takes the position) that Christ is the "leche" who makes whole, by means of his "pardoun." My point is not to sympathize with him but to understand him. He has enough intelligence to know the truth of what he has said. The actor or impostor can shift into truth just as easily as he can shift into a lie. Moreover, a neuter and a parasite who so desperately wants and needs healing would predictably refer to *the* Healer at some point, especially since he lives his life in carnal parody and imposture of the Healer—selling the latter's pardons to persons who are in fact from time to time healed. But the tragedy of such a poser is that he cannot hold this position for long; he knows his sickness too well—it has become almost comfortable for him. And so the Pardoner abandons "oure soules leche" and "his pardoun" so as to lapse back into the by now much more familiar role.

Hawking his pardons once again, the Pardoner confronts and affronts Herry Bailly (*PardT* C 941–45):

> "I rede that oure Hoost heere shal bigynne,
> For he is moost envoluped in synne.
> Com forth, sire Hoost, and offre first anon,
> And thou shalt kisse the relikes everychon,
> Ye, for a grote! Unbokele anon thy purs."

Much attention has been paid recently to the Pardoner's sexual affront of the Host.[21] While I recognize the validity of this position, I am also intrigued by the *truth* of the Pardoner's accusation. Whether Herry is the *most* "envoluped in synne" we might want to debate, but *that* he is "envoluped in synne" we can hardly deny: he swears outrageously, drinks, indulges games of chance (the meal at his inn for which the pilgrims are contending), backbites his wife (*MerT* E 2427–29), and gives in to rage. The Pardoner has read Herry very closely and read him very well. His intelligence continues awesome. The measure of how well he has read Herry is Herry's very rage. Herry reacts not only or most importantly to sexual effrontery but also and crucially to the bitter, sharp sting of truth. The Pardoner has penetrated the "envelope" ("envoluped in synne") of Herry's position or role or act—interpreted the *involucrum* of his position (and pose)[22]—and this penetration *does* threaten

Herry, not only sexually but also spiritually. Before the consummate actor his act is transparent. His envelope or covering or mask is like a set of easily decipherable codes for the master manipulator of codes.

Hence Herry's violence and attempt not only to penetrate the Pardoner's role but also to reduce him, to drag him down, to his positionless position, his sexless neutrality (*PardT* C 951–55):

> "But by the croys which that Seint Eleyne fond,
> I wolde I hadde thy coillons in myn hond
> In stide of relikes or of seintuarie.
> Lat kutte hem of, I wol thee helpe hem carie;
> They shul be shryned in an hogges toord!"

Whatever the Pardoner's sexuality, Herry's threat to his "coillons" questions that sexuality and hence the Pardoner's identity. And the question is enough, enough to expose the pose of the consummate poser: "this Pardoner answerde nat a word; / So wrooth he was, no word ne wolde he seye" (lines 956–57). At this moment the Pardoner is fixed in wrath, and it is the only position in which he can be fixed. "No word ne wolde he seye": of course not – words are the stuff of poses, and all poses have just been disposed of.

As the Knight of all the pilgrims occupies the most fixed position, so the Pardoner occupies the least. Indeed, it might be said that the opposition between the two in *The General Prologue* is that between fixed position (knight, soldier, noble, etc.) and no position at all. Therefore, when the Knight reconciles Herry and the Pardoner, a massive discrepancy opens up which in itself defines the Pardoner's tragedy. The very security of the Knight's and Herry's positions must oppress the Pardoner, who can only submit to the Knight's will because he has no position of his own. Exposed, the Pardoner disappears. In a kiss.

The importance of the Pardoner to *The Canterbury Tales*, if they are understood as a collection of the possible positions of poets and poetry, is that, consummate impostor, he occupies the extreme of "irreference." The Pardoner's very "self" is "counterfeit." If he "'wol noon of the apostles countrefete,'" that is because they are apostles and not because he does not or is not "countrefete." If the Wife of Bath would substitute herself for the allegorical plenitude of Scripture and exegesis, like a heretic, if the Merchant would annihilate that plenitude because it accuses and condemns his own poverty, the Pardoner, on the contrary, revels in it because it is an inexhaustible supply of masks, feints, sleights-of-hand, and gimmicks – an inexhaustible supply of counterfeit selves. Unlike the Wife, who has a self (and such a self) to sell, or the Merchant, who has no self, only his craft, the Pardoner has a multiplicity of selves whenever he wants them—he is a broken mirror whose fragments reflect a brilliant but forever incomplete identity. And everything the Pardoner says or does is a frantic effort to collect the fragments in the ultimately vain attempt to say, "I am."

Hence the insistent and finally pathetic "self"-referentiality, itself only imposture: "'for myn entente is nat but for to winne'" (*PardP* C 403). This declaration of his intent only proves the poverty of the Pardoner's content. In fact, it might plausibly be argued that the "character" of the Pardoner (understanding by the word "character" here the literary construct) is to be a character who has *only* a character. Chaucer, it may be, explores through the Pardoner the illusoriness of the boundary between inside and outside in phenomena so linguistic as "character." Any attempt to discover what makes the Pardoner tick, to get "inside" him, invariably meets with only more words, with only more "outside." The Pardoner seems continuously to transform content into intent, turning himself "inside out," through torrents of speech. Hence his "inside" is his "outside"; his "outside," his "inside." He is a "character" (itself only words) whose character is to be only words: we might subtitle his *Prologue* "Character and Its Dis/Contents." Where the boundary between inside and outside is pure illusion, where there are only words on words, where there is only "character," the character (and we as well) are dis-contented. Where there is no content, there is no meaning to content. Where there are only words on words, there is only endless reference, never meaning. If reference is the "gold" of signs (Chap. 1 above), then the Pardoner's gold is never minted. He never tells us what he means; or, if he does, as perhaps he does through the reference to Christ, "oure soules leche," he immediately takes it back—he is precisely *avaricious*. And just as the Old Man, probably a figure of avarice (Ginsberg 1976:91), is never understood, so is the Pardoner, "hoarding" *his* "meaning" or "content," never understood. And this because he only talks—it seems as if he could talk endlessly—and only talks so as to appropriate the coin of others to be *his* meaning, *his* content. His only content is his intent: coin, the coin of others—"'nobles or pens, whiche that be goode and trewe'" (*PardT* C 930). Hence his poverty (and the poverty of the avaricious). Just enough of the moral sense of "goode and trewe" lingers in the monetary and commercial sense that it is possible to hear the pathetic irony: "goode and trewe" coin is as close as the Pardoner comes to the good and the true. Meaning for the Pardoner is coin, and coin is meaning: this is both extreme literalism and extreme metaphoricity, a "stew" of language. More important, it is an appropriation of meaning to the self and its desires which exploits community. The conversion of the substance of language into the accident of coin is a materialization of desire which exploits the community's need for media of exchange. It is a radical assertion of the priority of the private precisely there where the private should cooperate with the public if community is to exist and flourish. But the community, the household, of Christendom, unable to allow for the peculiar privation of the Pardoner, will win no mercy from his relentless desire to practice his privacy upon it.

And yet the poet, for whom the private is also prior, does not thrive without a community. It is merely a vanity of Romanticism that the poet writes only for himself. The poet writes to be heard—and thus *for* a community. At the same time, however, it is true that the poem begins in the mind, "a fine and private place," and that "the mind, In the act of finding what will suffice, destroys / Romantic tenements of rose and ice" (Wallace Stevens, "Man and Bottle"). The tremendous anxiety inscribed in the Pardoner is the anxiety that from the mind to the community there is no translation—that the priority of the private in the world of art is absolute, so that no reconstruction follows the destruction of the tenements. And this is the anxiety that motivates even as it frustrates the Pardoner's problematic confession. He goes out of his way to betray his act and his pose to the pilgrims because he wants to involve them in his act and his pose—he wants to establish with them a sort of community of imposters, on his own terms (cf. Josipovici 1971:89-93). The Wife of Bath wants to be an "auctoritee" in whatever community she happens to live in; the Merchant does not give a damn about community; the Pardoner wants a community of his own—and tries for it with the pilgrims. For if they participate with him in his act and his pose, they thus bestow upon him the self he otherwise lacks and cannot possess. They make it possible for him to say "*I am* your pardoner" (*PardT* C 931-34):

> "It is an honour to everich that is heer
> That ye mowe have a suffisant pardoneer
> T'assoille yow, in contree as ye ryde,
> For aventures whiche that may bityde."

I am not so naïve as to think that the Pardoner's motives here are pure; they obviously are not. But I do believe that his *im*pure motive is the desire for an identity *as their pardoner*. In this regard, consider the extraordinary word "suffisant": it suggests something more than just "legitimate" or "authorized"; it suggests something like "I really am adequate, you know," a sentiment in which conviction and self-doubt keep uneasy company. The response which the Pardoner is seeking is not only nor perhaps most importantly "nobles or pens" but also something like "Yes, yes, well, tell us another—you really are quite good at it." What he gets instead, though, is violence—*violence because words do refer and refer, moreover, to the truth.* In the agonized privacy of his unredeemed (and just possibly unredeemable) self, the Pardoner, consummate impostor and artificer of roles and master of words though he be, has forgotten that words *always* refer. Herry Bailly's reaction is sufficient evidence of that. The word, even the word of death, refers. But words do not always or necessarily *translate* unless and until the community understands their intentionality and thus also their intrumentality.

If all instrumentality is narcissistic, then the Pardoner's is a narcissism so drastic as to be incapable of even an echo.[23] He would have the pilgrims so completely suppose his pose that they can only oppose him. He would have them identify so far with him that they would end being he: he exposes his gimmick, works his gimmick, then asks them to buy his gimmick—all of which assumes that *they are one with him, do not differ from him.* But they are not one with him, and they do most certainly differ from him. The Pardoner, in short, has made no effort to translate. Rather he supposes that by exposing his pose he can impose upon the pilgrims a will to repose in him their trust. I recognize that this play of words is too much; I intend it so. It helps me to demonstrate the Pardoner's excess. To turn on the pilgrims, as he does, expecting them to buy his gimmick, the Pardoner must suppose *not* that they are his but that they are *he.* The Merchant, by contrast, supposes that the pilgrims will become his, his property—his creatures seeing the world as he sees it—and Herry Bailly almost obliges him. The Pardoner, however, supposes that the pilgrims are so completely one with him that they will obey him even as he obeys himself. Such a supposition, of course, is psychotic. It precludes any effort of translation—of taking the positions of others so as to see how they see the world. It is the supposition of one so accustomed to posing and imposture that he has forgotten that people are more than their poses.

Something Chaucer never forgot. We revere Chaucer precisely because he was a master of taking the positions of others so as to see how they see the world. The Pardoner, in contrast, is exclusively about himself. The exemplum he tells is about the old man he meets everyday in his own body. The Pardoner does not translate. When he chooses Herry to begin his pardoning, it is not only the fact that his words refer to the truth that so distresses Herry but also the fact that he supposes that there is no difference between Herry and him. Truth and lie are horribly mixed. And the Pardoner is only talking to himself. Herry, of course, will have none of it—hence he fixes precisely on the most glaring difference between them when he talks back.

And people do talk back. Something else Chaucer never forgot.

Epilogue

Just as the senseless oppression of the superego lies at the root of the motivated imperatives of conscience, the passionate desire peculiar to man to impress his image in reality is the obscure basis of the rational mediations of the will.

(Jacques Lacan)

Representing is no longer a self-unconcealing for...[*das Sich-entbergen für*] but is a laying hold and grasping of.... What presences does not hold sway, but rather assault rules.

(Martin Heidegger)

As the study and systematization of empirical fact, science enables mankind to rise above the level of animal creation and to behave in a manner distinctively human, by relating means to ends in an ordered scheme of life. As such, it un-questionably has "its own good." The good of science, however, is limited by the fact that it fails to disclose an end other than that of mere adjustment, *ut conformemur huic saeculo*. It is thus incapable of satisfying the appetite for felicity to which mankind, by the very conditions of his being, necessarily aspires.

(Charles Norris Cochrane)

This perplexity, inherent in all consistent utilitarianism, . . . can be diagnosed theoretically as an innate incapacity to understand the distinction between utility and meaningfulness, which we express linguistically by distinguishing between "in order to" and "for the sake of." . . . The perplexity of utilitarianism is that it gets caught in the unending chain of means and ends without ever arriving at some principle which would justify the category of means and ends, that is, of utility itself. The "in order to" has become the content of the "for the sake of"; in other words, utility established as meaning generates meaninglessness. . . . It is because of these consequences that Plato, who at the end of his life recalls once more in the *Laws* the saying of Protagoras, replies with an almost paradoxical formula: not man — who because of his wants and talents wishes to use everything and therefore ends by depriving all things of their intrinsic worth — but "the god is the measure [even] of mere use objects."

(Hannah Arendt)

What, then, is truth? A mobile army of metaphors, metonyms, and anthropomorphisms – in short, a sum of human relations, which have been enhanced, transposed, and embellished poetically and rhetorically, and which after long use seem firm, canonical, and obligatory to a people: truths are illusions about which one has forgotten that this is what they are; metaphors which are worn out and without sensuous power; coins which have lost their pictures and now matter only as metal, no longer as coins. . . . to be truthful means using the customary metaphors – in moral terms: the obligation to lie according to a fixed convention, to lie herd-like in a style obligatory for all.

(Freidrich Nietzsche)

People of literary inclinations, I believe, have a natural jealousy of sociology because it seems to be in process of taking over from literature one of literature's most characteristic functions, the investigation and criticism of morals and manners. Yet it is but fair to remark that sociology has pre-empted only what literature has voluntarily surrendered.

(Lionel Trilling)

WO TASKS remain: one, to review the argument of this book; two, to open out the implications of that argument for certain contemporary questions and dilemmas. In both these tasks, initially, Shakespeare will be very helpful. In *Troilus and Cressida*, Shakespeare twice penetrates to the essence of Chaucer's vision in *Troylus and Criseyde*.[1] The first time he catches the quandary of value in a net of language so fine nothing escapes (2.2.51–60):

> Hector.   Brother, she is not worth what she doth cost
>   The keeping.
> Troilus.   What's aught but as 'tis valued?
> Hector.   But value dwells not in particular will:
>   It holds his estimate and dignity
>   As well wherein 'tis precious of itself
>   As in the prizer. 'Tis mad idolatry
>   To make the service greater than the god,
>   And the will dotes that is attributive
>   To what infectiously itself affects,
>   Without some image of th'affected merit.[2]

The error of Chaucer's Troylus is precisely this "mad idolatry": he makes his service of Criseyde far greater than her person can justify, even though her person is, we understand, unusually beautiful and attractive. The second time Shakespeare writes of something like the true, irreducible complexity of our condition of narcissism, instrumentality, and community (3.3.96–111):

> Ulysses.   A strange fellow here
>   Writes me that man, how dearly ever parted,
>   How much in having, or without or in,
>   Cannot make boast to have that which he hath,
>   Nor feels not what he owes, but by reflection;

As when his virtues, aiming upon others,
Heat them, and they retort that heat again
To the first [giver].
Achilles.   This is not strange, Ulysses.
The beauty that is borne here in the face
The bearer knows not, but commends itself
To others' eyes; nor doth the eye itself,
That most pure spirit of sense, behold itself,
Not going from itself; but eye to eye opposed
Salutes each other with each other's form;
For speculation turns not to itself
Till it hath travell'd, and is [mirror'd] there
Where it may see itself. This is not strange at all.[3]

More persuasively than any words I might find, this dialogue suggests that every person is Narcissus looking for his reflection, that he can find it only in a community, that position and positioning are crucial to self-discovery, that every person must use the creatures of this world to find himself, and, finally, that these creatures, whether things or other persons, must be *their own* if the user would truly know who *he* is—if he would be more than Narcissus (cf. Serres 1982:168, on "parasitism").

It comes as no surprise, of course, that Shakespeare understands Chaucer so well. Not only is he obviously a brilliant reader, but also Chaucer points Troylus's error clearly even as he is hardly chary of allusions to Narcissus, speculation, instrumentality, reflexivity, and exchange. But this is not all. Shakespeare also knows—as does Chaucer—that, if men need each other in order to be, this need—which, we remember, Aristotle says is the origin of money—is also the origin of serious, often inhuman abuses. If Shakespeare's play is a "problem play," it is so partly because no character uses any other character well. Perhaps for a moment, there is some kindness, but its motive, upon investigation, proves tainted with expediency (Ulysses, of course, is the incarnation of expediency) or vitiated by self-deception—though Cressida claims, "'My love admits no qualifying dross'" (4.4.9), we know better, in part, because, like Shakespeare, we have read Chaucer. Where all human relationships are, at one level or another, exploitative—Thersites observes, "'All the argument is a whore and a cuckold'" (2.3.68–69)—there can be no dramatic resolution in the proper sense. *King Lear* is not a "problem play"; it is a tragedy—Lear *loves* Cordelia.

Shakespeare readily perceived in *Troylus and Criseyde* Chaucer's agon with mediation. He doubtless saw—as can we, from the perspective of this book's argument—that Chaucer's principal angst concerned his own mediation between text and audience. As such, Chaucer's angst is a narratorial, technical and partly secularized, though for all this none the less serious, version of Dante's concern with communicating the by-definition incommunicable. Where Dante must be constantly sensitive to the narcissism of his instrumentality because he is mediating that which is transhuman and transimagery, Chaucer must be constantly sensitive to the narcissism of his instrumentality because he is mediating the irreducibly particular, circumstantially nuanced, nonsubstitutable personal position of another—the Wife of Bath, the Merchant, the Pardoner, and so on. Where Dante must not call God any *thing* in such a way as to suggest that that thing *equals* God, Chaucer must not represent his characters in such a way as *to present* them *as* merely *his*. Hence, just as Dante insists on himself so as the more faithfully to efface himself, so does Chaucer interpose himself between text and audience so as to force the audience to take the measure of him and thus the measure also of his characters, who thereby assume more truth and reality than they otherwise would possess. The matter can be put as follows, almost epigrammatically—and this is as close to a one-line summary of my book as I can come: what for Dante is a problem of the expression of transcendence is for Chaucer a problem of the transcendence of expression.

Modern theory has taught us that "expression" is a shibboleth in the vocabulary of criticism.[4] "Expression" wants to espouse the notion that a centered, self-contained, individual, and inviolable subjectivity expresses itself in writing; "expression" is very much a shibboleth of Romantic esthetics and poetics. Chaucer, quite the contrary, does not "express" himself; he tries, just the opposite, to de-center himself and thus enter into others, the Other. Chaucer's desire is to let the Other and others have their say, for "al that is writen is writen for oure doctrine" (Rom. 15.4; *Retraction* I 1083). Jacques Lacan writes:

> What I seek in speech is the response of the other. What constitutes me as subject is my question. In order to be recognized by the other, I utter what was only in view of what will be. In order to find him, I call him by a name that he must assume or refuse in order to reply to me. I identify myself in language, but only by losing myself in it like an object. What is realized in my history is not the past definite of what was, since it is no more, or even the present perfect of what has been in what I am, but the future anterior of what I shall have been for what I am in the process of becoming (Trans. Sheridan 1977:86).

Although this is a post-Freudian and modernist position, it is not without its obvious relevance for Chaucer and Dante. They too desire to understand how "I" is not "I" without the proposition "you." For Dante, who is the mightier intellect, this mystery is inseparable from the profounder if not also more momentous mystery of the Trinity, Three Persons in One. But Dante also shares with Chaucer, the less mighty intellect but no less loving human being, the concern with the more immediate social and political consequences which flow from "I's" need for "you." Both poets, in short, write comedies. Dante differs from Chaucer mainly in this, that he would write a "sacro poema," but Chaucer learns from Dante all the same that comedy (of the non-dramatic sort) presupposes minimally that the author alienate himself into a character – that is, that he make himself an otherness. (*Troylus and Criseyde*, the poem, is finally a comedy and not a tragedy because the character Chaucer emerges whole and new from the experience of the poem; were he not there, the poem, as well as the story, would be unrelieved tragedy).[5]

Chaucer, then, like Dante, is a character in his own comedy. As such, he supposes and also proposes that truth is less verification of the adequacy of word to thing than it is searching and cooperating for fidelity among persons, peace among men. To be in the comedy is already an act of faith and a quest for peace. What is important is not getting it right but getting it true – best if you can do both, but, failing that, do the latter. I am not here just playing with the two meanings of "trouthe" – verity and fidelity. I want much more, to suggest that the two meanings guard and preserve a wisdom we would do well to consider, and perhaps assume, in our own time, our own world. Here I lay down the putative objectivity of the scholar (which is so often a mask for rampant subjectivity anyway) to take up the position of advocate for faith and peace in a technological world. Now I want to extend and to apply Dante's and Chaucer's profound understanding of vision, versions, and positions to our own attitudes toward and uses of the creatures of this world.

Medieval men were hardly innocent of technology; a description of the efficiency of a Cistercian abbey would dispel any illusion that they were.[6] Thus they faced the same perilous quandary as do we: whether by technology to dominate Nature to destruction or by technology to cooperate with Nature for the improvement of life *and* the preservation of the earth. It is hard not to believe that wood was meant for fires, hard not to believe that water was meant to run downhill and generate power, hard not to believe that wind was meant to billow in sails, hard not to believe that the atom was meant to be split.[7] So much is the property of each, and its property is in part a thing's meaning – its, so to speak, "meant-to-be" (cf. Boyde 1981:60–62). But the property and the meaning of a thing lie as much in the community which uses it as in the thing: the community may decide to burn this stand of timber; it may decide to build houses with it; it may decide to let it stand. The question

before the community is, To what is the stand of timber referred? This question clears a space for much more difficult questions. What is the ground of
the referral? What are the community's motives? Does it seek dominance,
mastery, and the product of these states, or the security of the predictable
and the repeatable? Or does it seek cooperation, preservation, and
familiarity—activities in essence insecure because considerate of the
unknown? Is the community of Narcissus? Or is it of God?

So posed, the questions are scandalous and must give offense to many. But
Dante and Chaucer raise them, and they must be faced. Indeed, if I write
now in such a way as, in John Murray Cuddihy's terms, "to give offense"
(1978:1–24), it is because I am writing not out of "civil religion" or a "religion
of civility" but out of a specifically Christian apologetic which is *not* civil or
mannerly in the American sense of "tolerate all." And I do so for the one very
good reason that the argument which I have undertaken and the poems which
occasioned it demand that I do so. Both Dante and Chaucer are Christian
poets (which does not mean "ecclesiastical" poets),[8] and they both render account of their stewardship of the things of this world—taking no offense, as
far as I can see, at the embarrassing questions the man Jesus, called the
Christ, again and again posed. And as the day of our reckoning approaches,
whether with the Soviet Union or the unknowns of outer space, or the
melting of the polar ice, their accounts may be to our credit.

Supreme to my mind among Dante's many gifts is his capacity to let a thing
or a person be what it is or who he or she is—if I may borrow Heidegger's
term, to let essences essence (*Wesen*).[9] Thus, if a man chooses to falsify, as
Master Adam does, then Dante will let his falsity be, in putrid and putrifying
manifestation. Thus, a different case, if the sun rises in such a way as to offer
itself, for a few moments when the clouds are in just the right position, to
naked mortal sight, then Dante will let this vision of light be, in a crisply
morning manifestation (*Purg.* 30.22–27). Perhaps his clearest statement that
everyone and everything has an essence to essence occurs in the *Paradiso*
(8.142–48):

> "E se 'l mondo là giù ponesse mente
>   al fondamento che natura pone,
>   seguendo lui, avria buona la gente.
> Ma voi torcete a la religïone
>   tal che fia nato a cignersi la spada,
>   e fate re di tal ch'è da sermone;
> onde la traccia vostra è fuor di strada."

("And if the world there below would give heed to the foundation which

Nature lays, and followed it, it would have its people good. But you wrest to religion one born to gird on the sword, and you make a king of one that is fit for sermons; so that your track is off the road.")

This is dense and complicated poetry; it is much bound up with imagery and questions of divine intentionality and the seeming fortuitousness of history. I do not wish to ride roughshod over this imagery and these questions. I do, however, want to point out that here Dante clearly indicates that men have natures or essences or, if I may, properties. The nature or properties of a man may be hidden or secret; they may manifest themselves properly or distortedly according as history or fortune gives occasion; but every man *has* an essence; everything *has* an essence. And it is the essence of essences to essence — to come into the light, to appear.[10] This Dante knows as no other poet in the West knows.

Supreme among Chaucer's gifts, to my mind, is his capacity to catch human beings in those moments, moments of relations with others, when they most obscure or conceal or mistake who they are; he knows the myriad ways in which men and women try to avoid or simply misunderstand their essences. Hence, obviously, he has a large share of Dante's gift, just as, of course, Dante has a large share of his. Neither in fact could be without the other; but one gift does dominate in each man. And as Dante strives to let essences essence, Chaucer ponders the innumerable ways essences do not quite manage to appear as the essences they are, the way essences tend to show forth somehow as slightly bent. In essence, the Wife of Bath is a loving, extraordinarily energetic woman of great appetite; in appearance, she is a scheming sexpot somewhat past her prime, a bit sad. Chaucer is every bit as much a poet of the ideal, of essences, as Dante is; only, he sees the ideal, the essence, in its fallen and erratic, its self-deceiving and self-forgetting, though incarnate and redeemable, version — he sees it in this world, not in Hell or Purgatory or Paradise.

Each poet, because of his peculiar gifts and combination of gifts, came to understand that appearance, the essencing of essences, is paramount in life on earth. Because Narcissus cannot let the Other be, he is damned, and the poet must repudiate him, especially the poet of essences. The poet of essences must love not only himself but also others and, finally, others more than himself. The poet of essences, who "uses this world as if he used it not" (1 Cor. 7.31), seeks not dominion, mastery, and security but cooperation, preservation, and familiarity. He seeks the context and the relations in which everything may appear as what it is and every person may appear as who he is, even if, ironically, he appears as who he is not (as does the Pardoner, for example). The poet of essences seeks the "as" which is the "is" of each creature—the role or the character or the type in which that creature discovers who he is. And the poet of essences will not *impose* this "as" upon anyone's or anything's "is." Such imposition would be falsification and no less falsification for going by the name of—one of several possible names—technological accuracy. Getting it "right" is less important for the poet of essences than getting it "true." Getting it "right"—quantifiable, verifiable, predictable, and certain—will almost without fail preclude that indeterminacy, incertitude, openness, and spontaneity which is the space of the "true," the space where persons discover who they are, discover what a thing is. The tree is not falsified as lumber as long as the community remembers what the *tree* is; but if they forget the truth of the tree, then the accuracy of the lumber is the merest functional technology. And persons can live without that, without necessarily getting it "right," though it is convenient, comfortable, and sometimes beneficial to have it "right"; but persons cannot live without truth—without fidelity, trust, and peace. Without the latter, essences cannot essence; with only the former, technicity merely functions. Where there is love, even death can be endured, as the very ground and enfranchisement of essencing—the end of one appearance of essence and the beginning of another.[11] Where there is only sterile, technical equipment, respirators and pumps, existence may be prolonged, but life and essence and appearance are dismayed, undone. The poet of essences knows that love—fidelity, trust, and peace—must precede technicity and its dominion if these are to have any meaning. For love *lets* the Other be, love rejoices in the being of the Other, and thus love can chasten the relentless desire of technicity *to make* the other be...whatever. The poet of essences, of what something is or of who someone is, must be a love poet. So Dante, so Chaucer.

To judge from the love poets Dante and Chaucer, the poet of essences must also be a poet of money, as were they. This is to say, he must be a poet of exchange. And this because, ultimately, no thing is what it is, no person is who he or she is, without reference to other things, to other persons. *What* the stand of timber *is* depends on what the stand of timber is *referred to* precisely in the sense of *exchanged for*. If the stand of timber is referred to personal comfort and exchanged for that, then it is firewood—money having facilitated this reference-exchange by paying the laborers who cut down the trees. If the stand of timber is referred to natural beauty and exchanged for that, then it is a public or private forest or park—money having facilitated this reference-exchange by paying for the rights to preserve the stand *and* by paying for alternative building, heating, and writing materials. If a person is referred to indentured service and exchanged for that, then he is a slave—money having facilitated this reference-exchange by paying the slave trader his expenses of transport and feeding (such as it was). If a person is referred to God and ex-changed for Him, then he is a person, loved—money having facilitated this reference-exchange by paying for his sustenance, nurturance, and other material, hence also spiritual needs.

This latter position, I hope, shocks my readers; it is meant to anyway. If Dante and Chaucer are poets of money as well as of love, this is mainly because, as Christian poets, they understand that man's relations with God and his relations with other men under God are relations of exchange, of com-merce. So much, we can pause here to note, explains the insistence with which the man Jesus, called the Christ, returns to commercial and monetary imagery in His discourse—He understands that one must pay for what one chooses, that it is the structure of life to have to lay down if one would take up. Hence, if one wants a person—and I choose this example to take full ad-vantage of the *double entendre* in "want," namely, "need" and "desire"—one must pay the price of wanting: that is, one must pay the wanting as price; one must hand it over, lay it down, resign it, for only so will the wanting not threaten to replace the person. The wanting is paid to God, the Guarantor of the person, who then gives the person as and because He gives Himself in the person: He gives, because He is, that person's freedom to give himself or herself to the lover. The wanted, that is, the beloved, referred to God is thus exchanged for God, who becomes the beloved's love; God is the love with which the lover loved the beloved enough to refer him or her to God in the first place. So referred to and exchanged for God, the wanted, the beloved, knows himself or herself loved first and foremost for being himself or herself, and this knowledge, which is the love of God in the beloved and in the lover and in between them, is precisely the liberty to be, the free will of the be-loved, to essence, to appear, to come forth.[12] If I pay my wanting to God, then I may have the person, the being, of my beloved, which I possess as if I possessed it not (1 Cor. 7.30). Unlike Narcissus, I must not die *in* my want-ing, I must die *to* my wanting (cf. Rom. 6–8).

Thus we come to the curse on money, the negative feature of it which com-pels Dante's and Chaucer's separate but related interests. Money is the origin of artificial want (=need and desire). If need (=want and desire) is the origin of money (Aristotle's position), money, once it has come into existence to facilitate the exchanges which satisfy need, has no natural limit—as the modern world has learned: create debt and print more paper.[13] Money will in-crease forever. Increase forever, initially because human want knows no limit (other than the infinitely repeated and therefore "limitless limit" of need-surfeit-need-surfeit); increase forever eventually, however, because it becomes the artificial body of want itself. Money is the accumulation, the store, the endless supply of want.[14] Money, unlike wealth, hypostatizes and thus gives an illusory presence to the want which it is meant to help satisfy; consequently, the more money a man has, the more want he has. Although it looks like wealth or power or prestige or influence, he holds in his hands corrosive want, for, holding it in his hands, he *wants* to spend it—probably to acquire more of the same, or more of the want. To have money is to want; the more money, the more want. The medieval analysis of avarice is exact: all the avaricious wants is more of what he already has—to have (own) want (money) is to want. The only limit on money and its tyrannous illusion is the *un*natural limit of human will saying, "No, this is enough"; such a will—a will not stricken with "cieca cupidigia"—must be precisely "libero, dritto e sano."[15]

Money, my argument suggests, is preeminently the means which becomes an end. Money is accumulated want, without a referent, able to refer to anything or nothing, and therefore likely in the absence of anything else to refer to itself. If man's chief glory is instrumentality—man, the toolmaker—then his chief temptation is to let instruments, the means, become an end. He risks this temptation most seriously, and it is most visible, in the instruments money and language, which in a number of ways already resemble each other. Hence Dante's and Chaucer's fascination with money and language and with money as language, language as money. Both poets, committed to community and communication, do not want to see the means to community and communication become ends in themselves; among other casualties were this to happen would be poetry, the sapience of man, the means which is supremely meaning and meaningful.

"Al that is writen is writen for oure doctrine" (Rom. 15.4). So Chaucer in his *Retraction* (line 1083), a document which has troubled his readers almost from the very beginning.[16] The statement is peculiar: note its obvious, even obtrusive means-end structure—"al that is writen" is the means; "oure doctrine" is the end. The statement not only makes a sweeping claim but makes it in a very special, logical form. Chaucer claims, even though he goes on to "revoke" certain of his own works, that *all* that is written is a means to the end of our doctrine. Moreover, he adds, "and that is myn entente." I cannot, in this book, take *that* statement lightly. Even though Chaucer refers primarily to *The Parson's Tale* with the statement "al that is writen is writen for oure doctrine," it and the declaration of intent can hardly fail to reverberate further, as I do not doubt that Chaucer intended them to do. Note that he continues: "*Wherfore* I biseke yow mekely, for the mercy of God, that ye preye for me that Crist have mercy on me and foryeve me my giltes; and namely of my translacions and enditynges of worldly vanitees, the whiche I revoke in my retracciouns" (lines 1083–85; emphasis added). The "wherfore" is crucial:

"for this reason" (Davis 1979:170)—namely, *because* it is his intent to mean the end of doctrine—Chaucer prays for forgiveness for the works which he goes on to revoke. Having made his intent so clear by means of this logical connective, Chaucer then welcomes our raised eyebrows and quizzical bemusement. For if "*al* that is writen is writen for oure doctrine," and if Chaucer goes on, even in the case of some for the purpose of revocation, to list his own collected works, the suspicion must linger in the reader's mind that the poet may have intended to include his own works in that "al." Indeed, even those that are "revoked," for "to revoke" is as well "to call back" as it is "to cancel" (Sayce 1971:242). To be sure, it is primarily "to cancel," and these works *are* canceled—I am hardly denying that—but in canceling them, Chaucer is saying that something is amiss with them, and in saying that, he is effectively purging them calling them back—he is effectively warning his reader: Take care when you open *Troylus and Criseyde*, etc. And having thus purged them, he can let them lie, by implication, under the claim that "al that is writen is writen for oure doctrine"—he can, in short, add them to the list of "doctrinal" works.

Where, in fact, they belong if they remain means, which they are, and do not become ends. For if they remain means, then they will, by that very fact, be read for the end of doctrine: they will be searched for their meaning, not indulged solely for entertainment as ends in themselves. They will thus be approached as the sapience of man for communication in the community. They will be approached as poetry—poetry for present purposes includes fiction in prose—which possesses an intention to remember the intentions of men in times past so that there might be a means and a meaning for men in times to come. So approached, so used, they will figure as part of prudence, which includes memory as its first function (Yates 1966:35–36). And prudence it is, Dante and Chaucer would agree, which enables the sapience of man to chasten and to humanize the sciences of men—that essences might essence, appearances appear, being be.

Notes
Introduction

1. The position I sketch out in this introduction is variously informed, but the following works have the most to do with its shape and tone: Aers 1980; Alford 1977:941–51; Alford 1979:377–96; Allen and Moritz 1981; Arendt 1958:236–47; Arendt 1972:460–79; Arendt 1977–78:2, 84–110; Auerbach 1957:151–77; Barthes 1966:56–57, Barthes 1979:73–81; Bloch 1977:108–214; Coward and Ellis 1977:25–60; de Man 1971:20–34; Derrida 1974:6–16; Durling 1981:61–93; Heinzelman 1980; Mazzotta 1979:190 and Mazzotta, 1972:64–81; Murray 1978:25–80; Sennett 1978:43; Sennett 1980; Serres 1982; Shell 1978; Shell 1980:516–62; Sohn-Rethel 1978; Vance 1979:293–337.

2. Catto 1980:11–14; Cipolla 1956:20–21, 24; Duby 1974:150–52; Garrani 1967:101–106, 139; Le Goff 1977:171–73; Lopez 1976:63–70; Martines 1980:7–21, 72–86; Valerani 1915:197–220.

3. Cipolla 1956:24; Bec 1967:20–45.

4. Cipolla 1956:22–24; Lopez 1951:209–34.

5. *Politics* 1.3.16 [1257b]; in the "antiqua Translatio" of Aristotle's works, available in the thirteenth century, the relevant passage reads: "But on the contrary some find money a *madness* – a convention merely and nothing at all by nature," printed with his commentary on the *Politics* in Albertus Magnus, ed. Borgnet 1891:8, 49 (emphasis added); see also the fourteenth-century French translation by Nicole Oresme, *Le Livre de politiques d'Aristote* 1.12 (ed. Menut 1970:64).

6. A good illustration of this involvement is the elaborate distinction worked out by Francis's successors between ownership (*dominium*) and simple use (*usus*): "To 'own' property was to possess it in a dimension both legal and personal – as to own a house. . . . *Use* on the other hand is the contingent and insecure relationship with the necessities of life, such as food and clothing and sufficient shelter from the elements, enjoyed not by continuing legal right

but as charity and Providence might each day provide. The friars were *mendicants* precisely because they owned nothing, living from day to day only by the 'poor man's use' (*usus pauperis*)." Fleming 1977:77.

7. Martines 1980:79–84; see, in addition, Dante's own powerful *rima* no. 96, "Doglia mi reca ne lo core ardire," lines 85–126, ed. Barbi (*ED* 6:667–68); see also Peck 1980: 21–22, 29, 46, 72, 92–95.

8. Little 1978:36; Huizinga 1954:27–28.

9. Ed. Meiser 1880:32, lines 5–32, and 33, lines 1–2. If Boethius provides, so to speak, philosophical authority for the analogy, Horace provides, again so to speak, poetic authority: "It has always been accepted, and always will be, that words stamped with the mint-mark of the day should be brought into currency." *Ars poetica*, lines 57–59 (trans. Dorsch 1965:81); see also the commentary and further examples in Weinrich 1958:508–21.

10. *Ethics* E 1133a–b; for Grosseteste's version, see Kübel 1968–72:344–45; for Oresme's version, *Le Livre de éthiques d'Aristote* 5.11 (ed. Menut 1940:297).

11. This position would have scandalized some medieval theorists — Thomas Aquinas, for example, who held that money is a measure and that "thus formally considered, [it] is conceived as having one constant, fixed value — its legal face value." Noonan 1957:52. And yet, in the very defense of such a thesis, Nicole Oresme, a seminal economic theorist of the fourteenth century, will bear witness to its antithesis, or the position which I have just stated. See his *De moneta*, trans. Johnson 1956:12–23.

12. I am not a Marxist, but like any other educated person, I am aware of Marx and of his incontestable importance for modern thought, especially in his reflections on money, some of which bear quotation here as part of the introduction to this book: "Being the external, common *medium* and *faculty* for turning an *image* into *reality* and *reality* into a mere *image* (a faculty not springing from man as man or from human society as society), *money* transforms the *real essential powers of man and nature* into what are merely abstract conceits and therefore *imperfections* — into tormenting chimeras — just as it transforms *real imperfections and chimeras* — essential powers which are really impotent, which exist only in the imagination of the individual — into *real powers* and *faculties.* . . . it is the general *confounding* and *compounding* of all things — the world upside-down [a particularly Chaucerian observation, I might suggest] — the confounding and compounding of all natural and human qualities. . . . It makes contradictions embrace." Ed. Struick 1964:168–69. As a supplement to Marx's reflections, see Foucault 1973:175 (cf. Serres 1982:149–50, 163, 172); consider also Martines (1980:79), who quotes these lines from a Trecento lyric: "Florins clear your eyes and give you fires, / Turn

to facts all your desires / And into all the world's vast possibilities."

13. On the status of the ideal in Chaucer's poetry, consult Mann (1973:197), who gives a lucid and accurate description of a poetry which wishes *to preserve* the ideal without *falsifying* any of the complexity, good and bad, of human kind. The aim of my book, joining hers at this point, is to describe how Chaucer preserves the ideal intact even as it breaks into so many particular versions of itself.

14. See Derrida 1976:10–18: "The Signifier and Truth"; Lentricchia 1980:168–77.

15. Silverman 1953:329–36; McGalliard 1975:14–15; Fisher 1982:94–152.

16. See lines 1226, 1259, 1288, 1304, 1329, 1333, 1337 var., 1339, 1447, 1450, 1454, 1469, 1472, 1554, 1577, 1599; and consult Fisher 1965:168–70.

Chapter 1

1. Relevant studies include Brownlee 1978:201–206; Dragonetti 1965:85–146; Frappier 1959:134–58; Freud 1957:14.73–102; Köhler 1963:86–103; Lacan 1977:16–25; Miller 1977:263–79; Poirion 1970:153–66. I regret that I must omit from this book any discussion of the Narcissus and the exchange imagery in *Inferno* 32; this imagery is so extensive and so complex that I do not have the space to undertake an analysis of it here.

2. Ovid, of course—*Met.* 3.339–510—is responsible for this popularity. Basic studies of Narcissus in the Middle Ages include Goldin 1967:20–68 especially, and Vinge 1967:55–115. I follow Goldin and Alan Gunn (n. 13 below) in printing Narcissus when I refer to the character in Latin and Italian literature but Narcisus when I refer to him in Old French literature.

3. "Speculatio" is normally reserved for the early or novitiate stages of contemplation; see, e.g., Richard of St. Victor *Benjamin major* 5.14 (*PL.* 196:187; trans. Zinn 1979:335–36); see, further, the fundamental study by Javelet 1967:1.360, 384–90. Dante, we should note, does not strictly adhere to this distinction (see chap. 4 below).

4. The most authoritative argument for this turning inward, contemporary with Dante, is probably that of Saint Bonaventura, *Itinerarium mentis ad Deum* 3.1 (Quaracchi 5:303; trans. Boas 1953:22).

5. On the issue of a "just self-love" in medieval thought, see the excellent remarks by O'Donovan 1980:37–92 especially.

6. Besides Javelet's study, I have used Cacucci 1971:15–133; Lonergan 1967; Mussetter 1975; Sullivan 1963. Also important, though not directly concerned with Image theology, is Hofmann 1974:65–80.

7. Examples include *Par.* 1.89–90, 3.124–30, 14.82–84, 22.125–26,

31.97–99. See, further, Mazzeo 1958:1–24, 17 especially.

8. See Musa 1974:37–64; Herzman and Stephany 1978:39–65.

9. See Mayer 1974:261–67; "Die Dialektik von revelatio und velatio – Die Funktion des Enthüllens und des Verbergens des sacramentum incarnationis."

10. At *Met.* 3.464, Narcissus laments: "'Vror amore mei, flammas moueo' que feroque'" ("'I am on fire with love for my own self. It is I who kindle the flames with which I burn'"; Innes 1955:92). This is obviously figurative fire, and the "hardening" of such figurativity is, we shall see, a crucial part of Dante's strategy.

11. On reflection here, see Colish 1968:9–12, 315–41; Shoaf 1975:48–51 and n. 30.

12. Others include *Li Lais de Narcisse* and the *Ovide moralisé*; see Vinge 1967:58–66, 91–98.

13. See, further, the commentary by Gunn 1952:287–91.

14. On the considerable importance of the adjective *pesant*, see also Dragonetti 1965:108.

15. See, further, Dragonetti 1978:89–111; Eberle 1977:241–62.

16. See *Conf.* 7.7–14 (PL 32:739–44); also *De civitate Dei.* 11. 9 (CCSL 48:328–30), 11.22 (CCSL 48:340–41); *Enchiridion ad Laurentium de fide et spe et caritate* 4.14 (CCSL 46:55–56).

17. I rely on Battisti and Alessio 1954:s.v; and on *GDI* 10:782. I perhaps should make a special point of Dante's frequent recourse to etymology – another good example is *Inf.* 13.59, 62, "*Fede*rigo" and "fede" – since in this regard he is very much a man of his time and *not* "modern"; it is not that he "trusts" the etymon to "connect" with reality but that he takes seriously the question or, if you will, the problem of the "connection." The literature on etymology is extensive. A good starting place now is Brinkmann 1980:39–43 and n. 101 especially; see, further, Chamberlin 1977:18–43.

18. Cf. Dragonetti 1965:89, 139. Medieval theory would probably have understood this matter in terms of multivocity and equivocity; see Brinkmann 1980:179–81. Florence and the florin are named by the same word ("Fiorenza" – "fiorino": "fiore"), which is thus equivocal; and because of this equivocity, in part, it would be possible – to take an example which Dante doubtless confronted often in his life – for an avaricious man to reduce Florence to florins.

19. See Saint Thomas *Quaestiones disputatae de Veritate* 2.11(23); Spiazzi 1949:22; Cacucci 1971:75; see, further, pseudo-Dionysius the Areopagite *The Divine Names* 2.8 (PG 3:646; trans. Rolt 1940:75); also Saint John Chrysostom *Homilies on the Epistle to the Hebrews* 12.3 (PG 63:98; trans.

Keble 1975:424).

20. Saint Augustine is eloquent on this matter; see *De doctrina Christiana* 2.4.5 (*CCSL* 32:34; trans. Robertson 1958:36); consult also the commentary by Duchrow 1961:369–72.

21. *In libros politicorum* 1.7. par. 120; Spiazzi 1951:37; Bridrey 1906:373.

22. The phrase is ubiquitous: it will be found in Dante himself in *De vulgari eloquentia* 1.3.3 (*ED* 6:756); see, further, Borst 1959:2.2, 869–77; Engels 1963:87–114; Mengaldo 1978:165 n. 8; Rotta 1909:187.

23. For example, John Aurifaber (transcribed by Pinborg 1967:228); Roger Bacon (ed. Fredborg et al. 1978:128); John Dacus (Grubmüller 1975:1.217).

24. Cf. Quintilian *Institutio oratoria* 1.6.3: "Custom, however, is the most certain ruler of speech and of using language clearly—just as with money, whose form is public"; consider, further, the similar position of John Dacus *Summa grammatica* (Grubmüller 1975:1.217), who also speaks of "significatio publicata."

25. Cf. Saint Thomas, below, "in quibus proprie haec nomina dicuntur" ("wherein those expressions are properly employed"). See, further, Quintilian *Institutio oratoria* 8.6.5; Saint Augustine, *Contra mendacium* 10.24; and for a study of the "proper" in patristic denunciations of heretics, with copious documentation, see de Lubac 1961:3.99–113; consult also Mazzotta 1979:190; and cf. Serres 1982:139–46.

26. The phrase is Saint Augustine's: *Contra mendacium* 10.24 (*CSEL* 41:499); Isidore repeats it: *Etymologiae* 1.37.2; so does John Balbus: *Catholicon*, pt. 4, "de figuris," s.v. Consult, further, Pépin 1970:77, Pépin 1958:89–90; Chydenius 1960:8.

27. Chenu (trans. Taylor and Little) 1968:99; Curtius (trans. Trask) 1953:206; Demats 1973:5–60.

28. *Li Livres dou tresor* 2.29.2 (ed. Carmody 1975:199); Bridrey 1906:112.

29. On the whole issue of justice in commerce, in scholastic thought, see the excellent study by Langholm 1979:11–37.

30. Cf. the provocative remarks of Burckhardt 1968:22–46.

31. Cf. Aristotle *Metaphysics* 1006a21; Lacan 1975:127.

32. Dante confronted the problem most directly perhaps in the opposition between the "allegory of the poets" and the "allegory of the theologians"; the bibliography on this subject is vast, but convenient access to it is provided in Hollander 1969:57–103; Hollander 1976:91–136, 120–36 especially; the classic debate on the two allegories is, of course, that between Green 1957:118–28 and Singleton 1957:129–35.

33. Cf. Derrida 1974:14; Struever 1970:157 and n. 39.

34. *Policraticus* 8.5 (ed. Webb 1909:2.247); Vinge 1967:72–73.

35. On Dante's Platonism and, more specifically, his Neo-platonism, see Mazzeo 1960 (1977):92, 112; for a reasonable and well-spoken plea for more attention to Dante's Platonism and to Platonic influences on him, see Chiarenza 1978:207–12, 209 especially.

36. On the terms *via negativa* and *via affirmativa* and their relevance to Dante, see Williams 1943:8–12.

Chapter 2

1. On the insistent intertwining of error and resemblance, see Percy 1975:64–82: "Metaphor as Mistake."

2. For similar figures which Dante may well have known, see Horace *Odes* 2.2.13–16 (Bennett 1947: 110–11); Saint John Chrysostom *Homilies on the Epistle to the Hebrews* 2.5 (*PG* 63:25; trans. Keble 1975:374); Theoderich von St. Trond "De Nummo" 75–78; and, finally, Hugh of St. Cher 1621:7, fol. 227ra [*ad* II Tim. 3.2].

3. For the distinction of thirst, see *Met.* 3.415; for that of fire, 3.426; for that of images, 3.432, for example (also lines 416–17, 424, 463). Because of my exclusive focus on Narcissus in canto 30, I must omit many matters of great importance to the canto's structure and meaning–alchemy, for example, on which see Mussetter 1978:427–35, or, again, the matter of the "vineyard." At line 93, Master Adam is said to have "confini" ("confines"); at line 122–23, Sinon ridicules the "'acqua marcia / che 'l ventre innanzi a li occhi sì t'assiepa'" ("'the foul water that makes your belly thus a hedge before your eyes'")–there is a strong suggestion that Master Adam is an expanse of land. Moreover, as the allusion to Semele at the beginning of the canto might well suggest, he is grape-growing land–a caricature of Bacchus. And if Dante is implying that Master Adam, in his vast girth, resembles a vineyard, then I have little doubt that his motive is the affirmation of the *New* or *Second* Adam that "I am the true vine: and my Father is the husbandman" (John 15.1). I plan a full-length study of this imagery at a later date.

4. Extraordinary evidence for the medieval appreciation of this argument is found in Peter of Capua: "And of the first denarius–that is, the rational mind–the maker is God. And it bears the image of the king impressed on it, namely grace, and also the name of the king inscribed on it; whence also Christians are so called from Christ. Meanwhile, however, the image of God is deleted from this denarius. *And yet it retains the name, as in those who are false Christians.* And then the devil himself impresses on it his image; and so that denarius is false. Thus the devil falsifies the money of our mind. *Now, in false money, the superscription is indeed the same as it is with true money, but the*

matter is different; and danger derives from this. *Thus also a false Christian has
the same superscription as the true*, because either is called Christian; but the
matter of Christianity — that is, the impression of the image — is different in
each case: for the true Christian, the image of God; for the false, however, the
image of the devil; and from this especially derives danger. For there is no
more effective plague than an enemy who seems familiar and friendly. *But if
the superscription is scored off, so that they cannot be called Christians, manifestly
will they be recognized — even evidently — for false money*, and thus, lest harm
follow, more easily can precautions be taken." Peter of Capua *Rosa
alphabetica* (ed. Pitra 1855: 2.279; emphasis added). For the devil as falsifier
or counterfeiter, see, further, Javelet 1967:1.259. Finally, consider the helpful
observation by Hugh Kenner in *The Counterfeiters* (1968:30): "...the
counterfeiter's real purpose is to efface himself, like the Flaubertian artist, so
that we will draw the conclusion he wants us to draw about how his artifact
came into existence."

5. See Cassell 1976:2–5, Shoaf 1975:43–44.

6. Compare the equally fitting but perhaps more obvious *contrapasso* of
Bertran de Born, *Inf.* 28.142; see also Valerani 1915:206–209.

7. Compare Hugh of St. Victor's argument regarding those who falsely
pursue wisdom ("sapientia"): "What was without they cleaned, what was
within they left dirtied. And this was not wisdom; because it was not the
truth — *rather false, an image alone*," *In Ecclesiasten homiliae* 10 (*PL*
175:177–78; emphasis added). See, further, Javelet, 1967:1.256; the image is
false when *alone*, disjunct from any referent.

8. Dragonetti (1965:86) notes that the debate between Master Adam and
Sinon is technically in the form of a "tençon provençale."

9. See Shoaf 1975:34–35 for an analysis of the phrase in *Purg.* 2.

10. *De doctrina Christiana* 2.1.2 (*CCSL* 32:32–33; trans. Robertson
1958:34).

11. Freccero 1966:1–25; Freccero 1959:245–81; Mussetter 1977:39–52.

12. For "ragion" as "reason" in the structure of the soul, see *ED* 4:831–42,
sec. 5 especially; and *ED* 4:828–39 for the texts cited there.

13. So much is, time and again, the burden of Boethius's *De cons.*; see, for
example, book 2, pr. 1, 5; see also the commentary by Patch 1927:13–14,
33–34, 99.

14. Since I have suggested that Virgil is a figure of Reason, I am under some
obligation to answer the objections to such a suggestion entered now in
several places by T. K. Swing (Seung); see Bibliography. His position on the
Trinitarian structure of the *Commedia* is one which I find congenial at many
points but which finally I cannot embrace entirely. I am, for example, uncon-

vinced that the Trinity is the hero of the poem (1976:144). I am, on the other hand, attracted if not yet convinced by the argument that Virgil figures the Second Person of the Trinity; and when I suggest that Virgil is a figure of Reason, a position Seung has attacked, I do so on the assumption that Reason is here understood under the aspect of *Intellectus*, or the Son. To be sure, the Second Person of the Trinity is more than Reason, which is only one reflex of *Intellectus*, but it remains true that, in the exercise of Reason, man knows the Son. Of course, even in the most abstruse Trinitarian speculation of the Middle Ages, the mind is whole, one entity; and it may be that someday enough evidence will be to hand to suggest that Virgil figures the whole mind in its essential intelligence. Until such time, however, I am content with the *approximation* "figure of Reason." Cf., further, on "ratio," Javelet 1967:1.169–76.

Chapter 3

1. See Battisti and Alessio 1954: *trovare*[1] and *trovare*[2]; for "trovare" in the sense of "poetare," see *ED* 5:745; consult also Curtius (trans. Trask) 1953:154.

2. See *De vulgari eloquentia* 1.11.3 (*ED* 6:759), 2.13.5 (*ED* 6:771), and the commentary in *ED* 3:489, "inventio" s.v.

3. At 1.11.1 (*ED* 6:759); 1.15.1 (*ED* 6:761); 1.18.1 (*ED* 6:762).

4. The locus classicus for the topos of the "regio dissimilitudinis" is *Conf.* 7, 10, 16 (*PL* 32:742), where Augustine confesses, "And I realized I was far away from you in a region of unlikeness [sc. where things are unlike God]." In twelfth- and thirteenth-century versions of the topos, it serves Trinitarian psychologies of the soul and thus becomes important to doctrines of the reformation of the soul from the darkness of this life to the light of similitude with God. The bibliography is considerable, as might be expected; a convenient beginning point is Mussetter 1977:50–51 and notes 4, 13; see, further, Javelet 1967:1.266–85.

5. Conventionally in the Middle Ages, "sinistra dicitur miseria praesentis vitae" ("the left denotes the abjectness of this life"); Alain de Lille, *Distinctiones* (*PL* 210:946).

6. Mazzotta 1979:90–106, 92, for rhetoric as "ignis in ore."

7. Battisti and Alessio 1954: s.v.

8. Boyde 1981:271–79; Nardi 1949:260–83.

9. In support of this argument is the common gloss on the biblical "drachma" (Luke 15.4–10): "The drachma is human nature, as in the Gospel: 'I found the drachma which I had lost'—that is, I have reformed human

nature, which I had lost through its guilt," *Allegoriae universam in Sacram Scripturam*, ascribed to Adam Scotus (*PL* 112:906). As the "drachma" is human nature (which, unreformed, is mere dead matter), so Dante's "dramma" is the "weight" of that nature; and precisely that weight of dead matter must be reformed to likeness again with God – "reformavi humanam naturam, quam per culpam amiseram." See, further, Peter of Capua *Rosa alphabetica* (ed. Pitra 1955:2.280–81).

10. That Beatrice is somehow to be associated with Revelation is evident from her conduct of Dante through Paradise. That she is somehow to be associated with Scripture is perhaps less immediately evident but no less certain from her position at the center of the Pageant of Scripture and the Church in *Purg.* 20:82–154. Then, too, like Scripture, she is a mirror; see especially *Purg.* 31:121–23; for Scripture as a mirror, see Saint Augustine, *Enarrationes in Psalmos* 103.1.4 (*CCSL* 40:1476); and consult Bradley 1954:100–15.

11. In addition to the sense of "purpose," the word "arte" can mean "creative art": see, e.g., *Purg.* 31.49; *Par.* 27.91; *ED* 1:397–99.

12. In addition to Brownlee 1978:201–206, see Spraycar 1978:1–19.

13. *De Genesi contra Manichaeos* 2.4.5 (*PL* 34:198); see also Heb. 6.6–8; and Chrysostom's commentary, *Homilies on the Epistle to the Hebrews* 10.1–2 (*PG* 63:83–84; trans. Keble 1975:413–14); and Saint Ambrose *Hexameron* 6.7.42 (*PL* 14:258; trans. Savage 1961:255).

14. "But all symbolism harbors the curse of mediacy and is bound to obscure what it seeks to reveal," Cassirer (trans. Langer) 1946:7; Hartman 1970:4, 108.

15. On this matter, Ferguson 1975:842–64, is extremely helpful.

16. *De doctrina Christiana* 3.9.13 (*CCSL* 32:85; trans. Robertson 1958:87).

17. Edler 1934:226; Malusséna 1968:255–81. I do not at all intend to exclude other connotations of "promession" by insisting on its economic sense; see, in particular, the citation from Boethius (*De cons.* 3.8.1–3, 31–35) in Singleton 1973:2.2, 753.

18. See Nardi 1949:153–65; Nardi 1966:110–65.

19. For an eloquent statement of this position and one doubtless known to Dante, see Saint Augustine *Conf.* 7.20 (*PL* 32:746–47).

20. In the words of John Duns Scotus, defining the activity of love, "Amo: volo ut sis" ("I love: I will that you be"), quoted in and explicated by Arendt 1977–78:2.125–46, 144 especially; consult further the helpful explication by O'Donovan (1980:112–36) of Saint Augustine's understanding of the "regula amoris" ("your neighbor as yourself").

21. The problematic of "version(s)" in Dante's strategy, to which I will

return at the end of Part One, emerges from perhaps the central question of the poem, or How is a man *converted*? What does it mean to be turned? What constitutes a wrong turning? The best preparation for addressing this problematic is the study of the "-vert" group of words in Augustine's *Confessions* by Burke 1970:43–171, 62–65 especially; see also Shoaf 1981a:267–69. My own analysis must await the study of *Paradiso*, since Dante's conversion is not complete until, transhumanized Narcissus, he gazes on "nostra effige" in the Trinity (*Par.* 33.131).

Chapter 4

1. The following studies, in addition to Dragonetti 1965; Miller 1977; and Bradley 1954, have been of particular use in the preparation of my own: Freccero 1968:85–111; Grabes 1973:356–90 especially; Hugedé 1957; Leyerle 1977:280–308; Mazzeo 1960 (1977); Montgomery 1979:13–92, 52 especially; Murtaugh 1975:277–84; Petrocchi 1978.

2. Cf. the very different conclusions reached by Murtaugh 1975:280.

3. We can also grasp this issue a different way. Whether with true figures or false imaginings, Dante must eventually cease seeing and begin to reflect. He must transcend the nature of the eye which is to *construct* what it sees. Medieval optics understood that the eye never simply mirrors what it sees: "The power of ordinary construction I call it because in it the forms of things are able to appear. And this is a property of light, as is manifest in an ordinary, material mirror, which, through the nature of light, assumes the forms (lit: the intentions) of things, but does not, all the same, know them, because in it there is no living power actually directed to the exemplars of things; and thus it is not able to transform itself (lit: convert itself—invoking the Aristotelian notion of the identity of the knower and the known) beyond simple reception so that it might judge of the things themselves—which is possible in any simple, living being. For from the union of the active power [in the living being] with the exemplar to which it is directed follows delight, in which is conscious and cognitive life." Anonymous *Liber de intelligentiis* 10.1 (ed. Bäumker 1908:14), quoted, with comment, by Leisegang 1937:148 and Leisegang 1949:164; consult, further, de Bruyne 1946:3, 239–51. The eye, on the contrary, possesses a "power of ordinary construction" which is natural to it in a post-lapsarian state. Hence in order to "see" Paradise, Dante must transcend by coming into conscious control of this "power." The union, of which the *Liber* speaks, must become fully conscious, fully reflective. Dante must learn not to see but to reflect, where reflection is allowing for, or thinking about, what the eye "thinks it sees." Dis-figuring, then, is the trope which

figures the suspension and transcendence of the "virtus exemplaris." Consult, further, Miller 1977:275–78.

4. For "segnato" in the sense of "stamped," see *Inf.* 17.65; *Purg.* 8.82; 33.81; *Par.* 17.9; see also *ED* 5:127.

5. The word "tesoro" also possesses other important contexts which deserve attention. On the one hand, it is almost a commonplace that the memory is a treasury or treasure house—see, e.g., John of Salisbury *Metalogicon* 1.11.839a (ed. Webb 1929:29); Javelet 1967:1.181; Latini *Tresors* 1.16 (ed. Carmody 1975:30)–and Dante would have included memory among the faculties of "mente." On the other hand, the title of the major work of his former teacher, now damned, Brunetto Latini, is *Li Livres dou tresors*; and, I suspect, Dante is suggesting that his poem is a *tesoro* so as to supplant and transume his precursor. See, further, n. 16 below.

6. *In Joannis Euangelium* 40.9 (*CCSL* 36:355); and see, for an abundant collection of similar arguments from economics by Saint Augustine, Herz 1958:81, 121, 196–98, 200, 204–206, 213, 269.

7. I should make a special point of noting that the immediate reference of *Par.* 1.70–72, and especially of "essemplo," to the story of Glaucus, *Par.* 1.67–69, does not by any means preclude a larger reference to Dante's experience and to his poem as a whole.

8. A good orientation is provided by Pezzard 1953:2.219–35.

9. Consult on this matter Brinkmann 1980:169–98; Chenu 1955:75–79; Jeanneau 1957:35–100; Wetherbee 1972:36–48; Wetherbee 1973:111–12.

10. The figure of the candle possesses a rich prehistory which I can only mention in passing. See, e.g., Saint Bonaventura: ". . . where [sc. in the mirror of the mind] the light of truth is shining before our minds as in a candelabrum, for in it gleams the resplendent image of the most blessed Trinity"; *Itinerarium* 3.1; Quaracchi 5:303; trans. Boas 1953:22. I plan to pursue this matter further in a later study.

11. The literature on mysticism is, of course, vast. A very helpful starting point on the issue of "loss of self" and on the question of union is Johnston 1973:10–16; see also Zinn 1979:30–31. Because of the primacy of intellect and sight in Dante's theology (*Par.* 28.109–11), the moment of union must also be the moment of distinction. To my mind, Saint Bonaventura expresses this best at *Itinerarium* 6.6 (Quaracchi 5:311–12; trans. Boas 1953:42).

12. See Heb. 5.12–14; T. von Bavel 1957:255–67.

13. *Par.* 12.71, 73, 75; 14.104, 106, 108; 19.104, 106, 108; 32.83, 85, 87.

14. The phrase is Saint Augustine's, *In Joannis Euangelium* 29.6 (*CCSL* 36:287); he goes on: "Therefore, do not seek to understand so that you might believe but believe so that you might understand." The economic trope in his

affirmation is crucial; it appears again in a very similar and to Dante highly appropriate affirmation: "Some great thing it is we are to see, *since all our recompense is vision*; and this very great vision, it is our Lord Jesus Christ." *Enarrationes in Psalmos* 90.2.13; *CCSL* 39:1277; emphasis added.

15. *De Joseph* 8.45 (*PL* 14:692), and see also Ambrose's *De Patriarchis* 6.30 (*PL* 14:717); the trope which figures faith as money probably derives from Origen, *In Leviticum*, IV (*PG* 12:433–4; in Rufinus's Latin translation, ante 410 A.D.); see, further, for Saint Augustine's version of the trope, *Sermo* 216. III. 3 (*PL* 38:1078). Hugh of St. Victor *De Sacramentis* 1.10.9 (*PL* 176:342); Javelet 1967:1.378, 2.289. For faith as "umbra" ("image"), see Saint Bernard *Sermones in Cantica Canticorum* 31.8–10 (ed. Leclercq et al. 1957:1.224–26), especially 9: "And it is good that faith is a shadow, for it tempers the light to the eye's weakness and prepares the eye for the light"; trans. Walsh 1976:132; 48.6–7 (ed. Leclercq et al. 1958:2.70–71).

16. "The kingdom of heaven is like unto a treasure hidden in a field"; Matt. 13.44. Dante, of course, at the very beginning, likens Paradise to a "tesoro" (*Par.* 1.11). And biblical encyclopedias and "distinctiones" regularly gloss "thesaurus" as, in one sense, the treasures of Heaven: see, e.g., Bersuire *Repertorium morale* 6:1197–98: "The fourth thesaurus is that of heavenly opulence, and this is the thesaurus of the glory of paradise, in which God holds and keeps all His good, although He does not choose to reveal it in any way to any but his friends and familiars." See, further, *Allegoriae universam in Sacram Scripturam, PL* 112:1066.

17. No one has more penetratingly or eloquently exposed the curse on instrumentality than Arendt 1958:153–74; in addition to Arendt, Saint Augustine has played an important role in my thinking on this subject; see *De doctrina Christiana* 1.4.4 (*CCSL* 32:8); and the commentary by O'Donovan 1980:24–29. Also important has been Heidegger's understanding of the tool; *Being and Time* (trans. Macquarrie and Robinson) 1962:91–122. Let me note especially here that my use of the concept and the term "instrumentality" is independent of the medieval and Aristotelian notion of the *instrumental cause*; see Boyde 1981:52. The *instrumental cause* and instrumentality should *not* be confused. The one is a scientific explanation, while the other is a philosophical construct.

18. Augustine *De Trinitate* 12.9.14–10.15 (*CCSL* 50:368–69; emphasis added; trans. McKenna 1963:356-7).

19. *De doctrina Christiana* 1.4.4 (*CCSL* 32:8); *Enarrationes in Psalmos* 54.1 (*CCSL* 39:655); *De Trinitate* 11.6.10 (*CCSL* 50:345–46), 14.1.3 (*CCSL* 50a:424); *De libero arbitrio* 2.17 (*CCSL* 29:268); consult also O'Donovan 1980:36.

20. Twelfth-century thinkers, especially the Victorines, follow Saint Augustine in this matter. They recognize that the imagination clings to and is intertwined with images as the mind ascends through various stages of sensibles to speculation and contemplation; most representative probably is Richard of St. Victor—e.g., *Benjamin minor* 6 (*PL* 196:56; trans. Zinn 1979:58–59); *Benjamin major* 1.8 (*PL* 196:73–74; trans. Zinn 1979:165), 3.8 (*PL* 196:118; trans. Zinn 1979:233).

21. On the Augustinian notion of "commoda privata," see O'Donovan 1980:102–104.

22. The pattern is impressive: faith is money, hope is a flower, charity is a seal; all three, then, are intimately related to imagery and image making. And the three—if we would seek the purpose of the pattern—are frequently said to constitute the Image in man "de la Trinité créatrice"—see, e.g., Rupert of Deutz *In Jonam* 1 (*PL* 168:416); Gerhoh *In Psalmum* 1, pr. (*PL* 193:629–30); Hildebert of Lavardin *Sermones in Quadragesima* (*PL* 171:436); Javelet 1967:1.216, 2.186. Moreover: "That old Adam banishing himself from charity, hope, faith also defrauded his posterity and separated himself and them far from similitude with the blessed Trinity. The new Adam, however, reversing the steps, reforms us through faith, hope and charity to that same similitude"; Rupert of Deutz *De glorificatione Trinitatis et processione Sancti Spiritus* 6.19; (*PL* 169:138). As Dante passes his examinations on faith, hope, and charity, in the process the Image in him is being reformed to Similitude with God; at the same time the systematics of Narcissus and the problematic of poetic imagery are approaching their term. Note also that, in addition to testimony of reform through faith, hope, and charity, Rupert also asserts that Adam *defrauded* himself and his posterity of similitude; with such close similarity as this does Dante's Master Adam resemble his namesake—each guilty of fraud. See, further, Javelet 1967:1.339, 2.186, 267.

23. *De Trinitate* 5.16.17 (*CCSL* 50:227; emphasis added; trans. McKenna 1963:498).

24. Here I rely on the analysis by Richard Drake (1977:20–69) of the condition of being "beside oneself" as it figures in Augustine's *Confessions*.

25. According to *GDI* 1:347–48, the word *alquanto* in its adverbial sense means "un poco (come quantità, come durata)." For the sense "come quantità," see *Purg.* 5.20; among the ancient commentators, Benvenuto remarks "*alquanto circonspetta*, id est, paullulum considerate vel inspecta circum" (Biagi 1939:3.748).

26. For God as *painter* of the Image, see Saint Ambrose *Hexameron* 6.8.47 (*PL* 14:260–61; trans. Savage 1961:259–60).

27. Here, as the problematic of "version(s)" approaches its term, we should

recall, on the one hand, the Christian insistence on the necessity to "turn" toward the Good, to convert, and, on the other, Ovid's appeal, in vain, to Narcissus, "quod amas, *auertere*, perdes" ("only *turn aside* and you will lose what you love," 3.433; Innes 1955:92; emphasis added). Like Narcissus, then, Dante can *not* turn—recall, too, that his eyes are not "aversi" from the "vivo raggio" (33.77–78)—and yet unlike Narcissus, or, better, like Narcissus transhumanized, his gaze is fixed there where *not turning* is the measure of a *just self-love*. Having turned to the true Image, Dante need never turn from it again. Hence he both is and is not Narcissus, as the systematic allusions to Narcissus insist. Consult, further, on the theological sense of "version," Javelet 1967:1.379, 2.289.

28. Battisti and Alessio 1954: s.v.

29. In this, as in so many other cases, Dante's genius does not isolate itself from the achievements of his predecessors. In book 7, lines 34–42, of the *Anticlaudianus*, Alain de Lille writes (ed. Bossuat 1955:158): "Ex hiis materiam ductam Natura *monetat* / In speciem, uultus humani corporis aptans / Materie, cuius miratur turba decorem, / Parque suum stupet in terris decor ipse deorum. / Omnes *diuicias* forme diffundit in illo / Nature *prelarga* manus; post *munera pauper* / Pene fuit Natura parens que *dona* decoris, / Forme *thesauros* uultu deponit in uno. / Spirat in hac forma *Narcisus*" ("The material drawn from these Nature *mints* into something precious and fits the features of the human body to her material. Earth marvels at its beauty and the very beauty of the gods is astonished to behold its equal on earth. Nature's *bounteous hand* showers it with all *the riches* of beauty; having granted these *endowments* Mother Nature was almost *a pauper* since she has granted to one set of features her *gifts* of grace and *treasures* of beauty. In this beauty another *Narcissus* lives"); trans. Sheridan 1977:174; emphasis added. Note well that Nature coins the "novum hominem" whose soul Phronesis has brought back from Heaven; just so, "nostra effige" coins or stamps Dante anew with our image. Note further the insistence on wealth—"diuicias"; "praelarga"; "munera"-"pauper"-"dona"; "thesauros"—and just so, throughout the *Commedia*, Dante has structured the reformation of his image to likeness with God in terms of largesse and the gratuity of grace: faith, for example, is money; Paradise is a treasure in his mind. Finally, and most compellingly, Nature lavishes her wealth and the stamp of her coining on Narcissus; just so, Dante before "nostra effige" is Narcissus transhumanized.

Chapter 5

1. Note that I follow the convention of printing Troylus, principally to in-

sist on the very close relationship between Troy and Troylus. All quotations are from F. N. Robinson, *The Works of Geoffrey Chaucer*, 2d ed. (Boston: Houghton Mifflin Co., 1957).

Chapter 6

1. "Fals" often referred to counterfeit money in Chaucer's day; see *MED*, F:390, br. 5(a). That "fals" or "contrefete" was used of persons and their behavior is amply demonstrated by another of Chaucer's texts, which also, happily, confirms the reciprocity between the two words. In *LGW* 4, "The Legend of Hypsipyle and Medea," Chaucer complains of Jason: ". . . with thy contrefeted peyne and wo. / There othere falsen oon, thow falsest two!" (lines 1376–77)—Jason "betrays" the two not by falsifying *them*, of course, but by being himself "fals" or "contrefete," as is Criseyde, eventually, too. Since, moreover, the two words are reciprocal, Chaucer is free to use "fals" in *Troylus and Criseyde*, and not "contrefete," thus to insist on the connection with *Inferno* 30, which invariably uses "falso," "falsificando," "falsasti," etc. (see, e.g., *Inf.* 30.41, 73, 115).

In further confirmation of Chaucer's strategy in suggesting that Criseyde is a "fals" coin is the evidence in contemporary Latin sermon materials of the analogy between the human soul and a coin. For example, in the "Distinctiones" of William de Montibus (thirteenth century) the compiler lists eight properties of a coin, then argues that "ita etiam haec in iusto quolibet esse debent" ("thus these should also be in any just entity whatsoever") and proceeds thence to enumerate the application of these properties to the human soul. For example, a coin should possess "integritas," and "de tertio, ait Apostolus: Sit integer spiritus vester in vobis" (1 Thess. 5.23) ("concerning the third, the Apostle says: Let your spirit be whole within you"; MS Oxford Bodleian 419, fol. 21v). While the entire entry is too long to transcribe here, this example does suggest, I think, the kinds of associations and responses Chaucer could have assumed in his audiences familiar with Latin and/or vernacular sermons. Very similar evidence leading to the same conclusion is found in the "Distinctiones" of Odo of Chateauroux (d. 1273)—for example, in MS Troyes Bibliothèque Municipale 1089, fols. 126v–127r, 127v–128r.

2. Chaucer would have known this aspect of Juno from Macrobius (fl. ca. 400) *The Saturnalia* 1.12.30 (trans. Davies 1969:89), or from John Balbus (d. 1296) *Catholicon* (1460; reprint, 1971), s.v. "moneta."

3. See, e.g., 4.158–60; also 59, 146, 347 var., 485, 487, 559, 665, 878. I rely for my statistics here and elsewhere in Parts Two and Three on the Tatlock-Kennedy *Concordance* (1927; reprint, 1963). Other words and im-

ages which support the suggestions in "exchaunge" are "bought" (4.290–91; 5.965) and "purchase" (4.557; see chap. 9 n. 27 below for a discussion of this passage). More support derives from the lore that Troy shall fall for failure to pay a debt: "'Bycause [Lameadoun] nolde payen hem [Phebus and Neptunus] here hire, / The town of Troie shal ben set on-fire'" (4.124–26). Calkas recalls this point of lore in his plea with the Greeks for the exchange of Antenor for Criseyde; Chaucer positions the lore, then, where it will necessarily meld with other economic images. On the basis of this lore and the exchange of Criseyde, Troy, we might say, is bad at business. Bad faith in the one case and bad judgment in the other (Antenor proves a traitor, we remember) precipitates the downfall of Troy. If we would generalize from the evidence, we might suggest that it imputes to Troy a certain failure to understand and appreciate the nature and importance of exchange in human life – a certain failure to value the *community* which makes value and values possible.

4. It may be of crucial importance here that "Criseyde" means "daughter of gold," see Taylor 1980:296 n. 20. Although Chaucer may not have known this item of Greek, his coinage imagery and his allusions to Dante make the hypothesis that he did very attractive.

5. See especially Donaldson, "Criseide and Her Narrator" 1972:65–83.

Chapter 7

1. See Gordon 1970:27–60; Muscatine 1969:139; Payne 1963:205 and nn. 45–46.

Chapter 8

1. *Poetria nova* 43–45 (ed. Faral 1971:198; trans. Nims 1967:16–17).

2. See Arbusow 1963; Horace *Ars poetica* 361, and the commentary by Trimpi 1978:29–74.

3. Consult further Davis 1979:114. I hope to pursue further elsewhere the extent to which Chaucer modeled Pandarus on the contemporary character of lawyers or advocates. Obviously Pandarus is an "advocate" and a "representative" for Troylus; and if we consider only such medieval legal concepts as "Who does a thing through another – it is as if he did it himself, on his own" (Hofmann 1974:153), we can readily see the potential importance of the law for illuminating Chaucer's poem.

4. See B 2–4 and the excellent commentary by Yunck 1963.

5. See Krewitt 1971:231 (emphasis added); Brinkmann 1980:173–85.

6. *De planctu naturae*, pr. 4 (*PL* 210:453; trans. Moffat 1972:44); and see below, chap. 12 and n. 17.

7. *Anticlaudianus* 2.404–408 (ed. Bossuat 1955:84; trans. Sheridan 1977:85); *De nuptiis* 3.226 (ed. Dick 1925:83; trans. Stahl 1977:66).

8. The best study of "ingenium" is that by Wetherbee 1972:94–98, 116–18; see, further, Wetherbee 1976:45–64; also Nitzsche 1975.

9. Consider, further, in this regard, Troylus's "sickness" at the end of book 2 (lines 1527–33; emphasis added):

> Quod Troylus, "Iwis, thow nedeles
> Conseilest me that siklich I me *feyne*,
> *For I am sik in ernest*, douteles,
> So that wel neigh I sterve for the peyne."
> Quod Pandarus, "Thow shalt the bettre pleyne,
> And hast the lasse nede *to countrefete*,
> For hym men demen hoot that men seen swete."

Troylus feels that he is "sik in ernest" ("ernest" is a powerfully resonant word here), but he will in fact "feyne" another kind of sickness, concealing his love-sickness (see 2.1576 especially). Pandarus seems actually pleased to hear that Troylus is sick since, this being the case, he has "the lasse nede to countre-fete." Note well that, even though he *is* "sik in ernest," Troylus is *still* going, as Pandarus sees it, to "countrefete" (not "no need" but, crucially, "the lasse nede")—he is still going to behave in the image of his *auctor*, Pandarus, the supreme counterfeiter. This entire stanza is remarkable for the way in which it exposes the confusion and self-deceptions in which falsification embroils Pandarus and Troylus—"for him men demen fals that men seen lye." For a possible source and a helpful discussion of the scene, see Muscatine 1948:372–77. Yet another instance in which Troylus appears in the image of his maker, and one which can hardly go unmentioned, is when he, too, assumes the pose of "'swich a meene / As maken women unto men to comen'" and offers Pandarus whichever of his royal sisters pleases the latter most (3.407–13).

10. See especially 3.1562–82 and the remarks by Donaldson 1975:294–95 and by Muscatine 1969:138.

11. I should perhaps make a special point of noting that Ovid's stories are moral in themselves, before later medieval allegory reads them—Lycaon *is* a wolf, and his metamorphosis only fulfills the truth of his character. Medieval allegory, then, cultivates what is already evident in Ovid's text. On this crucial matter the finest remarks I know are those by Allen and Moritz 1981:14–20 and by Demats 1973:107–77.

12. See Rowland 1969:9; Carton 1979:47–61.

13. At lines 124, 303, 314, 449, 450, 606, 770; and see Hatcher 1973:316–18.

14. See, e.g., 2.579–81, 878, 1560–61, 1723–24; 3.124–26, 1165–66, 1184–89, 1226–29. In my text the two principal treatments of "entente" are in chap. 9 below. It almost goes without saying that this one term and its significance for Chaucer's poem deserve a study as long as this one, if not longer: in a sense, the *Troylus* is a poem about intentionality, moral and poetic intentionality alike.

15. At 3.310, 571. With this issue my work meets and joins that of Trimpi 1974:113–18, 117 especially: "For it is precisely through his release from ethical and historical circumstances that the artist can establish a temporary order of events and of emotions which has the power to increase the listener's understanding of the communal world after he has returned to it." Pandarus's falsification consists in just this: he does *not* have any such "release from ethical and historical circumstances" because he is imposing his images on real beings (real, that is, within the fiction)–he is still within "the communal world" when he practices his art. Early in Fellini's *Satyricon*, Vernacchio, the jester, as part of the entertainment he is staging, chops off the hand of a beggar, Muzio Scevola; assistants then take Scevola backstage and attach a golden hand to the bleeding stump; meanwhile, a child actor, in the role of Caesar, exclaims "'Now, through me, great Jove will restore that hand.'" Scevola is led back onstage, and the audience is properly awed by the spectacle. Here, from a great work of a modern master, is an example of the extreme of Pandarus's perversion of art–total disregard of the boundary between illusion and reality, between "the communal world" and the artist's "temporary order of events and of emotions."

Chapter 9

1. For the formula for tragedy, see *MkT* 7.1973–77, and, further, McAlpine 1978:86–115. For the formula for decorum, see Robinson's notes to lines 12–14 (1957:814) and line 103 of *SqT* (1957:718). For "clerkly" subservience, formulaic utterance is suggested by the paraphrase of the papal title "servus servorum Dei"; see, further, Robinson's note to *SqT* 15ff. (1957:814). The formula for erotic bliss is the most tenuous, but three other times in his poetry Chaucer uses the alliterative phrase "bathen in bliss" (*TC* 2.849; 4.208; *WBT* D 1253), and I suspect that he felt it as at least quasi-formulaic. For the formulaic appearance of detractors, the authority is the *Roman de la Rose* 7333–99, where Amis warns Amans against *Male Bouche*.

2. The most important medieval document in testimony of this understanding of economics among Chaucer and his contemporaries is Peter John Olivi (d. 1296) *Tractatus de emptione et venditione*; since this work figures

prominently in my analysis of *The Merchant's Tale*, I refer the reader to Part Three, chap. 12, for fuller discussion and bibliographical information.

3. Warrant for this manner of speaking and precedent for Chaucer's usage John of Salisbury provides in *Metalogicon* 2.20: "*In the mart* of the various branches of knowledge, free *mutual exchange of words* between one discipline and another ought to prevail, as observes Ulger, venerable Bishop of Angers. Liberality reigns in the marketplace of philosophers, *where words may be borrowed without restriction or charge.*" Webb 1929:100–101, 879ab; trans. McGarry 1955:122–23; emphasis added).

4. See Muscatine 1969:134–37; Payne 1963:211–13; Vance 1979:311–35.

5. See Mazzotta 1979:165–69; Poggioli 1957:313–58 (1966:61–77); Shoaf 1975:44–49.

6. "'Quel giorno più non vi leggemmo avante'" ("'that day we read no farther in it [the book of Lancelot]'"; *Inf.* 5.138) is perhaps by now one of the most famous lines in all of the *Inferno*. In the context of Saint Augustine's conversion (*Conf.* 8.12), Francesca's words define the Christian sense of misreading. Whereas Augustine, after obeying the child's command and reading Romans 13.13, 14, "had no wish to read more and no need to do so" because he had in that moment been converted, Paolo and Francesca read no further that day because they had been perverted. "'Galeotto fu 'l libro e chi lo scrisse'" ("'A Gallehault was the book and he who wrote it'"; *Inf.* 5.137). This line is hardly less famous; it has fathered some extraordinary reactions against literature—see Mazzotta 1979:160–72. But we may have been too quick to ignore the quotation marks: these are Francesca's and not necessarily Dante's words. She condemns book and author, and to be sure, Dante doubtless condemns *fin'amors* pseudo-transcendence, but he condemns Francesca, too—which is to say, he recognizes that the will of the reader is at least as guilty as the text of the book. So much indeed is clear from Augustine's experience. We need to remember that people *consent* to the mediations of a go-between. On the relevance of the Paolo and Francesca episode to the *Troylus*, see, further, Rowe 1976:153–54.

7. Earlier (1975:51) I claimed that it is. Mine was one of those reactions against literature fathered by *Inf.* 5.137. In now retracting my claim, I am not interested to exonerate language and literature of the "curse of mediacy" (chap. 3 n. 14 above), but I am concerned to insist that we cannot foist off on this curse our responsibility to life and death.

8. All readers of the poem, I think, recognize the Narrator's distance, paradoxically (but very humanly) combined with his affection for Criseyde—see especially the classic essay by Bloomfield 1957:14–26

(1961:196–210); Payne, in particular (1963:215–16), notes the increase and rigor of the distance in the last two books.

9. "E lo cielo di Venere si può comparare a la Rettorica per due pro- prietadi: l'una sì è la chiarezza del suo aspetto, che è soavissima a vedere più che altra stella" ("And the heaven of Venus may be compared with Rhetoric on account of two properties: one is the brightness of its aspect which is most pleasant to behold, more than that of any other star"; *Conv.* 2.13.13 (*ED* 6:699); cf. "Il Filostrato" 3.78.

10. On "concordia discors," see Rowe 1976:6–56, 6–11 especially; Kamin- sky 1980:70–71.

11. Payne (1963:77) notes this recall. Consider, also, Hugh of St. Victor *Didascalicon* 6.9: (". . . sometimes the letter is perfect, when, in order to signify what is said, nothing more than what has been set down needs to be added or taken away"; Buttimer 1939:126, 807B; trans. Taylor 1961:147; em- phasis added). In this sense, Chaucer's "littera" is hardly perfect, and "the things which are set down" certainly need augmentation or diminution – that is, *we* have to decide what is at stake here, we have to take a position of our own (cf. Introduction above).

12. Dante, recall, defaces or disfigures the known, the certain, false image so as to probe and expose it; Chaucer, the contrast with Dante clearly shows us, does not deface and rigorously avoids defacing because it is the structure of his subject, personality, to preclude such certainty. Criseyde *is* "fals," but she is a coin or a text only by analogy, and Chaucer will not mark her as did Pandarus, who treated her heart as if it were stone (2.1241).

13. There are, obviously, many allusions to religion, and to the Christian religion in particular, throughout the poem, especially because of the parallel between *fin'amors* and Christianity. My point is only the narrow but, I think, crucial one that nowhere in the poem before 4.1695 does the Narrator in his own voice quote Scripture.

14. Cf. David (1962:578): "Troilus' tragic error, if such an error can be called tragic, is to have tried to love a human being with an ideal spiritual love."

15. Consistently, the glosses on Saint Paul's "quae" ("*the things* which God hath prepared for them that love Him") understand them in terms of "treasure" ("thesaurus") or "reward" ("premium") – see, e.g., Peter of Capua *Rosa alphabetica* (ed. Pitra 1855:2.287); *Glossa ordinaria* 6: loc. cit. Here is a case, I think, in which exegesis is crucial to the meaning of Chaucer's text. In- stead of the rewards or treasures of the divine, Troylus enjoys (I intend the irony but no sarcasm) the "peynes" which attend the earthly treasure of Criseyde (a kind of coin, we know). The emphasis on treasure or reward and

the economic connotation also recall Matt. 6.21 ("For where thy treasure is, there is thy heart also") and, though more distantly, Matt. 13.44 ("The kingdom of heaven is like unto a treasure hidden in a field"). Chaucer's words do not reduce to the meanings associated with these verses, but these meanings are hardly irrelevant to his words.

16. On the "effictio," see Colby 1965:89–90, 99; Krewitt 1971:344.

17. Here I rely on but differ markedly from Lacan 1966:502 (trans. Sheridan 1977:153); Lacan 1973:185.

18. Cf. Donaldson 1972:53–59; Owen 1967:444.

19. Donaldson 1972:65–66, although, in all fairness to his and my argument as well, I should point out that here he is discussing the Narrator of Book 2.

20. "Troylus wel understod that she / Nas not so kynde as that hire oughte be" (5.1642–43) is not chastisement, to be sure, but it is far more critical than it would have been had Chaucer at this moment not opted for *indirect* discourse. He definitely agrees with Troylus.

21. Davis 1979:128; Cooper 1980:1–12.

22. Here I am in essential agreement and sympathy with McAlpine (1978:179): "Troylus' speech represents here exactly what its original represents in Cicero's 'Dream of Scipio': the highest vision of *pagan* wisdom." See also Reiss 1968:131–44; Kaminsky 1980:61–64.

23. Steadman (1972) provides the best study of Chaucer's sources for Troylus's translation to Heaven, pagan and philosophical and otherwise; see, further, Wood 1970:180–91.

24. The economic trope in "redemption" was very much alive throughout the Middle Ages; for evidence and discussion, see chap. 13 and nn. 8–11 below.

25. William Butler Yeats, "Crazy Jane Talks with the Bishop." The tension between art and life in Yeats can be informative for understanding the similar tension in Chaucer: if Yeats imagines "an agony of flame that cannot singe a sleeve" ("Byzantium"), Chaucer imagines a Pardoner who cannot pardon (only his office is efficacious in pardoning) – in each case, artifice precludes contact with reality, and in each case, agony is the result. See, further, Utley 1974:174–98.

26. For a different view, see Kelly 1975:225–31, 238–42.

27. For Criseyde's refusal to run away with Troylus and her reasons, see 4.1528–33, 1555–96; Troylus's report of Priam's will is very revealing (4.554–60; emphasis added):

> "I have ek thought, so it were hire assent,
> To axe hire at my fader, of his grace;
> Than thynke I, this were hire accusement,

> Syn wel I woot I may hire nought *purchace*.
> For syn my fader, in so heigh a place
> As *parlement*, hath hire *eschaunge* enseled,
> He nyl for me his *lettre* be repeled."

Besides yet another repetition of "eschaunge," the passage is remarkable for the way in which Troylus so easily lapses into economic parlance — "purchace." To be sure, the word can have a somewhat neutral sense of "obtain," but it would be arbitrary and self-defeating to deny its strong economic denotation. Troylus thinks of Criseyde as a commodity, too (along with everyone else in Troy at this point). Furthermore, the passage insists on speech in certain fascinating ways. "Parlement," as Bloch has pointed out (1977:139), is the place of *speech*, and Priam's "lettre" in this context is, of course, law. As Troylus sees it, this letter and this law in this place of speech definitely kill; and so it is hardly fanciful to recall Saint Paul's teaching that "the letter killeth, but the spirit quickeneth" (2. Cor. 3.6). Troylus, in a sense, is the victim of the letter. Not entirely of his own will but nonetheless consenting, he practices that literalism that Saint Augustine so deplores: "It is a servile infirmity to follow the letter and to take signs for the things that they signify," *De doctrina Christiana* 3.9.13. Troylus does, in fact, take the sign for the thing that it signifies — Criseyde, for transcendence and felicity. And, to be sure, we can understand why — she was, from all reports, a very beautiful woman. But if she is a sign — and he does treat her as if she were a sign — then she will surely kill if not referred to a meaning which transcends her. When Troylus first hears of her exchange for Antenor, "upon his beddes syde adown hym sette, / Ful lik a ded ymage" (4.234–35). The servant of the letter comes to resemble a dead image, to resemble what he serves (for the letter and the law are dead, working death; see Rom 7.10, 11). If Criseyde were treated as a woman, however beautiful, and not as some sort of goddess (an image, to be literalized), Troylus would in all important senses live; as it is, he is dead, and dead long before he dies. The precision of Chaucer's language moves me; and I cannot see refusing his meaning. Saint Augustine finishes the sentence I just quoted: "in the same way it is an evil of wandering error to interpret signs in a useless way" (*CCSL* 32:86; trans. Robertson 1958:87).

28. Saint Augustine time and again makes this point in *De doctrina Christiana*; see, e.g., 2.3.4 (*CCSL* 32:34), 2.24.37 (*CCSL* 32:59–60), 2.25.38 (*CCSL* 32:60).

29. Kaske 1980:114–18. Of course, an editor may emend, but the presence of an emendation marks the absence of a certified authorial signature.

30. The double meaning of "trouthe" in ME generates extraordinary com-

plexes of vision and understanding in ME poetry; see Burrow 1965:42–50.

31. See Galinsky 1968:31, who notes that "the development of the meaning of *cursus* reaches by 1355 the nuance of 'currency' in the monetary sense."

32. Such as Macrobius's *Commentary* on Cicero's "somnium Scipionis" or Lucan's *Pharsalia*; see Steadman 1972:42–65. For an excellent discussion of the *florilegium*, such as might have contained the kind of information Chaucer draws on here, see Rouse 1979:3–64; also *DSpir.* 5:468–69.

33. This distinction, apparently so minor that many might laugh at it, is in fact crucial, for Dante consistently, from the *Convivio* on through the *Commedia*, associates the eyes and smiles of Beatrice with "demonstrazione e persuasioni" (see, e.g., *Conv.* 3.8.6–12; *ED* 6:711). Smiles are reasonable and evidence of reason. Just so, Dante, reasonably, goes on to say, in *Paradiso*: "e quel consiglio per migliore approbo / che l'ha per meno; e chi ad altro pensa / chiamar si puote veramente probo" ("and that counsel I approve as best which holds it [sc. this earth] for least, and he whose thought is turned elsewhere may be called truly upright"; *Par.* 22.136–38), whereas Troylus, on the other hand, *un*reasonably damns the world.

34. The character of the Other World in *Aen.* 6 – the regret at the soul's return to the body, for example – is the most authoritative witness to this fact. See, further, the helpful remarks by Vossler 1929:1.192.

35. This sense of "matter" is continuous though not identical with that in French "matière de Bretagne" – see Kelly 1966; Kelly 1978: 155–56, 169, 229, 312. It is roughly the sense, as in medieval philosophy, of "principle of individuation": my matter makes me the individual I am (see *Conv.* 3.6.6; *ED* 6:709); my form gives that individuality identity. The form can be abstracted and known; hence Chaucer's usage. The matter, as such, is unknowable precisely because individual: that which cannot be divided (*in-dividu-um*) cannot be known. Translation of any sort always fails because, while it can recover the form, it can only betray the matter. When Criseyde is translated from Trojan into Greek, Troylus can know her "meaning" still, but he has lost precisely her matter, her body. And when that matter is "imposed upon" by another "to signify" *his* meaning, she in that moment loses her meaning for Troylus – "her name of trouthe / Is now fordon." "Trouthe," we can see, never was her name; rather, "Criseyde."

36. McAlpine 1978:245; Meech 1959:130.

37. Perhaps the most extraordinary medieval English witness to this truth is Will in *Piers Plowman*: he never understands in the singular – indeed, when he tries, he always winds up going astray again – and his dilemma is Everyman's dilemma of being unable to find in his decaying times a community which really serve understanding and truth – courts, markets, friars,

theologians, the family, what have you, all fail him.

Chapter 10

1. Cf. Kenner 1978:14: "For nothing is as dependent as Objectivity on language and the rituals of language, Objectivity which had promised to evade rhetoric and make the facts effect their own declaration." Part of what is at issue here is the fundamental datum of the positionality of language and hence of the self also; cf. Lacan (trans. Sheridan) 1977:84–86.

2. Cf. Scholes and Kellogg 1966:55; Wetherbee 1972:243.

3. Cf. Leicester 1980:220; Mann 1973:197.

4. Cf. Carton 1979:47–61; Mann 1973:7; Mehl 1974:173–89.

5. For a discussion of this pun and its usefulness for interpreting Chaucer, see Shoaf 1977:81.

6. Davis 1979:65; for the meaning "fiction," see *FrP* D 1279.

7. On the Augustinian notion "commoda privata," see O'Donovan 1980:102–104. I should take this opportunity to anticipate a probable objection to my use of the word true /"true." It should be obvious by now that part of my concern is to quarrel with both positivism and phenomenology precisely in regard to their positions on verification or truth. The former's position I reject basically for the same reasons as Kenner puts forth in *The Counterfeiters*, "The Gulliver Game": "positive" verification, as of the adequation of one word to one fact, ultimately dehumanizes because in it "the thing that is not can have no saying" (1968:139). The latter's position I reject because it seems to me still bound to the Cartesian *cogito* in the measure to which it privileges perception and the ego—see Rorty 1979:8–12; Heidegger (trans. Macquarrie and Robinson) 1962:122–35. Each of these positions, in its own way and for its own reasons, presupposes science as the standard for the measurement of truth (verification). My own position presupposes, on the contrary, the standard of sapience (wisdom), which measures truth for fidelity or loyalty to Being (this position is not Coleridgean: I do not privilege the Imagination; rather Memory is the mode of sapience as the measure of truth's fidelity to Being). To the various sciences of man invented (I agree with Foucault) in the eighteenth century, I would oppose poetry, here inclusive of theology and philosophy, as the sapience of man. I will expand on my position at length in the Epilogue. Here let me note only that true or designing fiction is bad fiction precisely because it is so clearly and immediately verifiable—i.e., its attack on someone or something can be verified. "True" or designed fiction, on the other hand, is not verifiable; it is rather contemplatable and dialecticalogical.

8. On the epithet "hende," see Donaldson 1972:17–20.

9. The basic meaning of the word is "requite" or "pay" or "reward"; see Davis 1979:116; *OED* Q:71–72.

10. For ethics in the category of positive justice, see Hugh of St. Victor *Didascalicon* 3.2 (trans. Taylor 1961:84, 209 n. 15); Hugh's position is common. It will be helpful to recall also *ST* 2a. 2ae. 58, 11, 3 (chap. 1 above), where Thomas writes: ". . . that justice is first of all and more commonly exercised in voluntary interchanges of things, such as buying and selling, where the expressions 'loss' and 'gain' are properly employed; *and yet they are transferred to all other matters of justice.* The same applies to the rendering to each one of what is his own" (emphasis added). Because justice is so obvious in commerce, commerce is obviously a relevant sphere of discourse for a meditation on justice—such as *The Canterbury Tales.* Consult, further, de Roover 1971:18–19.

11. Here I owe a pervasive debt to Derrida: the twin notions of "la différance" and "la différence" have played a large role in my thinking on the structure of *The Canterbury Tales.*

12. Theseus fails to control his household most obviously by failing to contain and define the power of love; for all his pronouncements, love still sets his house in disorder. Carpenter John obviously fails to control his household by having married someone far too young for him and by having subsequently provided her "likerous yë" someone to look upon. Symkyn in *The Reeve's Tale* fails to control his household not only by being unable to discipline his daughter but also by founding his prosperity upon theft. Finally, *The Cook's Tale* fragment: here perhaps it is enough to say that the word "household" hardly even applies.

13. For these pairings I am indebted to Patterson 1978:375–76.

14. The *oikonomia* of salvation, of redemption, judgment, etc., is a crucial concept in Christianity and especially in the Pauline Epistles; see, e.g., Eph. 1.10, 3.9. Consult, further, Saint John Chrysostom *Homilies on the Epistle to the Hebrews* 3.2, (PG 63:29), 4.6 (PG 63:41), 5.2 (PG 63:47); trans. Keble 1975:376, 385, 389.

15. John Balbus *Catholicon* (1460; reprint 1971), s.v.; Isidore *Etymologiae* 2.24.4.

16. Chaucer's contemporaries Langland and Gower shared this desire; see, e.g., *Piers Plowman* B 19.182; *Confessio Amantis* 2.2377.

17. The medieval "distinctio" is a collection of definitions or "distinctions" of biblical words or images; it originated as a preacher's tool, to facilitate the composition of sermons; we are only beginning to appreciate its importance for later medieval poetry. Two recent studies provide valuable introductions:

Brinkmann 1980:78–83; and Rouse and Rouse 1979:7–11.

18. Howard 1976:150–52, has suggested that *The General Prologue* to *The Canterbury Tales* might profitably be understood as an artificial memory system – see the remarkable study of such systems by Yates 1966:63–134. He notes that the likeliest structure would be: Knight: Squire, Yeoman, Prioress, Monk, Friar, Merchant; Clerk: Man of Law, Franklin, Guildsmen, Shipman, Physician, Wife; Parson and Plowman: Miller, Manciple, Reeve, Summoner, Pardoner, Host. In this system Knight, Clerk, Parson, and Plowman are obviously ideal types. Allen and Moritz 1981:89–91 have completed this suggestion by realizing that the ideal types are those that are, those that know, and those that do. These types, in turn, they note, are convenient to the obvious "distinctio" of Man as soul, mind, and body. In light of this "distinctio," it is possible to say that the content of *The Canterbury Tales* is Man: the pilgrims "add up" to Man – "These people are a normative array, sufficient for the definition of the category 'man'" (p. 90).

Chapter 11

1. On medieval "money of account," see Pirenne 1937:107–13.

2. In addition to Pirenne, I have consulted Bridbury 1962; Du Boulay 1970; Lopez 1976; Postan 1973:41–48, 186–213.

3. Specialized studies of these changes abound; convenient bibliographies are available in Du Boulay 1970:181–83; Miskimin 1975:171–79.

4. Fame, of course, was bought – see the comments by Delaney (1972:91–92) on the palace of Fame. But, it must be remembered, fame would also buy; see Du Boulay 1970:141.

5. See Bowden 1967:215; Carruthers 1979:209–22.

6. See, e.g., Isidore *Etymologiae* 8.3.1–2: "'Heresy,' in Greek, is so called from 'election' – namely, because anyone at all elects for himself what seems better to him. . . . therefore, it is called 'heresy,' the Greek word, from the meaning 'election' in that someone by his own will elects to himself what he will either for establishing it as a rule or for assuming it as a position." Consult, further, Mazzotta 1979:283–84; Leff 1967:1, 7–8. In support of the argument that the Wife of Bath is a "heretic" is the Clerk's allusion to "al hire *secte*" (*CIT* E 1171; emphasis added – and see Robinson's note [1957:712] for the debate over the word "secte"); see, further, Le Goff 1977:165. I would add that it does seem particularly fitting that the Clerk should be the one to suggest that she has set up her own "heretical" sect; after all, it would be his business to know.

7. See de Lubac 1961:3, 99–113; he also cites other labels for heretical

construction of Scripture, such as "proprius sensus," "propria pravitas," and "sensus perfidus."

8. See on this matter Casey 1976:237; Power 1926:432.

9. Ann S. Haskell (1977:2–3) describes "a fifteenth-century miniature in Froissart's Fourth Book of Chronicles...(Harley Ms. 4379, fol. 99)" which illustrates compellingly the Wife's predicament as a medieval woman: "The women in the scene are placed on the far side of the knights whom they accompany, making one of the ladies visible only from the waist up and the other three from the shoulders upward. All are dressed alike, and their plastic, expressionless faces, turned toward the knights, are identical. By contrast, the knights are depicted in the foreground of the scene, each wearing a highly individualized suit of armor, carrying a shield painted with his own coat of arms, and mounted on a horse covered with a cloth of ornate, distinctive pattern."

10. Medieval "privitee" was not the same as modern privacy; it was much more the deprivation of one's being in public and of the publicity of one's being. Consider, in the next century, the fate of Jacques d'Armagnac if he breaks his oath: he forfeits the privileges of his rank, and the king may move against him "'comme personne pure, privée, non aiant aucun privilleige, prerogative ou dignité, sans ce que pour ce faire soit besoing au Roy faire assembler sa court de parlement'" ("'as against a person merely, a private person, bearing no privilege, prerogative or dignity, without any intervening need for the king to summon his court of parliament'"; de Mandrot 1890:258; emphasis added). Of course, the oxymoron in "Goddes privitee" is part of Chaucer's irony in The Miller's Tale: strictly speaking, God, unlike wives, has no "privitee"; God is full of mystery, yes, but He is in no way deprived—indeed, His essence is the opposite of privation, or plenitude. See, further, Blodgett 1976:477–85.

11. For the medieval view of hoarding, engrossing or otherwise monopolizing goods, see O'Brien 1920:124–25. O'Brien's book, while it contains a wealth of useful information, is highly tendentious and must be used with caution; a very helpful check on O'Brien is de Roover 1971.

12. For the literature of misogyny and its ubiquity in the Middle Ages, see Utley 1944.

13. See Lentricchia 1980:169–70; Weiskell 1976:140–41.

14. Medieval grammar was aware that the trope is literally a "turning": "And it is so called from 'trope' because such a manner of speaking converts or exchanges words and their significations [for other meanings]"; John Balbus Catholicon (1460; reprint 1971), pt. 4, "de figuris," s.v.; the same definition will be found in Alain de Lille Distinctiones (PL 210:981); consult, further,

Brinkmann 1980:251; Nims 1974:215–30.

Chapter 12

1. Janet Smarr, "Chaucer and the *Decameron*: Some New Connections?" (Paper delivered at the Sixteenth International Congress on Medieval Studies, Western Michigan University, Kalamazoo, May 8, 1981).

2. See Noonan 1957:34–35; Olson 1961:259–63.

3. My argument is cast in so oblique and careful a way because of the re-cent, valuable study by Cahn (1980:81–119), an example of the kind of study Chaucer's poetry urgently needs. In this study evidence is adduced and care-fully weighed to show that words and phrases hitherto assumed to prove that the Merchant practices usury in fact prove only that he was in debt; it is the study's great merit to have clarified so much terminology so thoroughly. When, however, Cahn goes on to claim that "it is certain that [the Merchant] was neither a usurer nor a speculator" (p. 91), he seems, in my judgment, to err seriously in letting external evidence overrule the evidence of the poetry itself. The poetic evidence of Narrator identification with narrative matter in *The Merchant's Tale* should come first, and it suggests that the Merchant has in the past come by some familiarity with the practice of usury. Expressed negatively: Cahn's argument that various words and phrases do not prove usury does not mean that other evidence cannot suggest, if not prove, usury. Finally, although I rest no great weight on this notion, it is, I think, hard to imagine a businessman, medieval or modern, not practicing usury, at least oc-casionally, when circumstances permit.

4. See Noonan 1957:38–41; and for an exhaustive summary and analysis of the arguments against usury by an exact contemporary of Chaucer, see Oresme's translation of Aristotle's *Politics* 1.12 (ed. Menut 1970:66–68).

5. *ST*, 2a. 2ae. 78, 1, resp. Aristotle's teaching will be found principally in *Politics* 1.3.1256a–58b and is respresented in Oresme's translation in chaps. 10–13 of Book 1 (ed. Menut 1970:62–68).

6. The "etymology" is found in Paucapalea, in his paraphrase of the *Digest*'s (Roman law) definition of a loan in his commentary on Gratian's discussion (canon law) of usury; Noonan 1957:39; Baldwin 1970:1, 286–88.

7. See Oresme *Politiques* 1.12 (ed. Menut 1970:67); Noonan 1957:56–57; de Roover 1967:29.

8. See Baldwin 1970:1, 263–64; Spicciani 1977:211.

9. Petri Ioannis Olivi *Tractatus de emptione et venditione* (ed. Spicciani 1977:255, lines 50–70); see also de Roover 1967:18–20, on San Bernardino's dependence on Olivi.

10. Cf. Dragonetti 1978:103–11; Robertson 1962:99–103.

11. Macrobius *Commentary on the Dream of Scipio* 1.6.63–64 (ed. Eyssen-hardt 1868:498): ". . . once the seed has been deposited in the mint where man is coined, nature immediately begins to work her skill upon it so that on the seventh day she causes a sack to form around the embryo" (trans. Stahl 1952:112).

12. See Power 1975:16–19; Sheehan 1975.

13. See *Politics* 1.3.1256b, 8–20; Oresme *Politiques* 1.9–10 (ed. Menut 1970:62–64), where the distinction continues, though the terminology is variable.

14. See Burrow 1957:199–208; Economou 1965:251–57.

15. For a graphic portrayal of Nature at her forge, see Tuve 1966:324, fig. 107, 108; see, further, chap. 8 above.

16. See Alain de Lille *De planctu naturae* (PL 210:453, 431, 438, 447); also his *Anticlaudianus* 7.34, 2.410 (ed. Bossuat 1955:158, 84).

17. See *The Cosmographia of Bernardus Silvestris* 1.2 (trans. Wetherbee 1973:71–72, 146–47 nn. 29, 35); consult, further, Häring 1955:508–12; Häring 1956:46–49.

18. The most extraordinary evidence for this understanding of Nature is actually Chaucer's own version of his Platonic inheritance, in *The Physician's Tale* (C 11–22; emphasis added):

> "Lo! I, Nature,
> Thus kan I forme and peynte a creature,
> Whan that me list; *who kan me countrefete?*
> *Pigmalion noght, thogh he ay forge and bete,*
> Or *grave*, or *peynte*; for I dar wel seyn,
> Apelles, Zanzis, sholde werche in veyn
> Outher to grave, or peynte, or forge, or bete,
> *If they presumed me to countrefete.*
> For He that is the formere principal
> Hath maked me his vicaire general,
> *To forme and peynten erthely creaturis*
> *Right as me list. . . ."*

Although "countrefete" here means primarily "imitate" (see Robinson's note [1957:711] to *The Clerk's Tale*, line 743), the other meaning of "falsify" is distantly audible; and we could answer Nature's question, "The Merchant can, or thinks he can." Be that as it may, Nature's mandate is obviously generation.

19. For a helpful discussion of the name of the one character who is not a personification, or Damyan, see Brown 1968:273–77.

20. So John Balbus *Catholicon* (1460; reprint, 1971) s.v.; consider also the fourteenth-century *Book of Vices and Virtues* (ed. Francis 1942:22; emphasis added): "Þe enuyous may not *see* good bi oþere, ne *see* who-so helpeþ hym, no more þan a bake may suffre to *see* þe schynyng of þe sonne."

21. To my knowledge, nowhere else in *The Canterbury Tales* does Herry suggest that he has told or will tell a tale. I have checked myself against the Tatlock and Kennedy *Concordance*. Moreover, it seems fairly clear from Herry's remarks at the beginning of the pilgrimage that he does not intend to enter the contest as a participant (see especially *GP* A 805–806). Hence, when he *does* tell a tale, the occasion *is* unusual; and I suspect that the text depends on this fact to underscore the mesmeric and temporarily frightening powers of the Merchant's style: Herry would not be telling a tale if the Merchant had not almost hypnotized him.

22. On the *amplificatio* of *circumlocutio*, see Geoffrey of Vinsauf *Poetria nova* (ed. Faral 1971:204; trans. Nims 1967:24–25).

23. See also *MerT* E 1783–87; *Poetria nova* (ed. Faral 1971:205–11; trans. Nims 1967:25–32), where Geoffrey goes out of his way to emphasize the excellence of apostrophe as one of the modes of *amplificatio*.

24. See also *MerT* E 1729–39, 2031–37; Curtius (trans. Trask) 1953:162.

25. "[T]he dominant view of the Church was that usury resided only in a loan—'solum in mutuo cadit usura'—and the exchange was not a loan—'cambio non est mutuum'"; Cahn 1980:96.

26. Allegory, which includes irony among its tropes, is defined as "alieniloquium" by Isidore *Etymologiae* 1.37.22; see also the discussion by Allen 1971:7 nn. 6, 7.

27. My use of the word "fruit" looks to the famous distinction between "fruyt" and "chaf" (*NPT* B[2] 3443) and to the whole hermeneutical tradition which it represents; see, further, Brinkmann 1980:169–98.

28. *Conf.* 4.2 (*PL* 32:693); Burke 1970:49.

29. My example is also one of Saint Thomas's favorite examples for illustrating metaphor; see *ST* 1.13.6, resp.; 1a. 2ae. 88, resp.

30. That this was the medieval position Dante's *Inferno* and *Purgatorio* amply illustrate: in the former, lust is the first sin punished, in the latter, the last sin purged—in each case because it is the least culpable. Dante depends in this matter, as do most medieval thinkers, on the tradition which originates with Saint Gregory: "Carnal sins are of less guilt and greater infamy than spiritual sins"; quoted in Reade 1909:207.

31. *MED* L:932–35, s.v., br. 1a, 2c; Davis 1979:87–88.

32. On exegesis of the *Canticum Canticorum*, a good starting point is Leclercq (trans. Misrahi) 1961:106–109; for more detailed study, see Ohly 1958.

Chapter 13

1. A good starting place is Halverson 1970:184–202; see also Baugh 1977:128–31.

2. See, e.g., 1 Cor. 15.45–49, and for representative patristic comment, see Saint Augustine *Secundam Juliani responsionem, imperfectum opus* 2.87–91 (*PL* 45:1222–24).

3. Curry 1960:54–70; Miller 1955:180–99; McAlpine 1980:8–22; Rowland 1979:140–51; Elliott 1966:62–63; Donaldson 1980:9.

4. See Ginsberg 1976:77–78 and nn. 2–3.

5. For a helpful discussion of this scene, from a different point of view, see Kaske 1957:249–68.

6. Certainly one can argue that the Miller seems to have arrived at some such conclusion, given the vehemence of his reaction to the Knight's tale; and while the Miller is not the only type of reader *The Knight's Tale* can find, he certainly is one type—representing energy, humor, and the physical—and he is not lightly or condescendingly to be dismissed. I hope to develop further and to nuance more carefully my position on the Knight and his tale in a later study.

7. On these matters the essay by McAlpine (1980:14–19) is helpful. Consult further, in addition to Curry and Miller, Kellogg 1951:465–81; Kellogg and Haselmayer 1951:251–77.

8. On this matter I have relied on the article "Salvation" in *Sacramentum Mundi: An Encyclopedia of Theology*, 5:425–38, and on the extensive bibliographies cited there; also on the remarkable studies by Lyonnet 1970:61–184 and Sabourin 1970:203–24; and on Rivière 1928; Rivière 1934; and Aulén (trans. Hebert) 1957:82, 90. More generally, I am dependent upon Oberman 1977 and Ozment 1980.

9. *Enarrationes in Psalmos* 21.28 (*CCSL* 38:130); cited by Rivière 1928:107.

10. E.g., Saint Augustine *Enarrationes in Psalmos* 102.6 (*CCSL* 40:1456); Saint Anselm *Cur Deus Homo* (*PL* 158:426); Saint Thomas *ST* 3.48, 4, reply obj. 3; see, further, Vignaux 1934:52–61.

11. See Palmer 1959:336–51; Steadman 1965:4–7.

12. *Enarrationes in Psalmos* 95.5 (*CCSL* 39:1346).

13. The phrase is the common scholastic formula for distinguishing sacraments from other signs; see, e.g., *ST* 3.62, 1, ad resp. 1.

14. Notably Miller 1955:185–86; see also Halverson 1970:190.

15. I have tentatively sketched the relationship between language and seed in Chaucer's poetry in Shoaf 1979:56–57.

16. "Saffron" means "to season"; Davis 1979:125.

17. Ginsberg 1976:79–80; Nichols 1967:498–504.

18. See, e.g., Saint Jerome *In Osee* 3.13 (*PL* 25:937); Guibert of Nogent *Tropologiae in Osee, Amos, et Jeremia* 3.13 (*PL* 156:409); Rupert of Deutz *Commentaria in XII Prophetae Minores—In Osee* 6.13 (*PL* 168:196).

19. On the "descensus ad inferos" (or "infernum"), see MacCulloch 1930; Owen 1971.

20. E.g., Jerome (*PL* 25:937–38); Rupert (*PL* 168:197).

21. See, e.g., Howard 1976:367–68; McAlpine 1980:17.

22. ME "envoluped" derives from OF "envoluper" (Davis 1979:48), which itself derives directly from Latin "involucrum" (Godefroy, 3:311c); see, further, chap. 4 and n. 9 above.

23. Recall, in regard to this matter, that Herry Bailly, in one sense, precisely "echoes" the Merchant after the latter has finished his tale—he sounds just like the Merchant. The Pardoner, on the contrary, does not want anyone to sound like him; he wants everyone to be like him—the difference is that between a dictator and an actor.

Epilogue

1. On Shakespeare's relation to and use of Chaucer, consult Thompson 1978:111–65.

2. *The Riverside Shakespeare*, ed. Evans 1974:461; on the issue of value in the play, see, further, Rabkin 1967:31–63.

3. The text of *Troilus and Cressida* is peculiarly vexed: "[mirror'd]" in the present passage is a good example of the kinds of cruces the play contains; the First Folio and the Quarto show "married" rather than "[mirror'd]" which is supplied only in the Singer and Collier manuscripts. This sort of crux is insoluble short of a new text of the play suddenly turning up. But my reading of Chaucer's *TC* does lend weight to the choice of "[mirror'd]," since it suggests that Shakespeare too might have noted the emphasis on Narcissus in the poem.

4. On this matter I find particularly helpful the essay by Roland Barthes, "From Work to Text," and that by Michel Foucault, "What Is an Author?" in Harari 1979:73–82, 141–60, respectively. While I do not cede every position these essays take, I do think they are masterful in the isolation and definition of many problems.

5. For a discussion of this issue from the perspective of the late medieval ethical poetic, see Allen 1982:29–34, 288–300.

6. Such a description will be found in Gimpel 1976:3–7; consult, further, Le Goff 1977:162–80, "Métier et profession d'après les manuels de confesseurs du Moyen Age."

7. The first of these examples, wood for fires, I choose precisely because depletion of forests for technological purposes was a serious problem in the Middle Ages; see Gimpel 1976:75–80.

8. On this point, in regard to Chaucer, see Brewer 1976:229.

9. My use of *Wesen* here derives mainly from "The Question Concerning Technology" (trans. Lovitt) 1977:3–35; Lovitt gives a very helpful note on the term on pp. 3–4 of his translation; I also rely on the essay "The Age of the World Picture" (trans. Lovitt), 1977:115–54. By way of commentaries on Heidegger's thought, I have consulted Harries 1978:65–79; Mehta 1967:114–27.

10. This, of course, is the Heideggerean position. One of its heirs, perhaps the most valiant and certainly the most loyal, has been the political philosophy of Arendt. At the center of man's existence as she understands him is his desire and need to appear: "Could it not be that appearances are not there for the sake of the life process but, on the contrary, that the life process is there for the sake of appearances? Since we live in an *appearing* world, is it not much more plausible that the relevant and the meaningful in this world of ours should be located precisely on the surface?"; Arendt 1977–78:1.27. The entire argument surrounding these two questions – 1.24–30 – deserves and will repay close study.

11. Extraordinary witness to this truth may be seen in Michael Roemer's film *Dying* (1976), in which, at one point, the death of an old black minister is chronicled: he is seen at the last at home in his own bed with his entire family surrounding him as he departs; the peace, and the understanding, visible in the scene are moving. Consult, further, the discussion of the film by Ariès 1981:590–92.

12. If I may adapt Pascal's famous formula – "Console-toi, tu ne me [Jesus Christ] chercherais pas, si tu ne m'avais trouvé" ("Be comforted, you would not seek me had you not already found me"; *Pensées* no. 553) – "One would not love the beloved for the beloved's sake had not one already loved God in the beloved."

13. See Galbraith and Salinger 1978:77; Smith 1981:14–18, 25–27, 61. I think I should make a special point of noting here that my discussion is intentionally outside the boundaries of professional economics; I am, perhaps perversely, looking only for common sense, in ordinary language.

14. Wealth, on the other hand, is limited by the things of which it consists; and common sense suggests that it can be stored as capital insofar as not all wealth can be expended at once. On this commonsense understanding, it can also be noted that all societies are capitalistic, even the communist, where it is only a matter of different hands holding the capital.

15. Cf. the remarks on "pleonexia" (uncontrolled greed) and its Aristotelian context in MacIntyre 1981:145–46, 171.

16. See Sayce 1971:230–48 (237, 241–43, 245 especially).

Bibliography

Ancient, Medieval, and Renaissance Texts

Note: Proper names are modernized; translations follow the original works in a separate list; an edition which also contains a translation is listed only once.

Alain de Lille. *Anticlaudianus*. Ed. R. Bossuat. Paris: Librairie Philosophique J. Vrin, 1955.

————. *De planctu naturae*. Ed. Migne. *PL* 210:429–82.

————. *Distinctiones dictionum theologicarum*. Ed. Migne. *PL* 210:685–1012.

Alberich of Monte Cassino. *Flores rhetorici*. Ed. M. Inguanez and H. M. Willard. Miscellanea Cassinese, vol. 14. Montecassino, 1938.

Albert the Great. *Opera omnia 8. Super politicam*. Ed. A. Borgnet. Paris: Vives, 1891.

————. *Opera omnia 14.1. Supra ethica commentum et quaestiones*. Ed. William Kübel. Westphalia: Aschendorff, 1968–72.

Dante Alighieri. Note: All the texts which I have elected to quote are now conveniently available in the *Appendice* to the *Enciclopedia Dantesca*. 6:621–1002.

————. *Convivio*. Ed. G. Busnelli and G. Vandelli. Florence: Le Monnier, 1934–37. *ED* 6:677–751.

————. *De vulgari eloquentia*. Ed. Aristide Marigo. Florence: Le Monnier, 1948. *ED* 6:753–72.

————. *La Divina Commedia secondo l'antica vulgata*. Ed. Giorgio Petrocchi. Società Dantesca Italiana, Edizione Nazionale. Milano: Mondadori, 1966–67. *ED* 6:833–964.

————. *Rime*. Ed. Michele Barbi. Florence: R. Bemporad e Figlio, 1921. *ED* 6:645–76.

————. *La vita nuova*. Ed. Michele Barbi. Florence: Le Monnier, 1932. *ED* 6:621–43.

Allegoriae universam in Sacram Scripturam [attributed to Adam Scotus]. Ed. Migne. *PL* 112:849–1088.

Ambrose, Saint. *De Joseph*. Ed. Migne. *PL* 14:673–704.

————. *De Patriarchis*. Ed. Migne. *PL* 14:707–28.

————. *Hexameron*. Ed. Migne. *PL* 14:123–274.

Anselm, Saint. *Cur Deus homo*. Ed. Migne. *PL* 158:359–432.

Aquinas, Saint Thomas. *In libros politicorum Aristotelis expositio*. Ed. Raymund M. Spiazzi, O.P. Rome: Marietti, 1951.

————. *Quaestiones disputatae de Veritate*. Ed. Raymund M Spiazzi, O.P. Rome: Marietti, 1949.

————. *Summa theologiae*. Ed. and trans. Blackfriars. London: Eyre and Spottiswoode. New York: McGraw-Hill, various dates.

Aristotle. *Metaphysics*. Ed. and trans. Hugh Tredennick. Loeb Classical Library. Cambridge, Mass.: Harvard University Press, 1968.

————. *Nichomachean Ethics*. Ed. and trans. H. Rackham. Loeb Classical Library. Cambridge, Mass.: Harvard University Press, 1934.

————. *The Politics*. Ed. and trans. H. Rackham. Loeb Classical Library. Cambridge, Mass.: Harvard University Press, 1932.

Augustine, Saint. *Confessions*. Ed. Migne. *PL* 32:659–868.

————. *Contra Julianum*. Ed. Migne. *PL* 44:641–874.

————. *Contra mendacium*. Ed. Joseph Zycha. *CSEL* 41. Vienna: Tempsky, 1890.

————. *De civitate Dei*. Ed B. Dombart and A. Kalb. *CCSL* 47, 48.

————. *De doctrina Christiana*. Ed. J. Martin. *CCSL* 32:1–167.

————. *De Genesi contra Manichaeos*. Ed. Migne. *PL* 34:173–220.

————. *De libero arbitrio*. Ed. W. M. Green. *CCSL* 29:204–321.

————. *De Trinitate*. Ed. W. J. Mountain and Fr. Glorie. *CCSL* 50–50a.

————. *Enarrationes in Psalmos*. Ed. E. Dekkers and J. Fraipont. *CCSL* 38–40.

————. *Enchiridion ad Laurentium de fide et spe et caritate*. Ed. E. Evans. *CCSL* 46:20–114.

————. *Secundam responsionem Juliani*. Ed. Migne. *PL* 45:1049–1608.

————. *Sermones*. Ed. Migne. *PL* 38, 39, 46, 47.

Aurifaber, John. *Determinatio de modis significandi*. Transcribed Jan Pinborg. *Die Entwicklung der Sprachtheorie im Mittelalter*. Beiträge zur Geschichte der Philosophie and Theologie des Mittelalters, 42.2. Westphalia: Aschendorff, 1967.

Averroes. *On Plato's "Republic."* Trans. Ralph Lerner. Ithaca, N.Y.; Cornell University Press, 1974.

Bacon, Roger. "De Signis." Ed. K. M. Fredborg, Lauge Nielsen, and Jan Pinborg. "An Unedited Part of Roger Bacon's 'Opus Maius': 'De Signis.'" *Traditio* 34 (1978):75–136.

Balbus, John. *Catholicon*. Mainz. Reprint. London: Gregg International Publishers, 1971.

Bernard, Saint. *Opera omnia* 1. *Sermones super Cantica Canticorum 1–35*. Ed. J. Leclercq, C. H. Talbot, and H. M. Rochais. Rome: Editiones Cistercienses, 1957.

———. *Opera omnia* 2. *Sermones 36–86*. Ed. J. Leclercq et al. Rome: Editiones Cistercienses, 1958.

Bernardus Silvestris. *Cosmographia*. Ed. Peter Dronke. Textus Minores, vol. 53. Leiden: Brill, 1978.

Bersuire, Pierre. *Opera omnia*. Ed. John William Huisch and Peter Pütz. Cologne, 1730–31.

Biagi, Guido, ed. *"La Divina Commedia" nella figurazione artistica e nel secolare commento*. 3 vols. Turin: Unione Tipografico–Editrice Torinese, 1924–39.

Bible. "Paris Version" [13th century]. Ed. Migne. *PL* 28, 29. Trans. Douay-Rheims. London: Burns and Oates, 1964.

Boccaccio, Giovanni. *Il Filostrato*. Ed. Nathaniel E. Griffin and Arthur B. Myrick. 1929. Reprint. New York: Biblio and Tannen, 1967.

Boethius, Anicius Manlius Severinus. *De interpretatione*. Ed. Charles Meiser. Leipzig: Teubner, 1880.

———. *Philosophiae consolatio*. Ed. Ludwig Bieler. *CCSL* 94.1.

Bonaventura, Saint. *Opera omnia*. Ed. Collegium a S. Bonaventura. Quaracchi, 1882–1902. "Itinerarium mentis ad Deum." 5 (1891): 293–317.

The Book of Vices and Virtues. Ed. W. N. Francis. *EETS*, o.s. 217. London: Oxford University Press, 1942.

Chaucer, Geoffrey. *The Book of Troilus and Criseyde*. Ed. Robert K. Root. Princeton, N.J.: Princeton University Press, 1926.

———. *Chaucer's Poetry*. Ed. E. T. Donaldson. New York: Ronald Press, 1958.

———. *The Complete Poetry and Prose of Geoffrey Chaucer*. Ed. John H. Fisher. New York: Holt, Rinehart and Winston, 1977.

———. *Works*. Ed. F. N. Robinson. 2d ed. Boston: Houghton-Mifflin, 1957.

Dacus, John. *Summa grammatica*. Ed. A. Otto. *Johannis Daci opera*. Corpus philosophorum Danicorum medii aevi, vol. 1. Copenhagen, 1955.

Pseudo-Dionysius the Areopagite. *The Divine Names*. Ed. Migne. *PG* 3:586–996.

———. *Mystical Theology*. Ed. Migne. *PG* 3:997–1064.

Geoffrey of Vinsauf. *Poetria nova*. Ed. Edmond Faral. *Les Arts poétiques du XIIe et du XIIIe siècle*. 1924. Reprint. Paris: Champion, 1971. Pp. 197–262.

Gerhoh of Reichersberg. *Commentarium in Psalmos*. Ed. Migne. *PL* 193:619–1814.

Glossa ordinaria. Froben, 1498.

Gower, John. *Confessio Amantis*. Ed. G. C. Macaulay. *The Works of John Gower*. 4 vols. (vols. 2, 3). Oxford: Oxford University Press, 1899–1902.

Guibert of Nogent. *Tropologiae in Osee*. Ed. Migne. *PL* 156:341–416.

Guillaume de Lorris and Jean de Meun. *Le Roman de la Rose*. Ed. Félix Lecoy. 3 vols. Paris: Champion, 1966–74.

Hildebert of Lavardin. *Sermones in Quadragesima*. Ed. Migne. *PL* 171:423–76.

Horace. *Ars poetica*. Ed. H. Rushton Fairclough. Loeb Classical Library. Cambridge, Mass.: Harvard University Press, 1970.

———. *Odes and Epodes*. Ed. C. E. Bennett. Loeb Classical Library. Cambridge, Mass.: Harvard University Press, 1947.

Hugh of St. Cher. *Opera omnia in universum Vetus et Novum Testamentum*. Cologne: Johannes Gymnicus, 1621.

Hugh of St. Victor. *Didascalicon: de studio legendi*. Ed. Charles H. Buttimer. Washington, D.C.: Catholic University of America Press, 1939.

———. *Homiliae in Ecclesiasten*. Ed. Migne. *PL* 175:113–256.

Isidore, Saint. *Etymologiarum sive Originum Libri XX*. Ed. W. M. Lindsay. Oxford: Oxford University Press, 1971.

Jerome, Saint. *In Osee*. Ed. Migne. *PL* 25:815–946.

John Chrysostom, Saint. *Homilies on the Epistle to the Hebrews*. Ed. Migne. *PG* 63:9–236.

John of Salisbury. *Metalogicon*. Ed. Clement C. J. Webb. Oxford: Clarendon Press.

———. *Policraticus*. Ed. Clement C. J. Webb. Oxford: Clarendon Press, 1909.

Le Lais de Narcisse. Ed Martine Thiry-Stassin and Madeleine Tyssens. Bibliothèque de la faculté de philosophie et lettres de l'université de Liège, fasc. 211. Paris: Société d'édition "Les Belles Lettres." 1976.

Langland, William. *Piers Plowman: The B Version*. Ed. George Kane and E. T. Donaldson. London: Athlone, 1975.

Latini, Brunetto. *Li livres dou tresor*. Ed. Francis J. Carmody. 1948. Reprint. Geneva: Slatkine Reprints, 1975.

Macrobius. *Commentary on the Dream of Scipio*. Ed. Francis Eyssenhardt. Leipzig: Teubner, 1868.

———. *Saturnalia*. Ed. Jacob Willis. Leipzig: Teubner, 1963.

Martianus Capella. *De nuptiis philologiae et mercurii*. Ed. A. Dick. Rev. Jean Préaux. Reprint. Stuttgart: Teubner, 1969.

Migne, Jacques Paul, ed. *Patrologiae cursus completus: series graeca.* Paris, 1857–94.

———. *Patrologiae cursus completus: series latina.* Paris. 1844–64, with later printings.

Odo of Châteauroux [d. 1273]. *Super Psalterium.* MS Troyes Bibliothèque Municipale 1089. Saec. 13.

Olivi, Peter John. *Tractatus de emptione et venditione.* Ed. Amleto Spicciani. *La Mercatura e la formazione del prezzo nella riflessione teologica medioevale.* Atta della Accademia Nazionale dei Lincei, 8th ser., vol. 20, fasc. 3. Rome, 1977. Pp. 253–70.

Oresme, Nicole. *De moneta.* Ed. and trans. Charles Johnson. London: Thomas Nelson and Sons, 1956.

———. *Le Livre de éthiques d'Aristote.* Ed. Albert D. Menut. New York: G. E. Stechert and Co., 1940.

———. *Le Livre de politiques d'Aristote.* Ed. and trans. Albert D. Menut. *TAPS,* n.s. 60, pt. 6. 1970.

———. *Le Livre de yconomique d'Aristote.* Ed. and trans. Albert D. Menut. *TAPS,* n.s., 47, pt. 5 (1957): 783–853.

Origen. *In Leviticum.* Ed. Migne. *PG* 12:405–574.

Ovid. *Metamorphoses.* Ed. George LaFaye. 1930. Reprint. Paris: Société d'édition "Les Belles Lettres," 1972.

Ovide moralisé. Ed. C. de Boer. Koninklijke Akademie van Wetenschappen te Amsterdam. *Vorhandelingen, Afd. Letterkunde,* n.s. 15. 1915.

Pascal, Blaise. *Pensées.* 3 vols. *Oeuvres.* Ed. Léon Brunschvicg. Paris: Librairie Hachette, 1925.

Peter of Capua. *Rosa alphabetica.* Ed. J. B. Pitra. *Spicilegium solesmense.* 4 vols (vol. 2). Paris, 1855.

Peter of Celle. *Sermones.* Ed. Migne. *PL* 202:637–926.

Quintilian. *Institutio oratoria.* Ed. Jean Cousin. Paris: Société d'édition "Les Belles Lettres," 1975–80.

Richard of St. Victor. *Benjamin major.* Ed. Migne. *PL* 196:64–202.

———. *Benjamin minor.* Ed. Migne. *PL* 196:1–64.

Rupert of Deutz. *De glorificatione Trinitatis et processione Sancti Spiritus.* Ed. Migne. *PL* 169:13–202.

———. *In Jonam.* Ed. Migne. *PL* 168:339–440.

———. *In Osee.* Ed. Migne. *PL* 168:11–204.

Sacrum commercium Beati Francisci cum Domina Paupertate. Ed. Edoardo Alvisi. "Nota al canto XI (versi 43–75) de 'Paradiso' di Dante Alighieri." *Collezione di "Opuscoli Danteschi" inediti o rari,* vol. 12. Ed. G. L. Passerini. Città di Castello: S. Lapi, 1894.

281

Shakespeare, William. *The Riverside Shakespeare*. Ed. G. Blakemore Evans. 2 vols. Boston: Houghton Mifflin, 1974.

Theoderich von St. Trond. "De nummo." Ed. F. G. Otto. *Commentarii critici in codices Bibliothecae Gissensis*. Giessen: G. F. Heyeri, 1842. Pp. 163–98.

Virgil. *Aeneid*. Ed. H. Rushton Fairclough. 2 vols. Loeb Classical Library. Cambridge, Mass.: Harvard University Press, 1934.

William de Montibus [d. 1213]. *Distinctiones theologicum*. MS Oxford Bodleian 419. Saec. 13.

Pseudo-Witelo. *Liber de intelligentiis*. Ed. Clemens Bäumker. *Witelo: Ein Philosoph und Naturforscher des XIII Jahrhunderts*. Beiträge zur Geschichte der Philosophie des Mittelalters, 3.2. Münster: Aschendorff, 1908.

Translations of Ancient, Medieval, and Renaissance Texts

Note: Unless otherwise noted, translations in this book are my own. Acknowledgment of another translator follows immediately upon citation of the original. The one exception to this rule is the translation of Dante's *Commedia*. I use, without further acknowledgment, the translation by Singleton in the Bollingen series. When I alter his translation, as on occasion I do, for special emphasis, I note that I have done so. In my own translations, utility rather than elegance has been my goal; and if I have erred, it will be found, I believe, to have been on the side of the too literal.

Apostle, H. G. Aristotle. *The Nichomachean Ethics*. Dordrecht: D. Reidel, 1975.

Boas, George. Saint Bonaventura. *The Mind's Road to God*. Indianapolis, Ind.: Bobbs-Merrill, 1953.

Dahlberg, Charles. Guillaume de Lorris and Jean de Meun. *The Romance of the Rose*. Princeton, N.J.: Princeton University Press, 1971.

Davies, Percival V. Macrobius. *The Saturnalia*. New York: Columbia University Press, 1969.

Dorsch, T. S. Horace. *On the Art of Poetry: Classical Literary Criticism*. Harmondsworth: Penguin, 1965.

Fathers of the English Dominican Province. Saint Thomas. *Summa theologica*. London: R. and T. Washbourne, various dates.

Green, Richard H. Boethius. *The Consolation of Philosophy*. Indianapolis, Ind.: Bobbs-Merrill, 1962.

Innes, Mary M. Ovid. *The Metamorphoses*. Harmondsworth: Penguin, 1955.

Keble, T. Saint John Chrysostom. *Homilies on the Epistle to the Hebrews.* Revised with Introduction and Notes by Frederic Gardiner. A Select Library of the Nicene and Post-Nicene Fathers of the Christian Church, vol. 14. 1877. Reprint. Grand Rapids, Mich.: William B. Eerdmans, 1975.

Lerner, Ralph, *Averroes on Plato's "Republic."* Ithaca, N.Y.: Cornell University Press, 1974.

McGarry, Daniel D. John of Salisbury. *The Metalogicon.* Berkeley: University of California Press, 1955.

McKenna, Stephen, C.SS.R. Saint Augustine. *The Trinity.* Washington, D.C. Catholic University of America Press, 1963.

Michie, James. Horace. *Odes.* New York: Washington Square Press, 1963.

Moffat, Douglas M. Alain de Lille. *The Complaint of Nature.* Hamden, Conn.: Shoe String Press, 1972.

Nims, Sister Margaret F. Geoffrey of Vinsauf. *Poetria nova.* Toronto: Pontifical Institute of Medieval Studies, 1967.

Pine-Coffin, R. S. Saint Augustine. *Confessions.* Harmondsworth: Penguin, 1961.

Robertson, D. W., Jr. Saint Augustine. *On Christian Doctrine.* Indianapolis, Ind.: Bobbs-Merrill, 1958.

Rolt, C. E. Dionysius the Areopagite. *The Divine Names and the Mystical Theology.* London: SPCK, 1940.

Savage, John J. Saint Ambrose. *Hexameron.* New York: Fathers of the Church, 1961.

Sheridan, James J. Alain de Lille. *Anticlaudianus.* Toronto: Pontifical Institute of Medieval Studies, 1973.

Singleton, Charles S. Dante Alighieri, *The Divine Comedy.* Bollingen Series, no. 58. 3 vols. in 6. Princeton, N.J.: Princeton University Press, 1970–75.

Stahl, William H. Macrobius. *Commentary on the Dream of Scipio.* New York: Columbia University Press, 1952.

Taylor, Jerome. Hugh of St. Victor. *The Didascalicon of Hugh of St. Victor.* New York: Columbia University Press, 1961.

Walsh, Kilian, O.C.S.O. Saint Bernard. *On the Song of Songs I.* Spencer, Mass.: Cistercian Publications, 1971. *On the Song of Songs II.* Kalamazoo, Mich.: Cistercian Publications, 1976.

Wetherbee, Winthrop. *The Cosmographia of Bernardus Silvestris.* New York: Columbia University Press, 1973.

Zinn, Grover A. Richard of St. Victor. *The Twelve Patriarchs, The Mystical Ark, Book Three of the Trinity.* New York: Paulist Press, 1979.

Secondary Works

Aers, David. *Chaucer, Langland, and the Creative Imagination.* London: Routledge and Kegan Paul, 1980.

Alessio, Giovanni. See Battisti and Alessio.

Alford, John A. "Literature and Law in Medieval England." *PMLA* 92 (1977):941–51.

———. "Medicine in the Middle Ages: The Theory of a Profession." *CR* 23 (1979):377–96.

Alinei, Mario, ed. *A Linguistic Inventory of Thirteenth-Century Italian, II 5: Dante Alighieri, "La Commedia,"* ed. G. Petrocchi. Bologna: Il Mulino, 1971.

Allen, Judson B. *The Ethical Poetic of the Later Middle Ages: A Decorum of Convenient Distinctions.* Toronto: University of Toronto Press, 1982.

———. *The Friar as Critic.* Nashville, Tenn.: Vanderbilt University Press, 1971.

———, and Theresa Ann Moritz. *A Distinction of Stories: The Medieval Unity of Chaucer's Fair Chain of Narratives for Canterbury.* Columbus, Ohio: Ohio State University Press, 1981.

Anderson, William. *Dante the Maker.* London: Routledge and Kegan Paul, 1980.

Arbusow, Leonid. *Colores Rhetorici.* 2d ed. Ed. Helmut Peter. Göttingen: Vandenhoeck and Ruprecht, 1963.

Arendt, Hannah. *The Human Condition.* Chicago: University of Chicago Press, 1958.

———. *The Life of the Mind.* 2 vols. New York: Harcourt, Brace, Jovanovich, 1977–78.

———. *The Origins of Totalitarianism.* New York: World, 1972.

Ariès, Phillipe. *The Hour of Our Death.* New York: Knopf, 1981.

Atchity, Kenneth John. See Rimanelli and Atchity.

Auerbach, Eric. *Mimesis: The Representation of Reality in Western Literature.* Trans. Willard Trask. New York: Anchor Books, 1957.

Aulén, Gustaf. *Christus Victor: An Historical Study of the Three Main Types of the Idea of Atonement.* Trans. A. G. Hebert. New York: Macmillan, 1957.

Baldwin, John W. *Masters, Princes, and Merchants: The Social Views of Peter the Chanter and His Circle.* 2 vols. Princeton, N.J.: Princeton University Press, 1970.

Barney, Stephen A. "Troilus Bound." *Speculum* 47 (1972):445–58.

Barthes, Roland. *Critique et Vérité.* Paris: Éditions du Seuil, 1966.

———. "From Work to Text." In Josué V. Harari, ed. *Textual Strategies.* Ithaca, N.Y.: Cornell University Press, 1979. Pp. 73–81.

Bartholomew, Barbara. *Fortuna and Natura: A Reading of Three Chaucer Narratives.* The Hague: Mouton, 1966.

Battisti, Carlo, and Giovanni Alessio, eds. *Dizionario etimologico italiano.* 5 vols. Florence: G. Barbera, 1950–57.

Baugh, A. C. *Chaucer.* 2d ed. Goldentree Bibliographies. Arlington Heights, Ill.: AHM, 1977.

van Bavel, T., O.E.S.A. "L'humanité du Christ comme *lac parvulorum* et comme *via* dans la spiritualité de Saint Augustine." *Aug* 7 (1957):245–81.

Bec, Christian. *Les marchands écrivains à Florence, 1375–1434.* Civilisations et Sociétés, vol. 9. Paris: Mouton, 1967.

Benson, C. David. *The History of Troy in Middle English Literature: Guido delle Colonne's "Historia destructionis Troiae" in Medieval England.* Totowa, N.J.: Rowman and Littlefield, 1980.

Benveniste, Émile. *Problems in General Linguistics.* Trans. Mary E. Meek. Miami Linguistics Series, vol. 8. Coral Gables, Fla.: University of Miami Press, 1971.

Bloch, R. Howard. *Medieval French Literature and Law.* Berkeley: University of California Press, 1977.

Blodgett, E. D. "Chaucerian *Pryvetee* and the Opposition to Time." *Speculum* 51 (1976):477–93.

Bloomfield, Morton W. "Distance and Predestination in *Troilus and Criseyde*." *PMLA* 72 (1957):14–26. Reprinted in Richard J. Shoeck and Jerome Taylor, eds. *Chaucer Criticism.* 2 vols. Notre Dame, Ind.: University of Notre Dame Press, 1960, 1961. 2:196–210.

Borst, Arno. *Der Turmbau von Babel: Geschichte der Meinungen über Ursprung und Vielfalt der Sprachen und Völker.* 4 vols. in 6. Stuttgart: Anton Hiersemann, 1957–63.

Du Boulay, F. R. H. *An Age of Ambition: English Society in the Late Middle Ages.* London: Nelson, 1970.

Bowden, Muriel. *A Commentary on the General Prologue to the "Canterbury Tales."* 2d ed. London: Macmillan, 1967.

Boyde, Patrick. *Dante, Philomythes and Philosopher: Man in the Cosmos.* Cambridge: Cambridge University Press, 1981.

Bradley, Sister Ritamary, C.H.M. "Backgrounds of the Title *Speculum* in Mediaeval Literature." *Speculum* 29 (1954):100–15.

Brewer, D. S. Review of H. Gillmeister, *Discrecioun: Chaucer und die Via Regia.* *Anglia* 94 (1976):228–32.

Bridbury, A. R. *Economic Growth: England in the Later Middle Ages.* London: George Allen and Unwin, 1962.

Bridrey, Émile. *Nicole Oresme: La théorie de la monnaie au XIVe siècle.* Paris:

V. Giard et E. Brière, 1906.

Brinkmann, Hennig. *Mittelalterliche Hermeneutik*. Tübingen: Max Niemeyer, 1980.

Brown, Emerson, Jr. "Chaucer, the Merchant, and Their Tale: Getting Beyond Old Controversies: Part I." *ChauR* 13 (1978):141–56. "Part 2." *ChauR* 13 (1978):247–62.

———. "The *Merchant's Tale*: Why Is May Called 'Mayus'?" *ChauR* 2 (1968):273–77.

———. "The *Merchant's Tale*: January's 'Unlikly Elde.'" *NM* 74 (1973): 92–106.

Brownlee, Kevin. "Dante and Narcissus (*Purg.* XXX.76–99)." *Dante Studies* 96 (1978):201–206.

de Bruyne, Edgar. *Études d'esthétique médiévale*. 3 vols. Brugge: "De Tempel," 1946.

Bundy, Murray Wright. *The Theory of Imagination in Classical and Medieval Thought*. University of Illinois Studies in Language and Literature, vol. 12, nos. 2–3. Urbana: University of Illinois Press, 1927.

Burckhardt, Sigurd. *Shakespearean Meanings*. Princeton, N.J.: Princeton University Press, 1968.

Burke, Kenneth. *The Rhetoric of Religion: Studies in Logology*. Berkeley: University of California Press, 1970.

Burrow, John. "Irony in the Merchant's Tale." *Anglia* 75 (1957): 199–208.

———. *A Reading of "Sir Gawain and the Green Knight."* London: Routledge and Kegan Paul, 1965.

Cacucci, Francesco. *Teologia dell'immagine prospettive attuali*. Rev. ed. Rome: Edizioni i 7, 1971.

Cahn, Kenneth S. "Chaucer's Merchants and the Foreign Exchange: An Introduction to Medieval Finance." *SACh* 2 (1980):81–119.

Carroll, Berenice A., ed. *Liberating Women's History: Theoretical and Critical Essays*. Urbana: University of Illinois Press, 1976.

Carruthers, Mary. "The Wife of Bath and the Painting of Lions." *PMLA* 94 (1979):209–22.

Carton, Evan. "Complicity and Responsibility in Pandarus' Bed and Chaucer's Art." *PMLA* 94 (1979):47–61.

Casey, Kathleen. "The Cheshire Cat: Reconstructing the Experience of Medieval Woman." In Berenice A. Carroll ed. *Liberating Women's History: Theoretical and Critical Essays*. Urbana: University of Illinois Press, 1976. Pp. 224–49.

Cassell, Anthony K. "Failure, Pride and Conversion in *Inferno* 1: A Reinterpretation." *Dante Studies* 94 (1976):1–24.

Cassirer, Ernst. *Language and Myth.* Trans. Susanne K. Langer. New York: Dover, 1946.

Catto, Jeremy. "Florence, Tuscany, and the World of Dante." In Cecil Grayson, ed. *The World of Dante: Essays on Dante and His Times.* Oxford: Clarendon Press, 1980. Pp. 1–17.

Chamberlin, John S. *Increase and Multiply: Arts-of-Discourse Procedures in the Preaching of Donne.* Chapel Hill, N.C.: University of North Carolina Press, 1976. Pp. 1–91.

Chenu, Marie-Dominique, O.P. "*Involucrum*: le Mythe selon les théologiens médiévaux." *AHDLMA* 30 (1955):75–79.

―――. *Nature, Man, and Society in the Twelfth Century.* Trans. Jerome Taylor and Lester K. Little. Chicago: University of Chicago Press, 1968.

Chiarenza, Marguerite Mills. "The Singleton *Paradiso.*" *Dante Studies* 96 (1978):207–12.

Chydenius, Johann. *The Theory of Medieval Symbolism.* Societas scientiarum Fennica, commentationes humanarum litterarum 27.2. Helsingfors, 1960.

Cipolla, Carlo M. *Money, Prices, and Civilization in the Mediterranean World.* Princeton, N.J.: Princeton University Press, 1956.

Colby, Alice M. *The Portrait in Twelfth-Century French Literature: An Example of the Stylistic Originality of Chrétien de Troyes.* Geneva: Librarie Droz, 1965.

Colish, Marcia L. *The Mirror of Language.* New Haven, Conn.: Yale University Press, 1968.

Cooper, Geoffrey. "'Sely John' in the 'Legende' of the *Miller's Tale.*" *JEGP* 79 (1980):1–12.

Cormier, Raymond J., and Urban T. Holmes, eds. *Essays in Honor of Louis Francis Solano.* University of North Carolina Studies in the Romance Languages and Literatures, vol. 92. Chapel Hill: University of North Carolina Press, 1970.

Coward, Rosalind, and John Ellis. *Language and Materialism.* London: Routledge and Kegan Paul, 1977.

Crivelli, E. "Il vetro, gli specchi e gli occhiali ai tempi di Dante." *GD* 12 (1941):79–90.

Crump, C. G., and E. F. Jacob, eds. *The Legacy of the Middle Ages.* Oxford: Clarendon Press, 1926.

Cuddihy, John Murray. *No Offense.* New York: Seabury Press, 1978.

Curry, Walter Clyde. "The Pardoner's Secret." In *Chaucer and the Medieval Sciences.* 2d ed. New York: Barnes and Noble, 1960. Pp. 54–70.

Curtius, Ernst Robert. *European Literature and the Latin Middle Ages.* Trans.

Willard Trask. London: Routledge and Kegan Paul, 1953.

David, Alfred. "The Hero of the *Troilus*." *Speculum* 37 (1962):566–81.

Davis, Norman, et al., eds. *A Chaucer Glossary*. Oxford: Clarendon Press, 1979.

Delaney, Sheila. *Chaucer's House of Fame: The Poetics of Skeptical Fideism*. Chicago: University of Chicago Press, 1972.

Deleuze, Gilles. *Différence et répétition*. Paris: Presses Universitaires de France, 1968.

Demats, Paule. *Fabula: trois études de mythographie antique et médiévale*. Publications Romanes et Françaises, vol. 122. Geneva: Librairie Droz, 1973.

Derrida, Jacques. "Freud et la scène de l'écriture." In *L'Écriture et la différence*. Paris: Éditions du Seuil, 1967. Pp. 293–340. Trans. Alan Bass. Chicago: University of Chicago Press, 1978. Pp. 196–231.

———. *Of Grammatology*. Trans. Gayatri Chakravorty Spivak. Baltimore, Md.: Johns Hopkins University Press, 1976.

———. "White Mythology: Metaphor in the Text of Philosophy." *NLH* 6 (1974):5–74.

Dictionnaire de spiritualité. Marcel Viller, S.J., gen ed. Paris: Beauchesne, 1937–.

Donaldson, E. T. "Chaucer in the Twentieth Century." Presidential Address to the New Chaucer Society, 1979. *SACh* 2 (1980):7–13.

———. *Chaucer's Poetry*. New York: Ronald Press, 1958.

———. "Chaucer's Three 'P's': Pandarus, Pardoner, and Poet." *MQR* 14 (1975):282–301.

———. *Speaking of Chaucer*. New York: Norton, 1972.

Dragonetti, Roger. "Dante et Narcisse ou les faux-monnayeurs de l'image." *REI* 11 (1965):85–146.

———. "Pygmalion ou les pièges de la fiction dans le *Roman de la Rose*." *Orbis Mediaevalis: mélanges de langue et de littérature médiévales offerts à Reto Raduolf Bezzola*. Ed. Georges Güntert, Marc-Rene Jung, and Kurt Ringger. Berne: Éditions Francke, 1978. Pp. 89–111.

Drake, Richard F. "The Profession of the Coin: Studies in the Autobiographical Tradition." Ph.D. dissertation, Yale University, 1977.

Duchrow, Ulrich. "'Signum' and 'superbia' beim jungen Augustin (386–390)." *REA* 7 (1961):369–72.

Duby, Georges. *The Early Growth of the European Economy: Warriors and Peasants from the Seventh to the Twelfth Century*. Trans. Howard B. Clark. Ithaca, N.Y.: Cornell University Press, 1974.

Durling, Robert. "Deceit and Digestion in the Belly of Hell." In Stephen J.

Greenblatt, ed. *Allegory and Representation*. Selected Papers from the English Institute, 1979–80, n.s., no. 5. Baltimore, Md.: Johns Hopkins University Press, 1981. Pp. 61–93.

Eberle, Patricia J. "The Lovers' Glass: Nature's Discourse on Optics and the Optical Design of the *Romance of the Rose*." In John Leyerle, ed. *The Language of Love and the Visual Imagination in the High Middle Ages. UTQ* 46(1977):241–62.

Economou, George D. "Januarie's Sin Against Nature: The *Merchant's Tale* and the *Roman de la Rose*." *CL* 17 (1965):251–57.

Edler, Florence. *Glossary of Mediaeval Terms of Business, Italian Series, 1200–1600*. Cambridge, Mass.: Mediaeval Academy of America, 1934.

Elliott, Ralph W. V. "Our Host's 'Triacle': Some Observations on Chaucer's 'Pardoner's Tale.'" *REL* 7 (1966):61–73.

Ellis, John. See Coward and Ellis.

Enciclopedia Dantesca. 6 vols. Rome: Istituto della Enciclopedia Italiana, 1970–78.

Engels, J. "Origine, sens et survie du terme boécien 'secundum placitum.'" *Vivarium* 1 (1963):87–114.

Fellini, Federico. Satyricon. Ed. Dario Zanelli and trans. Eugene Walter and John Matthews. New York: Ballantine Books, 1970.

Ferguson, Margaret W. "St. Augustine's Region of Unlikeness: The Crossing of Exile and Language." *GR*, Winter, 1975, pp. 842–64.

Fish, Stanley. *Self-consuming Artifacts: The Experience of Seventeenth-Century Literature*. Berkeley: University of California Press, 1972.

Fisher, Ruth M. "'Cosyn' and 'Cosynage': Complicated Punning in Chaucer's 'Shipman's Tale'?" *N&Q* 210 (1965):168–70.

Fisher, Sheila M. "Chaucer's Poetic Alchemy: A Study of Value and Its Transformation in *The Canterbury Tales*." Ph.D. dissertation, Yale University, 1982.

Fleming, John V. *An Introduction to the Franciscan Literature of the Middle Ages*. Chicago: Franciscan Herald Press, 1977.

Foucault, Michel. *The Order of Things*. New York: Vintage, 1973.

———. "What Is an Author?" In Josué V. Harari, ed. *Textual Strategies*. Ithaca, N.Y.: Cornell University Press, 1979. Pp. 141–60.

Frappier, Jean. "Variations sur le thème du miroir, de Bernard de Ventadour à Maurice Scève." *CAIEF* 11 (1959):134–58.

Freccero, John. "Casella's Song." *Dante Studies* 91 (1973):73–80.

———. "Dante's Firm Foot and the Journey Without a Guide." *HThR* 52 (1959):245–81.

———. "Dante's Prologue Scene." *Dante Studies* 84 (1966):1–25.

————. "Medusa: The Letter and the Spirit." *YIS*, 1972, Pp. 1–18. Reprinted. ("Dante's Medusa: Allegory and Autobiography,") in *By Things Seen: Reference and Recognition in Medieval Thought*. Ed. D. L. Jeffrey. Ottawa: University of Ottawa Press, 1979. Pp. 33–46.

————. "Paradiso X: The Dance of the Stars." *Dante Studies* 86 (1968): 86–111.

————, ed. *Dante: A Collection of Critical Essays*. Englewood Cliffs, N.J.: Prentice-Hall, 1965.

Freud, Sigmund. "On Narcissism: An Introduction." *The Standard Edition of the Complete Psychological Works of Sigmund Freud*. Trans. and ed. James Strachey. London: Hogarth Press, 1957. 14:73–102.

Fromm, Hans; Wolfgang Harms; and Uwe Ruberg, eds. *Verbum et signum: Festschrift Friedrich Ohly*. 2 vols. Munich: Wilhelm Fink, 1975.

Galbraith, John Kenneth, and Nicole Salinger. *Almost Everyone's Guide to Economics*. Boston: Houghton Mifflin, 1978.

Galinsky, Hans. *Naturae cursus: Der Weg einer Antike kosmologischen Metapher von der Alten in die Neue Welt*. Studien zum Fortwirken der Antike, vol. 4. Heidelberg: Carl Winter, 1968.

Garrani, Giuseppe. *Il Pensiero di Dante in tema di economia monetaria e creditizia*. Palermo: Fondazione Culturale "Lauro Chiazzese," 1967.

Gilchrist, John. *The Church and Economic Activity in the Middle Ages*. New York: St. Martin's Press, 1969.

Gimpel, Jean, *The Medieval Machine: The Industrial Revolution of the Middle Ages*. Harmondsworth: Penguin, 1976.

Ginsberg, Warren. "Preaching and Avarice in the 'Pardoner's Tale.'" *Mediaevalia* 2 (1976):77–99.

Le Goff, Jacques. *Pour un autre moyen âge: temps, travail, et culture en Occident*. Paris: Éditions Gallimard, 1977.

Goldin, Frederick. *The Mirror of Narcissus in the Courtly Love Lyric*. Ithaca, N.Y.: Cornell University Press, 1967.

Gordon, Ida L. *The Double Sorrow of Troilus: A Study in Ambiguities in Troilus and Criseyde*. Oxford: Clarendon Press, 1970.

Grabes, Herbert. *Speculum, Mirror und Looking-Glass: Kontinuität und Originalität der Spiegelmetapher in den Buchtiteln des Mittelalters und der englischen Literatur des 13. bis 17. Jahrhunderts*. Buchreihe der Anglia, vol. 16. Tübingen: Max Niemeyer, 1973.

Grayson, Cecil, ed. *The World of Dante: Essays on Dante and His Times*. Oxford: Clarendon Press, 1980.

Green, Richard F. *Poets and Princepleasers: Literature and the English Court in the late Middle Ages*. Toronto: University of Toronto Press, 1980.

Green, Richard H. "Dante's 'Allegory of Poets' and the Medieval Theory of Poetic Fiction." *CL* 9 (1957):118–28.

Greenblatt, Stephen J., ed. *Allegory and Representation*. Selected Papers from the English Institute, 1979–80, n.s., no. 5. Baltimore, Md.: Johns Hopkins University Press, 1981.

Grubmüller, Klaus. "Etymologie als Schlüssel zur Welt? Bemerkungen zur Sprachtheorie des Mittelalters." In *Verbum et Signum: Festschrift Friedrich Ohly*. Ed. Hans Fromm, Wolfgang Harms, and Uwe Ruberg. 2 vols. Munich: Wilhelm Fink Verlag, 1975. 1:209–300.

Gunn, Alan M. F. *The Mirror of Love: A Reinterpretation of "The Romance of the Rose."* Lubbock, Texas: Texas Tech Press, 1952.

Halverson, John. "Chaucer's Pardoner and the Progress of Criticism." *ChauR* 4 (1970):184–202.

Harari, Josué V., ed. *Textual Strategies*. Ithaca, N.Y.: Cornell University Press, 1979.

Häring, Nikolaus, S.A.C. "Character, Signum und Signaculum." *Scholastik* 30 (1955):481–512; 31 (1956):41–69.

Harms, Wolfgang. See Fromm, Harms, and Ruberg.

Harries, Karsten. "Fundamental Ontology and the Search for Man's Place." In Michael Murray, ed. *Heidegger and Modern Philosophy: Critical Essays*. New Haven, Conn.: Yale University Press, 1978. Pp. 65–79.

Hartman, Geoffrey. *Beyond Formalism*. New Haven, Conn.: Yale University Press, 1970.

Haskell, Ann S. "The Portrayal of Women by Chaucer and His Age." In Marlene Springer, ed. *What Manner of Woman?* New York: New York University Press, 1977. Pp. 1–14.

Hatcher, Elizabeth R. "Chaucer and the Psychology of Fear: Troilus in Book V." *ELH* 40 (1973):307–24.

Heidegger, Martin. "The Age of the World Picture." In *The Question Concerning Technology*. Trans. William Lovitt. New York: Harper, 1977. Pp. 115–54.

———. *Being and Time*. Trans. John Macquarrie and Edward Robinson. New York: Harper, 1962.

———. *Poetry, Language, Thought*. Trans. Albert Hofstadter. New York: Harper, 1971.

———. *The Question Concerning Technology*. Trans. William Lovitt. New York: Harper, 1977.

Heinzelman, Kurt. *The Economics of the Imagination*. Boston: University of Massachusetts Press, 1980.

Herz, Martin. *Sacrum commercium: Eine begriffsgeschichtliche Studie zur*

Theologie der Römischen Liturgiesprache. Münchener Theologische Studien, 2.15. Munich: K. Zink, 1958.

Herzman, Ronald B., and William A. Stephany. "'O miseri seguaci': Sacramental Inversion in *Inferno* XIX." *Dante Studies* 96 (1978):39–65.

Hofmann, Hasso. *Repräsentation: Studien zur Wort- und Begriffsgeschichte von der Antike bis ins 19. Jahrhundert.* Berlin: Duncker and Humblot, 1974.

Hollander, Robert. *Allegory in Dante's "Comedy."* Princeton, N.J.: Princeton University Press, 1969.

————. "Dante *Theologus-Poeta.*" *Dante Studies* 94 (1976):91–136.

Holmes, U. T. See Cormier and Holmes.

Howard, Donald R. *The Idea of the Canterbury Tales.* Berkeley: University of California Press, 1976.

Hugedé, Norbert. *La Métaphore du miroir dans les Epîtres de saint Paul aux Corinthiens.* Neuchatel: Delachaux et Niestlé, 1957.

Huizinga, Johan. *The Waning of the Middle Ages.* New York: Doubleday, 1954.

Isaac, J., O.P. *Le "Peri Hermeneias" en Occident de Boèce à saint Thomas.* Bibliothèque Thomiste, vol. 29. Paris: Librairie Philosophique J. Vrin, 1953.

Jacob, E. F. See Crump and Jacob.

Javelet, Robert. *Image et ressemblance au douzième siècle.* 2 vols. Paris. Éditions Letouzey et Ané, 1967.

Jeauneau, Édouard. "L'Usage de la notion d' 'integumentum' à travers les gloses de Guillaume de Conches." *AHDLMA* 32 (1957):35–100.

Johnston, William, S.J. *The Cloud of Unknowing and the Book of Privy Counseling.* New York: Image Books, 1973.

Josipovici, Gabriel. *The World and the Book.* London: Macmillan, 1971.

Kaminsky, Alice R. *Chaucer's "Troilus and Criseyde" and the Critics.* Columbus, Ohio: Ohio University Press, 1980.

Kaske, R. E. "Chaucer and Medieval Allegory." *ELH* 30 (1963):175–92.

————. "*Clericus Adam* and Chaucer's *Adam Scriveyn.*" In Edward Vasta and Zacharias P. Thundy, eds. *Chaucerian Problems and Perspectives: Essays Presented to Paul E. Beichner, C.S.C.* Notre Dame, Ind.: University of Notre Dame Press, 1980. Pp. 114–18.

————. "The Knight's Interruption of the *Monk's Tale.*" *ELH* 24 (1957):249–68.

Kellogg, Alfred L. "An Augustinian Interpretation of Chaucer's Pardoner." *Speculum* 26 (1951):465–81. Reprinted in *Chaucer, Langland, Arthur.* New Brunswick, N.J.: Rutgers University Press, 1972. Pp. 245–68.

————. *Chaucer, Langland, Arthur.* New Brunswick: Rutgers University

Press, 1972.

————, and Louis A. Haselmayer. "Chaucer's Satire of the Pardoner." *PMLA* 66 (1951):251–77. Reprinted in Alfred L. Kellogg, *Chaucer, Langland, Arthur.* New Brunswick, N.J.: Rutgers University Press, 1972. Pp. 212–44.

Kellogg, R. See Scholes and Kellogg.

Kelly, Douglas. *Medieval Imagination: Rhetoric and the Poetry of Courtly Love.* Madison: University of Wisconsin Press, 1978.

————. *"Sens" and "Conjointure" in the "Chevalier de la charrette."* The Hague and Paris: Mouton, 1966.

Kelly, Henry Ansgar. *Love and Marriage in the Age of Chaucer.* Ithaca, N.Y.: Cornell University Press, 1975.

Kennedy, A. G. See Tatlock and Kennedy.

Kenner, Hugh. *The Counterfeiters.* Bloomington: Indiana University Press, 1968.

————. *Joyce's Voices.* Berkeley: University of California Press, 1978.

Kittredge, George Lyman. *Chaucer and His Poetry.* Cambridge, Mass.: Harvard University Press, 1939.

Köhler, Erich. "Narcisse, la Fontaine d'Amour et Guillaume de Lorris." *JS,* April–June, 1963, Pp. 86–103.

Kohut, Heinz. *The Restoration of the Self.* New York: International Universities Press, 1977.

Krewitt, Ulrich. *Metapher und tropische Rede in der Auffassung des Mittelalters.* Beihefte zum "Mittellateinischen Jahrbuch," vol. 7. Ratingen: A. Henn, 1971.

Lacan, Jacques. *Écrits: A Selection.* Trans. Alan Sheridan. New York: Norton, 1977.

————. "Le sujet et l'Autre: l'aliénation." *Le Séminaire* 11 (1973):185–96.

————. "Sur le narcissisme." *Le Séminaire* 1 (1975):125–35.

Langholm, Odd. *Price and Value in the Aristotelian Traditions: A Study in Scholastic Economic Sources.* Bergen: Universitets-Forlaget, 1979.

Leclercq, Jean. *The Love of Learning and the Desire for God.* Trans. Catharine Misrahi. New York: Fordham University Press, 1961.

Leff, Gordon. *Heresy in the Later Middle Ages.* 2 vols. New York: Barnes and Noble, 1967.

Leicester, H. Marshall, Jr. "The Art of Impersonation: A General Prologue to the *Canterbury Tales.*" *PMLA* 95 (1980):213–24.

Leisegang, Hans. "Die Erkenntnis Gottes im Spiegel der Seele und der Natur." *ZPF* 4 (1949):161–83. Also published as "La connaissance de Dieu au miroir de l'âme et de la nature." *RHPR* 17 (1937):145–77.

Lentricchia, Frank. *After the New Criticism*. Chicago: University of Chicago Press, 1980.

Levy, Madeleine. See Tigar and Levy.

Leyerle, John. "The Rose-Wheel Design and Dante's *Paradiso*." In John Leyerle, ed. *The Language of Love and the Visual Imagination in the High Middle Ages. UTQ* 46 (1977):280–308.

———, ed. *The Language of Love and the Visual Imagination in the High Middle Ages. UTQ* 46 (1977):185–308.

Little, Lester K. *Religious Poverty and the Profit Economy in Medieval Europe.* Ithaca, N.Y.: Cornell University Press, 1978.

Lonergan, Bernard, S.J. *Verbum: Word and Idea in Aquinas.* Notre Dame, Ind.: University of Notre Dame Press, 1967.

Lopez, Robert S. *The Commercial Revolution of the Middle Ages, 950–1350.* Cambridge: Cambridge University Press, 1976.

———. "The Dollar of the Middle Ages." *JEH* 11 (1951):209–34.

de Lubac, Henri. *Exégèse médiévale: les quatre sens de l'écriture.* 4 vols. Paris: Aubier, 1959–64.

Lyonnet, Stanislaus, S.J., and Léopold Sabourin, S.J. *Sin, Redemption, and Sacrifice: A Biblical and Patristic Study.* Rome: Biblical Institute Press, 1970.

McAlpine, Monica. *The Genre of "Troilus and Criseyde."* Ithaca, N.Y.: Cornell University Press, 1978.

———. "The Pardoner's Homosexuality and How It Matters." *PMLA* 95 (1980):8–22.

MacCulloch, John A. *The Harrowing of Hell.* Edinburgh: T. & T. Clark, 1930.

McGalliard, John C. "Characterization in Chaucer's *Shipman's Tale*." *PQ* 54 (1975):1–18.

MacIntyre, Alasdair. *After Virtue: A Study in Moral Theory.* Notre Dame, Ind.: University of Notre Dame Press, 1981.

Malausséna, P. "*Promissio Redemptionis*: le rachat des captifs Chrétiens en pays Musulman, à la fin du XIVe siècle." *AM* 80 (1968):255–81.

de Man, Paul. *Blindness and Insight: Essays in the Rhetoric of Contemporary Criticism.* New York: Oxford University Press, 1971.

———. "Nietzsche's Theory of Rhetoric." *Symposium* 28 (1974):33–51.

de Mandrot, B. "Jacques d'Armagnac, Duc de Nemours." *RH* 44 (1890): 241–312.

Mann, Jill. *Chaucer and Medieval Estates Satire.* Cambridge: Cambridge University Press, 1973.

Margulies, Cecile S. "The Marriages and the Wealth of the Wife of Bath." *MS* 24 (1962):210–16.

Martines, Lauro. *Power and Imagination: City-States in Renaissance Italy.* New York: Vintage Books, 1980.

Martinez, Ronald. "Dante the Counterfeiter: Ovid and Adam." Paper read at the Annual Meeting of the Midwest Modern Language Association Meeting, Oconomowoc, Wisconsin, November 6, 1981.

Marx, Karl. *Economic and Philosophic Manuscripts of 1844.* Ed. Dirk J. Struik. Trans. Martin Milligan. New York: International Publishers, 1964.

Massey, Irving. *The Gaping Pig: Literature and Metamorphosis.* Berkeley: University of California Press, 1976.

Mayer, Cornelius, O.S.A. *Die Zeichen in der geistigen Entwicklung und in der Theologie Augustins.* 2 vols. Cassiciacum, 24:1, 2. Würzburg: Augustinus-Verlag 1969, 1974.

Mazzeo, Joseph. *Medieval Cultural Tradition in Dante's "Comedy."* 1960. Reprint. Westport, Conn.: Greenwood Press, 1977.

———. *Structure and Thought in "Paradiso."* Ithaca, N.Y.: Cornell University Press, 1958.

Mazzotta, Giuseppe. *Dante, Poet of the Desert.* Princeton, N.J.: Princeton University Press, 1979.

———. "The Decameron: The Marginality of Literature." *UTQ* 42 (1972):64–81.

Meech, Sanford B. *Design in Chaucer's "Troilus."* Syracuse, N.Y.: University of Syracuse Press, 1959.

Mehl, Dieter. "The Audience of Chaucer's *Troilus and Criseyde.*" In Beryl Rowland, ed. *Chaucer and Middle English Studies: In Honour of Rossell Hope Robbins.* London: Allen and Unwin, 1974.

Mehta, J. L. *Martin Heidegger: The Way and the Vision.* Honolulu: University of Hawaii Press, 1967.

Meiss, Millard. *Painting in Florence and Siena After the Black Death: The Arts, Religion, and Society in the Mid-Fourteenth Century.* Princeton, N.J.: Princeton University Press, 1951.

Mengaldo, Pier Vincenzo. *Linguistica e retorica di Dante.* Saggi di Varia Umanità, vol. 21. Pisa: Nistri-Lischi, 1978.

Middleton, Anne. "Chaucer's 'New Men' and the Good of Literature in the *Canterbury Tales.*" In Edward Said, ed. *Literature and Society.* Selected Papers from the English Institute, 1978. Baltimore, Md.: Johns Hopkins University Press, 1980.

Miller, James L. "Three Mirrors of Dante's *Paradiso.*" In John Leyerle, ed. *The Language of Love and the Visual Imagination in the High Middle Ages.* *UTQ* 46 (1977):263–79.

Miller, Robert P. "Chaucer's Pardoner, the Scriptural Eunuch, and the

Pardoner's Tale." *Speculum* 30 (1955): 180–99. Reprinted in Richard J. Schoeck and Jerome Taylor, eds. *Chaucer Criticism*. 2 vols. Notre Dame, Ind.: University of Notre Dame Press, 1960, 1961. 1:221–44.

Minnis, Alastair. "'Authorial Role' and 'Literary Form' in Late Medieval Scriptural Exegesis." BGDSL 99 (1977):37–65.

Miskimin, H. A. *The Economy of Early Renaissance Europe, 1300–1460*. Cambridge: Cambridge University Press, 1969.

———. "Monetary Movements and Market Structure: Forces for Contraction in Fourteenth- and Fifteenth-Century England." *JEH* 24 (1964):470–90.

Montgomery, Robert. *The Reader's Eye: Studies in Didactic Literary Theory from Dante to Tasso*. Berkeley: University of California Press, 1979.

Moritz, Theresa Ann. See Allen and Moritz.

Murray, Alexander. *Reason and Society in the Middle Ages*. Oxford: Clarendon Press, 1978.

Murray, Michael, ed. *Heidegger and Modern Philosophy: Critical Essays*. New Haven, Conn.: Yale University Press, 1978.

Murtaugh, Daniel M. "'Figurando il paradiso': The Signs That Render Dante's Heaven." *PMLA* 90 (1975):277–84.

Musa, Mark. "From Measurement to Meaning: Simony." *Advent at the Gates: Dante's "Comedy."* Bloomington: Indiana University Press, 1974. Pp. 37–64.

Muscatine, Charles. *Chaucer and the French Tradition*. Berkeley: University of California Press, 1969.

———. "The Feigned Illness in Chaucer's *Troilus and Criseyde*." *MLN* 63 (1948):372–77.

Mussetter, Sally Ann. "Dante's Three Beasts and the *Imago Trinitatis*," *Dante Studies* 95 (1977):39–52.

———. "'Inferno XXX': Dante's Counterfeit Adam." *Traditio* 34 (1978):426–35.

———. "The Reformation of the Pilgrim to the Likeness of God: A Study of the Tropological Level of the *Divine Comedy* and *Piers Plowman* B." Ph.D. dissertation, Cornell University, 1975.

Nardi, Bruno. "Sull' interpretazione allegorica e sulla struttura della Commedia di Dante." In *Saggi e note di critica dantesca*. Milano: R. Ricciardi, 1966. Pp. 110–65.

———. "Sull' origine dell' anima umana." In *Dante e la cultura medievale*. 2d ed. Bari: Giusseppe Laterza & Figli, 1949. Pp. 260–83.

———. "La tragedia d'Ulisse." In *Dante e la cultura medievale*. 2d ed. Bari: Giuseppe Laterza & Figli, 1949. Pp. 153–65.

Nichols, Robert. "The Pardoner's Cake and Ale." *PMLA* 82 (1967):498–504.

Nims, Sister Margaret F. "Translatio: 'Difficult Statement' in Medieval Poetic Theory." *UTQ* 43 (1974):215–30.

Nitzsche, Jane Chance. *The Genius Figure in Antiquity and the Middle Ages.* New York: Columbia University Press, 1975.

Noonan, John T. *The Scholastic Analysis of Usury.* Cambridge, Mass.: Harvard University Press, 1957.

Oberman, Heiko A. *Werden und Wertung der Reformation.* Tübingen: Mohr, 1977.

O'Brien, George. *An Essay on Mediaeval Economic Teaching.* London: Longmans, Green, 1920.

O'Donovan, Oliver. *The Problem of Self-Love in St. Augustine.* New Haven, Conn.: Yale University Press, 1980.

Ohly, Friedrich. *Hohelied-Studien.* Wiesbaden: F. Steiner, 1958.

Olson, Glending. "Deschamps's *Art de Dictier* and Chaucer's Literary Environment." *Speculum* 48 (1973):714–23.

———. "Making and Poetry in the Age of Chaucer." *CL* 31 (1972):272–90.

Olson, Paul A. "Chaucer's Merchant and January's 'Hevene in erthe heere.'" *ELH* 28 (1961):203–14.

———. "The Merchant's Lombard Knight." *TSLL* 3 (1961):259–63.

Owen, Charles A., Jr. "The Problem of Free Will in Chaucer's Narrative." *PQ* 46 (1967):433–56.

Owen, D. D. R. *The Vision of Hell: Infernal Journeys in Medieval French Literature.* New York: Barnes and Noble, 1971.

Ozment, Steven. *The Age of Reform, 1250–1550.* New Haven, Conn.: Yale University Press, 1980.

Palmer, Paul F. *Sacraments and Forgiveness: History and Doctrinal Development of Penance, Extreme Unction and Indulgences.* Sources of Christian Theology, vol. 2. Westminster, Md.: Newman Press, 1959.

Patch, Howard R. *The Goddess Fortuna in Medieval Literature.* Cambridge, Mass.: Harvard University Press, 1927.

Patterson, Lee W. "Chaucerian Confession: Penitential Literature and the Pardoner." *M&H*, n.s. 7 (1976):153–73.

———. "The 'Parson's Tale' and the Quitting of the 'Canterbury Tales.'" *Traditio* 34 (1978):331–80.

Payne, F. Anne. *Chaucer and Menippean Satire.* Madison: University of Wisconsin Press, 1980.

Payne, R. O. *The Key of Remembrance.* New Haven, Conn.: Yale University Press, 1963.

Peck, George T. *The Fool of God: Jacopone da Todi.* University: University of Alabama Press, 1980.

Pépin, Jean. *Dante et la tradition de l'allégorie*. Montreal: Institut d'études médiévales, 1970.

———. *Mythe et allégorie*. Paris: Éditions Montaigne, 1958.

Percy, Walker. *The Message in the Bottle*. New York: Farrar, Straus, Giroux, 1975.

Petrocchi, Giorgio. *Il Paradiso di Dante*. Milan: Rizzoli, 1978.

Pezzard, André. "Adam Joyeux (Dante, *Paradis* XXVI 97–102)." *Mélanges de linguistique et de littérature romanes offerts à Mario Roques*. 2 vols. Bade: Éditions art et science, 1953. 2:219–35. Reprinted in *Dans le sillage de Dante*. Paris: Société d'études italiennes, 1975. Pp. 135–52.

Pirenne, Henri. *Economic and Social History of Medieval Europe*. Trans. I. E. Clegg. New York: Harcourt, Brace and World, 1937.

Poggioli, Renato. "Tragedy or Romance? A Reading of the Paolo and Francesca Episode in Dante's *Inferno*." *PMLA* 72 (1957):313–58. Reprinted (in abridged form) in John Freccero, ed. *Dante: A Collection of Critical Essays*. Englewood Cliffs, N.J.: Prentice-Hall, 1965.

Poirion, Daniel. "Narcisse et Pygmalion dans le *Roman de la Rose*." In Raymond I. Cormier and Urban T. Holmes, eds. *Essays in Honor of Louis Francis Solano*. University of North Carolina Studies in the Romance Languages and Literature, vol. 92. Chapel Hill: University of North Carolina Press, 1970. Pp. 153–66.

Postan, M. M. *Essays on Medieval Agriculture and General Problems of the Medieval Economy*. Cambridge: at the University Press, 1973.

Power, Eileen. *Medieval Women*. Ed. M. M. Postan. Cambridge: Cambridge University Press, 1975.

———. "The Position of Women." In C. G. Crump and E. F. Jacob, eds. *The Legacy of the Middle Ages*. Oxford: Clarendon Press, 1926.

Quinn, Esther C. *The Quest of Seth for the Oil of Life*. Chicago: University of Chicago Press, 1962.

Rabkin, Norman. *Shakespeare and the Common Understanding*. New York: Free Press, 1967.

Reade, W. H. V. *The Moral System of Dante's "Inferno."* Oxford: Clarendon Press, 1909.

Reiss, Edmund. "Troilus and the Failure of Understanding." *MLQ* 29 (1968):131–44.

Richard, Marcel. "Florilèges spirituels." *DSpir*. 5:435–512.

Rimanelli, Giose, and Kenneth John Atchity, eds. *Italian Literature: Roots and Branches: Essays in Honor of Thomas Goddard Bergin*. New Haven, Conn: Yale University Press, 1976.

Rivière, Jean. *Le Dogme de la rédemption au début du moyen âge.* Paris: Librairie Philosophique J. Vrin, 1934.

————. *Le Dogme de la rédemption chez saint Augustine.* Paris: Gabalda, 1928.

Robertson, D. W., Jr. *A Preface to Chaucer.* Princeton, N.J.: Princeton University Press, 1962.

de Roover, Raymond. *La Pensée économique des scolastiques: doctrines et méthodes.* Montreal: Institut d'études médiévales, 1971.

————. *San Bernardino of Siena and San' Antonio of Florence: The Two Great Economic Thinkers of the Middle Ages.* Boston: Kress Library of Business and Economics, 1967.

Rorty, Richard. *Philosophy and the Mirror of Nature.* Princeton, N.J.: Princeton University Press, 1979.

Rotta, Paolo. *La Filosofia del linguaggio nella Patristica e nella Scolastica.* Turin: Fratelli Bocca, 1909.

Rouse, Richard H., and Mary A. Rouse. *Preachers, Florilegia, and Sermons: Studies on the Manipulus florum of Thomas of Ireland.* Toronto: Pontifical Institute of Medieval Studies, 1979.

Rowe, Donald. *O Love! O Charite! Contraries Harmonized in Chaucer's "Troilus."* Carbondale: Southern Illinois University Press, 1976.

Rowland, Beryl. "Chaucer's Idea of the Pardoner." *ChauR* 14 (1979):140–54.

————. "Pandarus and the Fate of Tantalus." *OL* 24 (1969):3–15.

————, ed. *Chaucer and Middle English Studies: In Honour of Rossell Hope Robbins.* London: Allen and Unwin, 1974.

Ruberg, Uwe. See Fromm, Harms, and Ruberg.

Sabourin, L. See Lyonnet and Sabourin.

Said, Edward, ed. *Literature and Society.* Selected Papers from the English Institute, 1978. Baltimore, Md.: Johns Hopkins University Press, 1980.

"Salvation." In *Sacramentum mundi: An Encyclopedia of Theology.* 6 vols. New York: Herder and Herder, 1970. 5:425–38.

de Saussure, Ferdinand. *Course in General Linguistics.* Ed. Charles Bally and Albert Sechehaye, in collaboration with Albert Riedlinger. Trans. Wade Baskin. New York: McGraw-Hill, 1966.

Sayce, Olive. "Chaucer's 'Retractions': The Conclusion of the *Canterbury Tales* and Its Place in Literary Tradition." *MÆ* 40 (1971):230–48.

Scheps, Walter. "Chaucer's Numismatic Pardoner and the Personification of Avarice." *The Fourteenth Century: Acta of the Center for Medieval and Early Renaissance Studies,* vol. 4. Ed. Paul Szarmach and Bernard S. Levy. Binghamton, N.Y., 1977. Pp. 107–23.

Schoeck, Richard J., and Jerome Taylor, eds. *Chaucer Criticism.* 2 vols.

Notre Dame, Ind.: University of Notre Dame Press, 1960, 1961.

Scholes, Robert, and Robert Kellogg. *The Nature of Narrative*. New York: Oxford University Press, 1966.

Sennett, Richard. *Authority*. New York: Alfred A. Knopf, 1980.

———. *The Fall of Public Man*. New York: Vintage, 1978.

Serres, Michel. *The Parasite*. Trans. L. R. Schehr. Baltimore, Md.: Johns Hopkins University Press, 1982.

Seung. See Swing.

Sheehan, M. *Medieval Marriage*. Toronto: University of Toronto Press, 1975.

Shell, Marc. *The Economy of Literature*. Baltimore, Md.: Johns Hopkins University Press, 1978.

———. "Money and the Mind: The Economics of Translation in Goethe's *Faust*." *MLN* 95 (1980):516–62.

Shoaf, R. A. "'Auri sacra fames' and the Age of Gold: (*Purg.* 22. 40–41 and 148–150)." *Dante Studies* 96 (1978):195–99.

———. "Dante's *colombi* and the Figuralism of Hope in the *Divine Comedy*." *Dante Studies* 93 (1975):27–59.

———. "God's 'Malyse': Metaphor and Conversion in *Patience*." *JMRS* 11 (1981b):261–79.

———. "*Mutatio amoris*: Revision and Penitence in Chaucer's *The Book of the Duchess*." Ph.D. dissertation, Cornell University, 1977.

———. "Notes Toward Chaucer's Poetics of Translation." *SACh* 1 (1979):55–66.

———. "*Penitentia* and the Form of *The Book of the Duchess*." *Genre* 14 (1981a):163–89.

Silverman, Albert H. "Sex and Money in Chaucer's *Shipman's Tale*." *PQ* 32 (1953):329–36.

Singleton, Charles S. *Dante Studies I*. 1954. Reprint. Baltimore, Md.: Johns Hopkins University Press, 1977.

———. *Dante Studies II*. 1958. Reprint. Baltimore, Md.: Johns Hopkins University Press, 1977.

———. *An Essay on the Vita nuova*. 1948. Reprint. Baltimore, Md.: Johns Hopkins University Press, 1977.

———. "The Irreducible Dove." *Comparative Literature* 9 (1957):129–35.

Smarr, Janet. "Chaucer and the *Decameron*: Some New Connections?" Paper read at the Sixteenth International Congress on Medieval Studies, Western Michigan University, May 8, 1981.

Smith, Adam. *Paper Money*. New York: Summit Books, 1981.

Sohn-Rethel, Alfred. *Intellectual and Manual Labor: A Critique of Epistemo-*

logy. London: Macmillan, 1978.

Spicciani, Amleto. *La Mercatura e la formazione del prezzo nella riflessione teologica medioevale*. Atta della Accademia Nazionale dei Lincei, 8th ser., vol. 20, fasc. 3. Rome, 1977.

Spraycar, Rudy. "Dante's *lago del cor*." *Dante Studies* 96 (1978):1–19.

Springer, Marlene, ed. *What Manner of Woman?* New York: New York University Press, 1977.

Steadman, John M. "Chaucer's Pardoner and the *Thesaurus Meritorum*." *ELN* 3 (1965):4–7.

―――. *Disembodied Laughter: "Troilus" and the Apotheosis Tradition*. Berkeley: University of California Press, 1972.

Stephany, William A. See Herzman and Stephany.

Struever, Nancy S. *The Language of History in the Renaissance: Rhetoric and Historical Consciousness in Florentine Humanism*. Princeton, N.J.: Princeton University Press, 1970.

Sullivan, John E., O.P. *The Image of God: The Doctrine of St. Augustine and Its Influence*. Dubuque, Iowa: Priory Press, 1963.

Swing [Seung], T. K. "Bonaventure's Figural Exemplarism in Dante." In Giose Rimanelli and Kenneth John Atchity, *Italian Literature: Roots and Branches: Essays in Honor of Thomas Goddard Bergin*. New Haven, Conn.: Yale University Press, 1976.

―――. *Cultural Thematics: The Formation of the Faustian Ethos*. New Haven, Conn.: Yale University Press, 1976.

―――. *The Fragile Leaves of the Sibyl: Dante's Master Plan*. Westminster, Md.: Newman Press, 1962.

Taylor, Jerome. See Schoeck and Taylor.

Taylor, Karla. "Proverbs and the Authentication of Convention in 'Troilus and Criseyde.'" In Stephen A. Barney, ed. *Chaucer's Troilus: Essays in Criticism*. Hamden, Conn.: Archon, 1980. Pp. 277–96.

Tatlock, J. S. P., and A. G. Kennedy. *A Concordance to the Complete Works of Geoffrey Chaucer*. 1927. Reprint. Gloucester, Mass.: Peter Smith, 1963.

Thompson, Ann. *Shakespeare's Chaucer: A Study in Literary Origins*. New York: Barnes and Noble, 1978.

Thundy, Zacharias P. See Vasta and Thundy.

Tigar, Michael, and Madeleine Levy. *Law and the Rise of Capitalism*. New York: Monthly Review Press, 1979.

Trimpi, Wesley. "The Quality of Fiction: The Rhetorical Transmission of Literary Theory." *Traditio* 30 (1974):1–118.

―――. "Ut pictura poesis: The Argument for Stylistic Decorum." *Traditio* 34 (1978):29–74.

Tuve, Rosemund. *Allegorical Imagery.* Princeton, N.J.: Princeton University Press, 1966.

Utley, Francis Lee. *The Crooked Rib.* Columbus: Ohio State University Press, 1944.

―――. "Stylistic Ambivalence in Chaucer, Yeats, and Lucretius – The Cresting Wave and Its Undertow." *UR* 37 (1971):174–98.

Valerani, Flavio. "La Numismatica nella 'Divina Commedia.'" *RIN* 28 (1915):197–220.

Vance, Eugene. "Mervelous Signals: Poetics, Sign Theory, and Politics in Chaucer's *Troilus.*" *NLH* 10 (1979):293–337.

Vasta, Edward, and Zacharias P. Thundy, eds. *Chaucerian Problems and Perspectives: Essays Presented to Paul E. Beichner, C.S.C.* Notre Dame, Ind.: University of Notre Dame Press, 1980.

Vernon, W. W. *Readings on the "Paradiso" of Dante.* 2 vols. 1900. Reprint. New York: Books for Libraries Press, 1972.

―――. *Readings on the "Purgatorio" of Dante.* 2 vols. 3d ed. 1889. Rev. ed. London: Methuen, 1907.

Vignaux, Paul. *Justification et prédestination au XIVe siècle.* Paris: Ernest Leroux, 1934.

Vinge, Louise. *The Narcissus Theme in Western European Literature up to the Early Nineteenth Century.* Trans. Robert Dewsnap, Lisbeth Grönlund, Nigel Reeves, and Ingrid Söderberg-Reeves. Lund: Gleerups, 1967.

Vossler, Karl. *Mediaeval Culture: An Introduction to Dante and His Times.* Trans. William C. Lawton. 2 vols. New York: Harcourt, Brace, 1929.

Weinrich, Harold. "Münze und Wort: Untersuchungen an einen Bildfeld." *Romanica: Festschrift für Gerhard Rohlfs.* Ed. Heinrich Lausberg and Harald Weinrich. Halle: Max Niemeyer, 1958.

Weiskel, Thomas. *The Romantic Sublime: Studies in the Structure and Psychology of Transcendence.* Baltimore, Md.: Johns Hopkins University Press, 1976.

Wenzel, Siegfried. "Chaucer and the Language of Contemporary Preaching." *SP* 73 (1976):138–61.

Wetherbee, Winthrop. *Platonism and Poetry in the Twelfth Century.* Princeton, N.J.: Princeton University Press, 1972.

―――. "Some Twelfth-Century Literary Developments and the Classical Tradition." *SMC* 4 (1973):109–17.

―――. "The Theme of Imagination in Medieval Poetry and the Allegorical Figure 'Genius.'" *M&H*, n.s. 7 (1976):45–64.

Whallon, William. "Old Testament Poetry and the Homeric Epic." *CL* 18 (1966):113–31.

Williams, Charles. *The Figure of Beatrice*. London: Faber, 1943.

Wimsatt, William K. "The Concrete Universal." In *The Verbal Icon*. Lexington: University of Kentucky Press, 1954. Pp. 69–83.

Wood, Chauncey. *Chaucer and the Country of the Stars*. Princeton, N.J.: Princeton University Press, 1970.

Yates, Frances A. *The Art of Memory*. Harmondsworth: Penguin, 1966.

Yunck, John A. *The Lineage of Lady Mead*. Notre Dame, Ind.: University of Notre Dame Press, 1963.

Index

This index lists ancient and medieval authors; anonymous works; principal images, figures, persons, characters; major concepts; and modern authors cited in the text, but not those cited in the notes. Because of the organization of the book, which clearly indicates the main discussions of the works of Dante and Chaucer, only incidental references to these works are itemized in the index, under the name of the author.